# THE NAVARRE BIBLE

# MINOR PROPHETS

## VOLUMES IN THIS SERIES

**Standard Edition**

NEW TESTAMENT
St Matthew's Gospel
St Mark's Gospel
St Luke's Gospel
St John's Gospel
Acts of the Apostles
Romans and Galatians
Corinthians
Captivity Letters
Thessalonians and Pastoral Letters
Hebrews
Catholic Letters
Revelation

OLD TESTAMENT
The Pentateuch
Joshua–Kings [Historical Books 1]
Chronicles–Maccabees [Historical Books 2]
The Psalms and the Song of Solomon
Wisdom Books
Major Prophets
Minor Prophets

**Reader's (Composite) Edition**
The Gospels and Acts
The Letters of St Paul

**Compact Edition**
New Testament

# THE NAVARRE BIBLE

## Minor Prophets

The Books of Hosea, Joel, Amos, Obadiah, Jonah, Micah, Nahum,
Habakkuk, Zephaniah, Haggai, Zechariah and Malachi
in the Revised Standard Version and New Vulgate
with a commentary by members of the
Faculty of Theology of the University of Navarre

FOUR COURTS PRESS • DUBLIN
SCEPTER PUBLISHERS • NEW YORK

*Nihil obstat*: Jerome McCarthy, *censor deputatus*
*Imprimi potest*: Dermot, Archbishop of Dublin, 25 May 2005

Typeset by Carrigboy Typesetting Services for
FOUR COURTS PRESS LTD
7 Malpas Street, Dublin 8, Ireland
e-mail: info@four-courts-press.ie
http://www.four-courts-press.ie

*and in North America for*

SCEPTER PUBLISHERS, INC.
P.O. Box 211, New York, NY 10018–0004
e-mail: general@scepterpublishers.org
http://www.scepterpublishers.org

The translation of introductions and commentary was made by Michael Adams and Coilín Ó hAodha.

A catalogue record for this title is available from the British Library.

ISBN 1–85182–971–7 (Four Courts Press)
ISBN 1–59417–024–X (Scepter Publishers)

*Library of Congress Cataloging-in-Publication Data* [for first volume in this series]

Bible. O.T. English. Revised Standard. 1999.
  The Navarre Bible. – North American ed.
    p.   cm
  "The Books of Genesis, Exodus, Leviticus, Numbers, Deuteronomy in the Revised
    Standard Version and New Vulgate with a commentary by members of the
    Faculty of Theology of the University of Navarre."
  Includes bibliographical references.
  Contents: [1] The Pentateuch.
  ISBN 1–889334–21–9 (hardback: alk. paper)
I. Title.
  BS891.A1   1999.P75                                              99–23033
  221.7'7—dc21                                                        CIP

ACKNOWLEDGMENTS
Quotation from Vatican II documents are based on the translation in *Vatican Council II:
The Conciliar and Post Conciliar Documents*, ed. A. Flannery, OP (Dublin 1981).

The New Vulgate text of the Bible can be accessed via
http://www.vatican.va.archive/bible/index.htm

The English translation of the *Catechism of the Catholic Church* is copyright for Ireland
© 1994 Veritas Publishers and Libreria Editrice Vaticana. All rights reserved.

Printed and bound in Great Britain by MPG Books, Bodmin, Cornwall.

# Contents

# Contents

# Contents

# Table

## KINGS OF ISRAEL AND JUDAH
### *from the death of Soloman onwards*

| Kingdom of Israel | | Kingdom of Judah | | Prophets |
|---|---|---|---|---|
| 928–907 | Jeroboam | 931–911 | Rehoboam | |
| | | 911–908 | Abijam | |
| | | 908–867 | Asa | |
| 907–906 | Nadab | | | |
| 906–883 | Baasha | | | |
| 883–882 | Elah | | | |
| 882 | Zimri | | | |
| 882–871 | OMRI | | | |
| 873–852 | AHAB | | | |
| | | 870–846 | JEHOSHAPHAT | |
| 852–851 | Ahaziah | | | |
| 851–842 | Joram | 851–843* | Jehoram | |
| | | 843–842 | Ahaziah | |
| 842–814 | Jehu | 842–836 | Athaliah | |
| | | 836–798 | Joash | |
| 817–800 | Jehoahaz (Joahaz) | | | |
| 800–784 | (Jehoash) | | | |
| | | 798–769 | Amaziah | |
| 788–747* | JEROBOAM II | | | AMOS |
| | | 785–733* | AZARIAH (UZZIAH) | HOSEA |
| 747 | Zechariah | | | |
| 747 | Shallum | | | |
| 747–737 | Menahem | | | |
| 737–735 | Pekahiah | | | |
| 735–732 | Pekah | 759–743* | Jotham | |
| | | | | ISAIAH |
| 732–724 | Hoshea | 743–727 | Ahaz | |
| | | 727–698 | HEZEKIAH | MICAH |
| | | 698–642 | Manasseh | |
| | | | | NAHUM |
| | | 641–640 | Amon | |
| | | 639–609 | JOSIAH | ZEPHANIAH |
| | | | | JEREMIAH |
| | | 609 | Jehoahaz | |
| | | 608–598 | Jehoiakim | EZEKIEL |
| | | | | HABAKKUK |
| | | 597 | Jehoiachin | |
| | | 596–587 | Zedekiah | |
| | | Post-exile | | ZECHARIAH, HAGGAI |
| | | | | MALACHI |

*Note:* The biblical books listed on the right contain references to the period of the kings mentioned in the other columns, although some of those books were written later.

The more important kings' names are given in capital letters.

An asterisk indicates that the regnal years include years of regency.

For the dating of prophets Daniel, Joel, Obadiah, Jonah, see the introductions to these books.

# Preface and Preliminary Notes

The English edition of *The Navarre Bible: New Testament* was published in twelve volumes in 1985–92. These books have been constantly reprinted and have obtained a very wide acceptance. The present volume is the seventh and last in a companion series, *The Navarre Bible: Old Testament*.

The project of a new Spanish translation of the Bible, with commentary, was originally entrusted to the faculty of theology at the University of Navarre by St Josemaría Escrivá, the founder of Opus Dei and the university's first chancellor. Because it involved making a new translation of the Bible from the original languages, the Spanish original of this work was a much more substantial undertaking than might appear from the English edition.[1] The completion of the project was celebrated in Madrid in February 2005.

The main feature of the English edition, *The Navarre Bible*, is the commentary, that is, the notes and introductions provided by the editors; rarely very technical, these are designed to elucidate the spiritual and theological message of the Bible. Quotations from commentaries by the Fathers, and excerpts from other spiritual writers, not least St Josemaría Escrivá, are provided to show how they read Scripture and made it meaningful in their lives.

We consider ourselves fortunate in having the Revised Standard Version as the translation of Scripture and wish to record our appreciation for permission to use that text.[2]

The Standard Edition of *The Navarre Bible* includes the Western Church's official Latin version of the Bible, the *editio typica altera* of the New Vulgate (1986).

## PRELIMINARY NOTES

The headings in the biblical text have been provided by the editors (they are not taken from the RSV); this is true also of the cross references in the marginal notes. These headings are listed at the end of the volume to provide an overview of its content. *Some headings carry an asterisk*; this means there is an asterisked note below, more general than usual and one which examines the structure or content of an entire passage. To get an overview of each book, the reader may find it helpful to read the asterisked notes before reading the

---

**1.** *Sagrada Biblia: Antiguo Testamento. Libros proféticos* (Pamplona, 2002) at pp. 7–8 describes the principles governing its translation. **2.** Integral to which are the RSV footnotes, which are indicated by superior letters.

9

biblical text and the more specific notes. An asterisk *in the RSV text* refers the reader to the Explanatory Notes at the end of the book.

References in the margin of the biblical text or its headings point to parallel passages or other passages which deal with the same theme. References given in *italics* show the place in the New Testament which most directly touches on the subject. With the exception of the New Testament and Psalms, the marginal references are to the New Vulgate, that is, they are not normally adjusted (where applicable) to the RSV.

# Abbreviations

## 1. BOOK OF HOLY SCRIPTURE

| | | | |
|---|---|---|---|
| Acts | Acts of the Apostles | 1 Kings | 1 Kings |
| Amos | Amos | 2 Kings | 2 Kings |
| Bar | Baruch | Lam | Lamentations |
| 1 Chron | 1 Chronicles | Lev | Leviticus |
| 2 Chron | 2 Chronicles | Lk | Luke |
| Col | Colossians | 1 Mac | 1 Maccabees |
| 1 Cor | 1 Corinthians | 2 Mac | 2 Maccabees |
| 2 Cor | 2 Corinthians | Mal | Malachi |
| Dan | Daniel | Mic | Micah |
| Deut | Deuteronomy | Mk | Mark |
| Eccles | Ecclesiastes (Qoheleth) | Mt | Matthew |
| Esther | Esther | Nah | Nahum |
| Eph | Ephesians | Neh | Nehemiah |
| Ex | Exodus | Num | Numbers |
| Ezek | Ezekiel | Obad | Obadiah |
| Ezra | Ezra | 1 Pet | 1 Peter |
| Gal | Galatians | 2 Pet | 2 Peter |
| Gen | Genesis | Phil | Philippians |
| Hab | Habakkuk | Philem | Philemon |
| Hag | Haggai | Ps | Psalms |
| Heb | Hebrews | Prov | Proverbs |
| Hos | Hosea | Rev | Revelation (Apocalypse) |
| Is | Isaiah | Rom | Romans |
| Jas | James | Ruth | Ruth |
| Jer | Jeremiah | 1 Sam | 1 Samuel |
| Jn | John | 2 Sam | 2 Samuel |
| 1 Jn | 1 John | Sir | Sirach (Ecclesiasticus) |
| 2 Jn | 2 John | Song | Song of Solomon |
| 3 Jn | 3 John | 1 Thess | 1 Thessalonians |
| Job | Job | 2 Thess | 2 Thessalonians |
| Joel | Joel | 1 Tim | 1 Timothy |
| Jon | Jonah | 2 Tim | 2 Timothy |
| Josh | Joshua | Tit | Titus |
| Jud | Judith | Wis | Wisdom |
| Jude | Jude | Zech | Zechariah |
| Judg | Judges | Zeph | Zephaniah |

## 2. RSV ABBREVIATIONS

In the notes indicated by superior *letters* in the biblical text, the following abbreviations are used:

Cn     a correction made where the text has suffered in transmission and the versions provide no satisfactory restoration but the RSV Committee agrees with the judgment of competent scholars as to the most probable reconstruction of the original text

Heb    the Hebrew of the consonantal Masoretic Text of the Old Testament

Gk     Septuagint, Greek Version of the Old Testament

Lat    Latin Version of Tobit, Judith, and 2 Maccabees

Ms     manuscript

Mss    manuscripts

MT     the Hebrew of the pointed Masoretic Text of the Old Testament

Sam    Samaritan Hebrew text of the Old Testament

Syr    Syriac Version of the Old Testament

Tg     Targum

Vg     Vulgate, Latin Version of Old Testament

N.B. In the biblical text, the word LORD, when spelled with capital letters, stands for the divine name, Yhwh.

## 3. OTHER ABBREVIATIONS

| | | | |
|---|---|---|---|
| ad loc. | *ad locum*, commentary on this passage | Exhort. | Exhortation |
| AAA | *Acta Apostolicae Sedis* | f | and following (*pl.* ff) |
| Apost. | Apostolic | ibid. | *ibidem*, in the same place |
| can. | canon | in loc. | *in locum*, commentary on this passage |
| chap. | chapter | loc. | *locum*, place or passage |
| cf. | *confer*, compare | par. | parallel passages |
| CCC | *Catechism of the Catholic Church* | Past. | Pastoral |
| | | RSVCE | Revised Standard Version, Catholic Edition |
| Const. | Constitution | | |
| Decl. | Declaration | SCDF | Sacred Congregation for the Doctrine of the Faith |
| *Dz-Sch* | Denzinger-Schönmetzer, *Enchiridion Biblicum* (4th edition, Naples-Rome, 1961) | sess. | session |
| | | v. | verse (*pl.* vv.) |
| Enc. | Encyclical | | |

# The Prophetical Books of the Old Testament*

There are sixteen prophetical books in the biblical canon—four "major" (Isaiah, Jeremiah, Ezekiel and Daniel) and twelve "minor" works, a distinction referring only to their length: whereas each of the "major prophets" comprises an entire parchment roll, all the others take up only one—the Roll of the Twelve Prophets. In the Hebrew canon, the books of Deuteronomic history (Joshua, Judges, 1 & 2 Samuel, 1 & 2 Kings) are called "Earlier Prophets", and the name "Later Prophets" covers all the others (Isaiah, Jeremiah, Ezekiel and the Roll of the Twelve Prophets). Also, because it regards the prophetical books as teaching or commentary on the Law (the Pentateuch), the Hebrew canon places them immediately after the Pentateuch and before the books known as the "Writings". The book of Daniel, which was written after the "Prophets" collection was assembled, is included among the "Writings".[1] However, the Christian canon, which focuses on the *history of salvation*, sees the later prophets as being largely oriented towards a hopeful future that finds its fulfilment in Jesus Christ; hence it puts the prophetical books at the end of the canon and includes among them the book of Daniel, given its eschatological concerns. That is the order followed in the Navarre Bible, in line with the Septuagint Greek and the Latin versions. [The RSV places the two last historical books, 1 & 2 Maccabees, after the prophets.]

Both Jewish and Christian traditions hold the books of the prophets in high regard, because prophecy was an integral part of the religious heritage of ancient Israel and these books record the word of God addressed to his people through the oracles of the prophets.

## 1. PROPHETS AND PROPHETICAL BOOKS

The word "prophet" comes from the Greek *pro-phetes*, which means "to speak on behalf of someone," especially a god. It therefore has nothing to do with predicting the future, an activity described in Greek as *mantis*. The Hebrew word for *pro-phetes* is *nabî*, and its reference, too, is religious. *Nabî* came to mean "one chosen by God to speak in his name". The prophet is referred to in other ways in the Bible, in addition to *nabî*—for example, "man of God" (Josh 14:6; 1 Kings 17:18; 2 Kings 4:7), "man of the spirit" (Hos 9:7), "servant of

---

* This introductory essay also appears in *The Navarre Bible: Major Prophets*, pp. 11–26.
**1.** Cf. *The Navarre Bible: Psalms* and *Wisdom Books*, Introduction, p. 11.

the Lord" (2 Kings 9:7), all of which refer more to aspects of the prophet's personality.

a) In the Bible, the word "prophet" and its derivatives (prophecy, prophesying etc.) have quite a broad meaning, but all, primarily, refer to the idea of "speaking in the name of God", being his spokesman. We can see this, for example, in the opening words of the Letter to the Hebrews: "In many and various ways God spoke of old to our fathers by the prophets ..." ( Heb 1:1). The New Testament also describes as prophetical all those passages that refer to the future Messiah, be they in the Pentateuch, the Prophets or the Psalms, and it even goes so far as to consider the entire Old Testament as being prophetical (cf. Mt 2:23; Lk 18:13; Rom 1:2). The Church has inherited this way of speaking when she professes her faith in the Holy Spirit "who has spoken through the prophets" (Nicene-Constantinopolitan Creed).

Using this broad sense of the word, the Bible gives the title of "prophet" to Abraham (Gen 20:7), to Mary, the sister of Moses and Aaron (Ex 15:20), to the seventy elders of the people (Num 11:25–29), to Deborah, who judged Israel in the time of the judges (Judg 4:4), and, of course, to Moses, the very prototype of the prophet (Deut 18:15–18). Indeed, of him it goes so far as to say that "there has not arisen a prophet in Israel like Moses, whom the Lord knew face to face" (Deut 34:10).

People can receive messages in a variety of ways—some quite exceptional, such as visions, dreams, ecstasies etc.; others ordinary, such as incidents in the prophet's life, his alertness to see the significance of quite small things, etc. St Thomas Aquinas, who studied prophecy in depth, distinguishes four types of it in terms of the manner in which the prophet receives the message (the "species", in Thomistic language)—intellectually, by means of the imagination, by infused sight, or by natural sight. He regards the last-mentioned mode as the least perfect because it involves the least degree of direct intervention by God. He also deduces that the gift of prophecy is something transitory, unlike that of sanctifying grace; a person can be chosen to enunciate a specific oracle and never again speak in the name of God.[2]

b) As an institution proper to Israel, prophecy began during the very early days of the monarchy, at the shrines to which the Israelites went for answers to their questions and to discover what the Lord's will demanded of them. Samuel, a prophet in the temple of Shiloh (cf. 1 Sam 3:19-21), is considered to have been the earliest of the prophets (1 Sam 3:20) and later tradition raised him to the rank of intercessor (Ps 99:6; Acts 13:20), one who passed on the word of God (2 Chron 35:18), an upholder of the institutions of Israel (Sir 46:13–20) and the first herald of messianic times (Acts 3:24). Samuel is a prophet because he interprets God's will for the entire people, or for an individual chosen by God to undertake some important assignment: it is he

---

**2.** Cf. *Quodlib.*, 12,1.7, a. 26.

who anoints Saul and David; he spells out how the monarchy should operate; etc. From Samuel onwards, the prophet will have a public role in Israel, to make known God's will at key moments in the history of the people.

There were also "groups of prophets" associated with the shrines (though they often operated beyond their confines). These were communities of people who would enter into ecstatic trances by means of music, dancing and exaggerated gestures (1 Sam 10:5, 10–13). The Bible gives very little information about these groups, but they seem to have had some sort of internal structure and to have in general acted as a group. We know, for example, that at one point, when Saul had sent men to arrest David, Saul himself and his messengers actually took part in the ceremonies of a company of prophets that owed allegiance to Samuel (1 Sam 19:18–24).

In addition to what it has to say about temple prophets, the Bible also tells us about a number of individuals who, on occasion, acted as prophets. For example, Balaam spoke oracles (cf. Num 23:7–10; 18-24; 24:3–9, 15–25), even though he did not belong to the chosen people. Others, like Gad (1 Sam 22:5; 2 Sam 24:11–14, 18–19) and Nathan (2 Sam 7; 12:1–15), lived at court and were prophets of King David. Others, such as Abijah of Shiloh (1 Kings 11:29–39), Jehu (1 Kings 16:1–2) and Micaiah, son of Imlah (1 Kings 22:8–28), were court prophets in the Northern kingdom, where this type of prophetic office was more in evidence. Moreover, prophecy was an established ministry in the shrines at Jericho (2 Kings 2:4–5), Gilgal (2 Kings 4:38) and Bethel (1 Kings 13:11–24). Special mention should be made of the so-called charismatic prophets; these had no particular connexion with court or temple but they were very influential in the life of the people of Israel. Outstanding among these were Elijah (1 Kings 17–19; 2 Kings 1–2) and Elisha (2 Kings 1–13), who operated as prophets in the ninth century BC and had very considerable influence on the politics of the period and on the reform of religious life in Israel. To a greater or lesser extent, the Bible tells us about oracles or interventions by these men, but it does not attribute any written books or texts to them. They are prophets because the Bible tells us that they acted or transmitted their message in the name of God. After the fall of Samaria (722 BC) there were no prophets who were not also writers, or, if there were, they were not particularly influential.

c) The "writer prophets", that is, those who figure in the biblical canon, were, like those mentioned above, men who were conscious of being spokesmen of God; but what distinguishes them is the fact that their visions, oracles and careers, are recorded in writing. Strictly speaking, one should talk not of prophets but of "prophetical literature" or "prophetical books", meaning those writings which are attributed to a particular prophet and which have been handed down as such in the biblical canon. Many of these people exercised their prophetical office in the same way as the prophets mentioned earlier; others, perhaps, never actually preached, and there may even have been one prophet, Malachi, whose name was given to the book by a writer using a pseudonym. Be that as it may, the prophetical books (like the rest of Holy Scripture) are authoritative "on the grounds that, written under the inspiration of the Holy Spirit, they have God as their author, and have been handed on as such to the Church herself".[3]

In this edition, unless it is specifically stated to the contrary, when we speak of "prophets" and "prophetical books", we mean the same thing. As regards when the prophets lived: Amos, Hosea, Isaiah, and Micah belong to the eighth century BC; Nahum, Zephaniah, Habakkuk and Jeremiah, seventh to sixth century; Ezekiel, sixth century. Haggai, Zechariah and Malachi belong to the Persian period; Joel, Obadiah and Jonah are of a later period (it is difficult to be more specific). The book of Daniel was probably written a little before 165 BC.

d) In the New Testament, Jesus is the greatest and last messenger of God, and the eternal Word of the Father (Heb 1:1), although St Luke alone (and then only obliquely) applies to him the title of prophet (Lk 4:24; 13:33; cf. 7:16, 39; 9:8–19). The Church expresses her belief in this regard as follows: "Christ is the great prophet who proclaimed the kingdom of the Father both by the testimony of his life and by the power of his word. Until the full manifestation of his glory, he fulfills the prophetic office ...".[4]

For their part, the first people to embrace faith in Christ shared the conviction, widespread at the time, that prophecy would be a feature of the messianic age. Thus, we find them applying the title of prophet to such people as Anna, the prophetess in the temple (Lk 2:36), and John the Baptist (cf. Mt 11:9–11), who had a prominent role in signalling the dawning of the messianic age. In the aftermath of Pentecost, there were quite a number of Christians who "prophesied". These included Agabus (Acts 11:27–28; 21:10–11), the prophets of Antioch, among them Barnabas (Acts 13:2), the daughters of Philip (Acts 21:9), and many more whose names we do not know. In fact, St Paul praises the gift of prophecy that manifested itself in liturgical assemblies (1 Cor 11:4–5), and he pointed out that it was a gift to aspire to possess (1 Cor 14:1) because it helped to build up the whole Christian community (cf. 1 Cor 14:2–5). However, for that very reason, in order to protect the true charism of prophecy, the leaders of those communities were on their guard against false prophets (cf. 1 Jn 4:1–3) who might introduce erroneous teachings by claiming the authority of spokesmen of God.

The gift of prophecy survives in the Church, for "all the holy people of God shares also in the Church's prophetic office: it spreads abroad a living witness to him, especially by a life of faith and love and by offering to God a sacrifice of praise, the tribute of lips which praise his name (cf. Heb 13:15)".[5]

---

**3.** Vatican II, *Dei Verbum*, 11.  **4.** Vatican II, *Lumen gentium*, 35.  **5.** Ibid., 12.

## 2. HOW THE PROPHETICAL BOOKS CAME INTO BEING

The prophetical books, like many other books in ancient times, were not written all at one go. Like most of the books of the Bible, they went through an editing process over a period of time, until they reached the final stage and became part of the canon. Still, each book has a lot to do with the figure whose name it bears: first, because it contains the main elements of his teaching, but also because we know that some sections were written by the prophet himself (cf. Is 30:8), or by his amanuensis, as in the case of Baruch, who took dictation from Jeremiah. It will never be easy, or for that matter necessary, to work out which words of a book are the original words of the prophet, his *ipsissima verba*, but without doubt each book, as a whole, can be attributed to the original prophet or his circle of disciples.

Scholars usually point to there being three "layers" in the editorial compilation of these books, which correspond to three specific stages. Generally speaking (because the history of each book is different), we can say that one layer can be attributed to the prophet, one to the contribution of disciples, with the third layer, the literary structure, being the work of an editor who came later. The entire process was carried out under the inspiration of the Holy Spirit, who is the principal author of these books and of all Holy Scripture.

In general, the poetical sections of the books are attributed to the prophet himself, specifically those parts which are most expressive, such as, for example, the oracles against the neighbouring countries in Amos (Amos 1:3–2:8); the "confessions" of Jeremiah (Jer 12:1–6; 15:15–21; 20:7–18); the greater part of the Book of the Immanuel in Isaiah (Is 6–12); and many others to which we will draw attention in the commentaries.

The main work involved in creating the book is ascribed to the prophet's disciples—collecting and selecting the most significant oracles, giving them a literary form, writing the biographical sections in the third person, writing down the visions and details of the symbolic actions of the prophet. The disciples would have been responsible for the greater part of each book, given that it could take a lot of time and effort to do all that work. However, it is not always possible to work out the "itinerary" of an oracle from when it was first spoken by the prophet: maybe in the first instance it was transmitted among his immediate followers by being memorized and repeated orally, and was then linked up with other passages in the same tone or with similar content, and then, later still, found its way into small written collections or perhaps larger blocs of writings, until the book as we now know it was eventually produced.

Scholars see the final editor or redactor as being responsible for the book as such and for its final updating. For example, the oracles against the nations in Amos end with the prophecy pronounced against Israel (Amos 2:6–16), but the final redactor must have inserted a similar prophecy against Judah (Amos 2:4–5), because, once the Northern kingdom collapsed, only the people of the

South were in a position to receive the book by the prophet from Teko. In some cases, the final redactor collected and rearranged oracles which, though not those of the original prophet, did carry a message consistent with that in earlier texts; this could have occurred in the case of the book of Isaiah, which includes oracles from different periods but which are arranged in such a way that they make up a coherent book with a particular specific literary character to it. This last redactor played a very important role, because in addition to putting all the various elements together he gave them a unified style and a distinctive doctrinal focus. So, commentators are right to say, as they often do, that he performed the role of an author. To him also must be attributed the heading or title given to each book and the insertion of most of the references to when events took place.

From the literary point of view, prophetical books are different from others in that they retain the features of a public proclamation of the message. The prophet would normally address people in a speech, to move their hearts and to exhort them to mend their ways. Therefore, the most common form of prophetical expression is the oracle, that is, a solemn statement made in the name of God involving either denunciation or a promise of salvation. In the strict sense, an oracle is not a prediction of concrete events, but rather a proclamation of God's plan, which will always be realized. It is addressed to a particular individual (Amos 7:16–17) or, more often, a group of people or the whole nation (cf. Amos 4:1–3; 9–12). Oracles of salvation include the messianic and most of the eschatological oracles. There are also oracles expressed in the form of legal suits (*rîb:* see the notes on Is 1:10–20 and 1:2–31) between God and the people, designed to spell out the reasons for the punishment imposed by God (cf. Hos 2:4–10). In addition to oracles, the prophetical books contain songs (Is 5:1–2), hymns (Is 44:23), letters (Jer 29), wisdom teachings (Amos 5:21–24; Is 8:11–15), etc. The oracles are found side by side with narrative sections, such as accounts of the prophet's calling (Is 6:1–13; Jer 1:4–10), visions (Jer 1:11–14), dreams (Zech 1:7–17) and many other biographical or autobiographical references. Special mention should be made of symbolic actions, that is, "acted-out" oracles. These have nothing to do with magic performed to produce some desired result; they are simply designed to show by signs something that will happen in the future. For example, when Elijah poured water over the burnt offerings at Mount Carmel, he did not cause rainfall, but was imploring God to send it (cf. 1 Kings 18:25, 34–35); and when Jeremiah put the yoke around his neck (cf. Jer 27:2–22), this did not have the effect of plunging the people into slavery (in Babylon); it was an action he did to signal the slavery that awaited them. Almost all the writer prophets use this sort of oracle to help explain their message: Hosea made his matrimonial life a sign of God's love for his people (Hos 1–3), and Isaiah used the symbolic names of his sons (Is 7:3; 8:3) and that of Immanuel (Is 7:14) to proclaim the salvation that was to come. Jeremiah, for his part, employed symbolic actions of this sort more than his predecessors had done: among the examples we find in his work are: the spoiled piece of linen (Jer 13:1–11); the broken flask (Jer 19); the yoke around his neck (Jer 27; 28:10); the purchase of the field (Jer 32); the foundation of the throne of Nebuchadnezzar (Jer 43:8–13); and the book thrown into the Euphrates (Jer 51:59–64). Still, the greatest number of symbolic actions is to be found in Ezekiel, although, due to his style, it is not always easy to work out what they symbolize: his temporary loss of speech (Ezek 3:24–27; cf. 4:1–3); his acting-out of the siege of Jerusalem (Ezek 4:1–17); cutting his hair and beard (Ezek 5:1–3); venturing out with an exile's baggage (Ezek 12:1–16); eating bread with quaking (Ezek 12:17–20); not mourning the death of his wife (Ezek 24:15–27); the two sticks in his hand (Ezek 37:15–28); etc. New Testament prophets, too, carried out symbolic actions (as when Agabus predicted St Paul's imprisonment: Acts 21:11), but it must have occurred very seldom, because the Christian message has more to do with the proclamation of past events than with prophesying future ones (cf. Rom 10:14–18).

## 3. CONTENT

The message contained in the prophetical books covers all aspects of Israelite faith, but each prophet underlines and develops points of teaching that were of particular relevance to his contemporaries. This makes it difficult to summarize and synthesize the teaching of the prophets as a whole, for their writings extend over more than four centuries. The immediate concerns of Amos in the seventh century BC were different from those of Haggai and Zechariah (who lived towards the end of the sixth century) or those of Daniel (second-century). Even so, there are three points, that all the prophets stressed, more or less— belief in one God, the future messianic age, and ethical and social teaching.

a) *Monotheism* is the primary subject of the prophetical oracles. This involves not only the promotion of a single form of worship but also belief in the one, true God: there is no God but the Lord. The main points in their teaching in this regard are:

—God is the sovereign Lord of all human affairs. The God of Israel does not reside in a special *place*, where one must go to find him (in a pantheon, so to speak); nor is he essentially "the god of nature", whose seasons and fertility testify to his presence. Like the wise men (cf. Ps 29; 96; etc.) the prophets acknowledge the Lord (*Yhwh*) to be the ruler of the created universe, and, above all, the one who guides the course of history. It is he who determines victory or defeat, political success or exile, and everything is geared towards encouraging his people to "return" to him ( cf. Amos 4:4–12).

—God has a special relationship with Israel. In the book of Amos he is described as being a fellow wayfarer who reveals his secrets to his servants, the prophets (Amos 3:3–8), and in Hosea (eight century BC) we find the first mention of the Covenant in the books of the prophets (Hos 2:20; 6:7; 8:2). It is Hosea, too, who depicts the God-man relationship as being spousal (Hos 1–3) and that of father-and-son (Hos 11:1–14)—imagery that finds its way, via later prophetical books (cf. Jer 2:2), into the New Testament (cf. Mt 9:15; Rev 21:2).

—God is holy. Even though God has a close relationship with his people, he is not like them; he cannot be treated as being on a par with them; he cannot be "manipulated", not even by means of sacrifices and offerings. God stands above everything; he is the Most High—as Isaiah stresses so much (cf. Is 6:3). The holiness of the people, therefore, derives from their participating in the holiness of their God: their belief and its ethical demands mark them out as being different from other nations. God is the "Holy One of Israel" (Is 5:19–24), because, without ceasing to be the Most High, he has drawn near to his people.

—Punishment is interpreted as part of God's relationship with his people. If they fail to live up to the demands of their special calling, if their behaviour is no better than that of other nations, there is nothing for it but for God to chastise them (cf. Amos 3:2). That is the only way they can be brought back to the path of righteousness. God "visits" his people (that is, makes them pay the just price of their sins) in order to re-establish a proper relationship with them. That is what the prophets mean when they speak of the "day of the Lord" (cf. Amos 5:18–19; Zeph 1:7–18).

b) *Messianic hope* forms the very backbone of the prophetical books. Those from the pre-exilic period, as indeed the Psalms (Ps 2; 89), use Nathan's prophecy (2 Sam 7:14) to get across the idea that salvation will come through a descendant of David (*royal messianism*). But they never adopt a sycophantic attitude towards the king or use courtly forms of address or bestow divine titles on him or envision that he shall reign forever. The notion they have of the Messiah looks to the future, so that the reigning monarch pales into insignificance; they encourage the people to place their hopes in "the Lord's anointed", who is soon to come. Isaiah is the prophet who most often mentions the Davidic dynasty (cf. Is 7:13–17; 9:5–6; 11:1–5), and yet he never mentions the king by name. He applies grandiose, unheard-of titles to him, but in doing so he exalts the Lord's wondrous works more than the individual whom the Lord places at their centre. Micah, too, refers to the Davidic line without mentioning the king's name (Mic 5:1–5). And Jeremiah, who produced only one oracle about the future king, proclaims the coming of a descendant in the line of David who will rule with the justice and righteousness of the Lord (Jer 23:5–6). The king that all the prophets look forward to is someone who will live a life befitting a true son of God—not at all the sort of king they were familiar with.

The prophets of the exile period hardly ever speak in terms of royal Messiah: Ezekiel will not even give the title of "king" to the prince who will rule over a restored Israel and whom he sees as being a new "David" (Ezek

34:23–24). And in the years just before the return from exile we find it being said that God himself will bring salvation, without using intermediaries (Is 41:14)—a *messianism without a Messiah*. And sometimes we find the title of Messiah being given to any person who, acting in God's name, brings deliverance to Israel—even if he be a foreigner, as the Persian king Cyrus was (Is 45:1). But salvation will come about, primarily, through the people, or through someone born into it, a servant of the Lord who will achieve full freedom for himself and his fellow countrymen.

Among the last prophets, those of the period after the Exile, we find a spiritualization of messianism, which fits in very well with their teaching about the last days. This "eschatology" refers to their conviction that God will, in due course, save man once and for all, by means of Israel, his chosen people, who have a special role to play in the advent of salvation. Israel will judge the nations—in a scenario that prefigures God's last judgment (*the day of the Lord*) which will cover both Israel and all other nations. In the last of the prophetical books, things to do with the End take second place: the main emphasis is on the Messiah. According to Zechariah, God himself will come to rule over all the earth (cf. Zech 13:9), and the book of Daniel, where we find the figure of the "son of man", attests to the hope that God will give a humble person (read "the chosen people") a kingdom that will last forever and will encompass the whole world (Dan 7:13–14:27). In the New Testament we recognize Jesus to be the true Messiah, with all the features (and more) that the prophets attributed to the Messiah: he is the descendant of King David; he judges and redeems the world; he is the Son of man; and he takes on the features of Isaiah's Servant of the Lord in order to bring enduring salvation to all mankind.

c) *Ethical and social teaching*. The prophets, especially those prior to the Exile, lay much stress on the social implications of the faith. As heralds of God's teaching about his choice of Israel and about the Covenant, they exhort the people to obedience time and again. And because their contemporaries are losing their old ideals, exploiting the weaker members of society and adopting Gentile lifestyles, the prophets are not slow to reproach them for "forgetting God" (cf. Hos 2:13; Jer 2:32) and becoming like other peoples (cf. Hos 9:1).

Oppressive rulers come in for the severest criticism, and the prophets are at pains to stress divine preference for the "humble and lowly" (Zeph 3:12–13). In line with the thinking of the entire Old Testament, the prophets never consider material poverty as something desirable, much less as being an ideal. Poor people are not virtuous because they lack resources, but God has a special love for them because their poverty is often caused by the injustice of powerful, wealthy people. It is that type of poverty, the result of injustice, that the prophets seek to eliminate. Hence their continual insistence on the fact that justice and holiness are inescapable demands deriving from the Covenant.

The moral precepts preached by the prophets are those to be found in the Law, but the prophets are at pains to point out that good conduct must come from the heart. A clean heart is more imporant than external conformity to the Law (cf. Is 2:16–17; Ezek 11:19; 36:26); and from Jeremiah (cf. Jer 31:29–30) and Ezekiel (Ezek 18:1–4) onwards, great stress is laid on individual reponsibility: a person has to take responsibility for his own sins and not blame them on his forebears.

Finally, the prophets' message also stresses the importance of religious worship: it has to be performed properly, in the right spirit, as befitting the reverence due to God. They constantly criticize an external formalism in the practice of religion, and stress that there needs to be continuity between the worship rendered to God and the people's ethical and social life. A people that brings offerings to the Lord and professes faith in him in the sphere of the liturgy must make sure that it does not then turn around and deny him by misconduct and corruption in everyday life.

## 4. HISTORICAL BACKGROUND

The writer-prophets, from Amos down to Malachi, exercised their ministry over a long period of time—from the eighth century BC to the fourth century, or right into the second if one includes the book of Daniel. These were eventful years for Israel, as we know from the historical books of the Bible,[6] a period in which its fortunes changed radically. The Northern kingdom was dominant at first, under Omri and his successors, until it eventually decayed and then collapsed at the hands of the Assyrians (722 BC). Then came the heyday of the kingdom of Judah, in the reign of Hezekiah, and the religious reform led by Josiah (662 BC). But everything stopped abruptly with the invasion by Nebuchadnezzar. The king and all the most prominent members of the community were deported to Babylon (587 BC)—an exile that lasted fifty years; the exiles were allowed to return, thanks to King Cyrus' decree, but the country no longer had independence. Soon it came under the sway of the Persians (537–333 BC), and these were followed by the Greeks—the Lagid and the Seleucid kings (333–70 BC). From the time of the Babylonian captivity onwards, the Jews were never again independent, but they managed to maintain a strong religious life. All this is borne out in the prophetical books, which set out in an explicit way the historical background of each prophet. Being men of their time (and insightful interpreters of events), their writings contain many historical references, explicit and implicit, and these are very useful for dating an oracle or a book or part of a book.

a) *The prophets, interpreters of events.* The prophetical books tell us quite a lot about Israel's contacts with the peoples round about. We can see this in a literary genre found in all the main prophetical works—the "oracles against

---

6. Cf. *The Navarre Bible: Joshua–Kings*, Introduction, pp 14–18.

the nations" (Amos 1–2; Is 13–23; Zeph 2:4–15; Ezek 25–32; etc.); but there are frequent references also to the pagan nations in the minor prophets—for example, Nahum's oracles concerning Nineveh, and those of Obediah to do with Edom. All these oracles help to show the prophets' great interest in Israel's relationship with its pagan neighbours.

However, the prophets did not confine themselves to preaching about events in which they themselves played leading roles or which impinged on themselves more or less directly. they reflected deeply on all events and on the personalities involved, and pointed out the direction that history was taking. Their interpretation of events was based on three basic ideas—monotheism, God's election of Israel, and that the salvation he promised would apply to all mankind.

Because there is only one God, all human life and history is under his sway; he is in control of everything that happens. He guides the course of events; he is behind all the great and terrible events of history. Even so, people's faith in God can falter, especially at times of crisis, when some defeat or an invasion seems to be imminent, or actually takes place. When Israel is in difficulties (which is when it seeks protection from foreign nations or from foreign gods), a prophet is raised up to confirm them in the true faith: "'Do not seek Bethel and do not enter into Gilgal or cross over to Beer-sheba, for Gilgal shall surely go into exile, and Bethel shall come to naught.' Seek the Lord and live, lest he break out like fire in the house of Joseph, and it devour, with none to quench it for Bethel" (Amos 5:5–6).

Assyria, Babylon and Egypt are the main oppressors: these are evil and idolatrous nations, and yet everything goes well for them. If this is so, how can one say that the fate of nations is being determined by the Lord, the only God? It would seem, on the contrary, that the gods, the protectors of those nations, were getting the better of the Lord. However, the prophets do not agree at all: they tell us that God himself is behind those nations, he is using them to punish Israel as its sins deserve: "I will raise up against you a nation, O house of Israel, [says the Lord, the God of hosts], and they shall oppress you from the entrance of Hamath to the Brook of the Arabah" (Amos 6:14). In the oracles against the nations, as in other oracles, the prophets do not always predict specific future events but, rather, proclaim God's will, which is fulfilled in different ways at different times.

God in his wisdom shows special favour to the people of Israel. But this election does not mean that he isolates them from the rest of mankind or that he gives them special political privileges or a false security (cf. Amos 9:7); Israel should not think it is the greatest of nations (cf. Amos 7:2–5) or the richest (cf. Amos 6:2) or the strongest (cf. Amos 2:9). Israel is called to lead all the nations to share in the blessings and benefits that God bestows: "'Come, let us go up to the mountain of the Lord, to the house of the God of Jacob; that he may teach us his ways and that we may walk in his paths.' For out of Zion shall go forth the law, and the word of the Lord from Jerusalem" (Is 2:3 and

Mic 4:2). Israel is not the object of God's choice for its own benefit alone; that choice looks to all mankind, to all the nations. This idea comes across more clearly after the exile, when their experiences led them to reflect on the implications of their election by God. At that point we find God's relationship with his people being described in terms of an intimate and loving bond: "You, Israel, my servant, Jacob, whom I have chosen, the offspring of Abraham, my friend; you whom I took from the ends of the earth, and called from its farthest corners, saying to you, 'You are my servant, I have chosen you and not cast you off'; fear not for I am with you, be not dismayed, for I am your God" (Is 41:8–9).

Moreover, Israel has a close solidarity with the rest of mankind. In one of Zechariah's oracles of salvation, we are told how the history of the chosen people will impinge on others: "As you have been a byword of cursing among the nations, O house of Judah and house of Israel, so will I save you and you shall be a blessing. […] In those days ten men from the nations shall take hold of the robe of a Jew, saying, 'Let me go with you, for we have heard that God is with you'" (Zech 8:13, 23).

b) *Apocalyptic writing*. When it seems that the voice of the prophets can be heard no more, the word of God begins to express itself in a new way. In the darkest days of the Maccabees, after a long period that had seen no prophet in Israel, the book of Daniel came to be written. Although that book does link up with the earlier prophets, whom it explicitly cites (cf. Dan 9:2) or whom it copies when it comes to heavenly visions (cf. Ezek 1:3–4; Dan 8:2–3; etc.), its message and literary form are similar to what we find in other Jewish writings of the same period, or even earlier, which have not found their way into the Bible. It is an instance of what is called "apocalyptic" literature, two of whose features are that world history is seen as a continuum involving successive epochs, and the end of the world is nigh—the point when a new world will come into being and when even the dead (through resurrection) will live again. The book of Daniel is structured by real events, but the interpretation it offers of them is unlike that of earlier prophets, who concerned themselves with the fortunes of other nations only to the degree that they impacted on Israel at a particular juncture: the book of Daniel surveys the panorama of world history, which it divides into epochs and assesses from the standpoint of the final outcome—the establishment of the kingdom of God. The narratives in Daniel 2–7 show us the main periods of history, from Nebuchadnezzar to Antiochus IV Epiphanes, bringing in a new and hitherto unknown element as far as the Old Testament is concerned – the advent of the kingdom of God. The vision of the image or of the statue in chapter 2 is a superb description of the succession of empires—first, the Babylonian (gold), then that of the Medes (silver), followed by the Persian (bronze); then comes Alexander and the Greek empire, which, due to the continuous rivalry between Lagids and Seleucids, is depicted as iron mixed with clay. The final or eschatological stage is described in terms of a stone cut from a mountain: "The God of heaven will set up a kingdom which shall never be destroyed, [...] and it shall stand forever" (Dan 2:44). In chapter 7, where the visions of Daniel start, the author gives another description of the series of empires, from the Babylonian to the Seleucid, using wild beasts as imagery. It will all come to an end, and the climax will be the arrival of that "son of man", representing "the people of the saints of the Most High" who will be given "an everlasting kingdom, and all dominions shall serve and obey them" (Dan 7:27)

Daniel's prophecy, then, follows a historical schema, a highly stylized one consisting of three stages—past history (from Nebuchadnezzar to Antiochus), current events (a description of the persecution instigated by Antiochus, in great detail), and the definitive events at the End (a short account of the death of the oppressive king and the establishment of the Kingdom of God): see Daniel 7:17–23; 11:8–36; 11:40–12:3.

To sum up: although historical events provide the framework within which earlier modes of prophecy developed, the interpretation of history forms the literary base of apocalyptic writings. Earlier prophets buoyed up their listeners' hopes by means of oracles of denunciation and salvation, using contemporary events as a pretext for what they had to say. Apocalyptic writing achieves the same objective by proclaiming the catastrophe that will befall the whole world at the end of time—and which will be followed by salvation for those "written in the book", a salvation in which Gentiles and Israelites will share.

The focus of prophetical and apocalyptic writing on events of human history opens the way to a point in time when it will find fulfilment—when the New Testament will bear out everything found in the Old. The advent of the Messiah will mark the beginning of that fulfilment, the start of the last stage of history.

## 5. THE PROPHETS IN THE LIGHT OF THE NEW TESTAMENT

Apart from the Psalms, the prophetical books are, of all the Old Testament books, those that are to be found most often in the New, be it by way of explicit quotation or easily identifiable reference, or (as sometimes happens) allusions that are difficult to pin down.

As the *Catechism of the Catholic Church* explains, the prophetical books contain a message of hope and proclaim the ultimate salvation of all mankind: "Through the prophets, God forms his people in the hope of salvation, in the expectation of a new and everlasting Covenant intended for all ... (cf. Is 2:2–4; Jer 31:31–34; Heb 10:16). The prophets proclaim a radical redemption of the People of God, purification from all their infidelities (cf. Ezek 36), a salvation which will include all the nations (cf. Is 49:5–6; 53:11)."[7] In the New

---

7. *Catechism of the Catholic Church*, 64.

Testament we can see these expectations finding fulfilment in Jesus Christ—in his person and in his life and teaching, as St Matthew bears witness: "all this has taken place, that the scriptures of the prophets might be fulfilled" (Mt 26:56). The Gospels and the Letters of the apostles are well aware of the prophets and point out the ways their oracles find fulfilment: they show that they were referring to the present time; and that events have borne out what they predicted; and they use words of the prophets to confirm people in their faith in Jesus.

a) *The Christian meaning of the prophetic oracles.* As we know from biblical commentaries or *pesarim* discovered at Qumran, Jews of Jesus' time used to read the prophetical books in the light of events happening around them. The commentary in the book of Habakkuk (1 Qp Hab.), for example, does so, to explain Roman invasion and oppression (the Romans being the *Kittim* mentioned in Habakkuk). Similarly, the New Testament explains some passages by applying them to Jesus: in the synagogue of Nazareth, Jesus, after reading out Isaiah 61:1–2, openly says, "Today this scripture has been fulfilled in your hearing" (Lk 4:21). The book of the Acts tells us that the eunuch from the court of the Ethiopian queen asked Philip about the meaning of the fourth song of the Servant (Is 53:7–8), "and beginning with this scripture (Philip) told him the good news of Jesus" (Acts 8:35).

b) *The fulfilment of prophecies.* The New Testament writers never tried to prove that things contained in the prophetical writings were carried out to the last letter in the life of Jesus, as if the gift of prophecy was a form of magical foresight or fortune-telling. Rather, they saw Jesus as being the climax of salvation history: in him the ancient promises found fulfilment; the salvation which the prophets could only ever vaguely see had now come about in all its fullness.

The accounts of Christ's passion and infancy were, respectively, perhaps the first and last to be consigned to writing—the passion, death, and resurrection, because these underpinned the Christian faith; the birth and childhood of Christ, because they showed that Jesus was the Son of God. Various accounts contain references to the prophets in the repeated observation, "so that the scriptures might be fulfilled".

Apropos of Jesus' passion and death, we find the Gospels using the prophets to explain such episodes as his entry into Jerusalem on a donkey (Jn 12:14–15), the fact that his disciples fled from the garden of olives (Mt 26:30–31), the purchase of the potter's field with the thirty pieces of silver (Mt 27:7–10), the soldiers' dividing out Christ's garments (Jn 19:24), his side being pierced by a lance (Jn 19:36–37); and the whole sordid process of the passion (cf. Acts 3:18–24). Also, we quite often find puzzling events commented on through quotations from the prophets—for example, the reason for Christ's sentence, that is, the fact that he says he is the Son of man (Mt 26:64), the mention of his being "reckoned with transgressors" (Lk 22:37), the lament of the women of Jerusalem (Lk 23:26–30) and many little things that take on great significance when seen in the light of the Old Testament. Indeed, as Jesus himself told the disciples at Emmaus, the sufferings he underwent were necessary for the Messiah to enter into his glory, in keeping with what the prophets had said (Lk 24:25–26).

The infancy accounts of Matthew and Luke also carry many quotations from the prophets. Perhaps the most important one is that of the Immanu-el (Is 7:14), used to confirm the virginal conception and Person of Jesus, defining him, as it does, as "God with us" (cf. Mt 1:22–23 and Lk 1:30–31). St Matthew uses explicit quotations to justify, among other things, the fact that Bethlehem was the Messiah's birthplace (Mt 2:5), the flight into Egypt and the return from there (Mt 2:15), the slaughter of the innocents (Mt 2:17), and the return to Nazareth (Mt 2:23). St Luke prefers allusions and general references—in the announcement to Zechariah (Lk 1:17), in the *Magnificat* (Lk 1:47) and the *Benedictus* (Lk 1:76, 79), in the angels' hymn (Lk 2:14), and in that of Simeon (Lk 2:30–31).

The narrative of Jesus' public life also contains quotations from and references to the prophets, bearing out what Jesus himself said: "You search the scriptures [...] and it is they that bear witness to me" (Jn 5:39). And so, for example, a passage from Jeremiah is used by Jesus to justify his driving the merchants out of the temple (Mt 21:13), and he refers to Isaiah to explain why he speaks in parables (Mt 13:14) and to denounce the hypocrisy of the Pharisees (Mt 15:8).

c) *Confirmation of Christians in the faith.* The early Christians would have subscribed to the old adage that "What is not in the Torah [in the Bible] is not in the world".[8] They felt a need to support their belief in Christ, who died and rose from the dead, with passages from the Bible and particularly from the prophets. In the skeletal creed to be found in St Paul's First Letter to the Corinthians (it is probably the earliest of the creeds), we find the same refrain being repeated: "that Christ died *in accordance with the scriptures,* that he was buried, that he was raised on the third day *in accordance with the scriptures*" (1 Cor 15:3–4). The scriptures confirmed that Jesus rose from the dead in line with what the prophets, including Hosea and Isaiah, had announced (1 Cor 15:54–55). This way of reading the prophetical writings might sometimes seem to us to be not particularly "scholarly", but it shows the authority that the scriptures had for the early Christians (and for the Jews)—and how convinced early Christian communities were that the prophets' message about definitive salvation found its fulfilment in Christ Jesus, the Messiah and Saviour of all mankind.

The Fathers of the Church read the Bible in the same sort of way, and used the prophets as a source for their theology of Christ and the Church. St Irenaeus of Lyons, for example, who lived in the second century BC, makes a

---

8. Cf. *Mishnah, Abbot,* 5, 22.

subtle distinction between promise and prophecy. A promise is bound by the words in which it is expressed: the words are to be taken literally; whereas a prophecy goes beyond the confines of the meaning of the words and, referring as it does to Christ and the Church, it attains its full meaning when the events it describes take place. "If you wonder what changes the Lord effected when he came, know that everything was made new by his becoming present among us as it was foretold. For it was prophesied that the author of great change would come to renew and revitalize all mankind. The coming of a king is announced by servants sent out before him to prepare the people to receive their Lord. When the king stands before his subjects, they will be filled with the joy that was foretold and they will enjoy the freedom that comes from him and they will partake of his vision and listen to his preaching and rejoice in his gifts, and they will no longer wonder what changes the king will effect: for he brings himself and will grant to men all the gifts that have been foretold, gifts that the angels desire to know."[9]

---

**9.** *Adversus haereses*, 4, 34, 1.

# HOSEA

# Introduction

The book of Hosea comes first in the collection known as the "minor prophets", although chronologically it is the second book, coming after Amos. The position that Hosea is given shows the regard in which the book is held in both the Hebrew and the Christian canons.

The book is quite long but it tells us very little about Hosea himself, apart from some domestic troubles he experienced (1:2–9; 3:1–5). The book carries the title, "The word of the Lord that came to Hosea …" (1:1), which indicates that the author was more interested in passing on the words of the prophet than in telling us who the man was. From clues in the text, it appears that Hosea exercised his prophetical ministry in the last years of the reign of Jeroboam II of Israel (788–747 BC) and in the turbulent decades after the days of splendour that Jeroboam enjoyed. However, Hosea apparently knew nothing about the fall of Samaria in 721 BC. Therefore, he must have carried out his mission more or less between 750 and 725 BC.

The original text is not easy to read, being written in the dialect of the North. Still, the language of Hosea shows him to be a creative poet and a tender-hearted man; he is very conscious of God's love for his people, and he is able to express this by using daring imagery to catch the attention of his listeners.

## 1. STRUCTURE AND CONTENT

The book of Hosea is well worth reading as a record of the prophet's preaching over the course of twenty or more years of ministry. It is likely that one or a number of his listeners or disciples took down the prophet's teaching and gave it a structure that had more to do with the themes than with circumstances of each oracle and when it was spoken. Nowadays the general consensus is that by far the greater part of the book comes from Hosea himself. To that text, editor(s) would probably have added some linking passages etc.; Hosea was a prophet in the Northern kingdom (Israel), so the references to Judah may be later additions (cf. 1:1; 1:7; 1:10–12; 4:15a; 5:5; 6:11; 11:12b; 12:2), as also the words of warning at the end (14:9).

Leaving aside the title and the final exhortation (cf. 1:1 and 14:9), the book consists of two parts of unequal length. The first (1:2–3:5) deals with the prophet's mission and his marriage (and all its symbolism); this part is essential to understanding the overall message of Hosea. The second part (4:1–14:8), by far the longer, consists in a collection of oracles all to do in one way or another with God's faithfulness and the infidelity of Israel, that is, the Northern kingdom, Samaria or Ephraim. It is difficult to discern a clear structure in this collection, which takes up eleven chapters; but one could say that it has two sections to it. At two points, the oracles begin with a "legal pleading" or lawsuit (*rîb*) in which the Lord speaks (4:1, 4; 12:2), and on both occasions the oracles of denunciation conclude with verses about a future marked by blessing and reconciliation (11:8–11; 14:4–8); this pattern reproduces that found in the oracle in chapter 2, which sets the pattern for the whole book (2:2–23)—a "pleading" (2:2) followed by a denunciation and then the vision of a future when all will be well (2:2–13; 2:14–23). If we go along with this division, we should note that the second section of part two is more serene, more reflective, harking back to the origins of Israel and making the point that its identity as a people is linked to God's rescuing it from bondage in Egypt (cf. 12:5, 9; 13:4–5).

Dividing the book up in this way we have:

TITLE (1:1)

1. HOSEA'S MARRIAGE (1:2–3:5). This forms a homogeneous unit which contains the core of the book's message—namely, that the prophet's personal life (1:2–2:1; 3:1–5) is a symbol; the prophet uses his life as a metaphor for expressing God's feelings towards Israel (2:2–23).

2. THE SINS OF ISRAEL (4:1–11:11). This is a collection of all sorts of oracles indicting Israel for unfaithfulness. The sins condemned have to do with morality, public policy, idolatry and religious syncretism, divine worship, etc. They are denounced because they are all signs of waywardness, whereas love of God calls for total commitment; therefore, using the marriage metaphor set up in the first part of the book, the text now explains these sins as types of fornication. These chapters conclude with a beautiful poem in which God depicts himself to Israel not only as a solicitous husband but also as a tender, loving father.

3. ISRAEL'S UNFAITHFULNESS (11:12–14:8). These oracles denounce Israel for continuing to fall into the same sins—forgetting God, worshipping idols, and religious syncretism. We are told of another reason for God's love for Israel: even though Israel is as rebellious as his father Jacob, God's love goes back to his election of Jacob.

CONCLUDING ADMONITIONS (14:9).

## 2. COMPOSITION AND HISTORICAL BACKGROUND

The ministry of Hosea (covering approximately 750–725 BC) coincided with the prosperous reign of Jeroboam (788–747) and the years of strife that followed in the Northern kingdom: in little more than twenty years Israel had six kings, all of whom were deposed or assassinated; Pekahiah (737–735) was the only one to succeed to the throne by peaceful means. There are echoes of this anarchy to be found in the book (cf. 5:8–6:6; 7:3–7; etc.). The Assyrian empire contributed to this chaos; its kings Tiglath-pileser also known as Pul (745–727), and Shalmaneser V (727–722) both invaded Israel in their time, gained control over much of it, imposed heavy tribute and deported huge numbers of people. In 732 Tiglath-pileser deposed Pekah; and Shalmaneser deposed Hosea, the last king of Israel. Finally, Shalmaneser laid siege to Samaria, and his son, Sargon II, eventually took the city in 722–721, and the kingdom of Israel disappeared off the map. The book does not mention the fall of Samaria; but Syria's stranglehold on Israel can be seen from its pages.

Situated as it was between powerful empires like those of Assyria and Egypt, a small kingdom like Israel had to form political alliances or pay tribute as a vassal in order to survive. But, for Israel, political pacts involved a danger of compromising its commitment to the Lord, the God of Israel, and worshipping the gods of Israel's allies alongside him. It is this sort of religious syncretism that the prophet condemns (cf. 5:13; 7:11, etc.), and, in the opinion of the author of the book of Kings (cf. 2 Kings 17:7–23), it was one of the main causes of the eventual disappearance of Israel.

This syncretism was connected with an earlier one stemming from the Canaanite roots of the territory. Another frequent theme in Hosea is his denunciation of the cult of the Canaanite god, Baal; there were many who considered the worship of Baal and the worship of Yahweh to be compatible. To understand how this could happen, one needs to remember that when the chosen people settled Canaan in the time of the Judges (twelfth–eleventh century BC), they changed from being nomadic people to becoming tillers of the soil. They learned many of their agricultural skills from the Canaanites; but those skills and customs were steeped in the cult of Baal (held by the Canaanites to be a god of nature, lord of the rains, master of the seasons and of the mysteries of fertility) and Astarte, the wife of Baal and goddess of fertility. Moreover, through cultural contacts and a policy whereby some of the kings of the Northern kingdom entered into marriage alliances with Phoenician and Canaanite princesses, religious syncretism spread through Israel. Ancient shrines like Bethel and Gilgal became venues for harvest and other festivals where pagan rites were commonplace. And so it came about that many Israelites sought to combine their faith in the Lord with idolatrous practices (cf. 4:17–18; 8:11; etc.). The prophets of Israel dedicated their efforts to defending the purity of Yahwist religion, and its moral and cultic precepts.

This situation, together with the fact that Israel used to turn its back on God when things were going well, helps to explain the tone of the oracles in this book. Hosea does his very best to teach the people undiluted belief in the one true God and to make them see that they, and only they, have been singled out by the Lord to be his people. To get this message across, he does not resort to uttering awful threats; instead, he uses very tender, intimate images. Hosea is a great poet: he devises symbols and analogies and new ways of expressing God's love for his people that will be very influential on later prophets and make their mark on the history of Revelation. Some of the things he says are very daring and are charged with poetic power and deep feeling. God is a husband, father, physician and shepherd (2:19; 11:1; 7:1; 13:6); he is like a lion, a bear, a leopard or a lioness (5:14; 13:7–8). Israel is his wife, his son (2:19; 11:1); she is like a silly dove, a vine, a tamed heifer (7:11; 10:1, 10).

This imagery of Hosea's introduces us to the second context of the book—the story of the prophet's marriage. The first three chapters tell the story of Hosea's marriage to an unfaithful wife, his passionate love for her despite her infidelity, and their later reconciliation (something which was legally unthinkable at the time, and quite at odds with his wife's behaviour). The chain of events is so odd that even the earliest students of the text (Jewish and Christian) debated whether it has to do with things that actually happened in the life of the prophet (that he had in fact endured the bitter experience of his wife's infidelity) or whether the story is not a symbol, devised to convey just how unfaithful Israel has been. Most of the earlier commentators see it as a symbol; most of the modern ones think that the prophet did indeed have difficulties in his married life, which he used to symbolize the relationship between God and Israel. Be it based on real or imaginary events, the narrative bears witness to heartfelt love, where, despite the repeated infidelity of the loved one, the lover does not cease to love her, desires to love her as a wife and tries to attract her back so that they can live together in harmony.

The unique thing about Hosea's message is that the prophet identifies things happening in Israel (idolatry, syncretism, transgressions against the commandments, neglect of God in times of prosperity, etc.) as failures to keep the spousal covenant made between God and Israel. Just as Hosea's wife is untrue to her marriage covenant, Israel is unfaithful to the Covenant she made with the Lord. And when God asks the prophet to win back his wife's love by means of his own fidelity, the message also comes across that God never tires of forgiving; God is ever faithful, always ready to be re-united with his people.

Thus, the book uses this account of Hosea's marriage to communicate profound truths about the Covenant, about the exclusive commitment that Israel's election entails, about the "psychology" of God in his relations with human beings, etc.

## 3. MESSAGE

No prophet, not even Isaiah or Jeremiah, has equalled Hosea in the fervour with which he describes the mystery of God's love for his people. Jeremiah, particularly, and the lyrical Song of Songs have things to say about God's spousal love; but Hosea expounds it best of all—that is, until such time as the Son of God becomes man and actually shows us the love of God. Therein lies much of the originality and vigour of Hosea's enduring message—the fact that, as far back as the middle of the eight century BC, he anticipated the full Revelation of God in Jesus Christ, namely, the fact that God is, above all else, Love. But if one had to pin down Hosea's message any more than that, one would have to talk in terms of two new concepts—the spousal covenant, and steadfast love.

A covenant (the Hebrew word for it is *berith*) is, in the first instance, a pact or alliance made between individuals or nations (cf. Jer 2:2; 3:1–2, 6–10, 20; etc.). The Lord made a Covenant with Israel—a Covenant which Israel will break, but which the Lord will renew (10:4; 12:1). Going back over the early traditions of the people, Hosea says that it was during the exodus, in the wilderness, that God came to know Israel, made a covenant with him, and gave him the commandments (11:1; 12:13; 13:5). But the Covenant is not just a legal instrument, a pact; it is something more. The Covenant is first and foremost a loving initiative on God's part: God makes Israel his own son.[1] Moreover, in the light of his own marriage experience, the prophet teaches that the Covenant is also a spousal commitment, in which husband and wife make a commitment to love one another to the exclusion of anyone else. Therefore, Israel's infidelities and her prostitution, that is, her worship of alien gods,[2] provoke God's jealousy and anger; like a cheated lover, his passionate love changes to anger.[3] But God continues to love his spouse-people, his heart goes out to them (11:8), and their punishment is designed to lead them to conversion (2:14–23; 5:15). Hosea's depiction of God as a father and a husband enriches the concept of the Covenant: no longer is it something cut and dried; it is a permanent initiative on God's part; He offers the Covenant

---

**1.** During the exodus from Egypt, "when Israel was a child" (11:1). God loved him; he "took (him) in his arms" (11:3) and taught him to walk; he "fed (him)" (13:6); and led him to the promised land (12:14) which yields abundant fruit (10:1). **2.** Hosea teaches that even before entering the promised land Israel let herself be seduced by the abominable rites of Baal-peor (9:10), and continued to do so at Gilgal (4:15; 9:15; 12:11), in Gibe-ah (9:9; 10;9), in Bethel (Bet-Aven), (4:15; 5:8; 10:15) and in Samaria (8:5). Israel even went so far as to be contaminated by the belief that the Baals controlled fertility of the land and flocks and human beings (2:5; 7:14); Israel worshipped idols and offered sacrifices to them (4:13; 8:4, 10:1, 5; 11:2; 13:2; 14:8), and even took part in the practice of sacred prostitution in Canaanite fertility rites (4:11–14:1). **3.** Therefore, the prophet says that God will chase Israel like a hunter of birds (7:12), like a lion on the loose (5:14), like a bear robbed of her cubs (13:8); he will be like a moth to Ephraim and dry rot to Israel (5:12). He will destroy the places where idols are worshipped (10:2, 8); Israel's princes will die by the sword (7:16), its people will be deported (10:6), its fortress will be destroyed (10:14); and its king will perish (10:15).

and, when Israel breaks it, He offers it again. However, because the Covenant involves the kind of commitment that marriage does, breaking it is not just the transgression of a set of rules; it is a personal offence, a lack of love, infidelity and prostitution; it amounts to turning one's back on God.

The other idea that runs through the book of Hosea is that of the Lord's "steadfast love". As is true of all the prophetical books, Hosea's message is aimed at bringing about the people's conversion, their return to God. This conversion should not be a shallow, temporary phenomenon: it should be sincere; it must involve "knowing" the Lord better and being more faithful to him (cf. 6:1–6). The "logic", the process, of this conversion is what is new in Hosea. In the prophetical tradition, the process was: God chooses man; man sins; man has a change of heart; God forgives him. In the book of Hosea the last two stages are transposed: now, forgiveness precedes conversion. In this, Hosea is the great precursor of the New Testament, where even conversion is a gratuitous gift from God: "God shows his love for us in that while we were yet sinners Christ died for us" (Rom 5:8; cf. 1 Jn 4:10). St Paul is not saying here that conversion is unnecessary, but that it comes about as a response to the love of God, who is always ready to forgive us.

God's "steadfast love" for men and women can be seen not only in the changing circumstances described in the book; it comes across from the very language that the prophet uses, particularly in the terms that describe God's love for his people—"love", *'ahabá* (3:1; 11:1, 4; 14:4), and "steadfast love", *hesed* (2:19; 6:6; 10:12; 12:6). The first of these two words means love in the general sense—love between friends, between husband and wife, between God and human beings; mutual heartfelt love. The word *hesed* involves, along with love, the idea of mutual fidelity, a fidelity that is based in fact on love. When *hesed* is used to describe God's love for the human person, it means that his love endures despite betrayal and sin.

## 4. THE BOOK OF HOSEA IN THE LIGHT OF THE NEW TESTAMENT AND CHRISTIAN TRADITION

The sacred writers of the New Testament quote Hosea a number of times to show that his oracles found fulfilment in the life and teachings of Jesus, and to underline the Gospel message. Matthew 9:13 and 12:7 both report Jesus quoting the words of Hosea 6:6 ("I desire mercy [*hesed*], and not sacrifice"), an echo of which can also be found in Mark 12:33. Matthew 2:15 sees Hosea 11:1 fulfilled in the return of Joseph and the Child Jesus and Mary after the flight into Egypt; the "straight paths of the Lord" in Acts 13:10 is a turn of phrase similar to Hosea 14:9's "the ways of the Lord are right"; and 1 Corinthians 15:55 quotes Hosea 13:14 almost verbatim: "O death, where is thy victory? O death, where is thy sting?" The Revelation to John 6:16 uses the imagery of Hosea 10:8 where, in their despair, those unfaithful to the Lord call on the mountains to cover them; and the "great harlot" in Revelation 17 sends us back to Hosea 1:11–3:2. There are also some New Testament metaphors that seem to derive from Hosea—for example, that of Israel as the vineyard of the Lord (cf. Mt 21:33–43 and Hos 10:1—a metaphor that Isaiah also developed).

But Hosea's legacy to the New Testament can be seen not so much in its quotations from the book, as in the fact that Hosea is very clearly in line with the essential New Testament message—that "God is love"; God loves his people in spite of their unfaithfulness; he loves each person, in spite of his or her sins. Also, the marriage metaphor in Hosea is to be seen in New Testament passages where Christ is depicted as the bridegroom (cf. Mt 9:15 and par.; cf. Jn 3:28–29) or in which his love for the Church is used as a model for married love (cf. Eph 5:21–33). Finally, the idea of the gratuitousness of election and forgiveness endures in the Church, where each member of the faithful experiences divine predilection in an ongoing way.

Christian tradition, from the Fathers to the liturgy, has never lost sight of the book of Hosea. There are four great Patristic commentaries on the book—those by St Jerome (c.400), Theodoret of Mopsuestia (420), St Cyril of Alexandria (c.440) and Theodoret of Cyrus (c.460). Modern times have seen the publication of many useful studies focusing on the book's theological message—profound, touching and valid at all times.

## Title

2 Kings
14:28; 15:1
Joel 1:1; Mic 1:1
Jon 1:1; Zeph 1:1

1 [1]The word of the LORD that came to Hosea the son of Be-eri, in the days of Uzziah, Jotham, Ahaz, and Hezekiah, kings of Judah, and in the days of Jeroboam the son of Joash, king of Israel.

---

**1:1.** This heading, which must have been composed after the collapse of the (Northern) kingdom of Israel, lists, first, the kings of Judah (including the years of joint kingship: they are Uzziah [Azariah], 785–733, Jotham, 759–743, Ahaz, 743–727, and Hezekiah, 727–698) and then, one king of Israel, Jeroboam II, 788–747. It is surprising that four kings of Judah and only one of Israel are mentioned, for, as far as we know, Hosea ministered as a prophet in Israel, and the book also alludes to things that happened there after the reign of Jeroboam II. The reason for this weighting towards Judah is probably that the redactor of the book, who designed it for the inhabitants of Judah, wanted to emphasize that the prophet's message applied to them, too; it was moreover a message that had a lot in common with that of Isaiah, who certainly was a contemporary of the kings of Judah mentioned here.

*1:2–3:5. The three chapters that make up the first part of the book deal with Hosea's marriage and its symbolism. As in the case of other prophets—Isaiah and the names of his sons (Is 8:1–8), Jeremiah and his celibacy (Jer 16:1–9), Ezekiel and the death of his wife (Ezek 24:15–24)—a personal crisis becomes a symbol for something

much greater: just as Hosea loves his unfaithful wife, God loves his people; just as Hosea's faithfulness will bring his wife back, the Lord's faithfulness to Israel will win them back to Him, the one true God.

As readers follow the prophet's account of his marriage and its difficulties, they will discover other teachings as well. They can see, first of all, that God is faithful and merciful; he never ceases to love his sinful people or to forgive them. Also, God's Covenant with his people is not a legalistic affair, nor is it a relationship in which one party is an overlord and the other a vassal; it is (on God's part) a deep commitment. To convey this idea, the author uses the word *hesed*: "When in the Old Testament the word *hesed* is used of the Lord, this always occurs in connection with the covenant that God established with Israel. This covenant was, on God's part, a gift and a grace for Israel. Nevertheless, since, in harmony with the covenant entered into, God had made a commitment to respect it, *hesed* also acquired in a certain sense a legal content. The juridical commitment on God's part ceased to oblige whenever Israel broke the covenant and did not respect its conditions. But precisely at this point, *hesed*, in ceasing to be a juridical obligation, revealed its

---

[1] [1]Verbum Domini, quod factum est ad Osee filium Beeri in die bus Oziae, Ioatham, Achaz, Ezechiae regum Iudae, et in diebus Ieroboam filii Ioas regis Israel. [2]Principium verbi Domini per Osee. Dixit Dominus ad Osee: «Vade, sume tibi mulierem fornicationum / et filios fornicationum, / quia fornicans

# 1. HOSEA'S MARRIAGE*

**The prophet's mission and his marriage**

[2]When the LORD first spoke through Hosea, the LORD said to Hosea, "Go, take to yourself a wife of harlotry and have children of harlotry, for the land commits great harlotry by forsaking the LORD." [3]So he went and took Gomer the daughter of Diblaim, and she conceived and bore him a son.

---

deeper aspect: it showed itself as what it was at the beginning, that is, as love that gives, love more powerful than betrayal, grace stronger than sin" (John Paul II, *Dives in misericordia*, note 52).

These chapters may be difficult to follow not only because biographical details about Hosea are interwoven with what they symbolize (the relationship between God and his people) but also because it is sometimes difficult to work out the chronology: we are not given the whole story of the prophet's marriage but only those episodes that suit the message that the author wants to convey. To help solve these difficulties some scholars have even proposed changing the order in which the episodes appear; but it seems to make more sense to retain the text as it is and to remember that almost every phrase can be interpreted three ways—as a narrative about Hosea and his wife; as a symbol of the relationship between God and his people; and as a way to grasp the nature of God and his feelings towards his people and towards man in general. Looked at in this way, these chapters can be divided into three parts.

The book begins with an account of Hosea's marriage (1:2–9) and the sym-

bolic names of the three children. The meaning of the passage is clear: like the woman whom Hosea took as his wife, Israel is unfaithful, and the names given her three children reflect the effects of this infidelity: Israel is a violent nation, she is not the people of God, and she does not deserve God's compassion. But that is not the end of the story, for, in the next breath (1:10–12), we hear of a future time which will be the very opposite of what went before: Israel and Judah are great, they are God's people, and he does indeed take pity on them.

Then, a complaint (2:2) against the unfaithful wife, who forsakes her husband just as Israel flees from her Lord, marks the start of two passages on this theme. In the first (2:2–13) we are told how the Lord spies on Israel, and in the second (2:14–23) how he manages to draw her back, this wayward woman.

Finally (3:1–5), a passage written in the first person singular tells how the prophet and his wife are reconciled. This complements the biographical dimension of the opening account (1:2–9), but the most interesting thing about it is that it emphasizes what the whole passage is about—the fact that the initiative always lies with God; by

---

fornicatur terra a Domino». [3]Et abiit et accepit Gomer filiam Debelaim, quae concepit et peperit ei filium. [4]Et dixit Dominus ad eum: «Voca nomen eius "Iezrahel" quoniam adhuc modicum et visitabo /

1 Kings 18:45
2 Kings 9:1–10;
10:1–17; 17:3–16

2 Sam 1:18–19

1 Pet 2:10
2 Kings 19:35
Ps 20:8; Hos 14:4
Prov 21:31
Is 30:16
Zech 4:6; Mic 5:9

1 Pet 2:10

[4]And the LORD said to him, "Call his name Jezreel; for yet a little while, and I will punish the house of Jehu for the blood of Jezreel, and I will put an end to the kingdom of the house of Israel. [5]And on that day, I will break the bow of Israel in the valley of Jezreel."

[6]She conceived again and bore a daughter. And the LORD said to him, "Call her name Not pitied, for I will no more have pity on the house of Israel, to forgive them at all. [7]But I will have pity on the house of Judah, and I will deliver them by the LORD their God; I will not deliver them by bow, nor by sword, nor by war, nor by horses, nor by horsemen."

[8]When she had weaned Not pitied, she conceived and bore a son. [9]And the LORD said, "Call his name Not my people, for you are not my people and I am not your God."[a]

---

his faithfulness he will convert Israel, just as Hosea's fidelity wins back his unfaithful wife.

The interweaving of the marriage theme with that of the Covenant in these passages has much to say about the nature of Christian marriage: "Seeing God's covenant with Israel in the image of exclusive and faithful married love, the prophets prepared the Chosen People's conscience for a deepened understanding of the unity and indissolubility of marriage" (*Catechism of the Catholic Church*, 1611).

**1:2–9.** This very symbolic episode encapsulates the message of the book. The prophet's marriage and the symbolic names of his children form the crux of discussion and commentary on the text.

Many commentators have interpreted the prophet's marriage as being a symbol, on the grounds that it is difficult to see the Lord ordering someone to marry a prostitute (v. 2). That view would be an application of St Augustine's general principle: "In an inspired text, what cannot be understood literally or in accordance with noble customs and the truth of the faith must be read figuratively" (*De doctrina christiana*, 3, 33), and it is the stance taken by some authors in the Middle Ages, such as Rupert of Deutz, who interprets Hosea's marriage as an allegory (cf. his *Commentarii in prophetas minores*); medieval Jewish authors argue along the same lines, interpreting the whole piece as a vision: cf. Ibn Ezra, *Commentary on Hosea*, and Maimonides, *The Guide of the Perplexed*, 2, 32–46.

sanguinem Iezrahel super domum Iehu et cessare faciam regnum domus Israel; [5]et in illa die conteram arcum Israel in valle Iezrahel». [6]Et concepit adhuc et peperit filiam; et dixit ei: «Voca nomen eius "Absque misericordia", quia non addam ultra misereri domui Israel, ut ignoscam eis. [7]Et domui Iudae miserebor et salvabo eos in Domino Deo suo et non salvabo eos in arcu et gladio et in bello et in equis et in equitibus». [8]Et ablactavit eam, quae erat «Absque misericordia», et concepit et peperit filium. [9]Et dixit: «Voca nomen eius "Non populus meus", quia vos non populus meus, et ego "Non sum" vobis.

**a.** Gk: Heb *I am not yours*

However, because neither Hosea nor Gomer (v. 3) is a symbolic name, other commentators think that the passage refers to a real marriage. According to this interpretation, Hosea married a woman who had taken part in sacred prostitution in fertility rites at Canaanite temples. If so, there is a reference here to the sin of Israel: breaking her covenant commitment to the Lord, she played the harlot by adoring other gods. Those who subscribe to the "real marriage" interpretation concentrate on justifying Hosea's actions or God's command to him. For example, St Thomas Aquinas (*Summa theologiae*, 1–2, 100, a. 8) and St Jerome, while not going into the question as to whether the marriage was real or not, have no problem with the morality of the prophet's action: "We can find no fault with the prophet from what we read, because the prostitute [whom he marries] becomes an honest woman; on the contrary, we should praise him, for he has drawn good from evil. A good person is not tainted by his contact with an evildoer; in fact, the wicked one will be converted if he or she follows the good example they are given. Therefore, the prophet was not made unclean by his marriage to the adulteress; rather, she was purified by it. Above all, since Hosea did not act out of lust or sinfulness or at his own will, but in order to fulfill the command of God, we find that what we read as a human action on Hosea's part was in fact a spiritual work carried out by God" (St Jerome, *Commentarii in Osee*, 1, 3–4).

A third interpretation (which can explain God's command, Hosea's real marriage, and also how his mind works) meets with more favour nowadays. It argues that there was a real marriage but that Hosea's wife was not a prostitute when he married her. The book calls her a "wife of harlotry" (v. 2) because it is anticipating Gomer's later infidelity. This explanation is consistent with the application of the image to Israel: God chose her before she sinned and she can be called wanton in view of her later apostasy.

Irrespective of whether the text is describing a real marriage or not, the meaning is always clear: Israel has been unfaithful to her marriage covenant with her God, just as Gomer betrayed her marriage to Hosea. Her unfaithfulness also affects her children; they are called: "children of harlotry, for the land commits great harlotry by forsaking the Lord" (v. 2). As the prophet says later, "they sow the wind, and they shall reap the whirlwind" (v. 2): by forsaking her God, Israel renders herself unable to recover him, now or later. Hence the symbolism of the names which are given to the three children (vv. 4–9) and which stand for three "threats" by God to Israel. The first son, "Jezreel" (v. 4), reminds one of the murders in the valley of Jezreel (2 Kings 9:14–26, 30–37) instigated by Jehu, the founder of the Northern dynasty to which Jeroboam II (the king at this time) belonged and which would soon come to an end with the assassination of King Zechariah (2 Kings 15:8–12); the words "I will break the bow of Israel" mean that her army will cease to be of any use (cf. Gen 49:24; 2 Sam 1:18). Therefore, by the name Jezreel, God is saying that he

**Messianic promises of salvation**

Gen 22:17; 32:13; Jn 1:12 | Rom 9:26,27 — ¹⁰ᵇYet the number of the people of Israel shall be like the sand of the sea, which can be neither measured nor numbered; and in the place where it was said to them, "You are not my people," it shall be said to them,"Sons of the living God." ¹¹And the people of Judah and the people of Israel shall be gathered together, and they shall appoint for themselves one head; and they shall go up from the land, for great shall be the day of Jezreel.

Jer 3:18
Hos 1:4–9

Hos 2:24–25 — **2** ᶜ ¹Say to your brother,ᵈ "My people," and to your sister,ᵉ "She has obtained pity."

**The husband's treatment of his unfaithful wife**
²"Plead with your mother, plead—
for she is not my wife,
and I am not her husband—

---

will leave the country to its fate—and it will be a disastrous one. The name of the daughter, "Not pitied" (v. 6), symbolizes the fact that the Lord will show no further compassion to the Northern kingdom. Judah, however, will be shown pity (v. 7). The third child, "Not my people", stands for the fact that the Lord will break off his pact with the Northern people: he will treat them as if they were not his people (v. 9).

**1:10–2:1.** The previous oracle ended with God"s rejection of Israel, and this one promises rehabilitation. In the logic of the first three chapters of the book, as spelt out in the central poem (2:2–23), according to which God responds to Israel's infidelity by being faithful and merciful and thereby bringing about reconciliation, these three verses are a continuation of what is said in 3:1–5.

The prophecy announces a glorious restoration; the people will be reunited in the promised land (v. 11). The names given to the Israelite brother and sister (2:1) are the opposite of the three names used to curse her (1:4, 6, 9). The New Testament writers see this prospect of salvation as finding its fulfilment in the work of Jesus Christ who creates the new people of God, the Church. We find St Peter, for example, telling Christians from pagan backgrounds to praise God because "once you were no people but now you are God's people; once you had not received mercy but now you have received mercy" (1 Pet 2:10; cf. Rom 9:24–26).

**2:2–23.** This long poem contains the key to the book of Hosea. It explains the symbolism of the account of the poet's marriage contained in these three

**[2]** ¹Et erit numerus filiorum Israel / quasi arena maris, / quae sine mensura est et non numerabitur. / Et erit: in loco, ubi dicebatur eis: / "Non populus meus vos", / dicetur eis: "Filii Dei viventis". / ²Et congregabuntur filii Iudae / et filii Israel pariter / et ponent sibimet caput unum / et ascendent de terra,

**b.** Ch 2.1 in Heb   **c.** Ch 2.3 in Heb   **d.** Gk: Heb *brothers*   **e.** Gk Vg: Heb *sisters*

42

that she put away her harlotry from her face,
   and her adultery from between her breasts;
³lest I strip her naked

Is 47:2–3
Jer 6:8; 9:11; 13:22
Ezek 16:37–39

chapters; and it sums up the content and form of the oracles in the later part of the book. The poem begins (v. 2) with a complaint by Hosea about his wife (and therefore by God about his people); and it ends with the prospect of rehabilitation and blessing (vv. 14–23); the second and third parts in the book also begin with a charge laid by the Lord against his people (4:1; 12:2), and end with a promise of salvation. The message of these verses is perfectly clear. Like the prophet's wife, Israel has prostituted herself by worshipping other gods. The Lord spies on her and punishes her, to get her to return to him (vv. 2–13). But so great is his love for Israel that, despite her infidelity, he decides to woo her all over again, to draw her to himself, and thereby to embark on a new relationship with her in which all will be wonderful and there will never again be infidelity (vv. 14–23). This passage contains very rich teaching about the nature of God: the initiative is always his; he is not indifferent to the infidelity of his followers; if he watches what they do and punishes them, he does so to encourage them to come back to him. Moreover, if that does not work, he has another approach to fall back on: he can start again from the beginning; he can renew his relationships with his faithful and with all creation. The imagery used to describe the rehabilitation of Israel (vv. 14–23) is very rich and full of meaning; meditation on

this passage helps the reader to appreciate what God is really like.

The first part of the poem (vv. 2–13) begins with some words of complaint about the unfaithful wife who has left her husband and become a prostitute. However, the reader very soon sees that what is being said here also applies to Israel and the Lord. From v. 8 onwards, the perspective is slightly different: the dominant theme is the relationship between God and Israel, although the reader is also aware of the husband-wife relationship. In this way the sacred writer ensures that the reader can see the symbolism of the message; the whole story, the imagery, carries a message about the Lord and his people. The best example of the author's method is in the opening words (vv. 2–3), which summarize the passage. They declare that the marriage is over ("she is not my wife, and I am not her husband": v. 2) and give the reason why ("harlotry" and "adultery" in v. 2 mean the adornments, tattooes, amulets etc. worn by prostitutes and loose women: cf. Gen 38:15; Prov 7:10); there is also a reference to the way in which an adulterous wife was shunned (v. 3): stripping the woman of her garments is known to have formed part of the punishment of her crime according to some laws in force in the ancient East (cf. Is 47:2–3; Jer 13:22; Ezek 16:37–39; etc.). But then he moves directly onto the symbolic plane of God and Israel: the Israelites pay homage to the Canaanite fertility gods, yet there is only one God, the Creator of heaven and earth, who sends rain and makes things fertile. That God is the Lord: he can turn Israel into a parched land (v. 3). So, the faults that the prophet is condemning here are religious ones. He reproves the Israelites for their feast days in honour of Canaanite gods (vv. 11, 14); they think they ought to thank the Baals for bread and water and the produce of the earth (vv. 5, 9, 12), whereas all these things come in fact from the one God and Lord (v. 8).

The second part of the poem (vv. 14–23) speaks very directly about God and his people. It proclaims that a time of salvation is coming which will see the faithfulness of old fully restored, stronger than ever. It begins (vv. 14–15) by nostalgically recalling the secluded life that they enjoyed together in the wilderness, during the exodus from Egypt—depicted here as a sort of golden age in which the Lord was his people's only God (v. 14; cf. 11:1–4; Amos 5:25). That is why it mentions the Valley of Achor (v. 15), which, being near Jericho, was the access route to the promised land. It was the scene of a sin of infidelity, which God punished (cf. Josh 7:24–26); hence its name, which means misadventure, misfortune; but because it is the only route into the holy land, the Lord now calls it a "door of hope".

The text goes on (vv. 16–23) to describe the new Covenant that will be made "on that day" (vv. 16, 18, 21). The passage deals with two distinct themes: where the second person is used (vv. 16, 19–20), the spousal covenant is being described; where it is in the third person (vv. 17–18; 21–23), it is describing the effects that that covenant will have on the whole land. The first condition of the spousal covenant is that Israel will call her God "My husband" and not "My Baal" (v. 16). Baal is a word that can mean god, and also lord or husband. In wanting to be called "My husband", the Lord is rejecting any type of mixing of religions: the God of Israel is not one more god like the Baals; he is the only God there is. This exclusiveness in the area of married love, which transfers over into the Covenant, is spelt out in vv. 19–20: it will last forever, it will be made in "righteousness and in justice", that is, God will provide special protection to Israel (cf. Mic 6:5; Jer 23:6), and it will be in "steadfast love, and in mercy": the words that the text uses are *hesed* and *rahamim*, taking in, then, all the nuances of faithful love (cf. the note on Is 49:15).

Later verses uses the third person (vv. 17–18, 21–23) to describe the consequences that will flow from this renewed Covenant: all creation will enjoy the peace of Eden (v. 18), and the land of Israel will benefit most of all (vv. 21–23). Perhaps the most significant thing here is the use of the verb "to answer": when Israel "answers" (cf. v. 15) God's love, the heavens will answer the earth, and the earth will answer its fruits (vv. 21–22). What this means is that nothing will be barren, there will be no desire that goes unsatisfied; a proof of this is the new change of names (v. 23): names implying indictment are replaced by names of salvation.

and make her as in the day she was born,
and make her like a wilderness,
and set her like a parched land,
and slay her with thirst.

⁴Upon her children also I will have no pity,
because they are children of harlotry.

⁵For their mother has played the harlot;
she that conceived them has acted shamefully.
For she said, 'I will go after my lovers,
who give me my bread and my water,
my wool and my flax, my oil and my drink.'

⁶Therefore I will hedge up her[f] way with thorns;
and I will build a wall against her,
so that she cannot find her paths.

⁷She shall pursue her lovers,
but not overtake them;
and she shall seek them,
but shall not find them.
Then she shall say, 'I will go
and return to my first husband,
for it was better with me then than now.'

⁸And she did not know
that it was I who gave her
the grain, the wine, and the oil,
and who lavished upon her silver
and gold which they used for Baal.

⁹Therefore I will take back
my grain in its time,
and my wine in its season;
and I will take away my wool and my flax,
which were to cover her nakedness.

¹⁰Now I will uncover her lewdness
in the sight of her lovers,
and no one shall rescue her out of my hand.

¹¹And I will put an end to all her mirth,
her feasts, her new moons, her sabbaths,
and all her appointed feasts.

Job 3:23
Hos 1:2

Jer 2:25; 3:13;
44:17
Amos 2:4

Jer 2:23

Jer 3:22
Hos 6:1–3
Lk 15:17–18

Deut 7:13; 8:11–18
Ps 144:12

Ezek 16:37
Jn 10:29

2 Kings 4:23
Ps 80:13–19
Is 1:13–14; 5:5–6;
Jer 7:34
Amos 5:21–23; 8:5

---

/ quia magnus dies Iezrahel. / ³Dicite fratribus vestris: "Populus meus" / et sororibus vestris: "Misericordiam consecuta". / ⁴Contendite adversum matrem vestram; contendite, / quoniam ipsa non uxor mea, / et ego non vir eius; / auferat fornicationes suas a facie sua / et adulteria sua de medio uberum suorum, / ⁵ne forte exspoliem eam nudam / et statuam eam secundum diem nativitatis suae / et

**f.** Gk Syr: Heb *your*

¹²And I will lay waste her vines and her fig trees,
>    of which she said,
>    'These are my hire,
>      which my lovers have given me.'
> I will make them a forest,
>    and the beasts of the field shall devour them.

Ex 15:1–20
Josh 7:26
Jer 2:32
¹³And I will punish her for the feast days of the Baals
>    when she burned incense to them
> and decked herself with her ring and jewelry,
>    and went after her lovers,
>    and forgot me, says the LORD.

**Restoration and a new Covenant**
¹⁴"Therefore, behold, I will allure her,
>    and bring her into the wilderness,
>    and speak tenderly to her.

Ex 13:17;
Josh 7:24–26;
Is 65:10; Jer 2:2
¹⁵And there I will give her her vineyards,
>    and make the Valley of Achor a door of hope.
> And there she shall answer as in the days of her youth,
>    as at the time when she came out of the land of Egypt.

Lev 26:5;
Is 11:6–9;
Jer 23:6;
Ezek 34:25
¹⁶"And in that day, says the LORD, you will call me, 'My husband,' and no longer will you call me, 'My Baal.' ¹⁷For I will remove the names of the Baals from her mouth, and they shall be mentioned by name no more. Gen 9:8ff
Job 5:23; Is 2:4
Ezek 34:25
Hos 1:7 ¹⁸And I will make for you^g a covenant on that day with the beasts of the field, the birds of the air, and the creeping things of the ground; and I will abolish^h the bow, the sword, and

---

ponam eam quasi solitudinem / et statuam eam velut terram aridam / et interficiam eam siti. / ⁶Et filiorum illius non miserebor, / quoniam filii fornicationum sunt, / ⁷quia fornicata est mater eorum, / turpiter egit, quae concepit eos; / quia dixit: "Vadam post amatores meos, / qui dant panes mihi et aquas meas, / lanam meam et linum meum, / oleum meum et potum meum". / ⁸Propter hoc ecce ego saepiam / viam tuam spinis / et saepiam eam maceria, / et semitas suas non inveniet; / ⁹et sequetur amatores suos / et non apprehendet eos; / et quaeret eos et non inveniet / et dicet: "Vadam et revertar / ad virum meum priorem, / quia bene mihi erat tunc magis quam nunc". / ¹⁰Et haec nescivit quia ego / dedi ei frumentum et vinum et oleum / et argentum multiplicavi ei / et aurum, quae fecerunt Baal. / ¹¹Idcirco convertar et sumam / frumentum meum in tempore suo / et vinum meum in tempore suo; / et auferam lanam meam et linum meum, / quae operiebant pudenda eius, / ¹²et nunc revelabo ignominiam eius / in oculis amatorum eius, / et nullus est qui eruat eam de manu mea. / ¹³Et cessare faciam omne gaudium eius, / sollemnitatem eius, neomeniam eius, / sabbatum eius et omnia festa tempora eius; / ¹⁴et corrumpam vineam eius et ficum eius, / de quibus dixit: "Mercedes hae meae sunt, / quas dederunt mihi amatores mei". / Et ponam eas in saltum, / et comedet illas bestia agri. / ¹⁵Et visitabo super eam dies Baalim, / quibus accendebat incensum / et ornabatur inaure sua et monili suo / et ibat post amatores suos, / sed mei obliviscebatur, / dicit Dominus. / ¹⁶Propter hoc ecce ego lactabo eam / et ducam eam in solitudinem / et loquar ad cor eius; / ¹⁷et dabo ei vineas eius ex eodem loco / et vallem Achor, portam spei, / et respondebit ibi / iuxta dies iuventutis suae / et iuxta dies ascensionis suae de terra Aegypti. / ¹⁸Et erit:

**g.** Heb *them*   **h.** Heb *break*

war from the land; and I will make you lie down in safety. [19]And
I will betroth you to me for ever; I will betroth you to me in righteousness and in justice, in steadfast love, and in mercy. [20]I will
betroth you to me in faithfulness; and you shall know the LORD.
[21]"And in that day, says the LORD,
 I will answer the heavens
 and they shall answer the earth;
[22]and the earth shall answer the grain, the wine, and the oil,
 and they shall answer Jezreel;[i]
[23] and I will sow him[j] for myself in the land.
 And I will have pity on Not pitied,
 and I will say to Not my people, 'You are my people';
 and he shall say, 'Thou art my God.'"

*Ps 67:6; 85:12*

*Jer 31:27; Zech
10:9; 13:9; 1
Pet 2:10
Rom 9:25*

*Hos 1:4–9*

*1 Pet 2:10
Rom 9:25*

### Husband and wife reconciled

3 [1]And the LORD said to me, "Go again, love a woman who is
beloved of a paramour and is an adulteress; even as the LORD
loves the people of Israel, though they turn to other gods and love

*Jer 3:20; 7:18
Hos 1:2–3*

---

**3:1–5.** The text reverts here to the
biographical account, although this
time the story is told in the first person.
What the interpreter has to do here is
decide whether the passage deals with
another marriage, different from that in
1:2–9, or whether this is a further story
about the same marriage. The difficulties
arise from trying to work out who the
"woman who is beloved" is (v. 1) and
why money etc. is changing hands (v. 2).

 The "woman who is beloved of a
paramour and is an adultress" refers to
Gomer, the daughter of Diblaim (1:3),
and not to a new wife. The wording
"love a woman" (v.1) does not in itself
mean "marry her", so a new marriage is
not necessarily implied. Nor does the
fact that here he calls the woman an
"adulteress" (v.1) and that Gomer has
been described as a "wife of harlotry"
(1:2) mean necessarily that two different
women are involved. In psychological
terms, it doesn't matter: in both cases the
prophet loves an unfaithful woman who
doesn't deserve his love.

---

in die illa, / ait Dominus, / vocabis me: "Vir meus" / et non vocabis me ultra: "Baal meus". / [19]Et
auferam nomina Baalim de ore eius, / et non recordabitur ultra nominis eorum. / [20]Et percutiam eis
foedus in die illa / cum bestia agri et cum volucre caeli et cum reptili terrae; / et arcum et gladium et
bellum / conteram de terra / et cubare eos faciam confidenter. / [21]Et sponsabo te mihi in sempiternum;
/ et sponsabo te mihi in iustitia et iudicio / et in misericordia et miserationibus. / [22]Et sponsabo te mihi
in fide, / et cognosces Dominum. / [23]Et erit: in illa die exaudiam, / dicit Dominus, / exaudiam caelos,
/ et illi exaudient terram; / [24]et terra exaudiet / triticum et vinum et oleum, / et haec exaudient Iezrahel.
/ [25]Et seminabo eam mihi in terram / et miserebor eius, quae fuit "Absque misericordia"; / [26]et dicam
"Non populo meo": "Populus meus tu"; / et ipse dicet: "Deus meus es tu"».  **[3]** [1]Et dixit Dominus ad
me: «Adhuc vade, dilige mulierem dilectam amico et adulteram, sicut diligit Dominus filios Israel, et

**i.** That is *God sows*  **j.** Cn: Heb *her*

Jer 7:18 cakes of raisins." [2]So I bought her for fifteen shekels of silver and
Deut 21:11–13 a homer and a lethech of barley. [3]And I said to her, "You must
dwell as mine for many days; you shall not play the harlot, or
Ex 28:6
Hos 9:4; 10:3 belong to another man; so will I also be to you."[4]For the children
of Israel shall dwell many days without king or prince, without
Ex 23:24; 28:6 sacrifice or pillar, without ephod or teraphim. [5]Afterward the
1 Sam 15:22
Jer 30:9 children of Israel shall return and seek the LORD their God, and
Hos 2:9; 6:1; 14:2 David their king; and they shall come in fear to the LORD and to
his goodness in the latter days.

---

If the woman referred to here is Gomer, then it is difficult to work out why payment is mentioned (v. 2). Various theories have been put forward in this connexion, but none is very convincing. The best course seems to be to take the story as it comes: in ancient times, an adulterous wife separated from her husband would have had to survive on what her lovers gave her, like a prostitute, or else go back to her parents. To underscore even further his love for his unfaithful wife, the prophet goes so far as to hand over money to regain his rights over her, in an exaggerated show of his generosity and love.

Anyway, in the context of the book, this passage clearly has to do with reconciliation. The condition laid down for reconciliation is total fidelity (v. 3). Then, in the next verse the symbolism is set aside and the prophet spells out what reconciliation involves: it means doing without any human means of support "for many days", that is, for a long time—no king or prince (as in the early days of the chosen people, before the monarchy), no idolatrous cults, no fortune-telling.

Taken together, these three chapters are a valuable study of the love of God: "we have inherited from the Old Testament—as it were in a special synthesis—not only the wealth of expressions used by those books in order to define God's mercy, but also a specific and obviously anthropomorphic 'psychology' of God: the image of his anxious love, which in contact with evil, and in particular with the sin of the individual and of the people, is manifested as mercy" (John Paul II, *Dives in misericordia*, note 52). In the later books of the Bible, the implications of the spousal image of the love between God and man will be worked out in more detail. The first part of the book of Isaiah scarcely mentions it (cf. Is 1:21), but Jeremiah uses it a lot (Jer 2:2; 3:1–13) and Ezekiel develops two beautiful allegories with it (Ezek 16 and 23); and the second part of Isaiah depicts the restoration as the reconciliation of the unfaithful wife (Is 50:1; 54:6–7). This imagery provides the Song of Songs with its theological "credentials", so to speak. And the New Testament develops it further: Jesus is

---

ipsi respectant ad deos alienos et diligunt placentas uvarum». [2]Et emi eam mihi quindecim argenteis et choro hordei et dimidio choro hordei. [3]Et dixi ad eam: «Dies multos exspectabis me; non fornicaberis et non eris viro, neque ibo ego ad te». [4]Quia dies multos sedebunt filii Israel sine rege et sine principe

## 2. THE SINS OF ISRAEL*

**General corruption reproached**

**4** <sup>1</sup>Hear the word of the LORD, O people of Israel;
for the LORD has a controversy with the inhabitants of the land.

Is 1:8; 3:13–15
Jer 25:31; Hos
2:21–22; 12:3
Mic 6:1–5

---

the bridegroom, John the Baptist points out (Mt 2:19); the Kingdom of heaven is compared to a marriage feast (Mt 22:1–14; 25:1–13); Christian marriage is a "sacrament" of Christ's union with his Church (cf. Eph 5:25–33). But in the Ephesians text an important change is introduced: in Hosea, God "loves" the people like a husband who passionately loves his wife, whereas in St Paul "the husband should love" his wife as Christ loves his Church.

*4:1–11:11. This section is made up of a number of oracles arranged more by subject than by chronology. Like the central poem in the book (2:2–23) and the last section (11:12–14:8) it begins with an indictment (a "controversy"; Hebr. *rîb*, 4:1, 4) and ends with an announcement of eventual restoration (11:1–11).

The section starts with a series of oracles about the widespread corruption in the Northern kingdom; they are addressed to priests and prophets (4:4–8), the wayward people (4:9–19), the royal house and the rich (5:1–7). Immorality of various sorts is condemned, as well as religious aberrations (idolatry, syncretism). The prophet criticizes alliances with foreign countries

(5:8–15); they lead to pride and forgetfulness of God. Therefore, he calls on the people to return to the Lord with steadfast love (*hesed*), not just in external religious rites (6:1–7). God is the one who can remedy all ills, but he does punish past and present sins (6:8–7:12). This group of oracles ends with one placed on God's lips, reprimanding the people for their infidelity (7:13–16).

The following three chapters contain another series of oracles—not very different in theme from the previous ones. They criticize the religious and political policy of the kings and upper classes, and their ostentatious lifestyles (8:1–14); Israel is threatened with the prospect of exile (9:1–6)—a prophecy that earns Hosea persecution (9:7–9). The prophet recalls the ancient infidelity of the people at Baal-peor (9:10–14; cf. Num 25: 1–5) and their more recent sins at Gilgal (9:15–17; cf. Hos 4:15). In 10:1 there is a tentative anticipation, as it were, of Isaiah's song of the vineyard (Is 5:1–7) and of the parable of the murderous vineyard tenants (cf. Mt 21:33–44 and par.). This is followed by threats against various things to do with idolatrous cults (10:2–10), and Israel is reprimanded for being proud and for relying on her own strength (10:11–15).

---

et sine sacrificio et sine lapide et sine ephod et sine theraphim. <sup>5</sup>Et post haec revertentur filii Israel et quaerent Dominum Deum suum et David regem suum et pavebunt ad Dominum et ad bonum eius in fine dierum.   **[4]** <sup>1</sup>«Audite verbum Domini, / filii Israel, / quia iudicium Domino / cum habitatoribus terrae: / non est enim veritas, et non est benignitas, / et non est scientia Dei in terra; / <sup>2</sup>maledictum et

> There is no faithfulness or kindness,
>     and no knowledge of God in the land;
> Jer 7:9   ²there is swearing, lying, killing, stealing, and committing adultery;
>     they break all bounds and murder follows murder.

---

The section ends with a very touching oracle surveying the history of Israel from the viewpoint of God's love and compassion (1:1–11). Earlier, the prophet used marriage imagery to express the depth of God's love for his people; here he uses imagery connected with fatherhood.

**4:1–19.** This chapter begins and ends with a call to pay attention (v. 1; cf. 5:1). In the first stanza (vv. 1–3), the Lord "has a controversy with", indicts, the inhabitants of the land; in the second (vv. 4–8), the indictment is directed against priest (v. 4) and prophet (v. 5); finally (vv. 9–19), priest and people are told that they will be punished for their transgressions in the area of religious worship.

The sins of the people denounced here are moral faults, of two types— against God (v. 1) and against neighbour (v. 2), which includes all the sins on the two tablets of the Decalogue. These faults are regarded as so grievous that all creation bewails them. But the blame is directed against the priests, who have failed to teach the Law of God to the people (v. 6); worse still, they want the people to sin: that seems to be what v. 8 means. According to Leviticus 6:18–19, a priest who makes the people's sin offering is allowed to eat part of the offering; the text here censures priests who, instead of upbraiding the people for their sins, seem to wait for them to commit sins, so that they (the priests) will be assured of plenty of provisions from sin offerings. In both "indictments" there is a charge about there being "no knowledge of God" (vv. 1, 6). This word, as a noun and a verb (know, knowledge), occurs very often in Hosea and it sums up his entire exhortation. In the poem in chapter 2 about the relationship between the people and God, it was said that Israel, like the unfaithful wife, forsook her Lord, because she "did not know" he was her benefactor (2:8), and she is later told that, when things are restored eventually, she "shall know" the Lord (2:20). Knowing God means perceiving his true identity, and it leads to great intimacy with him and great righteousness. The New Testament contains the same idea: "Our faith rests on fear of the Lord and on patience, forbearance and self-control. If we practise these virtues in everything that concerns the Lord, we will also receive the gifts of wisdom, insight, knowledge and understanding. God has told us clearly through his prophets that he has no need of sacrifices, holocausts or offerings: *What need have I of all your many sacrifices?*" (*Epistula Barnabae*, 2).

In the last stanza (vv. 9–19) the sins condemned have to do mainly with

mendacium / et homicidium et furtum et adulterium inundaverunt, / et sanguis sanguinem tetigit. / ³Propter hoc lugebit terra, / et infirmabitur omnis, qui habitat in ea, / cum bestia agri et volucre caeli,

Jer 4:28
Zeph 1:3

³Therefore the land mourns,
    and all who dwell in it languish,
and also the beasts of the field,
    and the birds of the air;
    and even the fish of the sea are taken away.

## Priests and prophets reproached

⁴Yet let no one contend,
    and let none accuse,
    for with you is my contention, O priest.ᵏ
⁵You shall stumble by day,
    the prophet also shall stumble with you by night;
    and I will destroy your mother.
⁶My people are destroyed for lack of knowledge;
    because you have rejected knowledge,
    I reject you from being a priest to me.
And since you have forgotten the law of your God,
    I also will forget your children.

Ex 19:6
Is 5:13
Jer 5:4
Mal 2:1–9

religious worship. Sexual sins are mentioned, but one can see that they come within the context of idolatry and probably also religious syncretism, since the shrines mentioned are shrines of the Lord (v. 15) but the practices condemned are Canaanite ones. St Jerome has this to say about the warning to Judah in v. 15: "The core idea of the passage is as follows: Even if Israel has yielded to the prostitutes, and has named as priest of the gods anyone who presses gifts into her hand or the king's hand, you Judah, the homeland of Jerusalem, where the Levites practise the law according to the rites of the temple, should not follow the example of fornication shown by Oholah who was once your sister (cf. Ezek 23:4–5), adoring idols and worshipping God at the same time. Do not go into Gilgal, of which the prophet tells us: 'Every evil of theirs is in Gilgal' (Hos 9:15); where Saul was anointed king, and the people first made camp and carried out the second circumcision when they came out of the wilderness. Since that day, false worship has grown and spread from that place. And do not go up to Beth-aven, which was once called Bethel, where Jeroboam, son of Nabat, forged the golden calves, for it is not the House of God but a house of idols" (*Commentarii in Osee*, 4, 15–16).

/ sed et pisces maris auferentur. / ⁴Verumtamen non sit qui contendat / nec qui arguat, / sed tecum iudicium meum, sacerdos. / ⁵Et corrues plena die, / et corruet etiam propheta tecum nocte; / et perdam matrem tuam. / ⁶Perit populus meus, / eo quod non habuerit scientiam. / Quia tu scientiam reppulisti, / repellam te, ne sacerdotio fungaris mihi; / et quia oblitus es legis Dei tui, / obliviscar filiorum tuorum

**k.** Cn: Heb uncertain

Jer 2:11
Phil 3:19

7The more they increased,
the more they sinned against me;
I will change their glory into shame.

Lev 6:23; 10:17

8They feed on the sin of my people;
they are greedy for their iniquity.

### The people's apostasy

9And it shall be like people, like priest;
I will punish them for their ways,
and requite them for their deeds.

Lev 26:26
Mic 6:14

10They shall eat, but not be satisfied;
they shall play the harlot, but not multiply;
because they have forsaken the LORD
to cherish harlotry.

1 Kings 11:4

11Wine and new wine
take away the understanding.

Jer 2:27; 3:9
Hos 1:2; 2:6
Hab 2:19
Ezek 21:21

12My people inquire of a thing of wood,
and their staff gives them oracles.
For a spirit of harlotry has led them astray,
and they have left their God to play the harlot.

Deut 12:2
Is 1:29; 57:5
Ezek 6:13

13They sacrifice on the tops of the mountains,
and make offerings upon the hills,
under oak, poplar, and terebinth,
because their shade is good.

Therefore your daughters play the harlot,
and your brides commit adultery.

Deut 23:19

14I will not punish your daughters when they play the harlot,
nor your brides when they commit adultery;
for the men themselves go aside with harlots,
and sacrifice with cult prostitutes,
and a people without understanding shall come to ruin.

---

et ego. / 7Secundum multitudinem eorum, sic peccaverunt mihi; / gloriam eorum in ignominiam commutabo. / 8Peccatum populi mei comedunt / et ad iniquitatem eorum sublevabunt animas eorum. / 9Et erit sicut populus sic sacerdos; / et visitabo super eum vias eius / et opera eius reddam ei. / 10Et comedent et non saturabuntur; / fornicabuntur et non multiplicabuntur, / quoniam Dominum reliquerunt / in non custodiendo. / 11Fornicatio et vinum et ebrietas auferunt cor. / 12Populus meus in ligno suo interrogat, / et baculus eius annuntiat ei; / spiritus enim fornicationum decepit eos, / et fornicantur a Deo suo. / 13Super capita montium sacrificant / et super colles accendunt thymiama, / subtus quercum et populum et terebinthum, / quia bona est umbra eius; / ideo fornicantur filiae vestrae, / et sponsae vestrae adulterae sunt. / 14Non visitabo super filias vestras, / cum fuerint fornicatae, / et super sponsas vestras, / cum adulteraverint, / quoniam hi ipsi cum meretricibus secedunt / et cum prostibulis

<sup>15</sup>Though you play the harlot, O Israel,
  let not Judah become guilty.
Enter not into Gilgal,
  nor go up to Beth-aven,
  and swear not, "As the LORD lives."

Josh 7:12; 4:19
Hos 5:8
Amos 4:4; 8:14

<sup>16</sup>Like a stubborn heifer,
  Israel is stubborn;
can the LORD now feed them
  like a lamb in a broad pasture?

Jer 3:6; 31:18

<sup>17</sup>Ephraim is joined to idols,
  let him alone.
<sup>18</sup>A band$^l$ of drunkards, they give themselves to harlotry;
  they love shame more than their glory.$^m$
<sup>19</sup>A wind has wrapped them$^n$ in its wings,
  and they shall be ashamed because of their altars.$^o$

Hos 4:7; 6:4–6;
14:9
Amos 2:8

Jer 4:11–13
Amos 1:14

## Priests and rulers denounced

5 <sup>1</sup>Hear this, O priests!
  Give heed, O house of Israel!
Hearken, O house of the king!
  For the judgment pertains to you;
  for you have been a snare at Mizpah,

---

**5:1–15.** This new oracle begins with a call to listen; many prophetical passages begin like this, but in Hosea it happens only in 4:1 and here. It is not clear what situation the oracle refers to, but some clues in the text can help us to work it out.

The denunciation is aimed at the leaders of the people—priests, the house of Israel (=Northern kingdom) and the royal house (v. 1). The charge is one of prostitution (vv. 3, 4, 7), which in the language of Hosea means idolatry— the worship of gods other than the Lord. God's feelings as expressed by the prophet are very clear: "I know them but they do not know me" (cf. vv. 3–4). The sin that prevents them from knowing the Lord, from being converted to him, is pride (cf. v. 5), which stems from their

---

delubrorum sacrificant, / et populus non intellegens corruet. / <sup>15</sup>Si fornicaris tu, Israel, / non delinquat saltem Iuda; / et nolite ingredi in Galgala / et ne ascenderitis in Bethaven / neque iuraveritis: "Vivit Dominus". / <sup>16</sup>Quoniam sicut vacca lasciviens / Israel contumax est; / nunc pascet eos Dominus / quasi agnum in latitudine? / <sup>17</sup>Particeps idolorum Ephraim, / dimitte eum. / <sup>18</sup>Transiit convivium eorum, / fornicatione fornicati sunt, / diligunt vehementer / ignominiam impudicitiae. / <sup>19</sup>Ligabit spiritus eos in alis suis, / et confundentur a sacrificiis suis. **[5]** <sup>1</sup>Audite hoc, sacerdotes, / et attendite, domus Israel;

---

**l.** Cn: Heb uncertain  **m.** Cn Compare Gk: Heb of this line uncertain  **n.** Heb *her*  **o.** Gk Syr: Heb *sacrifices*

and a net spread upon Tabor.
²And they have made deep the pit of Shittim;ᴾ
but I will chastise all of them.

³I know Ephraim,
and Israel is not hid from me;
for now, O Ephraim, you have played the harlot,
Israel is defiled.

Jer 13:23<br>
Hos 1:2<br>
Amos 1:14

⁴Their deeds do not permit them
to return to their God.
For the spirit of harlotry is within them,
and they know not the LORD.

---

"deeds" (v. 4): Israel trusts in its deeds, not in the Lord.

The second part of the oracle (vv. 8–15) can shed more light on this sin of Israel's. The oracle seems to refer to the fratricidal wars between Judah and Israel (vv. 10–11), and the Northern kings' precarious grip on power, which led them to seek alliances with the Assyrians (v. 13; cf. 2 Kings 15:19). But in the circumstances of the time, no such alliance could be confined to the sphere of politics; it would also have religious implications (cf. e.g. 2 Kings 16:1–20); hence Hosea's opposition. It would seem that the sin he is denouncing is not lack of faith (as in Isaiah 7:5–9) but excessive tolerance—treating all religions as being on a par; whereas the Lord is a jealous lover, who does not want to share the love of his people with anyone else.

The Lord tells the people that these pacts will always fail. He will see to this because he wants Israel to "seek" him, not as proud, self-satisfied people (vv. 5–6) but out of a real sense of need and a desire for forgiveness (v. 10). That is what this passage is saying and it has become part of the ascetical tradition: "Devote some of your time to God, and rest in his presence. Enter the quiet of your soul; leave aside everything but God and whatever may help you to find him; close all the doors, and go in search of him. Say to Him, my soul, 'Lord, I seek your face.' And then, 'Lord, my God, teach my heart where to search for you and where to find you […]. Show me how to search for you, and how to show you to others who search for you; for I cannot seek you if you do not teach me, and I will not find you unless you reveal yourself to me. Filled with desire, I search for you, and searching for you increases my desire; filled with love, I find you, and finding you increases my love for you'" (St Anselm, *Proslogion*, 1).

---

/ et domus regis, auscultate, / quia vobis iudicium est; / quoniam laqueus facti estis pro Maspha / et rete expansum super Thabor. / ²Et foveam Settim profundam fecerunt; / ego autem castigabo vos omnes. / ³Ego scio Ephraim, / et Israel non est absconditus a me; / quia nunc fornicatus es, Ephraim, / contaminatus est Israel. / ⁴Non dabunt opera sua, / ut revertantur ad Deum suum, / quia spiritus

**p.** Cn: Heb uncertain

⁵The pride of Israel testifies to his face;
Ephraimq shall stumble in his guilt;
Judah also shall stumble with them.
⁶With their flocks and herds they shall go
to seek the LORD,
but they will not find him;
he has withdrawn from them.
⁷They have dealt faithlessly with the LORD,
for they have borne alien children.
Now the new moon shall devour them with their fields.

Hos 14:2
Amos 6:8

Prov 1:28
Is 1:11; 55:6
Amos 5:4; 8:11–12
Mic 6:5–6
Jn 7:34; 8:21

Hos 2:6

### Religious syncretism denounced
⁸Blow the horn in Gibe-ah,
the trumpet in Ramah.
Sound the alarm at Beth-aven;
tremble,r O Benjamin!
⁹Ephraim shall become a desolation
in the day of punishment;
among the tribes of Israel
I declare what is sure.
¹⁰The princes of Judah have become
like those who remove the landmark;
upon them I will pour out
my wrath like water.
¹¹Ephraim is oppressed, crushed in judgment,
because he was determined to go after vanity.s
¹²Therefore I am like a moth to Ephraim,
and like dry rot to the house of Judah.

Hos 4:15
Joel 2:1

Deut 19:14; 27:17

Is 50:9

fornicationis in medio eorum, / et Dominum non cognoverunt. / ⁵Et testatur arrogantia Israel in faciem suam, / et Israel et Ephraim ruent in iniquitate sua: / ruet etiam Iudas cum eis. / ⁶In gregibus suis et in armentis suis / vadent ad quaerendum Dominum / et non invenient; / subtraxit se ab eis. / ⁷In Dominum praevaricati sunt, / quia filios alienos genuerunt; / nunc devorabit eos uno mense cum partibus suis. / ⁸Clangite bucina in Gabaa, / tuba in Rama, / conclamate in Bethaven, / exterrete Beniamin. / ⁹Ephraim vastabitur in die correptionis; / in tribubus Israel annuntio rem certam. / ¹⁰Facti sunt principes Iudae / quasi transferentes terminos; / super eos effundam / quasi aquam iram meam. / ¹¹Oppressus est Ephraim, / fractum est ius, / quoniam voluit abire post sordem. / ¹²Et ego quasi sanies Ephraim, / et quasi putredo domui Iudae. / ¹³Et vidit Ephraim languorem suum, / et Iuda ulcus suum; / et abiit Ephraim ad Assyriam / et misit ad regem magnum; / sed et ipse non poterit sanare vos / nec solvere

q. Heb *Israel and Ephraim*   r. Cn Compare Gk: Heb *after you*   s. Gk: Heb *a command*

<sup>13</sup>When Ephraim saw his sickness,
> and Judah his wound,
> then Ephraim went to Assyria,
> and sent to the great king.<sup>t</sup>
> But he is not able to cure you
> or heal your wound.

1 Kings 15:19;
16:7–9
Hos 7:11; 8:9; 12:2

<sup>14</sup>For I will be like a lion to Ephraim,
> and like a young lion to the house of Judah.
> I, even I, will rend and go away,
> I will carry off, and none shall rescue.

Is 5:29
Hos 2:12
Amos 5:12

<sup>15</sup>I will return again to my place,
> until they acknowledge their guilt and seek my face,
> and in their distress they seek me, saying,

Deut 4:29–31
Jer 29:13
Amos 5:4

**True and false conversion—a call for love, not sacrifice**

6 <sup>1</sup>"Come, let us return to the LORD;
> for he has torn, that he may heal us;
> he has stricken, and he will bind us up.

<sup>2</sup>After two days he will revive us;
> on the third day he will raise us up,
> that we may live before him.

Ezek 37; Mt 16:21
Lk 9:22; 24:46
Jn 5:21; Acts 10:40
1 Cor 15:4

---

**6:1–7.** The call to seek the Lord at the end of the previous oracle (5:15) is responded to in 6:1–3. We hear the people speaking, led by their representatives (the prophet, or the priests). Having suffered (vv. 1–2), they are ready to repent and return to the Lord (v. 3). However, through the prophet the Lord tells them that their love should be steadfast (vv. 4 and 6 speak of *hesed*) but it is like dew or a morning cloud: it does not survive the heat of the day. The rather puzzling reference to "Adam" in v. 7

may mean the first man, but it could also be a city that stood at the entrance to the promised land where the waters of the Jordan were stopped to let the people cross (Josh 13:16); the meaning of the passage does not change much, whichever "Adam" is meant: the point is that transgression of the Covenant has a long history that extends back almost to the beginning; their faithfulness is as short-lived as the morning dew.

As against that, the Lord tells them where true worship lies—in steadfast

poterit vos ab ulcere. / <sup>14</sup>Quoniam ego quasi leaena Ephraim / et quasi catulus leonis domui Iudae; / ego, ego capiam et vadam, / tollam, et non est qui eruat. / <sup>15</sup>Vadens revertar ad locum meum, / donec poenas solvant / et quaerant faciem meam, / in tribulatione sua me desiderent. **[6]** <sup>1</sup>"Venite, et revertamur ad Dominum, / quia ipse laceravit et sanabit nos, / percussit et curabit nos. / <sup>2</sup>Vivificabit nos post duos dies, / in die tertia suscitabit nos, / et vivemus in conspectu eius. / <sup>3</sup>Sciamus sequamurque, /

**t.** Cn: Heb *a king that will contend*

[3]Let us know, let us press on to know the LORD;
  his going forth is sure as the dawn;
he will come to us as the showers,
  as the spring rains that water the earth."

Deut 11:14
Ps 72:6; 143:6
Is 54:13; Mic 5:2
Lk 1:78; Jas 5:7

[4]What shall I do with you, O Ephraim?
  What shall I do with you, O Judah?
Your love is like a morning cloud,
  like the dew that goes early away.
[5]Therefore I have hewn them by the prophets,
  I have slain them by the words of my mouth,
  and my judgment goes forth as the light.[u]

Hos 13:3

Jer 1:10; 5:14
Hos 2:11

---

love and "knowledge of God" (v. 6). The first words of this verse have had a considerable impact on Christian tradition, because they get to the heart of what religion is all about, and because our Lord quotes them more than once (cf. Mt 9:13; 12:7) to underscore his teaching that God judges not to condemn but to save: "For their own good, God demanded of the Israelites not sacrifices and holocausts, but faith, obedience and righteousness. He revealed his will through the words of the prophet Hosea: *I desire steadfast love and not sacrifice, the knowledge of God rather than burnt offerings* (Hos 6:6). The Lord gives further advice, saying: *And if you had known what this means, 'I desire mercy, and not sacrifice,' you would not have condemned the guiltless* (Mt 12:7); and thus bears witness on behalf of the prophets, who preached the truth, against all those who threw their ignorance in the faces of God's servants" (St Irenaeus, *Adversus haerseses*, 4, 17, 4).

In v. 2, the words "after two days he will revive us; on the third day he will raise us up" is a way of saying that the event described will happen in a short period of time. Some Christian writers beginning with Tertullian read the verse as referring to Christ's burial and resurrection; but the New Testament never quotes the verse as a prophecy. However, one cannot completely rule out Hosea 6:2 having a connexion with the New Testament wording "on the third day he arose according to the scriptures" (cf. 1 Cor 15:4) and with what Jesus said when he appeared in the cenacle (Lk 24:46); cf. *Catechism of the Catholic Church*, 627.

---

ut cognoscamus Dominum. / Quasi diluculum praeparatus est egressus eius, / et veniet quasi imber nobis temporaneus, / quasi imber serotinus irrigans terram". / [4]Quid faciam tibi, Ephraim? / Quid faciam tibi, Iuda? / Caritas vestra quasi nubes matutina / et quasi ros mane pertransiens. / [5]Propter hoc dolavi per prophetas, / occidi eos in verbis oris mei, / sed ius meum quasi lux egredietur; / [6]quia

**u.** Gk Syr: Heb *thy judgment goes forth*

*Mt 9:13; 12:7*
Mk 12:33
Amos 5:21
Hos 2:21–22; 8:1

⁶For I desire steadfast love and not sacrifice,
the knowledge of God, rather than burnt offerings.

⁷But at^v Adam they transgressed the covenant;
there they dealt faithlessly with me.

### Punishment for evildoing
⁸Gilead is a city of evildoers,
tracked with blood.

Jer 11:19
Hos 7:1

⁹As robbers lie in wait^w for a man,
so the priests are banded together;^x
they murder on the way to Shechem,
yea, they commit villainy.
¹⁰In the house of Israel I have seen a horrible thing;
Ephraim's harlotry is there, Israel is defiled.

¹¹For you also, O Judah, a harvest is appointed.

When I would restore the fortunes of my people,

---

**6:8–7:16.** It is difficult to work out where the oracles start and finish in this book; but in this particular passage we can distinguish four denunciations— two general oracles against priests and leaders for forsaking the Lord (6:8–11; 7:13–16) and, set within them, two others inveighing against court intrigue (7:1–7) and alliances with other nations (7:8–12). All four oracles are about the failure to obey the Lord: be it in religious worship, politics or prayer, Israel pays no heed to her God.

The first oracle (6:8–11) takes priests to task: they are like a band of murderous robbers (6:9). (Gilead is a region; but sometimes it is given as another name for the shrine at Bethel.) The prophet does not specify exactly what sin is being referred to here, other than the general idolatry into which the priests have led Israel.

The second oracle (7:1–7) is a condemnation of the conspirators and regicides responsible for the turmoil in the North at the time. Menahem killed King Shallum and took the throne (reigning from 747 to 737); he was succeeded by his son Pekahiah (737– 735), who was killed by Pekah, a captain

caritatem volo et non sacrificium, / et scientiam Dei plus quam holocausta. / ⁷Ipsi autem in Adam transgressi sunt pactum; / ibi praevaricati sunt in me. / ⁸Galaad civitas operantium iniquitatem / maculata sanguine. / ⁹Et quasi insidiantes virum latrones / caterva sacerdotum; / in via interficiunt pergentes Sichem, / vere scelus operantur. / ¹⁰In domo Israel vidi horrendum: / ibi fornicationes Ephraim, / contaminatus est Israel. / ¹¹Sed et tibi, Iuda, parata est messis, / cum convertero sortem

**v.** Cn: Heb *like*   **w.** Cn: Heb uncertain   **x.** Syr: Heb *a company*

**The people and their leaders denounced for wickedness**

7 <sup>1</sup>when I would heal Israel,
the corruption of Ephraim is revealed,
and the wicked deeds of Samaria;
for they deal falsely,
the thief breaks in,
and the bandits raid without.
<sup>2</sup>But they do not consider
that I remember all their evil works.
Now their deeds encompass them,
they are before my face.
<sup>3</sup>By their wickedness they make the king glad,
and the princes by their treachery.

Ps 90:8
Mal 3:16

---

in his army, who reigned from 735 to 732. When 2 Kings 15:13–31 covers these events it assesses the various kings in just the way Hosea does (7:7): none of them had any respect for the Law of the Lord. In this denunciation here, the prophet uses the allegory of bread-making: the baker, that is, the king, fails to watch the oven, that is, the conspiring princes: so he is responsible for the fact that the dough (the situation of the kingdom, probably) becomes overheated and intractable.

The third oracle (7:8–12) is a prophetic denunciation of the policy of making pacts with foreign countries. What the oracle says is very like what an earlier oracle says (cf. 5:1–15 and note); political alliances with foreigners were never merely that: they always ended with Israel's religion being contaminated and the Lord being neglected. Here again Hosea uses a parable—that of the "cake not turned"; the underneath part gets burnt but the top remains

uncooked: in other words, the pacts with Assyria and Egypt are useless: they damage one part of Israel and do no good to the other; Israel, like a silly pigeon (cf. v. 11), has gone looking for strange novelties instead of returning to her Lord; now he is going to hunt her and chastise her (v. 12). This passage must have been very vivid to Hosea's contemporaries; they knew how badly things were going for them, and it was all their own fault. The prophet is not detached from what is happening around him; it grieves him deeply. And when we read these words now, they spur us to check whether personally or collectively we are not as empty-headed as Ephraim; maybe we, too, fail to see the hand of God in the world we live in.

The last oracle (7:13–16) gives an overview of what has gone before. Israel has so often acted without reference to God, and come to harm in the process; there are lessons here for all of us.

---

populi mei. **[7]** <sup>1</sup>Cum sanare vellem Israel, / revelata est iniquitas Ephraim / et malitia Samariae, / quia operati sunt mendacium; / et fur ingressus est, / foris autem spoliat turma latronum. / <sup>2</sup>Et non dicunt in cordibus suis / omnem malitiam eorum me recordari. / Nunc circumdederunt eos opera sua,

⁴They are all adulterers;
    they are like a heated oven,
  whose baker ceases to stir the fire,
    from the kneading of the dough until it is leavened.
⁵On the day of our king the princes
    became sick with the heat of wine;
  he stretched out his hand with mockers.
⁶For like an oven their hearts burn[y] with intrigue;
    all night their anger smoulders;
  in the morning it blazes like a flaming fire.
⁷All of them are hot as an oven,
    and they devour their rulers.
All their kings have fallen;
    and none of them calls upon me.

## Israel's quest for foreign help

⁸Ephraim mixes himself with the peoples;
    Ephraim is a cake not turned.

Hos 5:12
Rev 3:17

⁹Aliens devour his strength,
    and he knows it not;
gray hairs are sprinkled upon him,
    and he knows it not.

Is 9:13–14
Amos 4:6–11
Hos 5:5

¹⁰The pride of Israel witnesses against him;
    yet they do not return to the LORD their God,
  nor seek him, for all this.

2 Kings 17:4
Hos 11:11; 12:1

¹¹Ephraim is like a dove,
    silly and without sense,
  calling to Egypt, going to Assyria.
¹²As they go, I will spread over them my net;
    I will bring them down like birds of the air;
  I will chastise them for their wicked deeds.[z]

---

/ coram facie mea facta sunt. / ³In malitia sua laetificaverunt regem et in mendaciis suis principes. / ⁴Omnes adulterantes; / quasi clibanus succensus illi, / pistor cessat excitare ignem / a commixtione fermenti, donec fermentetur totum. / ⁵Die regis nostri / infirmi facti sunt principes ardore vini, / quod apprehendit protervos. / ⁶Quia applicuerunt quasi clibanum cor suum / in insidiando; / tota nocte dormivit ira eorum, / mane ipsa ardet quasi ignis flammae. / ⁷Omnes calefacti sunt quasi clibanus / et devorant iudices suos. / Omnes reges eorum ceciderunt; / non est qui clamet in eis ad me. / ⁸Ephraim in populis ipse commiscebatur; / Ephraim factus est subcinericius panis, qui non reversatur. / ⁹Comederunt alieni robur eius, / et ipse nescit; / sed et cani effusi sunt in eo, / et ipse ignorat. / ¹⁰Et testatur superbia Israel in faciem suam, / nec reversi sunt ad Dominum Deum suum / et non quaesierunt eum in omnibus his. / ¹¹Et factus est Ephraim quasi columba / insipiens non habens sensum: /

y. Gk Syr: Heb *brought near*   z. Cn: Heb *according to the report to their congregation*

## A severe reproach

¹³Woe to them, for they have strayed from me!
  Destruction to them, for they have rebelled against me!
 I would redeem them,
  but they speak lies against me.

¹⁴They do not cry to me from the heart,
  but they wail upon their beds;
 for grain and wine they gash themselves,
  they rebel against me.
¹⁵Although I trained and strengthened their arms,
  yet they devise evil against me.
¹⁶They turn to Baal;ᵃ
  they are like a treacherous bow,
 their princes shall fall by the sword
  because of the insolence of their tongue.
 This shall be their derision in the land of Egypt.

Ps 78:57; 73:9
Hos 9:3

## Kings and princes condemned

8 ¹Set the trumpet to your lips,
  forᵇ a vulture is over the house of the LORD,
 because they have broken my covenant,
  and transgressed my law.

Jer 6:17
Ezek 3:17
Hos 5:8; 6:7
Joel 2:1

---

**8:1–14.** This passage begins and ends with imperatives (v. 1; cf. 9:1). The first stanza (vv. 1–7) gives God's order to Hosea to be his herald (to blow the trumpet or horn), to warn against impending danger: a vulture is hovering over "the house of the Lord", probably a reference to the shrine at Bethel (v. 1). The people respond ("My God": v. 2) and back their cry for help by saying that he should hear them because they acknowledge him as their God: "we Israel know thee."

But the Lord, through the prophet, says that that is not so: Israel does not know him, for it has "spurned the good" (v. 3). The prophet denounces two sins here: they have acted without

---

Aegyptum invocabant, / ad Assyrios abierunt. / ¹²Et cum profecti fuerint, / expandam super eos rete meum; / quasi volucrem caeli detraham eos, corripiam eos secundum auditionem coetus eorum. / ¹³Vae eis, quoniam recesserunt a me! / Vastabuntur, quia praevaricati sunt in me. / Et ego redimam eos, / cum ipsi locuti sint contra me mendacia? / ¹⁴Et non clamaverunt ad me in corde suo, / sed ululabant in cubilibus suis; / super triticum et vinum se incidebant, / contumaces sunt adversum me. / ¹⁵Et ego erudivi eos et confortavi brachia eorum, / et in me cogitaverunt malitiam. / ¹⁶Convertuntur ad eum, qui non prodest, / facti sunt quasi arcus dolosus; / cadent in gladio principes eorum / propter execrationem linguae suae: ista subsannatio eorum in terra Aegypti. [8] ¹In gutture tuo sit tuba! / Quasi aquila super domum Domini / pro eo quod transgressi sunt foedus meum / et legem meam praevaricati sunt. / ²Me

**a.** Cn: Heb uncertain  **b.** Cn: Heb *as*

Jer 14:8–9
Hos 6:1–3

²To me they cry,
   My God, we Israel know thee.
³Israel has spurned the good;
   the enemy shall pursue him.

1 Sam 8:1; 11:12
1 Kings 12:20
2 Kings 15:13,17,23

⁴They made kings, but not through me.
   They set up princes, but without my knowledge.

---

reference to God, by appointing kings "but not through me" (v. 4); and they have made idols of silver and gold (the golden calf of Samaria gets special mention: vv. 4–5). These are grievous sins; therefore, having sown the wind, "they shall reap the whirlwind", to quote the proverb, and a short wisdom maxim tells them what punishment awaits them (vv. 6–7).

The punishment announced in v. 7 (being "devoured by aliens") has already befallen Israel in the first verse of the second stanza (vv. 8–14), which denounces foreign pacts (vv. 9–10) and the idolatry that Israel falls into as a consequence of them (vv. 11–13). The prophet begins by saying that the alliances that Israel tries to make with foreign powers, involving probably tribute to the king of Assyria (vv. 8–10), will be to no avail. What these three verses seem to be saying is that Israel now tries to make alliances that are at odds with its true nature: inevitably, they will take its freedom away. The oracle goes on to denounce the effects that these pacts will have on worship of the Lord: there will be an increased number of places of worship but, because Canaanite rites will be mixed in with Yahwist ones, the religious services, far from expiating

sins, will multiply them (v. 11). Moreover, even the offerings that they do make to the Lord will not be pleasing to him, for they will not be backed up by fulfilment of the Law of the Lord (vv. 12–13). The same point is being made as in 6:6: "Outward sacrifice, to be genuine, must be the expression of spiritual sacrifice: 'The sacrifice acceptable to God is a broken spirit ...' (Ps 51:19). The prophets of the Old Covenant often denounced sacrifices that were not from the heart or not coupled with love of neighbour" (*Catechism of the Catholic Church*, 2100). So, the prophet sees that Israel needs to be cleansed; hence the threat that "they shall return to Egypt", that is, become enslaved once again.

The last verse re-introduces the idea of "forgetting God". By building palaces and fortresses, Israel is showing that he "has forgotten his Maker", that is, does not put his trust in him; if Assyria "devours" part of the nation's land (vv. 8–9), the fire of God will "devour" the strongholds, on which it had relied (v. 14). "Forgetting God" is a favourite theme of Hosea's (cf. 2:13; 4:6), but the threat of destruction by fire is repeated a number of times in Amos (cf. Amos 1:4, 7, 10, 12; 2:5).

invocant: "Deus meus"; / cognovimus te, Israel. / ³Proiecit Israel bonum; / inimicus persequetur eum. / ⁴Ipsi constituerunt reges, et non ex me; / principes constituerunt, et non cognovi: / argentum suum

With their silver and gold they made idols
    for their own destruction.
[5]I have[c] spurned your calf, O Samaria.
    My anger burns against them.
How long will it be
    till they are pure [6]in Israel?[d]

A workman made it;
    it is not God.
The calf of Samaria
    shall be broken to pieces.[e]

[7]For they sow the wind,
    and they shall reap the whirlwind.
The standing grain has no heads,
    it shall yield no meal;
if it were to yield,
    aliens would devour it.

**Israel ruined by relying on foreign help**
[8]Israel is swallowed up;
    already they are among the nations
    as a useless vessel.
[9]For they have gone up to Assyria,
    a wild ass wandering alone;
    Ephraim has hired lovers.
[10]Though they hire allies among the nations,
    I will soon gather them up.
And they shall cease[f] for a little while
    from anointing[g] king and princes.

*Marginal references:*

1 Kings 12:28,32

Ex 20:4; 34:17

Job 4:8; Prov 22:8
Hos 10:13; Gal 6:7

2 Kings 15:19
Ezek 16:32–34,41
Hos 5:13; 7:11

---

et aurum suum / fecerunt sibi idola, / ut interirent. / [5]Proiectus est vitulus tuus, Samaria; / iratus est furor meus in eos. / Usquequo non poterunt emundari? / [6]Quia ex Israel et ipse est: / artifex fecit illum, / et non est Deus; / quoniam in scintillas erit / vitulus Samariae. / [7]Quia ventum seminabunt / et turbinem metent; / cum culmus non sit in eo, / germen non faciet farinam: / quod et si fecerit, / alieni comedent eam. / [8]Devoratus est Israel, / nunc factus est in nationibus / quasi vas immundum. / [9]Quia ipsi ascenderunt ad Assyriam, onager est solitarius sibi; / Ephraim autem munera dederunt amatoribus. / [10]Sed et cum mercede conduxerint nationes, / nunc compellam eos, / et trement paulisper sub onere regis principum. / [11]Cum multiplicaret Ephraim altaria pro peccato, / factae sunt ei arae in peccatum. / [12]Scribebam ei multiplices leges meas; / velut alienae computatae sunt. / [13]Hostias amant, / immolant carnes et comedunt; / sed Dominus non suscipiet eas. / Nunc recordabitur iniquitatis eorum / et visitabit peccata eorum: / ipsi in Aegyptum convertentur. / [14]Et oblitus est Israel factoris sui / et aedificavit delubra; / et Iudas multiplicavit urbes munitas. / Et mittam ignem in civitates eius, / et devorabit aedes illius.

**c.** Heb *He has*  **d.** Gk: Heb *for from Israel*  **e.** Or *shall go up in flames*  **f.** Gk: Heb *begin*  **g.** Gk: Heb *burden*

[11]Because Ephraim has multiplied altars for sinning,
    they have become to him altars for sinning.

Deut 4:6,8    [12]Were I to write for him my laws by ten thousands,
    they would be regarded as a strange thing.

Deut 28:68
Hos 6:6; 9:3,9;
11:5; Amos 5:22

[13]They love sacrifice;[h]
    they sacrifice flesh and eat it;
    but the LORD has no delight in them.
Now he will remember their iniquity,
    and punish their sins;
    they shall return to Egypt.

Deut 32:15:18
Amos 2:5

[14]For Israel has forgotten his Maker,
    and built palaces;
and Judah has multiplied fortified cities;
    but I will send a fire upon his cities,
    and it shall devour his strongholds.

## Threat of exile

9 [1]Rejoice not, O Israel!
    Exult not[i] like the peoples;
for you have played the harlot, forsaking your God.
    You have loved a harlot's hire
    upon all threshing floors.

Hos 2:11    [2]Threshing floor and winevat shall not feed them,
    and the new wine shall fail them.

Jer 2:7; Dan 1:8
Hos 8:13; 11:5

[3]They shall not remain in the land of the LORD;
    but Ephraim shall return to Egypt,
    and they shall eat unclean food in Assyria.

Deut 26:14    [4]They shall not pour libations of wine to the LORD;
    and they shall not please him with their sacrifices.

---

**9:1–17.** This chapter is made up of stanzas about a future deportation (vv. 1–6), the prophet as God's watchman (vv. 7–9), and God's reaction to Israel's unfaithfulness (vv. 10–14; 15–17).

The opening verses are linked with the previous chapter, dealing as they do with the theme of Ephraim's (Israel's) return to Egypt (v. 3). The prophet's warning about not rejoicing (v. 1) has

[9] [1]Noli laetari, Israel; / noli exsultare sicut populi, / quia fornicatus es a Deo tuo, / dilexisti mercedem super omnes areas tritici. / [2]Area et torcular non pascet eos, / et vinum mentietur eis. / [3]Non manebunt in terra Domini. / revertetur Ephraim in Aegyptum, / et in Assyria pollutum comedent. / [4]Non libabunt Domino vinum, / et non placebunt ei sacrificia eorum; / quasi panis lugentium erunt eis: / omnes, qui

**h.** Cn: Heb uncertain    **i.** Gk: Heb *to exultation*

Their bread[j] shall be like mourners' bread;
  all who eat of it shall be defiled;
for their bread shall be for their hunger only;
  it shall not come to the house of the LORD.

---

to do with the harvest festivals, imbued with the Canaanite fertility rites so severely condemned by Hosea as "harlot's hire" (v. 1). All this will cause God to expel Ephraim from "the land of the Lord" (v. 3). Once they are in a foreign country, they will not be able to make offerings to God on feast days (vv. 4–5), for the sacred vessels used for the worship of the Lord will have been left behind in Israel; weeds will cover them over. The prophet is using poetic language to describe the evil of idolatry, and the punishment that will befall the Israelites and the liturgical vessels etc. of which they are so proud.

The passage about the prophet as a watchman (vv. 7–9) is unclear in the Hebrew text. Early translations did little to clarify it. But the main idea is that Hosea, like Amos and Jeremiah, meets with hostility from the people; they reject his message and call him a fool, a madman (cf. v. 7). In this sense Hosea is a figure of Christ and a forerunner of many saints who have had to say things that were not at all welcome to those who take no notice of God. The passage reminds us of our duty to speak out and to live faithful lives, even if that makes us unpopular.

The last verses (vv. 10–17) express how deceived God feels. The passage seems to be a dialogue between God (vv. 10, 13, 15–16) and the prophet (vv. 14, 17). Basically the idea is that the Israel of Hosea's time has inherited the sins of Israel of old, and shares the guilt of them. The prophet reminds them about Baal-peor (v. 10) and Gilgal (v. 15)—the former, the epitome of Israel's religious infidelities (cf. Num 25:1–5; Jer 11:13); and Gilgal being the place where Saul disobeyed the Lord, and which later became the centre of schismatic religious worship (it is mentioned in that connexion in 4:15). God has been deeply deceived, hence the severity of their chastisement; the prophet shares God's feeling (vv. 14, 17). The end of the passage (v. 17) reveals that Israel's fate will be like what they suffered before entering the promised land: they will be wanderers among the nations (cf. Jer 49:5).

---

comedent eum, contaminabuntur, / quia panis eorum erit tantummodo pro vita ipsorum; / non intrabit in domum Domini. / [5]Quid facietis in die sollemni, / in die festivitatis Domini? / [6]Ecce enim profecti sunt a vastitate; / Aegyptus congregabit eos, / Memphis sepeliet eos: / desiderabile argentum eorum / urtica hereditabit, / spina in tabernaculis eorum. / [7]Venerunt dies visitationis, / venerunt dies retributionis: / sciat Israel! / "Stultus—clamet—est propheta; / insanus vir spiritalis". / Secundum multitudinem iniquitatis tuae / multae sunt inimicitiae tuae. / [8]Speculatur Ephraim, populus Dei mei, prophetam; / laqueus aucupis super omnes vias eius, / inimicitiae in ipsa domo Dei eius. / [9]Profunde peccaverunt / sicut in diebus Gabaa; / recordabitur iniquitatis eorum / et visitabit peccata eorum. / [10]Quasi uvas in deserto / inveni Israel, / quasi prima poma ficulneae in initio eius / vidi patres vestros;

j. Cn: Heb *to them*

⁵What will you do on the day of appointed festival,
  and on the day of the feast of the LORD?
⁶For behold, they are going to Assyria;[k]
  Egypt shall gather them,
  Memphis shall bury them.
  Nettles shall possess their precious things of silver;
  thorns shall be in their tents.

## The prophet is persecuted

Amos 3:2
Jn 10:20

⁷The days of punishment have come,
  the days of recompense have come;
  Israel shall know it.
  The prophet is a fool,
  the man of the spirit is mad,
  because of your great iniquity
  and great hatred.

Jer 20:1–6
Amos 7:10–17

⁸The prophet is the watchman of Ephraim,
  the people of my God,
  yet a fowler's snare is on all his ways,
  and hatred in the house of his God.

Judg 19
Hos 8:13

⁹They have deeply corrupted themselves
  as in the days of Gibe-ah:
  he will remember their iniquity,
  he will punish their sins.

## The crime at Baal-peor

Num 23:28;
25:1–5
Deut 32:10
Jer 2:5; 24:2
Hos 2:16
Lk 13:6

¹⁰Like grapes in the wilderness,
  I found Israel.
  Like the first fruit on the fig tree,
  in its first season,
  I saw your fathers.
  But they came to Baal-peor,
  and consecrated themselves to Baal,[l]
  and became detestable like the thing they loved.

Deut 28:18

¹¹Ephraim's glory shall fly away like a bird—
  no birth, no pregnancy, no conception!

Deut 32:25

¹²Even if they bring up children,
  I will bereave them till none is left.

---

/ ipsi autem intraverunt ad Baalphegor / et se consecraverunt Confusioni / et facti sunt abominabiles / sicut id, quod dilexerunt. / ¹¹Ephraim quasi avis avolabit gloria eorum, / a partu et ab utero et a conceptu. / ¹²Quod si et enutrierint filios suos, / absque liberis eos faciam, absque hominibus; / sed et

**k.** Cn: Heb *from destruction*  **l.** Heb *shame*

Woe to them
    when I depart from them!
[13]Ephraim's sons, as I have seen, are destined for a prey;[m]
    Ephraim must lead forth his sons to slaughter.
[14]Give them, O LORD—
    what wilt thou give?
Give them a miscarrying womb
    and dry breasts.

Lk 23:19

### Evil done in Gilgal

[15]Every evil of theirs is in Gilgal;
    there I began to hate them.
Because of the wickedness of their deeds
    I will drive them out of my house.
I will love them no more;
    all their princes are rebels.

Hos 4:15

[16]Ephraim is stricken,
    their root is dried up,
they shall bear no fruit.
Even though they bring forth,
    I will slay their beloved children.
[17]My God will cast them off,
    because they have not hearkened to him;
they shall be wanderers among the nations.

Hos 9:12
Amos 2:9
Mt 21:10
Lk 13:6

Gen 4:14
Deut 28:64–65
Jer 49:5

### Israel's idolatry

**10** [1]Israel is a luxuriant vine
    that yields its fruit.

Ex 23:24
Deut 32:15
Is 5:1; Hos 4:10
Mt 21:33–34

---

**10:1–15.** Verses 1–2 summarize the underlying point in the passage: the wealthier Israel becomes, the more corrupt she is. The verbs "to increase" (v. 1) and "to bear guilt" (v. 2) are in direct contrast to one another. The "We

vae eis, / cum recessero ab eis! / [13]Ephraim, ut vidi, in venationem posuit sibi filios suos, / et Ephraim educit ad interfectorem filios suos. / [14]"Da eis, Domine! Quid dabis eis? / Da eis vulvam sine liberis et ubera arentia!". / [15]Omnes nequitiae eorum in Galgala, / profecto ibi exosos habui eos. / Propter malitiam operum eorum / de domo mea eiciam eos. / Non addam ut diligam eos; / omnes principes eorum rebelles. / [16]Percussus est Ephraim, / radix eorum exsiccata est, / fructum nequaquam facient; / quod si et genuerint, / interficiam amantissima uteri eorum». / [17]Abiciet eos Deus meus, / quia non audierunt eum; / et erunt vagi in nationibus». **[10]** [1]Vitis frondosa Israel, / fructum producens sibi; / secundum multitudinem fructus sui multiplicavit altaria, / iuxta ubertatem terrae suae / decoravit simulacra. / [2]Divisum est cor eorum, / nunc poenas solvent; / ipse confringet aras eorum, /

**m.** Cn Compare Gk: Heb uncertain

Mk 21:33–34
Mk 12:1–12
Lk 20:9–19

The more his fruit increased
  the more altars he built;
as his country improved
  he improved his pillars.
[2]Their heart is false;
  now they must bear their guilt.
The LORD[n] will break down their altars,
  and destroy their pillars.

---

have no king" (v. 3) and the king's being "like a chip on the face of the waters" (v. 7) refer to the instability of the monarchy in the Northern kingdom: the period between 747 (when Jeroboam II died) to 721 (when Samaria fell to the Assyrians) saw a succession of six kings, who were puppets of Assyria or were assassinated by usurpers. Hosea is quite right when he says they had no king to rule them. The results of this anarchy are mentioned in vv. 4–8—lots of empty talk, contracts with no substance to them, unjust legal decisions; and the result of it all will be that Assyria will destroy Israel's altars, the monarchy will perish, and the people will despair. Verses 9–10 probably hark back to the war when all the tribes turned on the tribe of Benjamin to avenge the crime committed at Gibe-ah (cf. Judg 19:1–20:48). Hosea must have regarded that crime and the war it led to (in which the tribe of Benjamin was almost wiped out) as an archetype of the infamy and cruelty that became so prevalent in later years. Verse 8 is quoted by our Lord when He meets the women of Jerusalem on his way to

Calvary (cf. Lk 23:20), and also in Revelation 6:16, in the scene where the sixth seal is opened. The whole passage is a reminder that material progress can also have negative consequences: "Holy Scripture teaches the human family what the experience of the ages confirms—that while human progress is a great advantage to man, it brings with it a strong temptation. For when the order of values is jumbled, and bad is mixed with the good, individuals and groups pay heed solely to their own interests, and not to those of others" (Vatican II, *Gaudium et spes*, 37).

The second stanza comprises a parable (vv. 11–13) which recalls the first days of Israel, the years in the wilderness, as being a golden age the stanza continues (vv. 13–15) with a passage that reveals how disappointed God feels; there are references here to recent events—the siege of Beth-arbel by Shalman, a Moabite king (v. 14) and unlawful cults at Bethel (v. 15; note **w**). The underlying theme is that of the whole book: the people put their trust in their own resources (cf. v. 13), neglecting to seek the Lord (cf. v. 12).

---

depopulabitur simulacra eorum. / [3]Profecto nunc dicent: / «Non est rex nobis; / non enim timemus Dominum, / et rex quid faciet nobis?». / [4]Loqui verba, iurare in vanum, / ferire foedus; / et germinabit quasi venenum ius / super sulcos agri. / [5]De vitulo Bethaven / trement habitatores Samariae; / quia luget

**n.** Heb *he*

[3] For now they will say:
"We have no king,
for we fear not the LORD,
and a king, what could he do for us?"
[4] They utter mere words;

Amos 6:12

with empty oaths they make covenants;
so judgment springs up like poisonous weeds
in the furrows of the field.
[5] The inhabitants of Samaria tremble
for the calf[o] of Beth-aven.

Hos 8:5; 14:15
Rev 18:14

Its people shall mourn for it,
and its idolatrous priests shall wail[p] over it,
over its glory which has departed from it.
[6] Yea, the thing itself shall be carried to Assyria,
as tribute to the great king.[q]
Ephraim shall be put to shame,
and Israel shall be ashamed of his idol.[r]

[7] Samaria's king shall perish,
like a chip on the face of the waters.
[8] The high places of Aven, the sin of Israel,
shall be destroyed.

2 Kings 23:15
Is 2:10
Hos 4:13

Thorn and thistle shall grow up
on their altars;
and they shall say to the mountains, Cover us,
and to the hills, Fall upon us.

Lk 23:30
Rev 6:16

[9] From the days of Gibe-ah, you have sinned, O Israel;
there they have continued.
Shall not war overtake them in Gibe-ah?

Hos 9:9

[10] I will come[s] against the wayward people to chastise them;
and nations shall be gathered against them
when they are chastised[t] for their double iniquity.

---

super eum populus eius; / dum sacerdotes eius super eum / exsultant in gloria eius; / vere migrabit ab eo. / [6]Siquidem et ipse in Assyriam delatus est, / munus regi magno; / confusio Ephraim capiet, / et confundetur Israel in consilio suo. / [7]Perit Samaria, / rex eius quasi festuca super faciem aquae. / [8]Et disperdentur excelsa impietatis, / peccatum Israel; / spina et tribulus ascendet / super aras eorum, / et dicent montibus: «Operite nos!» / et collibus: «Cadite super nos!». / [9]Ex diebus Gabaa peccavit Israel; / ibi perstiterunt. / Non comprehendet eos in Gabaa / proelium super filios iniquitatis? / [10]«Iuxta desiderium meum corripiam eos; / congregabuntur super eos populi, / cum corripientur propter duas iniquitates suas. / [11]Ephraim vitula docta, / diligens trituram. / Et ego transivi super pulchritudinem colli

**o.** Gk Syr: Heb *calves*     **p.** Cn: Heb *exult*     **q.** Cn: Heb *a king that will contend*     **r.** Cn: Heb *counsel*
**s.** Cn Compare Gk: Heb *in my desire*     **t.** Gk: Heb *bound*

**Israel reproached for its pride**

Jer 2:20; 5:5
Hos 4:16
Mt 11:29–30

[11]Ephraim was a trained heifer
 that loved to thresh,
 and I spared her fair neck;
but I will put Ephraim to the yoke,
 Judah must plough,
 Jacob must harrow for himself.

Is 45:8; Jer 4:3
Hos 2:21; Mic 6:8
Gal 6:8; *2 Cor 9:10*

[12]Sow for yourselves righteousness,
 reap the fruit[u] of steadfast love;
 break up your fallow ground,
for it is the time to seek the LORD,
 that he may come and rain salvation upon you.

Is 31:1

[13]You have ploughed iniquity,
 you have reaped injustice,
 you have eaten the fruit of lies.
Because you have trusted in your chariots[v]
 and in the multitude of your warriors,

Hos 14:1
Lk 19:44

[14]therefore the tumult of war shall arise among your people,
 and all your fortresses shall be destroyed,
as Shalman destroyed Beth-arbel on the day of battle;
 mothers were dashed in pieces with their children.
[15]Thus it shall be done to you, O house of Israel,[w]
 because of your great wickedness.
In the storm[x] the king of Israel
 shall be utterly cut off.

**When Israel was a child**

Ex 4:22–23
Jer 2:1–9
*Mt 2:15*

**11** [1]When Israel was a child, I loved him,
 and out of Egypt I called my son.

---

**11:1–11.** The second part of the book of Hosea ends with this very touching passage summing up, once again, the relationship between God and his people: the Lord is faithful, whereas Israel is not; but the Lord, true to his nature (v. 9), proclaims that he will bless Israel once more. The Christian

eius; / iunxi Ephraim aratro, / arabit Iudas, / sarriet sibi Iacob. / [12]Seminate vobis in iustitia, / metite secundum caritatem; / innovate vobis novale. / Tempus est requirendi Dominum, / donec veniat, ut pluat vobis iustitiam. / [13]Arastis impietatem, / iniquitatem messuistis, / comedistis frugem mendacii, / quia confisus es in curribus tuis, / in multitudine fortium tuorum. / [14]Consurget tumultus in populo tuo, / et omnes munitiones tuae vastabuntur, / sicut vastavit Salman Betharbeel / in die proelii, / matre super filios allisa. / [15]Sic faciet vobis Bethel / propter maximam nequitiam vestram. / Mane interibit rex Israel.   **[11]** [1]Cum puer esset Israel, dilexi eum / et ex Aegypto vocavi filium meum. / [2]Quanto magis

**u.** Gk: Heb *according to*   **v.** Gk: Heb *way*   **w.** Gk: Heb *O Bethel*   **x.** Cn: Heb *dawn*

²The more I[y] called them,
    the more they went from me;[z]
they kept sacrificing to the Baals,
    and burning incense to idols.

---

reader will immediately notice in v. 1 a line that is applied to Jesus in the New Testament (Mt 2:15).

What is new about this poem is the fact that whereas previously God's faithfulness was described as being like that of a husband, here God is depicted as a father: "God's love for Israel is compared to a father's love for his son (Hos 11:11). His love for his people is stronger than a mother's for her children. God loves his people more than a bridegroom his beloved (Is 62:4–5); his love will be victorious over even the worst infidelities and will extend to his most precious gift: 'God so loved the world that he gave his only Son' (Jn 3:16)" (*Catechism of the Catholic Church*, 219).

With the exception of v. 10, the oracle is placed on the lips of the Lord, to underscore God's relationship with his people. From the very first (v. 1), the Lord loved Israel as his own son, and from the first Israel rebelled (v. 2); the Lord reared him (v. 3), showing every sign of attention (v. 4: literally "cords of man" as distinct from the reins used for animals), but Israel is bent on forsaking his Lord (v. 7). Then, in a burst of anger, the Lord decides to chastise his people; they shall become slaves once more (vv. 5–6). But this anger does not last long, because, "even when the Lord is exasperated by the infidelity of his people and thinks of finishing with it, it is still his tenderness and generous love for those who are his own which overcomes his anger" (John Paul II, *Dives in misericordia*, 4).

This oracle shows the full extent of God's paternal affection. In the opening chapters God's love for Israel was compared with the distraught, impassioned love of a husband for his unfaithful wife; here it is depicted as a father's love for his son: he cannot not love him, even if the son proves ungrateful. The very thought of abandoning Israel breaks God's heart (cf. v. 8). What the prophet is doing here is telling us something about God's "psychology": God's love for his people, and ultimately for every human being, exceeds human loves—parental and spousal (these, in fact, are only partial reflections of divine love): "God is pure spirit in which there is no place for the difference between the sexes. But the respective 'perfections' of a man and woman reflect something of the infinite perfection of God: those of a mother and those of a father and husband" (*Catechism of the Catholic Church*, 370).

---

vocabam eos, / tanto recesserunt a facie mea; / ipsi Baalim immolabant / et simulacris sacrificabant. / ³Et ego dirigebam gressus Ephraim, / portabam eos in brachiis meis, / et nescierunt quod curarem eos. / ⁴In funiculis humanitatis trahebam eos, / in vinculis caritatis; / et fui eis, quasi qui elevant infantem

**y.** Gk: Heb *they*   **z.** Gk: Heb *them*

Ex 15:26
Deut 1:31

<sup>3</sup>Yet it was I who taught Ephraim to walk,
I took them up in my<sup>a</sup> arms;
but they did not know that I healed them.

Deut 8:16

<sup>4</sup>I led them with cords of compassion,<sup>b</sup>
with the bands of love,
and I became to them as one
who eases the yoke on their jaws,
and I bent down to them and fed them.

Hos 8:13; 9:3

<sup>5</sup>They shall return to the land of Egypt,
and Assyria shall be their king,
because they have refused to return to me.
<sup>6</sup>The sword shall rage against their cities,
consume the bars of their gates,
and devour them in their fortresses.<sup>c</sup>

Deut 32:36
1 Kings 18:25–29

<sup>7</sup>My people are bent on turning away from me;<sup>d</sup>
so they are appointed to the yoke,
and none shall remove it.

Gen 19:24–25
Deut 29:23; 32–36
Jer 9:7–8

<sup>8</sup>How can I give you up, O Ephraim!
How can I hand you over, O Israel!
How can I make you like Admah!
How can I treat you like Zeboiim!
My heart recoils within me,
my compassion grows warm and tender.

---

This oracle of salvation is rounded off by the final verses. God forgives Israel; it is only right that he should: he is God (v. 9). The wonderful thing about this passage is that God's forgiveness comes before Israel's conversion: his initial love, and the later reconciliation, are initiatives of God.

Conversion (vv. 11–12) stems from God's prior love.

St Matthew's Gospel (2:15) sees the prophecy in Hosea 11:1 being fulfilled in the flight into Egypt and subsequent return: according to the evangelist, Jesus, in his life, embodies the history of his people, and in him God fulfils his

ad maxillas suas, / et declinavi ad eum, ut vesceretur. / <sup>5</sup>Revertetur in terram Aegypti, / et Assur ipse rex eius, / quoniam noluerunt converti. / <sup>6</sup>Saeviet gladius in civitatibus eius / et consumet garrulos eius / et comedet eos propter consilia eorum. / <sup>7</sup>Populus meus pendet ad praevaricandum contra me; / vocant eum ad altum, sed simul non erigunt eum. / <sup>8</sup>Quomodo dabo te, Ephraim, / tradam te, Israel? / Quomodo dabo te sicut Adama, / ponam te ut Seboim? / Convertitur in me cor meum, / simul exardescit miseratio mea. / <sup>9</sup>Non faciam furorem irae meae, / non convertar, ut disperdam Ephraim, / quoniam Deus ego / et non homo, / in medio tui Sanctus / et non veniam in terrore. / <sup>10</sup>Post Dominum

**a.** Gk Syr Vg: Heb *his*   **b.** Heb *man*   **c.** Cn: Heb *counsels*   **d.** The meaning of the Hebrew is uncertain

⁹I will not execute my fierce anger,
  I will not again destroy Ephraim;
for I am God and not man,
  the Holy One in your midst,
  and I will not come to destroy.ᵉ

Num 23:19
Is 54:8
Jer 31:20
Ezek 18:23:32
Wis 1:13

¹⁰They shall go after the LORD,
  he will roar like a lion;
yea, he will roar,
  and his sons shall come trembling from the west;
¹¹they shall come trembling like birds from Egypt,
  and like doves from the land of Assyria;
  and I will return them to their homes, says the LORD.
¹²ᶠEphraim has encompassed me with lies,
  and the house of Israel with deceit;
but Judah is still known byᵍ God,
  and is faithful to the Holy One.

Jer 25:30
Amos 1:2
Rev 10:3

Ezek 37:21–23

---

ancient promises to renew the people of Israel.

*11:12–14:9. The third part of the book begins with another "indictment" (*rîb*) (12:2) and also ends with a restoration oracle (14:4–9). The sins condemned here are not very different from those denounced in the previous part—idolatry, pacts with foreign countries, neglect of the Lord when times are good, etc. However, the historical background seems to be different. In the previous part one could identify the reigns of Menahem, Pekahiah and Pekah (the period 747–732: cf. 2 Kings 15:13–31); here we seem to be in the last stage of the Northern kingdom, in the times of King Hoshea (733–724), shortly before the fall of Samaria.

However, the most interesting thing about this section is the fact that Hosea goes right back to the beginnings of the people, to accuse his fellow-citizens of being as inconsistent as their father Jacob, who was not a very trustworthy man (11:12–12:14), and to remind them that they owe their nationhood, their identity, to the Lord, the only God, when he delivered them from Egypt (12:9; 13:4).

11:12–12:14. This is a well-honed piece that recalls events during the time of the patriarchs and then applies them to the contemporary situation, drawing clear and vivid lessons. This passage is very important from the point of view of the history of composition of the Old Testament text. Hosea ministered very

ambulabunt; / quasi leo rugiet, / quia ipse rugiet, / et in tremore accurrent filii ab occidente. / ¹¹Et avolabunt quasi avis ex Aegypto / et quasi columba de terra Assyriae; / et collocabo eos in domibus suis, / dicit Dominus.  **[12]** ¹Circumdedit me in fraude Ephraim, / et in dolo domus Israel; / —Iudas

e. Cn: Heb *into the city*  f. Ch 12.1 in Heb  g. Cn Compare Gk: Heb *roams with*

## 3. ISRAEL'S UNFAITHFULNESS*

**Israel and Judah steeped in crime**

12 ¹Ephraim herds the wind,
and pursues the east wind all day long;
they multiply falsehood and violence;
they make a bargain with Assyria,
and oil is carried to Egypt.

---

early on (around the middle of the eighth century BC) and things that he says show that he was very familiar with the history of Jacob and of some other tribes; the book of Hosea is an important source for understanding how the Pentateuch took shape.

Hosea is acutely aware of the solidarity between the early generations of Israel and his own generation. Thus, in 12:4–5 we are told that Jacob "met God at Bethel and there God spoke with him [see note **h**]—the Lord the God of hosts, the Lord is his name." The prophet considers that, by speaking to Jacob, God spoke to all generations of Jacob. Some modern, Western, translations [including the RSV] correct the Hebrew "God spoke with us" (v. 4) to "God spoke with him"; by doing so they miss the sense (and theology) of solidarity contained in the original text: the prophet is reading the encounter with Jacob as perfectly applicable to the people as a whole in later generations. This sense of solidarity found in the Old Testament carries on into the New. To take just one example (Heb 7:9–10): "one might even say that Levi himself, who receives tithes, paid tithes

through Abraham, for he was still in the loins of his ancestor when Melchizedek met him."

The line or argument in this oracle is fairly clear: Israel is deceitful and is trying to make pacts with foreign countries (11:12–12:1), which is not surprising, for he is like his father, Jacob, a supplanter from his mother's womb (v. 3). Like his father, too, Israel strives against God, and then seeks his blessing (v. 4). In this vein, the prophet alternates reproaches, promises of reconciliation, and threats with references to past or recent events (12:6–14) —mention of the conquest of Canaan (with a play on words, for Canaan means "trader") (12:7); criticism of Ephraim (12:8); reference to the unicity and majesty of God by using his name, "the Lord", *Yhwh* (12:9); and mention of the sins committed at Gilead and Gilgal (12:11). Finally, the prophet recalls Jacob again (when he fled to Aram: 12:12; cf. Gen 29), whom he contrasts with Moses (12:13), though he does not mention the latter by name: he calls him "a prophet" (12:13) because it was through the prophets that the transcendent Lord guided and

---

autem, dum adhuc vagatur, est cum Deo / et cum Sancto fidelis»—. / ²Ephraim pascit ventum / et sequitur aestum; / tota die mendacium et violentiam multiplicat / et foedus cum Assyriis init / et oleum

[2]The LORD has an indictment against Judah,
    and will punish Jacob according to his ways,
    and requite him according to his deeds.

Hos 4:1

### Biblical history recalled

[3]In the womb he took his brother by the heel,
    and in his manhood he strove with God.
[4]He strove with the angel and prevailed,
    he wept and sought his favour.
He met God at Bethel,
    and there God spoke with him[h]—
[5]the LORD the God of hosts,
    the LORD is his name:
[6]"So you, by the help of your God, return,
    hold fast to love and justice,
    and wait continually for your God."

Gen 25:26<br>Is 43:27<br>Gen 28:10–22;<br>32:24–28<br><br><br><br><br>Amos 4:13<br><br>Jas 4:8

[7]A trader, in whose hands are false balances,
    he loves to oppress.
[8]Ephraim has said, "Ah, but I am rich,
    I have gained wealth for myself":
but all his riches can never offset[i]
    the guilt he has incurred.
[9]I am the LORD your God
    from the land of Egypt;
I will again make you dwell in tents,
    as in the days of the appointed feast.

Deut 25:13<br><br>Lk 12:16–21<br>Rev 3:17–18<br><br><br>Ex 20:2<br>Hos 2:16; 13:4

---

guides his people (12:10). The conclusion is inescapable: Ephraim deserves punishment for its sins (12:14).

The historical circumstances discernible within the oracle are very like those of the previous oracles—pacts with foreign countries (12:1), faults against love and justice (12:6), neglect of God in times of prosperity (12:8), etc. It is rather odd that Judah should be mentioned in 12:2: some authors think that this was inserted later to apply Hosea's prophecy to the kingdom of Judah, after the Northern kingdom had collapsed.

in Aegyptum fert. / [3]Iudicium ergo Domini cum Iuda, / et visitatio super Iacob; / iuxta vias eius et iuxta opera eius reddet ei. / [4]In utero supplantavit fratrem suum / et in robore suo luctatus est cum Deo. / [5]Et luctatus est cum angelo et praevaluit; / flevit et deprecatus est eum. / In Bethel invenit eum / et ibi locutus est nobiscum / [6]Dominus, Deus exercituum: / Dominus memoriale eius. / [7]«Et tu ad Deum tuum converteris; / caritatem et iudicium custodi / et spera in Deo tuo semper». / [8]Chanaan, in manu eius statera dolosa, / fraudem diligit. / [9]Et dixit Ephraim: «Verumtamen dives effectus sum, / inveni

**h.** Gk Syr: Heb *us*   **i.** Cn Compare Gk: Heb obscure

Hos 6:5 ¹⁰I spoke to the prophets;
it was I who multiplied visions,
and through the prophets gave parables.

Hos 4:15; 6:8; 9:15 ¹¹If there is iniquity in Gilead
they shall surely come to nought;
if in Gilgal they sacrifice bulls,
their altars also shall be like stone heaps
on the furrows of the field.

Gen 29 ¹²(Jacob fled to the land of Aram,
there Israel did service for a wife,
and for a wife he herded sheep.)

¹³By a prophet the LORD brought Israel up from Egypt,
and by a prophet he was preserved.

Ex 3:7–10;
12:50–51
Deut 18:15,18
¹⁴Ephraim has given bitter provocation;
so his LORD will leave his bloodguilt upon him,
and will turn back upon him his reproaches.

### Sins of idolatry

**13** ¹When Ephraim spoke, men trembled;
he was exalted in Israel;
but he incurred guilt through Baal and died.

---

**13:1–16.** This passage forms a unit with its four oracles about judgment and punishment. The oracle that follows it (cf. 14:1) begins with a call to conversion. The four oracles are: a condemnation of Ephraim for its idolatry (vv. 1–3); words of the Lord recalling all he has done for his people and telling them they will be chastised for their ingratitude (vv. 4–8); two rhetorical questions spelling out how it is inevitable that Israel should collapse and its monarchy disappear (vv. 9–11); a prophecy about the death and destruction of Ephraim (vv. 12–15) which concludes with a sentence of condemnation (v. 16).

The first two oracles condemn the sins of Israel with which the prophet is only too familiar—idolatry (v. 2) and indifference to God in times of prosperity (v. 6). In view of these sins, the Lord, now (vv. 4–5) as before (12:9), proclaims his right to be the

opes mihi, / omnes labores mei non invenient mihi / iniquitatem, quam peccavi». / ¹⁰«Ego autem Dominus, Deus tuus / ex terra Aegypti; / adhuc sedere te faciam in tabernaculis, / sicut in diebus conventus. / ¹¹Et loquar ad prophetas / et ego visionem multiplicabo / et in manu prophetarum proponam similitudines». / ¹²Si Galaad iniquitas fuerat, / prorsus inanes facti sunt; / in Galgala bobus immolantes, / etiam altaria eorum erunt quasi acervi / super sulcos agri. / ¹³Fugit Iacob in regionem Aram; / et servivit Israel pro uxore / et pro uxore custos fuit. / ¹⁴Per prophetam autem eduxit Dominus / Israel de Aegypto, / et per prophetam custoditus est. / ¹⁵Ad iracundiam provocavit Ephraim amarissime, / sed sanguinem eius super eum relinquet / et opprobrium eius retribuet ei Dominus suus. [13] ¹Loquente Ephraim, horror factus est; / dux erat in Israel. / Et deliquit in Baal / et mortuus est. /

<sup>2</sup>And now they sin more and more,
  and make for themselves molten images,
idols skilfully made of their silver,
  all of them the work of craftsmen.
Sacrifice to these, they say.<sup>j</sup>
  Men kiss calves!
<sup>3</sup>Therefore they shall be like the morning mist
  or like the dew that goes early away,
like the chaff that swirls from the threshing floor
  or like smoke from a window.

**Punishment to come**
<sup>4</sup>I am the LORD your God
  from the land of Egypt;
you know no God but me,
  and besides me there is no saviour.

*1 Kings 12:27,32; 19:18*

*Hos 6:4*
*Zeph 2:2*
*Is 17:13; 41:16*
*Jas 4:14*

*Ex 20:2*
*Deut 5:6; 32:37–39*
*Hos 12:10*

---

God of Israel: "I am the Lord your God from the land of Egypt." The wording used in this oracle is reminiscent of that used at the start of the ten commandments (cf. Ex 20:2 and note; Deut 5:6). It expresses the radical monotheism of Israel that is part of its very identity: if they lose God, they also lose their right to be a people: they relapse into the state of bondage they were in before God took them into his care. Hence the importance of truly knowing God (v. 4): "Man's glory and dignity stem from his knowing where true greatness lies, and his striving to join himself to it, seeking the glory that flows from the Lord of glory" (St Basil, *De humilitate*, 3).

The radical nature of Israel's sin (it has betrayed its very origin) also explains why its punishment should be so severe; this is spelt out in the two next oracles: Israel is going to be destroyed (v. 9), it will have no king (v. 13), no fruits to enjoy (v. 15); worse still, its fall will be bloody (v. 16). It is possible that in uttering these oracles the prophet sees the imminent fall of King Hoshea (vv. 9–11) —in an ironic play on words, for Hoshea means "God saves"—and of the kingdom of Israel, whose capital is Samaria (v. 16) in the year 721 (cf. 2 Kings 17:1–6). The second part of 13:14, with some changes and a meaning different to that read here, is evoked by St Paul (1 Cor 15:54) to demonstrate Christ's victory over death.

---

<sup>2</sup>Et nunc addunt ad peccandum / faciuntque sibi conflatile de argento suo, / secundum intellegentiam suam simulacra; / factura artificum totum est. / «His —ipsi dicunt— immolate!». / Homines vitulos osculantur. / <sup>3</sup>Idcirco erunt quasi nubes matutina / et sicut ros matutinus praeteriens, / sicut palea turbine rapta ex area / et sicut fumus de fumario. / <sup>4</sup>«Ego autem Dominus, Deus tuus / ex terra Aegypti; / et

**j.** Gk: Heb *to these they say sacrifices of*

Deut 2:7; 8:15
Is 43:11

5It was I who knew you in the wilderness,
 in the land of drought;

Deut 32:15

6but when they had fed[k] to the full,
 they were filled, and their heart was lifted up;
 therefore they forgot me.

Hos 5:14
Rev 13:2

7So I will be to them like a lion,
 like a leopard I will lurk beside the way.

2 Sam 17:8

8I will fall upon them like a bear robbed of her cubs,
 I will tear open their breast,
and there I will devour them like a lion,
 as a wild beast would rend them.

### The end of the monarchy foretold

9I will destroy you, O Israel;
 who[l] can help you?

1 Sam 8:5,19;
15:22,23

10Where[m] now is your king, to save you;
 where are all[n] your princes,[o] to defend you[p]—
those of whom you said,
 "Give me a king and princes"?

1 Sam 8:7,22
Hos 10:15

11I have given you kings in my anger,
 and I have taken them away in my wrath.

### The downfall of Ephraim

Deut 32:34–35

12The iniquity of Ephraim is bound up,
 his sin is kept in store.

Is 26:17–18; 37:3

13The pangs of childbirth come for him,
 but he is an unwise son;
for now he does not present himself
 at the mouth of the womb.

Is 25:8; Ezek 37:1–14
Hos 6:2; 1 Cor 15:55
Rev 6:8

14Shall I ransom them from the power of Sheol?
 Shall I redeem them from Death?

---

Deum absque me nescies, / et salvator non est praeter me. / 5Ego pavi te in deserto, / in terra ardenti solitudinis. / 6Iuxta pascua sua saturati sunt / et saturati elevaverunt cor suum, / propterea obliti sunt mei. / 7Et ego ero eis quasi leaena, / sicut pardus iuxta viam insidiabor. / 8Occurram eis quasi ursa, raptis catulis, / et dirumpam claustrum cordis eorum: / et consumam eos ibi quasi leo; / bestia agri scindet eos. / 9Perdo te, Israel; / quis est auxiliator tuus? / 10Ubinam est rex tuus, / ut salvet te in omnibus urbibus tuis, / et iudices tui, de quibus dixisti: / "Da mihi regem et principes"? / 11Do tibi regem in furore meo / et aufero in indignatione mea. / 12Colligata est iniquitas Ephraim, / absconditum peccatum eius. / 13Dolores parturientis venient ei; / erit filius non sapiens: / suo enim tempore non stabit / in ore vulvae. / 14De manu inferni liberabo eos, / de morte redimam eos? / Ubi pestilentiae tuae, o

**k.** Cn: Heb *according to their pasture* **l.** Gk Syr: Heb *for in me* **m.** Gk Syr Vg: Heb *I will be*
**n.** Cn: Heb *in all* **o.** Cn: Heb *cities* **p.** Cn Compare Gk: Heb *and your judges*

O Death, where<sup>q</sup> are your plagues?
O Sheol, where<sup>q</sup> is your destruction?
Compassion is hid from my eyes.

<sup>15</sup>Though he may flourish as the reed plant,<sup>r</sup>
    the east wind, the wind of the LORD, shall come,
    rising from the wilderness;
and his fountain shall dry up,
    his spring shall be parched;
it shall strip his treasury
    of every precious thing.

Hos 12:2

<sup>16s</sup>Samaria shall bear her guilt,
    because she has rebelled against her God;
they shall fall by the sword,
    their little ones shall be dashed in pieces,
    and their pregnant women ripped open.

Hos 7:1; 10:14
Amos 1:13
Lk 19:44

### Call to conversion

**14** <sup>1</sup>Return, O Israel, to the LORD your God,
    for you have stumbled because of your iniquity.

Hos 5:5

---

**14:1–8.** The last oracle follows the pattern of the whole book: the denunciation of Israel's infidelity is followed by a blessing from the Lord. This happened in the episode from Hosea's personal life at the start of the book (1:2–2:1), in the central poems (2:2–23), and in the first part of the oracles (4:1–11:11). The novelty of this oracle lies in the fact that previously salvation and forgiveness were offered by the Lord spontaneously and generously, without Israel's being asked for anything; whereas here (vv. 1–3) the prophet entreats Israel to be converted so that God may heal her unfaithfulness (v. 4).

In the oracle, both the prophet (vv. 1–3) and the Lord (vv. 4–8) speak. The words of the prophet are a call to conversion (v. 1) and a prayer proper to a penitential liturgy (vv. 2–3) in which the sins of Israel are expressly mentioned—reliance on foreign pacts rather than on the Lord, and revering manmade idols as if they were God.

The Lord's words (vv. 4–8) benevolently offer the people reconciliation and a cure for their unfaithfulness. They speak of a golden age of love between the Lord and his people; all sorts of attractive imagery are used: the dew, the fragrance of Lebanon, the

---

mors? / Ubi pestis tua, inferne? / Consolatio abscondita est ab oculis meis». / <sup>15</sup>Dum ipse inter fratres fructificat, / veniet ventus urens, ventus Domini / de deserto ascendens, / et siccabit venas eius / et desolabit fontem eius. / Ipse diripiet thesaurum, / omne vas desiderabile.　**[14]** <sup>1</sup>Poenas solvet Samaria, / quoniam rebellavit contra Deum suum: / in gladio peribunt, / parvuli eorum elidentur, / et praegnantes

**q.** Gk Syr: Heb *I will be*　**r.** Cn: Heb *among brothers*　**s.** Ch 14.1 in Heb

Ps 32:1; 50:14
Heb 13:15

²Take with you words
and return to the LORD;
say to him,
"Take away all iniquity;
accept that which is good
and we will render
the fruit[t] of our lips.

Ps 10:4
Is 30:2,16; 31:1
Hos 2:18–19;
5:13; 7:11; 12:2

³Assyria shall not save us,
we will not ride upon horses;
and we will say no more, 'Our God,'
to the work of our hands.
In thee the orphan finds mercy."

Is 26:19
Hos 1:6; 2:16–25;
9:15

⁴I will heal their faithlessness;
I will love them freely,
for my anger has turned from them.

Mic 5:6–7

⁵I will be as the dew to Israel;
he shall blossom as the lily,
he shall strike root as the poplar;[u]

Is 27:6

⁶his shoots shall spread out;
his beauty shall be like the olive,
and his fragrance like Lebanon.
⁷They shall return and dwell beneath my[v] shadow,
they shall flourish as a garden;[w]
they shall blossom as the vine,
their fragrance shall be like the wine of Lebanon.

---

grain (note **w**) and the vine stand for the good things that the Lord, and not the Baals, bestows on the people; the Lord is depicted as a cypress, evergreen; that is, he is stable and enduring. So, the book's conclusion is clear: since the Lord loves them so deeply, there is nothing that the people can do but respond: "The love of the Beloved or, to put it better, the Beloved who is love, loves only love and faithfulness. Do not resist his love. Can we stop loving the one who is Love in person? Can the one who is Love by his very nature be unloved?" (St Bernard, *In Cantica Canticorum*, 83, 5).

discindentur. / ²Convertere, Israel, ad Dominum Deum tuum, / quoniam corruisti in iniquitate tua. / ³Tollite vobiscum verba / et convertimini ad Dominum; / dicite ei: «Omnem aufer iniquitatem / et accipe bonum, / et reddemus fructum labiorum nostrorum. / ⁴Assyria non salvabit nos; / super equum non ascendemus / nec vocabimus ultra: "Deos nostros!" / opera manuum nostrarum, / quia in te misericordiam consequetur pupillus». / ⁵«Sanabo praevaricationem eorum, / diligam eos spontanee, / quia aversus est furor meus ab eis. / ⁶Ero quasi ros pro Israel; / germinabit quasi lilium / et mittet radices suas ut Libanus. / ⁷Expandentur rami eius; / et erit quasi oliva gloria eius, / et odor eius ut

**t.** Gk Syr: Heb *bulls*    **u.** Cn: Heb *Lebanon*    **v.** Heb *his*    **w.** Cn: Heb *they shall grow grain*

Hos 4:17
2 Cor 6:16

[8]O Ephraim, what have I to do with idols?
  It is I who answer and look after you.[x]
I am like an evergreen cypress,
  from me comes your fruit.

## A word to the wise

Deut 32:4
Ps 107:43
Prov 4:7;
10:29

[9]Whoever is wise, let him understand these things;
  whoever is discerning, let him know them;
for the ways of the LORD are right,
  and the upright walk in them,
  but transgressors stumble in them.

---

**14:9.** The last verses of the book are a piece of wisdom writing. They are somewhat reminiscent of Deuteronomy 32:4, Psalm 107:43 and Proverbs 4:7. They invite us to read the book by applying its message to our own circumstances.

Libani. / [8]Convertentur sedentes in umbra mea, / colent triticum / et germinabunt quasi vinea; / memoriale eius sicut vinum Libani. / [9]Ephraim, quid ei ultra idola? / Ego exaudio et respicio in eum. / Ego ut abies virens: / ex me fructus tuus invenitur». / [10]Qui sapiens est, intellegat ista; / intellegens sciat haec! / Quia rectae viae Domini, / et iusti ambulabunt in eis; / praevaricatores vero corruent in eis.

**x.** Heb *him*

# JOEL

# Introduction

In the Hebrew collection of the minor prophets and in the Latin versions, the book of Joel comes second, after Hosea and before Amos; whereas in the Greek version of the Septuagint it comes fourth. The position given to Joel in the Hebrew Bible may be due to the fact that in one of the last verses of Joel (Joel 3:16a) and at the start of Amos (Amos 1:2a), these words occur: "The Lord roars from Zion, and utters his voice from Jerusalem." Maybe, when the texts of the minor prophets were being assembled for the Hebrew Bible, the editors wanted their readers to read Amos' oracles in the light of Joel's. One would need to add that in the last chapter of Joel (Joel 3:4–8) is found the oracle against Tyre, Sidon and Philistia that is also in Amos' first oracle against the nations (Amos 1:6–10). In any event, the position given to Joel in the Hebrew canon and the book's announcement of the outpouring of the Holy Spirit signal Joel's importance in the Old Testament. Its importance increases in the light of the New.

We know nothing about Joel himself other than what is said or can be deduced from the text. "Joel" means "The Lord is God". In the title of the book it says that he was the son of Pethuel. And from the text in general we can see that the author lived and preached in Judah (1: 6), that he was familiar with the liturgy and day-to-day affairs of the temple (2:1, 15, 23), and that he was very conscious of the state of affairs in his country (1:5, 11, 13–14).

## 1. STRUCTURE AND CONTENT

Scholars generally agree that from a literary point of view the text divides into two parts (1:2–2:17 and 2:18–3:21); but there is no consensus as to whether each part was written separately and then the two parts brought together, or whether from the very start the book was a sort of diptych designed as such.

The first part is mainly narrative, with tones of lamentation. A plague of locusts (1:2–12) is seen as a scourge from God, meant to urge the people to conversion and penance (1:13–20). The account of the plague serves to underscore the power of God, and the people are urged to do penance in order to have the Lord take pity on them. In 1:8 Judah is compared to a young virgin wearing sackcloth, grieving and doing penance for her lost bridegroom. The bridegroom is none other than the Lord who, in the times of the patriarchs, took a virgin for his wife—Israel, unstained by idolatry. Then the prophet announces the nearness of the "day of the Lord" (2:1–2). The locust plague is depicted as an invading army that devours all before it (2:3–11). This first part of the book ends with a further call to conversion (2:12–16).

The second part is largely in the style of eschatological-salvation writing: the people of God and their land should not fear, for the Lord will rescue them from all misfortune and give them all manner of good things (2:18–27). More than that—he "will pour out (his) spirit on all flesh" (2:28). This verse is one of the two hinges on which the book turns, the other being the "day of the Lord" (1:15; 2:1, 11; 3:1; 3:14), the day when wickedness will be punished (1:15; 2:1–3), and God's power will be manifested by portents (2:30) and judgment (3:12–14). Verses 17–18 of chapter 2 act as the link between the two parts of the book.

The book can be said to have this structure:

1. A TIME OF MISFORTUNE (1:2–2:17). This part begins with a description of how the country is devastated by a plague of locusts (1:2–12), leading the prophet to preach conversion and penance (1:13–20), for "the day of the Lord" is nigh (2:1–2). Then the same pattern is repeated—a description of invasion by a "great and powerful people" (2:2–11), followed by an exhortation to a solemn assembly of penance (2:12–16), presided over by priests (2:17).

2. THE OUTPOURING OF THE SPIRIT, AND THE DAY OF THE LORD (2:18–3:21). In response to the people's penance, the Lord causes the plague to cease (2:18–20), future prosperity is announced (2:21–26), and the promise is given that the Lord will dwell among his people (2:27). Further blessings are announced—the outpouring of the Spirit (2:28–32), the judgment of the nations (3:1–8), a call to the holy war of peace (3:9–13), the final, great day of the Lord (3:14–17) which will see the restoration of the eschatological Jerusalem (3:18–21).

## 2. COMPOSITION AND HISTORICAL BACKGROUND

The book contains few references that might indicate when it was written, and those that there are are imprecise. Furthermore, there are two distinct sections to the book and these may come from different periods. So, we cannot be quite sure when to date it. Some scholars give great importance to little things that suggest it was composed very early on, around the ninth or eighth century BC. Others focus more on internal clues that could indicate it was written after the return from the Babylonian exile—to be more precise, in the decades around the year 400 BC; they say this because the book contains details that fit in with the way the Jewish community was organized as a result of the Nehemiah-Ezra reforms (at the start of the fourth century BC), when the monarchy was no longer part of the equation and a hierarchy of priests governed the life of Judah.

In addition to scanty historical references, there are literary and thematic aspects running right through the book that clearly have parallels in other prophetical writings—those of Amos, Hosea, Isaiah, Micah, Zephaniah, Ezekiel and Obadiah. Comparative studies seem to prove that the book of Joel was inspired by these, and not vice-versa. For all these reasons, modern scholarship inclines towards the date we have already mentioned—around the year 400 BC.

## 3. MESSAGE

Joel has left us a valuable legacy in two key areas of Revelation. The first part of it is summed up in 2:13: "Rend your hearts and not your garments. Return to the Lord, your God, for he is gracious and wonderful"; the second, in 2:28–29: "I will pour out my spirit on all flesh; your sons and daughters shall prophesy ...". True conversion and the promise of the Spirit are at the very heart of Joel's message.

The key to the whole book is the theme of "the day of the Lord", a phrase that actually appears five times (1:15; 2:1, 11, 32; 3:14). When the prophets speak of "the day of the Lord" they mean a special intervention by God in human history, particularly in the affairs of the chosen people. But that day has two aspects to it: on the one hand, it is Judgment Day, the day when the nations will be judged (this carries connotations of destruction-purification and chastisement); on the other, it is the day of divine salvation for those who have suffered injustice and oppression.

We can see this dual meaning in Joel. The passage about the plague of locusts (1:4–20) stresses the dark side. The poem in 2:1–11 gives an interpretation of the plague: the invading nation stands for God's army, charged with delivering divine punishment. That being so, the prophet then issues a message about penance (2:12–16). With 2:17–18 (man's penance and God's response) we see the other side of the coin: the day of the Lord is a day of salvation, involving all kinds of things maybe at the same time—the outpouring of the Spirit (2:28), cosmic commotion (2:30–32; 3:15–16); judgment of the unbelieving nations (3:1–8); a call to the nations to rally at Zion, and a call to peace (3:9–13); the restoration of Zion, and an abundance of good things (3:18–21): the whole scene transcends the real conditions of this world and involves a complete re-creation, with the Lord dwelling in the midst of his people (3:15–18).

This teaching covers part of the prophetical and apocalyptic message. Therefore, it would seem more appropriate to the period after the return from exile, when the message of the prophets was beginning to sink in and people's expectations had begun to focus on the End time rather than on the precarious rehabilitation of the chosen people in what was, after all, only a small province of the Persian empire.

## 4. THE BOOK OF JOEL IN THE LIGHT OF THE NEW TESTAMENT

Even though it is a short book, it has considerable resonance in the New Testament. St Mark quotes 3:13 (almost word for word) at the end of the parable about the seed that grows into a large shrub (Mk 4:26–29). The Gospel of St John (Jn 1:5; 8:12; 13:30; 20:1) in its depiction of darkness and night as elements hostile to Christ, contains echoes of 2:2. In his dialogue with the Samaritan woman, Jesus speaks to her about the living water that he will give her and that will spring up into eternal life (Jn 4:13–14), a passage reminiscent of 3:18.

There are other New Testament passages that contain explicit and important references to Joel. In his account of the day of Pentecost, in Acts 2:17–21, Luke records, at the end of St Peter's speech, a literal quotation from the oracle in Joel 2:28–32, which he sees as being fulfilled by the outpouring of the Holy Spirit on those present—the Christian community. In Romans 10:12–13, St Paul uses Joel 2:32a when expounding on the universal reach of the Gospel, with no distinction between Jew and Greek; and the same verse underlies Galatians 3:28; 6:15. Finally, Joel 2:4–6 inspired the vision of the blowing of the fifth trumpet and the plague of locusts in the Revelation to John (Rev 9:7–12).

Fathers of the Church and early Christian writers, in both East and West, commented on or quoted from Joel. The liturgy of the Church makes extensive use of some passages from Joel, which is indicative of how she interprets and applies this prophetical book. For example, Joel 2:12–18 is the first reading in the Ash Wednesday Mass, and Joel 2:13 and 2:17 are antiphons recited or sung during the imposition of the ashes. In the harvest thanksgiving Mass, Joel 2:21–27 is taken as the first reading. In the Mass for the vigil of Pentecost, Joel 2:28–32 is an optional first reading, and that text is also used in the rite for the sacrament of Confirmation.

**Title**

# 1 ¹The word of the LORD that came to Joel, the son of Pethuel:

## 1. A TIME OF MISFORTUNE*

**The land devastated by a locust plague**
²Hear this, you aged men,
  give ear, all inhabitants of the land!
Has such a thing happened in your days,
  or in the days of your fathers?

---

**1:1.** For St Jerome (cf. the prologue to his *Commentarii in Ioelem*) there is something to be said for putting Joel at the start of the minor prophets, after Hosea, as the Hebrew Bible does, particularly if one takes account of the etymology of "Joel" which, according to Jerome, means "he who begins". Modern scholars, too, see the books of Hosea and Joel as being an introduction to the minor prophets: Hosea, a Northern prophet, is God's messenger and a man faithful to the Covenant like the patriarchs; Joel, a Southern prophet, complements that message of compassion and love by announcing the outpouring of the Spirit of God. In this way the two books act as entrance pillars to the collection.

*1:2–2:17.** These verses form the first part of the book. They invite the listener to make an examination of conscience and to reflect on the sad events of the time. A few words of introduction (1:2–4) try to focus the listeners' attention on the speech that follows: the people need to ask themselves why there has been a terrible invasion of locusts that has devastated the country, harming them and the land (1:5–12). If they manage to work out the answer, their only recourse is conversion and penance (1:13–14): the misfortunes that beset them are a sign that the "day of the Lord" is coming (1:15). The situation is dire (1:16–18). The prophet beseeches the Lord for help (1:19–20).

The day of the Lord is at hand, a day of "darkness and gloom" (2:1–2). The plague of locusts is described as being like an invasion by a ferocious army (2:3–11); it is reminiscent of the eighth plague of Egypt (cf. Ex 10:13–15) and the description of the terrifying theophany on Mount Sinai (cf. Ex 19–20). The first part of the book ends with a new call to conversion: only the Lord can save them from disaster (2:12–17).

**1:2–12.** This is a poem of lamentation and warning addressed to various groups in society. The prophet reviews the situation after the plague of locusts; that plague is a sign that God's punish-

---

[1] ¹Verbum Domini, quod factum est ad Ioel filium Phatuel. ²Audite hoc, senes, / et auribus percipite, omnes habitatores terrae, / si factum est istud in diebus vestris / aut in diebus patrum vestrorum. /

³Tell your children of it,
and let your children tell their children,
and their children another generation.

Deut 28:38
Ps 105:34–35
Amos 4:9; 7:1
Mal 3:11

⁴What the cutting locust left,
the swarming locust has eaten.
What the swarming locust left,
the hopping locust has eaten,
and what the hopping locust left,
the destroying locust has eaten.

---

ment for sin will soon befall them. It is difficult to work out whether the terms in v. 4 refer to four species of locusts or simply four stages in the locust's development. A locust plague is particularly devastating for a farming community.

In v. 8 Judah is compared to a young virgin dressed in sackcloth, bewailing the death of her intended: "No one other than God is meant here, who, in Abraham, Isaac, and Jacob, took as his bride a virgin who was free from any taint of idolatry [...]. Thus the Apostle says to all believers: *I feel a divine jealousy for you, for I betrothed you to Christ to present you as a pure bride to her one husband* (2 Cor 11:2). While the bridegroom is with his bride, there will be no fasting (cf. Mt 9:15), nor lamenting, nor tears wept for the absent groom. But when the bridegroom is attacked, the bride will cry and wail, and dress in sackcloth and ashes and wear a belt of rope around her waist" (St Jerome, *Commentarii in Ioelem*, 1, 8).

But the main imagery that the prophet uses here is drawn from agriculture: Judah is quite denuded; there is no produce, not even enough for the temple offerings (v. 9). It is no surprise to find spiritual writers using this same imagery in relation to the duties of pastors and apostles: "We cannot deny that a great deal remains to be done. On one occasion, when he was looking perhaps at the swaying wheat-fields, Jesus said to his disciples: 'The harvest is plentiful, but the labourers are few; pray therefore the Lord of the harvest to send out labourers into his harvest' (Mt 9:38) Now, as then, labourers are needed to bear 'the burden of the day and the scorching heat' (Mt 20:12). And if we, the labourers, are not faithful, there will come to pass what was described by the prophet Joel: 'The fields are laid waste, the ground mourns; because the grain is destroyed, the wine fails, the oil languishes. Be confounded, O tillers of the soil, wail, O winedressers, for the wheat and the barley, because the harvest of the field has perished' (Joel 1:10–11)" (St Josemaría Escrivá, *Christ Is Passing By*, 158).

---

³Super hoc filiis vestris narrate, / et filii vestri filiis suis, / et filii eorum generationi alterae. / ⁴Residuum erucae comedit locusta, / et residuum locustae comedit bruchus, / et residuum bruchi comedit gryllus.

⁵Awake, you drunkards, and weep;
  and wail, all you drinkers of wine,
because of the sweet wine,
  for it is cut off from your mouth.
⁶For a nation has come up against my land,
  powerful and without number;
its teeth are lion's teeth,
  and it has the fangs of a lioness.
⁷It has laid waste my vines,
  and splintered my fig trees;
it has stripped off their bark and thrown it down;
  their branches are made white.

⁸Lament like a virgin girded with sackcloth
  for the bridegroom of her youth.
⁹The cereal offering and the drink offering are cut off
  from the house of the LORD.
The priests mourn,
  the ministers of the LORD.
¹⁰The fields are laid waste,
  the ground mourns;
because the grain is destroyed,
  the wine fails,
  the oil languishes.

¹¹Be confounded, O tillers of the soil,
  wail, O vinedressers,
for the wheat and the barley;
  because the harvest of the field has perished.
¹²The vine withers,
  the fig tree languishes.
Pomegranate, palm, and apple,
  all the trees of the field are withered;
and gladness fails
  from the sons of men.

Deut 28:39
Is 5:11

Jer 46:23
Rev 9:8

Is 5:1
Nahum 2:3

Prov 2:17
Jer 3:4

Hos 4:3

Is 16:10; 24:11
Jer 25:10; 48:33
Amos 4:7–9

---

/ ⁵Expergiscimini, ebrii, et flete, / et ululate, omnes, qui bibitis vinum, / propter mustum, / quoniam periit ab ore vestro. / ⁶Gens enim ascendit super terram meam / fortis et innumerabilis; / dentes eius ut dentes leonis, / et molares leaenae sunt ei. / ⁷Posuit vineam meam in desertum / et ficum meam in lignum confractum; / nudans spoliavit eam et proiecit, / albi facti sunt rami eius. / ⁸Plange, quasi virgo accincta sacco / super virum pubertatis suae. / ⁹Periit oblatio et libatio / de domo Domini; / luxerunt sacerdotes / ministri Domini. / ¹⁰Depopulata est regio; / luxit humus, / quoniam devastatum est triticum, / defecit mustum, / elanguit oleum. / ¹¹Confundemini, agricolae, / ululate, vinitores, / super frumento et hordeo, / quia periit messis agri. / ¹²Vinea exaruit, / et ficus elanguit, / malogranatum et palma et

Jud 4:14
2 Sam 12:16
1 Kings 21:27
Joel 1:8
**Call to repentance and prayer**

<sup>13</sup>Gird on sackcloth and lament, O priests,
    wail, O ministers of the altar.
Go in, pass the night in sackcloth,
    O ministers of my God!
Because cereal offering and drink offering
    are withheld from the house of your God.

Lev 23:27–36
1 Kings 21:9
2 Chron 20:9
<sup>14</sup>Sanctify a fast,
    call a solemn assembly.

---

**1:13–20.** In the form of a poem, the prophet appeals for public conversion and penance to entreat God to take pity on the people and the land. "Go in, pass the night in sackcloth" (v. 13)—the same language as is used to describe the penance done by David when his son was fatally ill (cf. 2 Sam 12:16), and, in general, the sign of deep mourning (cf. 1 Kings 21:27, when King Ahab is warned of what will befall him). Judith 4:8ff mentions priests, people and even livestock wearing sackcloth. "Sanctify a fast" (v. 14), that is, declare a holy fast, a penitential rite to move God to mercy; other Old Testament references to this are to be found in 1 Kings 21:9 and Jonah 3:5–9.

The basic purpose of these acts of penance is given in v. 15 with a play on words: the "day of the Lord" is near; it comes as destruction, as a scourge, *shod*, from the Almighty, *Shaddai*. Verses 16–18 show that the people admit that their punishment is deserved; this prepares the way for the prophet's prayer that follows. In it, Joel cries to the Lord on behalf of the community (v. 19)—

and not only he: "even the flocks of sheep" sigh to God in a mute prayer.

It is significant that the priests are the first to be called to penance (v. 13). They should be the first to lament—before calling others (elders, all the inhabitants) to do so (v. 14). This is something embedded in the tradition of the Bible and of the Church—the idea that ministers should set a good example: "Those who have been called to wait on the table of the Lord should be praiseworthy, shining examples of righteousness, unmarked by any stain or taint of sinfulness. They should live upright lives, as salt of the earth, for their own sake and for the sake of others, giving good example by their behaviour and deeds, as the light of the world. They should be mindful of the warning made by the divine teacher Christ Jesus to his apostles and disciples, and all of their successors, priests and teachers: *You are the salt of the earth; but if salt has lost its taste, how shall its saltness be restored?* (Mt 5:13)" (St John Capistrano, *Mirror of the Clergy*, 1, in the *Divine Office*, Readings, 23 October).

malum / et omnia ligna agri aruerunt, / quia evanuit gaudium / a filiis hominum. / <sup>13</sup>Accingite vos et plangite, sacerdotes; / ululate, ministri altaris. / Ingredimini, cubate in sacco, / ministri Dei mei, / quoniam interiit de domo Dei vestri / oblatio et libatio. / <sup>14</sup>Sanctificate ieiunium, / vocate coetum, /

Gather the elders
    and all the inhabitants of the land
to the house of the L<small>ORD</small> your God;
    and cry to the L<small>ORD</small>.

Joel 2:15
Jon 3:5–9

<sup>15</sup>Alas for the day!
    For the day of the L<small>ORD</small> is near,
    and as destruction from the Almighty it comes.
<sup>16</sup>Is not the food cut off
    before our eyes,
joy and gladness
    from the house of our God?

Is 13:6
Jer 46:10
Ezek 30:2–3

<sup>17</sup>The seed shrivels under the clods,<sup>a</sup>
    the storehouses are desolate;
the granaries are ruined
    because the grain has failed.
<sup>18</sup>How the beasts groan!
    The herds of cattle are perplexed
because there is no pasture for them;
    even the flocks of sheep are dismayed.

Hos 4:3; 13:15

## 2. THE OUTPOURING OF THE SPIRIT
## AND THE DAY OF THE LORD*

**The Lord's response: the plague ceases**
<sup>19</sup>Unto thee, O L<small>ORD</small>, I cry.
    For fire has devoured
    the pastures of the wilderness,
and flame has burned
    all the trees of the field.
<sup>20</sup>Even the wild beasts cry to thee
    because the water brooks are dried up,
and fire has devoured
    the pastures of the wilderness.

---

congregate senes, / omnes habitatores terrae / in domum Dei vestri, / et clamate ad Dominum: / <sup>15</sup>«Heu diei! / Quia prope est dies Domini, / et quasi vastitas a potente veniet. / <sup>16</sup>Numquid non coram oculis vestris / alimenta perierunt, / de domo Dei nostri / laetitia et exsultatio?». / <sup>17</sup>Computruerunt semina / subtus glebas suas, / demolita sunt horrea, / dissipatae sunt apothecae, / eo quod exaruit triticum. / <sup>18</sup>Quid ingemuit animal, / perterrita sunt armenta boum, / quia non est pascua eis? / Sed et greges pecorum disperierunt. / <sup>19</sup>Ad te, Domine, clamo, / quia ignis comedit / pascua deserti, / et flamma

**a.** Heb uncertain

Joel 1:15
Zeph 1:15
Jn 8:12

**The day of the Lord is coming "after darkness"**

**2** ¹Blow the trumpet in Zion;
sound the alarm on my holy mountain!
Let all the inhabitants of the land tremble,
for the day of the LORD is coming, it is near,

---

**2:1–11.** From the literary point of view, and also by virtue of their theme, these verses form a well-defined poem: this is signalled by the use of what is called "inclusion": cf. the reference to the day of the Lord in the first and last verses. The poem describes how God manifests his presence among his people, arriving with all the trappings of power. The passage is reminiscent of the account of the theophany on Mount Sinai (Ex 19:16–25; Deut 4:9–14) and of prophetical texts, too (Zeph 1:15; Is 13:8; etc.). It is all designed to make people conscious of the Lord's transcendence and power, in order to bring about a change of heart: only God can chastise them and by so doing rescue them from their anguish.

The first two verses are a call to attention. The trumpet or horn was blown mainly on two occasions—as an alarm in times of war, or to call an assembly; here, as in the parallel passage of Zephaniah 1:15–16, it is an alarm call. The "day of the Lord" (v. 1) arrives like a terrible army with all the panoply of war. St John's Gospel, in the prologue (Jn 1:5) and elsewhere (8:12; 13:30; 20:1; etc.), uses language similar to that found here (v. 2), depicting darkness and night as elements hostile to Christ.

Verses 3–11 elaborate on the first vision (1:6). The language and imagery here are typical of apocalyptic writing. The comparison of locusts to horses (v. 4) is to be found elsewhere in the Old Testament (cf. Job 39:19–20) and will later be found in the book of Revelation at the blast of the fifth trumpet when the army of locusts appears (vv. 4–9; cf. Rev 9:1–7). The earthquake and thunder and darkened sun and moon (vv. 10–11) have clear parallels in Isaiah 13:10, 13. Nahum 1:6 also speaks about the day of the Lord being unendurable (v. 11; cf. Rev 6:17). The sacred writer uses this vivid, bold imagery to show the gravity of sin and the need for conversion. His words are a permanent reminder to us to be prepared, because we not know when that day will come: "The uncertainty that surrounds the coming of the day of judgment provides us with two reasons to remain ever vigilant. First, if a man does not know whether it will arrive within his lifetime, he is given cause to be constantly prepared. Secondly, since man is responsible not only for himself, but also for his family, people, nation, and the whole Church, whose lifetimes extend far beyond the lifetime of one man, he must be vigilant, so that the Lord will not come and find people unprepared" (St Thomas Aquinas, *Summa theologiae*, Suppl. 88, 4).

---

succendit / omnia ligna agri. / ²⁰Sed et bestiae agri / suspirant ad te, / quoniam exsiccati sunt fontes aquarum, / et ignis devoravit / pascua deserti.  **[2]** ¹Canite tuba in Sion, / ululate in monte sancto meo;

<sup>2</sup>a day of darkness and gloom,
 a day of clouds and thick darkness!

Amos 5:17–20
Joel 1:6
Jn 1:5; 8:12;
13:30; 20:1

**Invasion by a "powerful people"**

Like blackness there is spread upon the mountains
 a great and powerful people;
their like has never been from of old,
 nor will be again after them
 through the years of all generations.

Mt 24:21
Mk 13:19

<sup>3</sup>Fire devours before them,
 and behind them a flame burns.
The land is like the garden of Eden before them,
 but after them a desolate wilderness,
 and nothing escapes them.

Gen 2:8
Ezek 28:13
Joel 1:19

<sup>4</sup>Their appearance is like the appearance of horses,
 and like war horses they run.
<sup>5</sup>As with the rumbling of chariots,
 they leap on the tops of the mountains,
like the crackling of a flame of fire
 devouring the stubble,
like a powerful army
 drawn up for battle.

Job 39:19–20
Rev 9:7,9

<sup>6</sup>Before them peoples are in anguish,
 all faces grow pale.
<sup>7</sup>Like warriors they charge,
 like soldiers they scale the wall.
They march each on his way,
 they do not swerve<sup>b</sup> from their paths.
<sup>8</sup>They do not jostle one another,
 each marches in his path;

Is 13:8
Nahum 2:11

---

/ conturbentur omnes habitatores terrae, / quia venit dies Domini, / quia prope est. / <sup>2</sup>Dies tenebrarum et caliginis, / dies nubis et turbinis; / quasi aurora expansa super montes / populus multus et fortis: / similis ei non fuit a principio, / et post eum non erit / usque in annos generationis et generationis. / <sup>3</sup>Ante faciem eius ignis vorat, / et post eum exurit flamma. / Quasi hortus Eden terra coram eo, / et post eum solitudo deserti; / neque est quod effugiat eum. / <sup>4</sup>Quasi aspectus equorum aspectus eorum, / et quasi equites sic current. / <sup>5</sup>Sicut sonitus quadrigarum / super capita montium exsiliunt, / sicut sonitus flammae ignis / devorantis stipulam, / velut populus fortis / praeparatus ad proelium. / <sup>6</sup>A facie eius cruciabuntur populi, / omnes vultus candentes. / <sup>7</sup>Sicut fortes currunt, / quasi viri bellatores ascendunt murum; / unusquisque in viis suis graditur, / et non declinant a semitis suis. / <sup>8</sup>Unusquisque fratrem

**b.** Gk Syr Vg: Heb *take a pledge*

they burst through the weapons
and are not halted.
⁹They leap upon the city,
they run upon the walls;
they climb up into the houses,
they enter through the windows like a thief.

Joel 3:4,16; 4:15–16
Mt 24:29
Rev 6:12; 9:2

¹⁰The earth quakes before them,
the heavens tremble.
The sun and the moon are darkened,
and the stars withdraw their shining.

Nahum 1:6
Mal 3:2,23
Rev 6:17

¹¹The LORD utters his voice
before his army,
for his host is exceedingly great;
he that executes his word is powerful.
For the day of the LORD is great and very terrible;
who can endure it?

**An urgent call to repentance**

Deut 4:29,30
1 Sam 7:3
Hos 12:7

¹²"Yet even now," says the LORD,
"return to me with all your heart,
with fasting, with weeping, and with mourning;

Ex 34:6–7; Is 58:5–7
Amos 5:21

¹³ and rend your hearts and not your garments."
Return to the LORD, your God,

---

**2:12–17.** The first part of the book ends with a general exhortation to conversion: there is an oracle of the Lord ("says the Lord": v. 12), where the prophet makes an appeal on behalf of God; and then he specifically mentions the priests' duty to do penance and offer prayers. Central to these words of warning is v. 13, which spells out what makes conversion last—God's compassion and man's sincere determination. St Jerome comments: "*Return to me with all your heart:* show your repentance and inner conversion through fasting, mourning and tears. By fasting now, your hunger will be satisfied later; mourning now, one day you will laugh; weeping now, you shall be consoled. The custom of rending one's garments at times of sorrow or adversity is well-

---

suum non coarctat, / singuli in calle suo ambulant, / per media tela prorumpunt / sine intermissione. / ⁹Urbem ingrediuntur, / in murum discurrunt, / domos conscendunt, / per fenestras intrant quasi fur. / ¹⁰A facie eius contremuit terra, / moti sunt caeli, / sol et luna obtenebrati sunt, / et stellae retraxerunt splendorem suum. / ¹¹Et Dominus dedit vocem suam ante faciem exercitus sui, / quia multa sunt nimis castra eius, / quia fortia et facientia verbum eius; / magnus enim dies Domini / et terribilis valde, et quis sustinebit eum? / ¹²«Nunc ergo, / dicit Dominus, / convertimini ad me in toto corde vestro, / in ieiunio et in fletu et in planctu; / ¹³et scindite corda vestra et non vestimenta vestra, / et convertimini ad Dominum Deum vestrum, / quia benignus et misericors est, / patiens et multae misericordiae et

for he is gracious and merciful,
slow to anger, and abounding in steadfast love,
and repents of evil.
<sup>14</sup>Who knows whether he will not turn and repent,
and leave a blessing behind him,
a cereal offering and a drink offering
for the LORD, your God?

Is 65:8
Hag 2:19
Amos 5:14
Jon 3:9
Mal 3:10

<sup>15</sup>Blow the trumpet in Zion;
sanctify a fast;
call a solemn assembly;
<sup>16</sup> gather the people.
Sanctify the congregation;
assemble the elders;
gather the children,
even nursing infants.
Let the bridegroom leave his room,
and the bride her chamber.

Joel 1:14; 2:1

Ex 19:10,22
Deut 24:5
1 Cor 7:5

**The priests entreat the Lord**
<sup>17</sup>Between the vestibule and the altar
let the priests, the ministers of the LORD, weep
and say, "Spare thy people, O LORD,
and make not thy heritage a reproach,
a byword among the nations.

Ex 32:11–12
Deut 9:26–27
1 Mac 7:36–38
Ps 42:11; 79:10
Ezek 8:16; Mic 7:10
Mal 2:17; Mt 23:15

---

established: the high priest tore his robes to show the gravity of the Saviour's crime; and, according to the Acts of the Apostles, Paul and Barnabas ripped their tunics when they heard blasphemous words being spoken. But I tell you to rend not your garments, but your hearts that are filled with sin. The heart, like wineskins, does not tear of its own accord: it must be deliberately torn. When you have rent your heart in this way, return to the Lord, your God, from whom you have strayed by your sins. Never doubt his forgiveness, for no matter how many and grave your past sins have been, he will pardon you from the abundance of his mercy" (*Commentarii in Ioelem*, 2, 12ff).

**2:17.** This verse (which the liturgy of the Church uses as a call to penance on Ash Wednesday) acts as a conclusion to the first part of the book: a change of heart, backed up by sincere acts of

placabilis super malitia». / <sup>14</sup>Quis scit, si convertatur et ignoscat / et relinquat post se benedictionem, / oblationem et libationem / Domino Deo vestro? / <sup>15</sup>Canite tuba in Sion, / sanctificate ieiunium, vocate coetum; / congregate populum, sanctificate conventum, / coadunate senes, / <sup>16</sup>congregate parvulos et sugentes ubera, / egrediatur sponsus de cubili suo, / et sponsa de thalamo suo. / <sup>17</sup>Inter vestibulum et altare plorent / sacerdotes ministri Domini / et dicant: «Parce, Domine, populo tuo / et ne des

> Why should they say among the peoples,
> 'Where is their God?'"

Deut 4:24   <sup>18</sup>Then the LORD became jealous for his land,
    and had pity on his people.
Deut 11:14   <sup>19</sup>The LORD answered and said to his people,
    "Behold, I am sending to you

---

penance, can cause God to stay his hand and spare his people any more affliction. The words that open the second part of the book (v. 18) tell us of the Lord's response; from then on, hope is on the horizon: "God does not let himself be outdone in generosity. Be sure that he grants faithfulness to those who give themselves to him" (St Josemaría Escrivá, *The Forge*, 623).

\*2:18–3:21. The second part of the book is all about salvation. The Lord's compassion (2:18) is shown by the message he sends via the prophet to the people in response to their conversion: "The Lord answered and said to his people" (2:19). On the Lord's behalf the prophet encourages Judah and Jerusalem, telling them that they have no reason to be afraid, for the Lord is going to deliver them from their afflictions and provide them with every sort of earthly good (symbolized here by the produce of the earth—grain, wine, oil: 2:19–27).

But the high point will be when God pours out his "spirit on all flesh ..." (2:28). The outpouring of the Spirit is the definitive sign that the "day of the Lord" has come. That "day" is mentioned five times in the book (1:15;

2:1, 11, 31; 3:14), each time with greater emphasis. The day of the Lord is an End time when a number of things will happen: wickedness will be punished (1:15; 2:1–3); the power of the Lord will be manifested by portents in the heavens and on earth (2:30–31); and, above all, it is the day when the Lord will judge all nations (3:1–8).

2:18–27. This first oracle in the second part of the book shows God's response to the people's good reaction to the earlier oracles. Therefore, it acts as a preface to the salvation text that follows. Earlier, the people (1:13–19) and even animals (1:20) beseeched God to relieve them of the locusts (1:2–12); now, the Lord promises to heap good things upon the people (vv. 23, 26), the fields (vv. 24–25) and the beasts of the field (v. 22). But the best news of all comes in the last verse: whereas previously it could be asked, "Where is their God?" (2:17), now the people can reply that God is in their midst (v. 27). The call to rejoice (v. 21), and the presence of the Lord among them (v. 27), remind the Christian reader of the account of the Annunciation to Mary (Lk 1:26–33) where these oracles of salvation, in fact, find fulfilment.

hereditatem tuam in opprobrium, / ut dominentur eis nationes». / Quare dicent in populis: / «Ubi est Deus eorum»? / <sup>18</sup>Zelatus est Dominus terram suam / et pepercit populo suo. / <sup>19</sup>Et respondit Dominus

grain, wine, and oil,
and you will be satisfied;
and I will no more make you
a reproach among the nations.

<sup></sup>20"I will remove the northerner far from you,
and drive him into a parched and desolate land,
his front into the eastern sea,
and his rear into the western sea;
the stench and foul smell of him will rise,
for he has done great things.

Deut 11:24
Jer 1:14; Is 34:3
Ezek 47:18
Amos 4:10
Zech 14:8

## Prosperity will return

21"Fear not, O land;
be glad and rejoice,
for the LORD has done great things!
22Fear not, you beasts of the field,
for the pastures of the wilderness are green;
the tree bears its fruit,
the fig tree and vine give their full yield.

23"Be glad, O sons of Zion,
and rejoice in the LORD, your God;
for he has given the early rain for your vindication,
he has poured down for you abundant rain,
the early and the latter rain, as before.

24"The threshing floors shall be full of grain,
the vats shall overflow with wine and oil.
25I will restore to you the years
which the swarming locust has eaten,
the hopper, the destroyer, and the cutter,
my great army, which I sent among you.

Deut 11:14

Joel 1:4

---

et dixit populo suo: / «Ecce ego mittam vobis / frumentum et vinum et oleum, / et replebimini eis; /
et non dabo vos ultra / opprobrium in gentibus. / 20Et eum, qui ab aquilone est, / procul faciam a vobis
/ et expellam eum in terram / inviam et desertam: / facies eius contra mare orientale, / et extremum eius
ad mare occidentale; / et ascendet foetor eius, / et ascendet putredo eius, / quia magna operatus est. /
21Noli timere, terra; / exsulta et laetare, / quoniam magna Dominus operatus est. / 22Nolite timere,
animalia regionis, / quia germinaverunt pascua deserti, / quia lignum attulit fructum suum, / ficus et
vinea dederunt divitias suas. / 23Et, filii Sion, exsultate / et laetamini in Domino Deo vestro, / quia dedit
vobis / pluviam iustitiae / et descendere fecit ad vos / imbrem matutinum et serotinum sicut prius. / 24Et
implebuntur areae frumento, / et redundabunt torcularia / vino et oleo; / 25et reddam vobis annos, / quos

²⁶"You shall eat in plenty and be satisfied,
    and praise the name of the LORD your God,
    who has dealt wondrously with you.
And my people shall never again be put to shame.
²⁷You shall know that I am in the midst of Israel,
    and that I, the LORD, am your God and there is none else.
And my people shall never again
    be put to shame.

Lev 26:11,12
Is 42:8; 45:5
Ezek 39:22
Hos 11:9

**The Spirit poured out**

Num 11:25–30
Is 32:15;
44:3; 54:13
Ezek 39:29
Zech 12:10
*Acts 2:17–21*

²⁸ᶜ"And it shall come to pass afterward,
    that I will pour out my spirit on all flesh;
your sons and your daughters shall prophesy,
    your old men shall dream dreams,
    and your young men shall see visions.

---

**2:28–32.** This is the great passage about the outpouring of the Holy Spirit. The word "afterward" in v. 28 marks the transition from the material benefits described in the previous verses to spiritual benefits. The outpouring of the Spirit involves charismatic and prophetical gifts primarily (moral gifts derive from these). This infusion of the Spirit is the fulfilment of an ancient promise, found in Numbers 11:16–30: "Gather for me seventy men of the elders of Israel, [...] and I will take some of the spirit which is upon you and put it upon them. [...] Would that all the Lord's people were prophets, that the Lord would put his spirit upon them!" This hope is accentuated in Joel, for now no limits are placed on who will benefit from it—elders, young people, and even servants (vv. 28–29). And the Lord will once more perform wondrous things through them (v. 30), like those done by prophets in the strict sense (cf. Deut 13:2; etc.).

St Peter sees this promise being fulfilled when the Holy Spirit is poured out on the day of Pentecost (Acts 2:1–21). "Peter turns to this passage from Joel to explain the significance of what has occurred, and the signs which those present have seen: 'the pouring out of the Holy Spirit'. It is a supernatural work of God, carried out with the signs typical of the coming of the Lord, as they were foretold by the prophets and realized in the New Testament with the coming of Christ" (John Paul II, Address, 8 November 1989). Therefore, too, in the tradition of

---

comedit locusta, bruchus / et gryllus et eruca, / exercitus meus magnus, / quem misi in vos. / ²⁶Et comedetis vescentes et saturabimini / et laudabitis nomen Domini Dei vestri, / qui mirabilia fecit vobiscum; / et non confundetur populus meus in sempiternum. / ²⁷Et scietis quia in medio Israel ego sum, / et ego Dominus Deus vester, / et non est amplius; / et non confundetur populus meus in aeternum». **[3]** ¹Et erit post haec: / effundam spiritum meum super omnem carnem, / et prophetabunt

**c.** Ch 3.1 in Heb

<sup>29</sup>Even upon the menservants and maidservants
in those days, I will pour out my spirit.
<sup>30</sup>"And I will give portents in the heavens and on the
earth, blood and fire and columns of smoke. <sup>31</sup>The sun shall
be turned to darkness, and the moon to blood, before the
great and terrible day of the LORD comes. <sup>32</sup>And it shall
come to pass that all who call upon the name of the LORD
shall be delivered; for in Mount Zion and in Jerusalem
there shall be those who escape, as the LORD has said, and
among the survivors shall be those whom the LORD calls.

Rev 8:7
Joel 2:11; Mt 24:29;
Mk 13:24; Rev 6:12; 9:2
Is 1:9; 10:21;
11:11,16; Jer 31:7
Mic 4:7; 5:0,7–8
Zech 8:6–12; Obad 17;
*Rom 10:13*; Rev 14:1

**The nations will be judged**

**3**<sup>d</sup> <sup>1</sup>"For behold, in those days and at that time,
when I restore the fortunes of Judah and Jerusalem,

Jer 30:3
Ezek 38:14

---

the Church, this descent of the Holy
Spirit is seen as an extension of his
descent on Jesus in the river Jordan:
"God promised through the mouths of
his prophets that in the last days he
would pour out his Spirit on all his servants, and that they too would prophesy.
Thus, the Spirit of God descended on
the Son of God, who had become the
Son of man, so that by remaining within
him, he would inhabit the heart of mankind and animate all the works carried
out by the hands of God, fulfilling the
will of the Father through all men and
making all men new—new creations in
Christ. Luke tells us that after the ascen-
sion of the Lord, the Spirit descended on
the apostles at Pentecost, to restore men
to new life and to bring the new covenant
to completion. Therefore, the disciples

praised God in all the tongues of men,
laying all peoples open to the action
of the Spirit and all nations open to
the power and authority of God" (St
Irenaeus, *Adversus haereses*, 3, 17, 1–2).

**3:1–8.** The restoration of the people of
God brings with it the judgment of the
nations who have been hostile to them.
The prophet singles out for special
mention Israel's neighbours on the
Mediterranean coast (v. 4), accusing
them of stealing Israel's land and
trafficking in its people.

The prophet sets the Judgment in the
valley of Jehoshapat (v. 2), a name that
means "The Lord judges" (v. 2). A little
further on (3:14), it will be called the
valley of Jarush, that is, of the decision,
or sentencing, of the nations. It is not

filii vestri et filiae vestrae, / senes vestri somnia somniabunt, / et iuvenes vestri visiones videbunt; / <sup>2</sup>sed
et super servos meos et ancillas / in diebus illis effundam spiritum meum. / <sup>3</sup>Et dabo prodigia in caelo
et in terra, / sanguinem et ignem et columnas fumi; / <sup>4</sup>sol convertetur in tenebras, / et luna in
sanguinem, / antequam veniat dies Domini / magnus et horribilis. / <sup>5</sup>Et erit: / omnis, qui invocaverit
nomen Domini, salvus erit, / quia in monte Sion et in Ierusalem / erit salvatio, sicut dixit Dominus, / et
in residuis, quos Dominus vocaverit. **[4]** <sup>1</sup>Quia ecce in diebus illis / et in tempore illo, / cum

**d.** Ch 4.1 in Heb

Is 66:16
Ezek 38:22
Zeph 3:8
Zech 14:2–4

Obad 11
Nahum 3:10

[2]I will gather all the nations and bring them down to the valley of Jehoshaphat, and I will enter into judgment with them there, on account of my people and my heritage Israel, because they have scattered them among the nations, and have divided up my land, [3]and have cast lots for my people, and have given a boy for a harlot, and have sold a girl for wine, and have drunk it.

[4]"What are you to me, O Tyre and Sidon, and all the regions of Philistia? Are you paying me back for something? If you are paying me back, I will requite your deed upon your own head swiftly and speedily. [5]For you have taken my silver and my gold, and have carried my rich treasures into your temples.[e] [6]You have sold the people of Judah and Jerusalem to the Greeks, removing them far from their own border. [7]But now I will stir them up from the place to which you have sold them, and I will requite your

Is 22:25
Obad 18

deed upon your own head. [8]I will sell your sons and your daughters into the hand of the sons of Judah, and they will sell them to the Sabeans, to a nation far off; for the LORD has spoken."

---

clear whether Joel is referring to a specific place or not. From the fourth century onwards a Jewish and Christian (and later Islamic) tradition identifies this place as being the part of the Kidron (or, Cedron) valley that separates the Mount of Olives from the temple of Jerusalem. In apocryphal writings, the Kidron became the valley of the Last Judgment. These eschatological connexions help to explain why so many tombs are to be found in this area. However, other authors think that there is no such valley. In any event, the passage has to do with divine judgment, and therefore is a call to repentance:

"My brothers, since we are offered the great opportunity to repent and be converted, while there is still time, let us turn to the Lord who calls to us and desires to gather us to himself. If we spurn earthly pleasures and strive to overcome our sinful desires, we will receive the mercy of Jesus. Remember always that the day of judgment is coming, as hot as a furnace, when the heavens will be dissolved and the earth will melt like lead in the fire, and all our deeds, even our most secret thoughts, will be laid bare" (Pseudo-Clement, *Epistula II ad Corinthios*, 15, 10–15).

convertero sortem / Iudae et Ierusalem, / [2]congregabo omnes gentes / et deducam eas in vallem Iosaphat / et disceptabo cum eis ibi / super populo meo et hereditate mea Israel, / quos disperserunt in nationibus, / et terram meam diviserunt. / [3]Et super populum meum miserunt sortem; / et dederunt puerum pro meretrice / et puellam vendiderunt pro vino, ut biberent. [4]Verum quid vobis et mihi, Tyrus et Sidon et omnes termini Philisthaeae? Numquid ultionem vos reddetis mihi? Et si ulciscimini vos contra me, cito velociter reddam ultionem vestram super caput vestrum. [5]Argentum enim meum et aurum tulistis et pretiosa bona mea intulistis in delubra vestra. [6]Et filios Iudae et filios Ierusalem vendidistis filiis Graecorum, ut longe faceretis eos de finibus suis. [7]Ecce ego suscitabo eos de loco, in quo vendidistis eos, et reddam ultionem vestram in caput vestrum. [8]Et vendam filios vestros et filias

**e.** Or *palaces*

## A call to battle

⁹Proclaim this among the nations:
  Prepare war,
    stir up the mighty men.
  Let all the men of war draw near,
    let them come up.
¹⁰Beat your ploughshares into swords,
  and your pruning hooks into spears;
  let the weak say, "I am a warrior."

Ezek 38:29
Zech 14:2

Is 2:4

¹¹Hasten and come,
  all you nations round about,
    gather yourselves there.
  Bring down thy warriors, O LORD.
¹²Let the nations bestir themselves,
  and come up to the valley of Jehoshaphat;
  for there I will sit to judge
    all the nations round about.

2 Chron 20:26–30
Ps 96:13
Is 2:4
Mic 4:3

¹³Put in the sickle,
  for the harvest is ripe.
  Go in, tread,
  for the wine press is full.
  The vats overflow,
  for their wickedness is great.

Is 17:5; 63:1–6
Mk 4:29
Rev 14:15,18–20

---

**3:9–13.** "Prepare war": literally, "sanctify war", that is, "declare holy war": war was regarded as a holy action, to be prefaced by ritual offerings (cf. 1 Sam 7:8–10); soldiers are even called "consecrated ones" (cf. Is 13:3). Verse 10 uses the same imagery as Isaiah 2:4 (swords–ploughshares, spears–pruning hooks) but the meaning is reversed; the people must arm for battle. The battlefield will again be the valley of Jehoshapat, where the Judgment will take place, and therefore victory will go to the Lord and his faithful.

---

vestras in manibus filiorum Iudae; et venumdabunt eos Sabaeis, genti longinquae, quia Dominus locutus est. ⁹Clamate hoc in gentibus, / sanctificate bellum, / suscitate robustos; / accedant, ascendant / omnes viri bellatores. / ¹⁰Concidite vomeres vestros in gladios / et falces vestras in lanceas; / infirmus dicat: / «Fortis ego sum». / ¹¹Erumpite et venite, / omnes gentes de circuitu, / et congregamini ibi! / Deduc, Domine, robustos tuos! / ¹²Consurgant et ascendant gentes / in vallem Iosaphat, / quia ibi sedebo, ut iudicem / omnes gentes in circuitu. / ¹³Mittite falces, / quoniam maturavit messis; / venite et premite, / quia plenum est torcular: / exuberant torcularia, / quia magna est malitia eorum. /

**The day of the Lord**

Is 17:12
Joel 4:2

<sup>14</sup>Multitudes, multitudes,
in the valley of decision!
For the day of the LORD is near
in the valley of decision.

Joel 2:10; Mt 24:29
Mk 13:24; Rev 6:12f

<sup>15</sup>The sun and the moon are darkened,
and the stars withdraw their shining.

Ps 46:2; Jer 25:30
Amos 1:2

<sup>16</sup>And the LORD roars from Zion,
and utters his voice from Jerusalem,
and the heavens and the earth shake.
But the LORD is a refuge to his people,
a stronghold to the people of Israel.

Is 2:4; Ezek 38:23
Joel 2:27; Zech 14:21
Rev 21:27; 22:15

<sup>17</sup>"So you shall know that I am the LORD your God,
who dwell in Zion, my holy mountain.
And Jerusalem shall be holy
and strangers shall never again pass through it.

---

**3:14–17.** The preceding verses were really a preparation for this final oracle which describes the Judgment and the victory of the Lord. "The valley of decision" (v. 14) is the same valley as that of Jehoshapat. The judgment that takes place on the day of the Lord is compared to a harvesting; the Lord will save his faithful, and destroy his enemies. The *Catechism of the Catholic Church*, 1040 uses this passage, along with Daniel 7:10 and Malachi 3:19, in its teaching about the Last Judgment (cf. the note on Jer 51:56) in which God the Father "through his Son Jesus Christ [...] will pronounce the final word on all history. We shall know the ultimate meaning of the whole work of creation and of the entire economy of salvation, and understand the marvellous ways by which his Providence led everything towards its final end".

The core of the oracle is vv. 16–17, when Joel sees the Lord presiding over Jerusalem and protecting his people, whose refuge and strength he is (cf. Ps 46). This picture of the Lord dwelling in his temple in Jerusalem recurs throughout biblical tradition and is probably in the background of what the fourth Gospel says about the Word, who was God and "dwelt among us" (Jn 1:14). Similarly, the reference in v. 17 which makes Jerusalem a holy place through which strangers must not pass (cf. also Is 52:1; Jer 31:40; Zech 9:8) later gave rise to there being a "dividing wall" (cf. Eph 2:14) that prevented

---

<sup>14</sup>Populi, populi / in valle Decisionis, / quia iuxta est dies Domini / in valle Decisionis. / <sup>15</sup>Sol et luna obtenebrati sunt, / et stellae retraxerunt splendorem suum. / <sup>16</sup>Et Dominus de Sion rugiet / et de Ierusalem dabit vocem suam; / et movebuntur caeli et terra, / et Dominus refugium populo suo / et fortitudo filiis Israel. / <sup>17</sup>Et scietis quia ego Dominus Deus vester / habitans in Sion monte sancto meo;

## The future glory of Israel

[18]"And in that day
   the mountains shall drip sweet wine,
      and the hills shall flow with milk,
   and all the stream beds of Judah
      shall flow with water;
   and a fountain shall come forth from the house of the LORD
      and water the valley of Shittim.

Num 25:1; Is 30:25
Ezek 47:1–12
Zech 14:8; Jn 7:38

---

outsiders from entering the temple proper, under pain of death. This is the wall that St Paul sees as being symbolically broken down by Christ's sacrifice, which removed any distinction between Jew and Gentile "that he might create in himself one new man in place of the two, so making peace, and might reconcile both to God in one body through the cross, thereby bringing the hostility to an end" (Eph 2:16). "The passion of the Saviour made peace between the circumcised and the uncircumcised. The Saviour undid the enmity that ran like a dividing wall between the circumcised and the uncircumcised, so that the Jew could no longer condemn the Gentile, basing his righteousness on the power of circumcision, nor could the Gentile denounce the Jew, asserting his superiority by the fact that he is uncircumcised, that is, a pagan. Both are re-made, and live out the faith of the one true God in Christ" (Ambrosiaster, *Ad Ephesios,* 2, 14).

**3:18–21.** The book ends with a vision of the eschatological Jerusalem in the new golden age. Three themes typical of Joel are raised in these verses.

Judah's afflictions (the locust plague, and the hunger and devastation that it brought) are here offset by an idyllic, Eden-like picture where Judah is a garden full of good things, of sweet wine and milk (v. 18). The same imagery and themes are to be found in Isaiah 30:25; Ezekiel 47:1–12; and Zechariah 14:8; the theme of living water will be taken up later by St John (cf. Jn 4:10–15; Rev 22:1). Judah will be most fertile, but God's vengeance will be wreaked on Egypt and Edom (symbolizing Israel's enemies); they will now be the ones to suffer devastation.

Finally (vv. 20–21) comes the promise that never again will there be exile (Judah and Jerusalem will always be inhabited), and "the Lord will dwell in Zion" (cf. v. 21)—which is their dearest wish. The entire book of Joel has been working up to this outcome. This passage is used most notably by St John in his vision of the messianic Jerusalem coming down from heaven ("He carried me away to a great, high mountain and showed me the holy city, Jerusalem coming down out of heaven, having the glory of God": Rev 21:10–11); and it is an image of the heartfelt hope of all mankind.

---

/ et erit Ierusalem locus sanctus, / et alieni non transibunt per eam amplius. / [18]Et erit in die illa: / stillabunt montes mustum, / et colles fluent lacte; / et per omnes rivos Iudae ibunt aquae, / et fons de

Ex 25:12
Rev 11:8

19"Egypt shall become a desolation
    and Edom a desolate wilderness,
for the violence done to the people of Judah,
    because they have shed innocent blood in their land.
20But Judah shall be inhabited for ever,
    and Jerusalem to all generations.

Jer 17:25
Ezek 27:25

21I will avenge their blood, and I will not clear the guilty,[g]
    for the LORD dwells in Zion."

---

domo Domini egredietur. / et irrigabit torrentem Settim. / 19Aegyptus in desolationem erit, / et Idumaea in desertum desolationis, / pro eo quod inique egerint in filios Iudae / et effuderint sanguinem innocentem in terra eorum. / 20Et Iuda in aeternum habitabitur, / et Ierusalem in generationem et generationem; / 21et vindicabo sanguinem eorum, quem non relinquam impunitum; / et Dominus commoratur in Sion.

**g.** Gk Syr: Heb *I will hold innocent their blood which I have not held innocent*

# AMOS

# Introduction

The book of Amos comes third in the Hebrew collection of minor prophets—which is also its place in the Christian canon; but the Septuagint puts it second, after Hosea. However, chronologically, Amos is the first of the "writer" prophets, followed (a few years later) by Hosea and then by such outstanding prophets as Isaiah and Jeremiah. Still, there are reasons for placing the book of Amos after Joel: it begins with oracles against the nations around Israel which also appear in Joel and, more specifically, with the words, "The Lord roars from Zion …"; and its message has to do with conversion, a theme much to the fore in Joel also.

Amos is of special interest on account of two closely connected things—his calling and his preaching. Amos did not come from a family with a prophetical tradition (cf. the note on 7:14); the Lord suddenly intervened in his life by sending him out to preach; and he was a native of Tekoa, which was in the Southern kingdom, and yet his mission was to the Northern kingdom. The Lord chose to make him his spokesman, to stir up people's consciences. His preaching has to do mainly with two subjects—the defence of the poor and needy against exploitation by the rich and powerful; and the need for external rites and worship to move people's hearts and encourage them to mend their ways: liturgical ceremony must not be used as a fig-leaf to cover exploitation.

It is evident from the book that although Amos came from a rural background, he was a man of some culture. He is well able to express himself, and does not mince his words.

## 1. STRUCTURE AND CONTENT

The book divides naturally into three parts, with an introduction and a conclusion:

INTRODUCTION (1:1–2). This consists of a title and an oracle that is a kind of summary of the book.

1. JUDGMENT OF THE NEIGHBOURING COUNTRIES, AND OF JUDAH AND ISRAEL (1:3–2:16). This is a collection of oracles against a series of nations, taking them to task for their sins; it culminates with an oracle against Israel (2:6–16), the longest of them all.

109

2. ISRAEL WARNED AND THREATENED (3:1–6:14). This consists of six oracles against Israel, condemning social injustice and aberrations in the practice of worship; their religious service is pretentious and superficial.

3. SERIES OF PROPHETICAL VISIONS (7:1–9:10). Using a series of metaphors (locusts, fire, a plumb line, fruit, the fall of the sanctuary), in five visions the prophet tells what the future holds for Israel if it does not abandon its empty way of life and show God due respect.

CONCLUSION. MESSIANIC REPARATION (9:11–15). The book ends with words of encouragement. Exile does await Israel—but so does restoration, for the Lord will repair the "fallen booth" of David (cf. 9:11).

Each part of the book is made up of a number of separate pieces, sometimes in different styles or from different genres—oracles, threats, allegories, visions, doxologies, "day of the Lord", promises of restoration, etc. A feature of the first part is the use of the wording, "For three transgressions ... and for four I will not revoke the punishment" (this occurs systematically in 1:3, 6, 9, 11, 13; 2:1, 4, 6). The three-plus-four formula crops up in other biblical books, but in the wisdom writings, not in the prophets—Proverbs 30:15, 18, 21, 29 and Sirach 26:5; in Sirach 26:28 the formula changes to two-plus-three; there are a few other instances where the numbers differ but in all cases the second number is greater than the first: it is a device designed to help memorization.

## 2. COMPOSITION AND HISTORICAL BACKGROUND

Amos must have been born around the start of the reigns of Uzziah in Judah (785–733 BC) and Jeroboam II in Israel (788–747). It was a period when both kingdoms enjoyed unparalleled peace and prosperity (the North-South division had occurred in 931, Israel was to collapse in 721 and Judah in 587). This material prosperity occurred at a time when the two main empires (Assyria and Egypt) were in decline, as was Syria—which meant that the small countries along the east coast of the Mediterranean were not under pressure. Israel, in fact, managed to extend its borders to south and east, at the expense of nations bordering on the Arabian desert.

But, in the Northern kingdom, particularly, this new-found prosperity was enjoyed by the upper classes only: rulers, landlords and the merchant class increasingly exploited the poor and defenceless. The upper classes of Israel attributed their peace and prosperity to their own resourcefulness and to the splendour of the liturgy at the main sanctuaries in the kingdom—Bethel and Gilgal. God, they thought, must be pleased with them, for things were going well, at least for the powerful in society. Religious practice had become a matter of ostentatious liturgies and elaborate festivals; but these were empty things; they did not impinge on people's consciences; religion had no influence on morality: for many of the rich and powerful it became a sort of camouflage that allowed them to do whatever they chose. The net result of this was great social injustice—not in any sense the way things should be among the people of God, who were supposed to be ruled by the ethical principles and the commandments spelt out in the Law.

This was the situation in which Amos received his call and was sent to preach in the Northern kingdom. It was inevitable that he should inveigh against the injustice practised by corrupt rulers, judges, business people (5:7, 10–12; 6:1–14) and, it seems, even well-to-do women (4:1–3)—and should do so very forthrightly, without being cowed by the prospect of opposition or trying to curry favour. It was not long before the guilty parties reacted.

The situation is encapsulated in the altercation between Amos and Amaziah, the priest of Bethel. Amaziah sent a message to the king telling him that Amos was conspiring against him (the king) by denouncing injustice and threatening divine punishment (7:10–17); he tells "the prophet" to go back home, to Judah, and leave them in peace. This tension between Amos' preaching and Amaziah's rejection of it anticipates (by eight hundred years) the opposition shown by the chief priests to Jesus' ministry: in Jesus' case, too, the clergy resorted to the civil authorities to do away with the "revolutionary" who criticized the status quo.

In order of time, Amos was the first of the "writer prophets". Some scholars wonder whether he did not set certain literary and thematic parameters for the prophets who came after him, such as Hosea, Isaiah etc. The most prominent features of his style are the oracles against the nations and against the chosen people itself (in the case of Amos, against the kingdom of Israel); the inclusion of pieces of wisdom writing (3:3–6); the use of contrasts and opposites (cf. e.g. 5:11–24); analogies taken from ordinary life (in Amos' case, from rural life, particularly: cf. e.g. 2:13; 4:7–9; 7:1; 8:1–2; 9:9); the attribution of human feelings to God, as when God "hates" and "despises" (cf. 5:21); etc. Literary devices favoured by Amos include: capturing the listener's attention by asking questions (cf. 2:11; 3:3–6; 5:18b, 20, etc.); plays on words or vowels within words (5:5); irony (4:4–5); etc.

Amos' language is direct; it has spark and vigour, and is expressed logically; he has a good command of language, though he does not compare with Isaiah. Modern scholarship, for the most part, agrees that the greater part of the book records the words of the prophet, spoken around the middle of the eighth century BC. Doubts have been raised about some passages—the oracles against Tyre (1:9–10), Edom (1:11–12) and Judah (2:4–5); the three doxologies (4:13; 5:8–9; 9:5–6); and some short pieces which could have been written up later by disciples of Amos when the book as such was being assembled—for example, the heading (1:1), the introduction (1:2) and the conclusion (9:11–15). But the texts of the book that have come down to us (the Hebrew and the early translations) are all consistent with its having only one author.

There is less agreement among scholars as to when exactly the final redaction of the text (as we have it today) took place. The theories put forward suggest around the end of the sixth century BC, on the basis of the sort of historical circumstances in which one would expect it to have been written— that is, about two centuries after the time when Amos preached, even though, as has been said, the bulk of the material, oral or written, comes from the prophet himself.

The original Hebrew text of the book is in good condition and easy to read; a few passages present some difficulty, but they are not important—2:7; 3:12; 5:6, 26; 7:2; 8:1. The early translations are very close to the Hebrew text; they manage to keep its tone, and introduce no variants of any significance.

## 3. MESSAGE

The teaching contained in the book goes beyond the context in which Amos worked: it is part of the ever-valid Revelation of the Old and New Testament. The One God, whose preferred title is *Yhwh Sebaoth*, the Lord of hosts, of armies, or of the heavens, is the only Lord and Governor. There is no limit to his power; he rules the forces of nature and the destinies of peoples (5:8–9; 6:1–2, 14; 9:7–8; etc.); he is just in his judgments over individuals and nations (1:3–2:6); he chose Israel for his very own (3:2), but all other nations belong to him too (9:7). The people of Israel should not pride themselves on the fact that they are the object of God's special choice: their election is, rather, a responsibility: they have to give an account of themselves; if they rebel and sin, they will be punished as they deserve (9:9–10).

Many of Amos' contemporaries had a very shallow understanding of spiritual and social life (a common human failing even nowadays): they thought that God could be placated if they went through the motions of religious observance—as if the Lord were a Baal, just another Canaanite god. In his preaching, Amos taught that true religion must involve being just and fair towards one's fellow men; religion without morality is not possible. Amos was very outspoken in his criticism of the well-to-do for the way they treated the poor and defenceless. The Israelites thought that God's election of them, and the Covenant, meant that God was duty-bound to look after them; Amos turns their thinking on its head: the main obligation lies with the people. He stresses that worship of God and justice towards others must go hand-in-hand—and that justice must be weighted in favour of the poor, the humble and the weak.

Amos' mission was that of a prophet, not just that of a wise man. Thus, we find that his utterances include grave warnings: if Israel fails to practise justice, if abuses against the underprivileged are not corrected, then God will judge the guilty severely, and there will be no going back on that judgment. Divine judgment is described as "the day of the Lord" (2:16; 3:14; 4:2; 5:18–20; 8:9–13; 9:11–13). People think that the day of the Lord will be the day when they receive their reward (5:18a); Amos tells them that there is another side to it; it will be a day for sentencing, a day of darkness and gloom. Still, the day of punishment will not be wholly dark: God in his compassion will bring salvation (5:15; 9:11–15). The theme of the day of the Lord will soon become a constant and essential theme in prophetical preaching.[1]

Echoes of Amos' message (and even his turns of phrase) can be found in other prophetical texts. His influence on Hosea, Joel, Jeremiah and Zephaniah is clear to see. For example, mention of false balances (8:5) occurs also in Hosea 12:8; the pride of Jacob (6:8) has its parallel in the pride of Israel in Hosea 5:5; both Amos (5:5) and Hosea (4:15) call Bethel "Beth-aven", "house of nothing". Amos 1:2 depicts the Lord as roaring from Zion, as Joel does in 3:16. Many other examples could be cited.

## 4. THE BOOK OF AMOS IN THE LIGHT OF THE NEW TESTAMENT

The words of Amos are echoed in a number of places in the New Testament. For example, the parables of the rich fool (Lk 12:16–21), who promises himself a life of ease, and that of Lazarus and the rich man (Lk 16:19–31), who does nothing for the poor, remind us of Amos 3:15 and 6:1. Acts 15:16–17 quotes Amos 9:11–12, following the Septuagint text rather than the Hebrew. Acts 7:42b–43 is a quotation from Amos 5:25–27, which also follows the Septuagint. The Letter of St James (Jas 5:1–5) contains warnings to the rich that are reminiscent of Amos' criticism of the rich and powerful (2:6–8; 4:1; etc.).

The two most prominent early Christian commentaries on Amos are those of St Cyril of Alexandra and St Jerome. But pastors and writers of all periods have availed themselves of the book of Amos as an inspired source for their defence of the poor and helpless. In recent decades, more recourse has been made to Amos, borrowing what he has to say about social justice and applying it to the circumstances of underdeveloped nations, particularly in Latin America and Africa.

---

1. Cf. e.g. Is 2:11; 11:11; 30:26; Jer 30:7–17; Joel 1:15; 3:4; 4:1; Zeph 1:14–18; Mal 3:19–23.

### Title and introduction

2 Sam 14:2
2 Kings 15:1;
14:23; Amos 8:8;
9:5; Zech 14:4–5
Is 33:9; Jer 25:30
Joel 4:16
Nahum 1:4
Rev 10:3

1 <sup>1</sup>The words of Amos, who was among the shepherds of Tekoa, which he saw concerning Israel in the days of Uzziah king of Judah and in the days of Jeroboam the son of Joash, king of Israel, two years<sup>a</sup> before the earthquake. <sup>2</sup>And he said:
"The LORD roars from Zion,
   and utters his voice from Jerusalem;
the pastures of the shepherds mourn,
   and the top of Carmel withers."

## 1. JUDGMENT OF THE NEIGHBOURING COUNTRIES, AND OF JUDAH AND ISRAEL*

### Against Damascus

2 Kings 10:33
Is 17:1–3
Jer 49:23–27
Amos 1:6,9,11;
2:1,4

<sup>3</sup>Thus says the LORD:
"For three transgressions of Damascus,
   and for four, I will not revoke the punishment;<sup>b</sup>
because they have threshed Gilead
   with threshing sledges of iron.

---

**1:1–2.** "Uzziah", also known as Azariah, was king of Judah from 785 to 733 BC (cf. 2 Kings 15:1–7). "Jeroboam II" reigned in Israel from 788 to 747 (2 Kings 14:23–29). The "earthquake" mentioned here (v. 1) must have been very severe: it was mentioned, years later, in Zechariah 14:4–5; from excavations in upper Galilee, archaeologists can confidently date it to around the year 760.

The passage clearly distinguishes the existence of two kingdoms—Israel (in the north) and Judah (in the south). The name Israel is used 23 times in Amos to designate the Northern king-dom; on one occasion (9:14) it is used to indicate the chosen people as a whole. Verse 2 shows that the Lord is present in a special way in Zion (that is, Jerusalem), and from there rules over the entire people—from Judah to "Carmel", that is, he rules over Israel, too.

**\*1:3–2:16.** This first part of the book is made up of eight oracles—six against the neighbouring countries, one against Judah, and another, longer, one against Israel. Each oracle begins with "Thus says the Lord," which is followed by another unvaried formula: "For three

---

[1] <sup>1</sup>Verba Amos, qui fuit in pastoribus de Thecua; quae vidit super Israel in diebus Oziae regis Iudae et in diebus Ieroboam filii Ioas regis Israel, duobus annis ante terraemotum. <sup>2</sup>Et dixit: / «Dominus de Sion rugit / et de Ierusalem dat vocem suam; / et lugent pascua pastorum, / et exsiccatur vertex

**a.** Or *during two years*  **b.** Heb *cause it to return*

⁴So I will send a fire upon the house of Hazael,
and it shall devour the strongholds of Ben-hadad.

⁵I will break the bar of Damascus,
and cut off the inhabitants from the Valley of Aven,ᶜ
and him that holds the sceptre from Beth-eden;
and the people of Syria shall go into exile to Kir," says the LORD.

2 Kings 8:12;
10:32–33; 13:3,7

2 Kings 16:9

### Against the Philistines

⁶Thus says the LORD:

Josh 13:2
2 Chron
21:16–17; 28:18

---

transgressions of ... and for four, I will not revoke the punishment."

There is no mention in these oracles of Assyria or Egypt. If, as archaeology seems to show, the earthquake (v. 1) happened around 760, and the prophet began his preaching about two years before then, it makes sense for the oracle not to mention those two great empires, for (though they would soon recover) they were in decline at this particular time and their influence was not being felt in Israel or the lands around it.

**1:3–2:3.** These six oracles are directed against the countries neighbouring on Israel and Judah. They are condemned for such crimes as cruelty in conquest (1:3), reducing whole peoples to slavery or deporting them (1:6, 9), breaking pacts (1:9), ruthlessness towards another nation (1:11), violence against women (1:13), etc. The Lord will punish these nations for their wickedness, for he is the one who judges and rules over not only the chosen people but all nations; he is the Lord of the heavens and the

earth and of all mankind, as will be spelt out later in 9:5–10. The Hebrew word translated as "transgressions" (*pesha'îm*) implies the idea of rebellion: by committing these crimes, the nations are rebelling against the Lord.

In the first two oracles, the sentence is handed down against the rulers. Thus, 1:5 and 1:8 specifically mention "him that holds the sceptre" or words to that effect. Amos' attitude seems to be that injustices should be laid at the door of those in authority. Those who hold public office must attend in the first instance to the administration of justice: "Those who are suited or can become suited should prepare themselves for the difficult, but at the same time, the very noble art of politics, and should seek to practise this art without regard for their own interests or for material advantages. With integrity and wisdom, they must take action against any form of injustice and tyranny, against arbitrary domination by an individual or a political party and any intolerance" (Vatican II, *Gaudium et spes*, 75).

---

Carmeli». / ³Haec dicit Dominus: / «Super tribus sceleribus Damasci / et super quattuor verbum non revocabo: / eo quod trituraverint in plaustris ferreis Galaad, / ⁴mittam ignem in domum Hazael, / et devorabit aedes Benadad; / ⁵conteram vectem Damasci / et disperdam habitatorem de Biceataven / et tenentem sceptrum de Betheden; / et transferetur populus Syriae Cir», / dicit Dominus. / ⁶Haec dicit

**c.** Or *On*

Jer 47:1,5
Zeph 2:4–7
Zech 9:5
Rev 2:1

"For three transgressions of Gaza,
    and for four, I will not revoke the punishment;[b]
because they carried into exile a whole people
    to deliver them up to Edom.
[7]So I will send a fire upon the wall of Gaza,
    and it shall devour her strongholds.

2 Chron 26:6

[8]I will cut off the inhabitants from Ashdod,
    and him that holds the sceptre from Ashkelon;
I will turn my hand against Ekron;
    and the remnant of the Philistines shall perish," says the
    Lord GOD.

## Against Phoenicia

2 Sam 5:11
Is 23
Ezek 26–28

[9]Thus says the LORD:
"For three transgressions of Tyre,
    and for four, I will not revoke the punishment;
because they delivered up a whole people to Edom,
    and did not remember the covenant of brotherhood.

1 Kings 5:26;
9:11–14

[10]So I will send a fire upon the wall of Tyre,
    and it shall devour her strongholds."

## Against Edom

Gen 27:41
Num 20:14–21,23
Ps 137:7; Is 34
Jer 27:3; 49:7–22
Ezek 25:12–14; 35

[11]Thus says the LORD:
"For three transgressions of Edom,
    and for four, I will not revoke the punishment;[b]
because he pursued his brother with the sword,
    and cast off all pity,
and his anger tore perpetually,
    and he kept his wrath[d] for ever.
[12]So I will send a fire upon Teman,
    and it shall devour the strongholds of Bozrah."

---

Dominus: / «Super tribus sceleribus Gazae / et super quattuor verbum non revocabo: / eo quod transtulerint captivitatem perfectam, / ut traderent eam in Edom, / [7]mittam ignem in murum Gazae, / et devorabit aedes eius; / [8]disperdam habitatorem de Azoto / et tenentem sceptrum de Ascalone; / convertam manum meam super Accaron, / et peribunt reliqui Philisthinorum», / dicit Dominus Deus. / [9]Haec dicit Dominus: / «Super tribus sceleribus Tyri / et super quattuor verbum non revocabo: / eo quod tradiderint captivitatem perfectam in Edom / et non sint recordati foederis fratrum, / [10]mittam ignem in murum Tyri, / et devorabit aedes eius». / [11]Haec dicit Dominus: / «Super tribus sceleribus Edom / et super quattuor verbum non revocabo: / eo quod persecutus sit in gladio fratrem suum / et violaverit misericordiam eius / et tenuerit ultra furorem suum / et indignationem suam servaverit usque in finem, / [12]mittam ignem in Theman, / et devorabit aedes Bosrae». / [13]Haec dicit Dominus: / «Super tribus sceleribus filiorum Ammon / et super quattuor verbum non revocabo: / eo quod dissecuerint

---

**b.** Heb *cause it to return*   **d.** Gk Syr Vg: Heb *his wrath kept*

## Against Ammon

<sup>13</sup>Thus says the LORD:

"For three transgressions of the Ammonites,
and for four, I will not revoke the punishment;<sup>b</sup>
because they have ripped up women with child in Gilead,
that they might enlarge their border.
<sup>14</sup>So I will kindle a fire in the wall of Rabbah,
and it shall devour her strongholds,
with shouting in the day of battle,
with a tempest in the day of the whirlwind;
<sup>15</sup>and their king shall go into exile,
he and his princes together," says the LORD.

## Against Moab

**2** <sup>1</sup>Thus says the LORD:
"For three transgressions of Moab,
and for four, I will not revoke the punishment;<sup>b</sup>
because he burned to lime
the bones of the king of Edom.
<sup>2</sup>So I will send a fire upon Moab,
and it shall devour the strongholds of Kerioth,
and Moab shall die amid uproar,
amid shouting and the sound of the trumpet;
<sup>3</sup>I will cut off the ruler from its midst,
and will slay all its princes with him," says the LORD.

## Against Judah

<sup>4</sup>Thus says the LORD:

*Marginal references:*
Deut 2:19
2 Kings 8:12;
15:16; Jer 49:1–6
Ezek 25:1–7
Zeph 2:8–11
Hos 14:1

Is 28:2

Num 20:36
2 Kings 3:27
Is 15–16; Jer 48
Ezek 25:8–11
Zeph 2:8–11

---

**2:4–16.** This passage contains a brief oracle on Judah (vv. 4–5) and another on Israel (vv. 6–16). The oracle against Judah is less severe than the previous ones and the one in vv. 6–16, which are more generic in tone; for this reason, some authors think that it must be a later addition. It reproaches Judah for breaking the commandments of the Law and for being unfaithful to God.

The oracle against Israel, on the other hand, is much longer and more

praegnantes Galaad / ad dilatandum terminum suum, / <sup>14</sup>succendam ignem in muro Rabba, / et devorabit aedes eius in ululatu in die belli / et in turbine in die procellae; / <sup>15</sup>et ibit rex eorum in captivitatem, / ipse et principes eius simul», / dicit Dominus. [2] <sup>1</sup>Haec dicit Dominus: / «Super tribus sceleribus Moab / et super quattuor verbum non revocabo: / eo quod incenderit ossa regis Edom / usque ad cinerem, / <sup>2</sup>mittam ignem in Moab, / et devorabit aedes Carioth, / et morietur in tumultu Moab, / in clamore et voce tubae; / <sup>3</sup>disperdam iudicem de medio eius / et omnes principes eius interficiam cum eo», / dicit Dominus. / <sup>4</sup>Haec dicit Dominus: / «Super tribus sceleribus Iudae / et super quattuor verbum

**b.** Heb *cause it to return*

Lev 26:14–15<br>Is 5:24; Jer 7:28<br>Ezek 20:18,30

"For three transgressions of Judah,
> and for four, I will not revoke the punishment;[e]
because they have rejected the law of the LORD,
> and have not kept his statutes,
but their lies have led them astray,
> after which their fathers walked.

Hos 8:14

[5]So I will send a fire upon Judah,
> and it shall devour the strongholds of Jerusalem."

## Against Israel

Lev 25:39–42<br>Amos 8:6

[6]Thus says the LORD:
"For three transgressions of Israel,

---

explicit. It mentions Israel's transgressions (and then punishment) and also the benefits that the people have received from God. These transgressions will be referred to throughout the book (cf. 3:1–9:10). They were largely to do with injustice towards the poor (synonymous with the righteous: cf. v. 6) and the needy (vv. 6–7); incest or idolatry (v. 7) and aberrant forms of worship (v. 8). They commit these crimes, forgetting how good God has been to them— setting them free from bondage in Egypt (v. 10), giving them the promised land (v. 10), and providing them with prophets and Nazirites to be their guides (v. 11). But Israel is proud and ungrateful, and will be punished. This punishment will be so all-embracing and so sudden that none will be able to escape or resist it (vv. 14–16).

St Jerome, commenting on v. 14, considers the example of Israel's pride for the benefit of his readers. Those will feel devoid of strength who "trust in their own strength and do not rely on the mercy of God, as Scripture tells us: 'I will destroy the wisdom of the wise, and the cleverness of the clever I will thwart' (1 Cor 1:19; cf. Is 29:14). Authentic wisdom cannot be destroyed nor knowledge of the truth undone, but the wisdom of those who believe themselves to be wise and who trust only in their own understanding will perish. The mighty man who shall not save his life (cf. Amos 2:14) dies because he is not dressed in the armour of an apostle. He bears a shield, but it is not the shield of faith; he has girded his loins, but not with the truth; he wears a suit of armour, but it is not the armour of righteousness; he carries a sword, but it is not the sword of salvation. This mighty warrior cannot be made holy by his battles nor wage the war of the Lord" (St Jerome, *Commentarii in Amos*, 2, 13–16).

---

non revocabo: / eo quod abiecerint legem Domini / et mandata eius non custodierint / —deceperunt enim eos idola sua, / post quae abierant patres eorum— / [5]mittam ignem in Iudam, / et devorabit aedes Ierusalem». / [6]Haec dicit Dominus: / «Super tribus sceleribus Israel / et super quattuor verbum non

**e.** Heb *cause it to return*

and for four, I will not revoke the punishment;<sup>e</sup>
because they sell the righteous for silver,
and the needy for a pair of shoes—
<sup>7</sup>they that trample the head of the poor into the dust of the earth,
and turn aside the way of the afflicted;
a man and his father go in to the same maiden,
so that my holy name is profaned;
<sup>8</sup>they lay themselves down beside every altar
upon garments taken in pledge;
and in the house of their God they drink
the wine of those who have been fined.

<sup>9</sup>"Yet I destroyed the Amorite before them,
whose height was like the height of the cedars,
and who was as strong as the oaks;
I destroyed his fruit above,
and his roots beneath.
<sup>10</sup>Also I brought you up out of the land of Egypt,
and led you forty years in the wilderness,
to possess the land of the Amorite.
<sup>11</sup>And I raised up some of your sons for prophets,
and some of your young men for Nazirites.
Is it not indeed so, O people of Israel?" says the LORD.

<sup>12</sup>"But you made the Nazirites drink wine,
and commanded the prophets,
saying, 'You shall not prophesy.'
<sup>13</sup>"Behold, I will press you down in your place,
as a cart full of sheaves presses down.
<sup>14</sup>Flight shall perish from the swift,
and the strong shall not retain his strength,
nor shall the mighty save his life;
<sup>15</sup>he who handles the bow shall not stand,

Deut 23:19;
27:20; Is 3:15

Ex 22:26
Deut 24:12–13

Num 21:21–25
Deut 7:1; 9:1–2
Josh 24:8
Job 18:16
Hos 9:16

Deut 2:7

Num 6:1–2
Deut 18:18

1 Kings 22:8,27
Is 30:10
Jer 11:21
Amos 1:3;
7:12–13

Amos 9:1

Amos 5:18

---

revocabo: / eo quod vendiderint pro argento iustum / et pauperem pro calceamentis; / <sup>7</sup>qui contriverint super pulverem terrae capita pauperum / et viam humilium declinaverint, / et filius ac pater eius iverint ad puellam, / ut violarent nomen sanctum meum; / <sup>8</sup>et super vestimentis pignoratis accubuerint / iuxta omne altare / et vinum damnatorum biberint / in domo Dei sui. / <sup>9</sup>Ego autem exterminaveram / Amorraeum a facie eorum, / cuius altitudo sicut altitudo cedrorum, / et fortitudo quasi quercuum; / exterminaveram fructum eius desuper / et radices eius subter. / <sup>10</sup>Ego ascendere vos feci / de terra Aegypti / et duxi vos in deserto / quadraginta annis, / ut possideretis terram Amorraei; / <sup>11</sup>et suscitavi de filiis vestris prophetas et de iuvenibus vestris nazaraeos. / Numquid non ita est, filii Israel?, / dicit Dominus. / <sup>12</sup>Et propinastis nazaraeis vinum / et prophetis mandastis dicentes: / "Ne prophetetis". / <sup>13</sup>Ecce ego comprimam vos ad solum, / sicut comprimit plaustrum / onustum feno; / <sup>14</sup>deerit fuga a veloce, / et fortis non firmabit virtutem suam, / et robustus non salvabit animam suam; / <sup>15</sup>tenens arcum

and he who is swift of foot shall not save himself,
nor shall he who rides the horse save his life;

Mk 14:52 ¹⁶and he who is stout of heart among the mighty
shall flee away naked in that day," says the LORD.

## 2. ISRAEL WARNED AND THREATENED*

**Election and punishment of Israel**

3 ¹Hear this word that the LORD has spoken against you, O people of Israel, against the whole family which I brought up out of the land of Egypt:

Deut 7:6      ²"You only have I known
Ezek 9:4–6          of all the families of the earth;
Dan 9:2
Mt 10:15;      therefore I will punish you
11:20–24          for all your iniquities.

---

*3:1–6:14. The second (and longest) part of the book contains denunciations of Israel and predictions about how her sins will be punished. It consists of three oracles, each beginning with "Hear this word ..." (3:1; 4:1; 5:1), and three others containing the words "O you ..." or "Woe to you" (5:7, 18; 6:1). In terms of content, all these oracles are a development of the oracle against Israel that closed the previous section (2:6–16).

This part begins with a new interpretation of the meaning of God's choice of Israel. The oracles are about that election. The Israelites think that their pilgrimages to the popular shrines of Bethel and Gilgal (where they make voluntary offerings and give tithes, 4:4–5, and assemble for festivals, 5:21–25) mean that they have fulfilled their religious duties and are in a good standing before God. They are living in prosperous times: what better proof that God is pleased with them. Material prosperity was more marked in Israel than in Judah, but, still, life was reasonably good under Uzziah. However, this material well-being went hand in hand with social injustice—oppression of the poor and needy, and a contradiction between formal religious acts and personal morality.

This is the context in which Amos preaches and utters his prophetic denouncements: quite a lot of people are getting richer, but the ranks of the poor are being swelled all the time; the rich and powerful are exploiting the poor, and are refusing them justice; attendance at religious ceremonies in Bethel and Gilgal (schismatic sanctuaries, for the

non stabit, / et velox pedibus suis non salvabitur; / ascensor equi non salvabit animam suam, / ¹⁶et fortissimus corde inter robustos / nudus fugiet in illa die», / dicit Dominus.    [3] ¹Audite verbum hoc, quod locutus est Dominus super vos, filii Israel, super omnem cognationem, quam eduxi de terra Aegypti, dicens: ²«Tantummodo vos cognovi / ex omnibus cognationibus terrae; / idcirco visitabo super

### The prophet, a messenger of the Lord

<sup>3</sup>"Do two walk together,
unless they have made an appointment?
<sup>4</sup>Does a lion roar in the forest,
when he has no prey?
Does a young lion cry out from his den,
if he has taken nothing?

---

temple of Jerusalem was the only proper place of worship) did not affect people's hearts; it did not provoke them to resolve to amend their lives; they were deceiving themselves, trusting in God without having grounds for doing so, and believed (wrongly) that they were absolved from their sins.

**3:1–8.** God's choice of Israel is very vividly described here. Amos does not use the term "covenant" or "steadfast love" to describe God's attitude towards Israel (those are terms often found in other prophetical texts); but he does make it clear that the Lord's commitment to his people is a single-minded one: "You only have I known of all the families of the earth" (v. 2). This election means that Israel has special duties towards God—and that God takes special care of Israel (cf. v. 3). And so St Jerome comments on the verse as follows: "You only I have known of all the people of the earth; therefore I will visit your iniquities upon you (cf. Amos 3:2): 'For the Lord disciplines him whom he loves, and chastises every son whom he receives' (Heb 12:6). God says that *I will visit*, not 'I will punish', for the coming of the Lord is both punishment and cure;

and, he says, *I will visit all of their iniquities*: all shall be chastised and none shall remain uncured" (*Commentarii in Amos*, 3, 1–2).

A little further on, this teaching is rounded off with a sapiential consideration (vv. 3–8). The Lord addresses Israel by means of his prophets. All events have a cause that one cannot perceive, but they do point to their cause: when two people go walking together it is a sign that they have previously arranged to do so (v. 3); the roar of the lion shows that he has caught his prey or is about to do so (v. 4), etc. So, the conclusion to be drawn is clear (cf. v. 8): if Amos is prophesying, he is doing so because the Lord has spoken and man must take heed. In a way, this verse is a kind of parallel to what Amos says to the priest of Bethel (cf. 7:14–15): it is the Lord who has sent him to prophesy; God is the one who has taken the initiative: "The literal meaning of these words is as follows: If all the animals of the earth are terrified and tremble at the sound of the lion's roar, how can we not prophesy when the Lord bids us speak and tell the people of the torments that await them?" (St Jerome, *Commentarii in Amos*, 3, 3–8).

---

vos / omnes iniquitates vestras. / <sup>3</sup>Numquid ambulabunt duo pariter, nisi convenerint? / <sup>4</sup>Numquid rugiet leo in saltu, / nisi habuerit praedam? / Numquid dabit catulus leonis vocem de cubili suo, / nisi

⁵Does a bird fall in a snare on the earth,
    when there is no trap for it?
Does a snare spring up from the ground,
    when it has taken nothing?
⁶Is a trumpet blown in a city,
    and the people are not afraid?
Does evil befall a city,
    unless the LORD has done it?
⁷Surely the Lord GOD does nothing,
    without revealing his secret
    to his servants the prophets.
⁸The lion has roared;
    who will not fear?
The Lord GOD has spoken;
    who can but prophesy?"

*Marginal references:*
Is 45:7
Joel 2:1
Gen 6:13; 18, 17–21; Jer 7:25
Rev 1:11; 10:7
Amos 7:14–15
Jer 20:7–9
Rev 10:3

## Oracle against Samaria

Zeph 3:8
Amos 2:6–8

⁹Proclaim to the strongholds in Assyria,f
    and to the strongholds in the land of Egypt,
and say, "Assemble yourselves upon the mountains of Samaria,
    and see the great tumults within her,
    and the oppressions in her midst."

---

**3:9–15.** The crimes and aberrations of Samaria will be preached near and far —in Ashdod (note **f**), which some Greek versions and the New Vulgate translate as "Assyria", and in distant Egypt (vv. 9–10). The prophet directs his attack against those who live opulent lives: they have fine houses for summer and winter (cf. v. 15) but all that they store up is violence and plunder (cf. v. 10); they are neglectful in regard to divine worship (the "horns of the altar" were corner pieces that jutted out; they were smeared with the blood of victims: v. 14), and are not upright in their dealings (v. 10). On account of all this, Israel itself will be plundered (v. 11) and reduced to almost nothing (v. 12). The imagery used here (what is left of Israel will be no more than a shepherd could save from a lion's attack on the flock) leads one to think that Amos may be referring to the "remnant" of Israel, a recurring motif in prophetical preaching (cf. 5:3, 15; 9:8; Is 4:3; etc.). In spite of its sins, Israel will not be totally destroyed; a remnant will be saved, from which the Lord will renew his people.

---

aliquid apprehenderit? / ⁵Numquid cadet avis super terram / absque laqueo? / Numquid laxatur laqueus de terra, antequam quid ceperit? / ⁶Si clanget tuba in civitate, / populus non expavescet? / Si erit malum in civitate, / nonne Dominus fecit? / ⁷Nihil enim faciet Dominus Deus, / nisi revelaverit secretum suum / ad servos suos prophetas. / ⁸Leo rugit, / quis non timebit? / Dominus Deus locutus est, / quis non prophetabit? / ⁹Auditum facite in aedibus Assyriae / et in aedibus terrae Aegypti / et dicite:

**f.** Gk: Heb *Ashdod*

[10]"They do not know how to do right," says the LORD,
"those who store up violence and robbery in their strongholds."
[11]Therefore thus says the Lord GOD:                                2 Kings 17:3–6
"An adversary shall surround the land,
and bring down your defences from you,
and your strongholds shall be plundered."

[12]Thus says the LORD: "As the shepherd rescues from the         Gen 31:39
mouth of the lion two legs, or a piece of an ear, so shall the people   Ex 22:12
of Israel who dwell in Samaria be rescued, with the corner of a
couch and part[g] of a bed."

## Oracle against Bethel and domestic luxury

[13]"Hear, and testify against the house of Jacob,"                 1 Sam 1:3
says the Lord GOD, the God of hosts,
[14]"that on the day I punish Israel for his transgressions,        Ex 27:2
I will punish the altars of Bethel,                                 1 Kings 12:29–
and the horns of the altar shall be cut off                         30; 13:1–5; Hos
and fall to the ground.                                             10:15; 12:5
[15]I will smite the winter house with the summer house;           1 Kings 22:39
and the houses of ivory shall perish,
and the great houses[h] shall come to an end," says the LORD.

## Against the women of Samaria

4 [1]"Hear this word, you cows of Bashan,                           Is 3:16–24;
who are in the mountain of Samaria,                                 5:11–12;
                                                                    32:9–14
                                                                    Hos 5:11

---

**4:1–3.** This is a short but very vivid oracle. Bashan was an area famous for its grazing lands and herds of cattle. These well-to-do women are perfectly content, like cows in clover, but they fail to see that they will end up like the cows of Bashan—being herded off to be sacrificed.

"Congregamini super montes Samariae"; / et videte insanias multas in medio eius / et oppressos in sinu eius. / [10]Et nescierunt facere rectum, / dicit Dominus, / thesaurizantes violentiam et rapinas / in aedibus suis». / [11]Propterea haec dicit Dominus Deus: / «Inimicus circumdabit terram, / et detrahetur ex te fortitudo tua, / et diripientur aedes tuae». / [12]Haec dicit Dominus: / «Quomodo si eruat pastor de ore leonis / duo crura aut extremum auriculae, sic eruentur filii Israel, / qui habitant in Samaria, / in margine lectuli / et in Damasci grabato. / [13]Audite et contestamini in domo Iacob, / dicit Dominus, Deus exercituum: / [14]In die cum visitavero praevaricationes Israel, / super eum visitabo et super altaria Bethel, / et amputabuntur cornua altaris / et cadent in terram; / [15]et percutiam domum hiemalem / cum domo aestiva, / et peribunt domus eburneae, / et dissipabuntur aedes magnae», / dicit Dominus. [4] [1]Audite verbum hoc, / vaccae Basan, / quae estis in monte Samariae, / quae opprimitis egenos / et

**g.** The meaning of the Hebrew word is uncertain   **h.** Or *many houses*

who oppress the poor, who crush the needy,
who say to their husbands, "Bring, that we may drink!'

Lev 17:1
Ps 89:36

²The Lord GOD has sworn by his holiness
that, behold, the days are coming upon you,
when they shall take you away with hooks,
even the last of you with fishhooks.
³And you shall go out through the breaches,
every one straight before her;
and you shall be cast forth into Harmon," says the LORD.

**Israel reproached**

Deut 14:28; 26:12
1 Kings 12:26–33
2 Kings 2:1
Hos 4:15

⁴"Come to Bethel, and transgress;
to Gilgal, and multiply transgression;
bring your sacrifices every morning,
your tithes every three days;

---

The word *'adonîm* (v. 1b) could be translated as "husbands" or as "lords, masters". St Jerome translates it as "masters" and goes on to interpret the oracle: "The prophet directs his words to the leaders of Israel and all the leading men among the ten tribes, who had given themselves over to lives of pleasure, greed and robbery, to exhort them to listen to the word of God, and to remind them of what they already know: they are not oxen that pull the plough, but fat cows of the herd [...]; that is, they are not beasts whose life is to labour in the fields, but animals to be sacrificed and consumed" (*Commentarii in Amos*, 4, 1–3). But most commentators prefer to translate *'adonîm* as "husbands": that reading means that the oracle is addressed to the women of Samaria, telling them that they are just as much to blame as their husbands for the oppression of the poor (cf. v. 1).

**4:4–5.** This is another short, very sarcastic, oracle, against the irregular forms of worship at Bethel and Gilgal. In each of these sanctuaries Jeroboam I (931–910) had put up a statue of a golden calf, thereby completing the schism between the kingdom of Israel and the temple of Jerusalem (cf. 1 Kings 12:26–33). That was why rites at those shrines were considered idolatrous. Amos may be parodying here the sermons given by priests at these shrines. He is poking fun at the fact that the priests are punctilious about ritual cleanness, but turn a blind eye to the moral misconduct of those who come to the shrines; they ignore the link between true religion and morality: "Poor Israel! How quickly her captivity approaches! The Assyrian army stands near. Do whatever you desire: debase yourself among the idols; the greater your sin and shame, the more just shall be my punishment" (St Jerome, *Commentarii in Amos*, 4, 4–6).

vexatis pauperes, / quae dicitis dominis vestris: / «Affer, ut bibamus». / ²Iuravit Dominus Deus / in sanctitate sua: / «Ecce dies venient super vos, / et levabunt vos in contis / et posteros vestros in hamis piscatoriis; / ³et per aperturas exibitis altera contra alteram / et proiciemini in Armon», / dicit Dominus. / ⁴«Venite in Bethel et impie agite, / ad Galgalam et multiplicate praevaricationem; / et offerte mane

⁵offer a sacrifice of thanksgiving of that which is leavened,
and proclaim freewill offerings, publish them;
for so you love to do, O people of Israel!" says the Lord GOD.

Ex 35:29<br>Lev 7:11,13;<br>22:18; 23:17<br>Mt 6:2; 23:5

**The Lord's warnings have gone unheeded**

⁶"I gave you cleanness of teeth in all your cities,
and lack of bread in all your places,
yet you did not return to me," says the LORD.

Lev 26:14–39<br>Wis 12:2,10

⁷"And I also withheld the rain from you
when there were yet three months to the harvest;
I would send rain upon one city,
and send no rain upon another city;
one field would be rained upon,
and the field on which it did not rain withered;
⁸so two or three cities wandered to one city
to drink water, and were not satisfied;
yet you did not return to me," says the LORD.

Jer 14:1–6

⁹"I smote you with blight and mildew;
I laid waste[i] your gardens and your vineyards;

Deut 28:22<br>1 Kings 8:37<br>Joel 1:4

---

**4:6–12.** This oracle has a regular rhythm to it—each of the Lord's actions ends with the sort of refrain you find in a poem: "… yet you did not return to me, says the Lord" (vv. 6, 8, 9, 10, 11). The actions taken by the Lord (withdrawing food, drought, blight, destruction of cities) are reminiscent of the plagues of Egypt; but, most of all, they demonstrate the Lord's sovereignty over nature. This is the same message as is contained in the doxologies: God, the Lord of Israel, is the only one who has power over all creation: no Baal, no Canaanite god, has any such power. The point is also made that the punishment sent by God is aimed at bringing about the people's conversion. When they saw all these awful things happen, the Israelites should have had a change of heart. But they did not: Israel's sin is that of pride and self-sufficiency; therefore, it is time to get ready for judgment and punishment (v. 12; cf. 3:1).

victimas vestras, / tribus diebus decimas vestras, / ⁵et sacrificate de fermentato laudem / et vocate voluntarias oblationes et annuntiate; / sic enim diligitis, filii Israel», / dicit Dominus Deus. / ⁶«Unde et ego dedi vobis / vacuitatem dentium in cunctis urbibus vestris / et indigentiam panis in omnibus locis vestris; / et non estis reversi ad me», / dicit Dominus. / ⁷«Ego quoque prohibui a vobis imbrem, / cum adhuc tres menses superessent usque ad messem; / et plui super unam civitatem / et super alteram civitatem non plui: pars una compluta est, / et pars, super quam non plui, aruit. / ⁸Tunc fugiebant duae, tres civitates / ad unam civitatem, ut biberent aquam, / et non satiabantur; / sed non redistis ad me», / dicit Dominus. / ⁹«Percussi vos in vento urente et in aurugine; / multitudinem hortorum vestrorum et

**i.** Cn: Heb *the multitude of*

your fig trees and your olive trees the locust devoured;
yet you did not return to me," says the LORD.

Ex 9:1–7
Deut 7:15
2 Kings 13:7
Is 34:2–3

10"I sent among you a pestilence after the manner of Egypt;
I slew your young men with the sword;
I carried away your horses;[j]
and I made the stench of your camp go up into your nostrils;
yet you did not return to me," says the LORD.

Gen 19:1
Is 13:19;
34:2–3
Zech 3:2
Jude 7

11"I overthrew some of you,
as when God overthrew Sodom and Gomorrah,
and you were as a brand plucked out of the burning;
yet you did not return to me," says the LORD.

Mal 3:1–2

12"Therefore thus I will do to you, O Israel;
because I will do this to you,
prepare to meet your God, O Israel!"

### Doxology

Jer 32:18
Hos 12:6
Amos 3:7;
5:8,27; 9:6

13For lo, he who forms the mountains, and creates the wind,
and declares to man what is his thought;
who makes the morning darkness,
and treads on the heights of the earth—
the LORD, the God of hosts, is his name!

---

**4:13.** This is the first of three doxologies (hymns of praise) in this book (the others being 5:8–9; 9:5–6). These few lines in the form of a hymn celebrate the power of God over all creatures— even over those things that man finds most awesome. This celebration of the greatness of God is also a confession of faith in the Lord. In the New Testament the same literary form (the doxology) is used to confess the divinity of Jesus (Rom 16:25–27; 2 Pet 3:17–18; etc.); it is a form of praise to God often found in Christian liturgy.

The first part of the verse says that the Lord is he who "creates the wind". Because these two words (*bārā*, to create, and *ruāḥ*, spirit or wind) are the

vinearum vestrarum, / ficeta vestra et oliveta vestra / comedit eruca; / sed non redistis ad me», / dicit Dominus. / 10«Misi in vos pestem / sicut pestem Aegypti, / percussi in gladio iuvenes vestros, / captis equis vestris; / et ascendere feci putredinem / castrorum vestrorum in nares vestras; / sed non redistis ad me», / dicit Dominus. / 11«Subverti vos, / sicut subvertit Deus Sodomam et Gomorram, / et facti estis quasi torris / raptus ab incendio; / sed non redistis ad me», / dicit Dominus. / 12Quapropter haec faciam tibi, Israel, / et quia haec faciam tibi, / praeparare in occursum Dei tui, Israel; / 13quia ecce formans montes et creans ventum / et annuntians homini cogitationem eius, / faciens auroram et tenebras / et

**j.** Heb *with the captivity of your horses*

## Lament for Israel

5 [1] Hear this word which I take up over you in lamentation, O
house of Israel:

[2] "Fallen, no more to rise,
is the virgin Israel;
forsaken on her land,
with none to raise her up."

Is 47:1; 37:22

---

same ones as are used in the account of creation (Gen 1:1–2) to describe the action of God, and the Holy Spirit, some heretics tried to deduce from the passage in Amos that the Holy Spirit was not God but was a being created by him and subordinate to him. That may explain why, although the verse as such may not seem very important, it received a lot of attention from Fathers of the Church—St Athanasius, Didymus the Blind, etc. St Ambrose has this to say: "The heretics used to argue that the Holy Spirit was a created being, and many based their assertions on what Amos said about creation of the wind [...]. But so that you would know he was referring to the winds of storm and weather, Amos said: *he ... forms the mountains and creates the wind*, for all natural phenomena are created. But the Holy Spirit is eternal, and those who argue that he is created cannot say that he is created every day as the winds are" (*De Spiritu Sancto*, 2, 6, 48–51).

**5:1–9.** In different parts of chapter 5 we find all the main themes touched on in Amos' preaching. However, they are not dealt with in a very orderly way; so, what we have here is probably a collection of short oracles delivered at different times.

These nine oracles form three groups. The first group (vv. 1–3) is an elegy or lament over what is soon to befall Israel. As happens in some other prophetical texts, the people are compared to a virgin (cf. Is 23:12; 37:22) who sees that there is nothing to be done for her.

The second unit (vv. 4–7) carries a clear message: Israel must seek the Lord if she wants to have life (vv. 4, 6). This seeking the Lord is (the oracles make quite clear) the opposite of seeking God in the sanctuaries of Bethel etc. (v. 5). The prophet mentions two schismatic sanctuaries of the North; and he makes a play on words: *Gilgal* sounds like *galah* (going into captivity or exile), and *Beth-el*, house of God, is like *aven* or *Beth-aven* (house of nothing, house of iniquity: cf. Hos 4:15). Surprisingly, he also mentions a Southern sanctuary—*Beer-sheba*. What the prophet appears to be saying is that a relationship with God must be based on sincerity, not on religious rites *per se*. And a clear proof of a person's sincerity in his search for God is his respect for justice and righteousness (v. 7).

gradiens super excelsa terrae; / Dominus, Deus exercituum, nomen eius. **[5]** [1]Audite verbum istud, / quod ego levo super vos, / planctum, domus Israel: / [2]Cecidit, non adiciet ut resurgat / virgo Israel; /

<sup>3</sup>For thus says the Lord GOD:
"The city that went forth a thousand
  shall have a hundred left,
and that which went forth a hundred
  shall have ten left
  to the house of Israel."

### "Seek me and live," says the Lord

Is 55:6    <sup>4</sup>For thus says the LORD to the house of Israel:
Hos 10:12    "Seek me and live;

Hos 4:15        <sup>5</sup>but do not seek Bethel,
Amos 4:4;    and do not enter into Gilgal
  8:14          or cross over to Beer-sheba;
for Gilgal shall surely go into exile,
  and Bethel shall come to nought."

<sup>6</sup>Seek the LORD and live,
  lest he break out like fire in the house of Joseph,
  and it devour, with none to quench it for Bethel,
<sup>7</sup>O you who turn justice to wormwood,
  and cast down righteousness to the earth!

### Doxology

Job 4:13; 9:9;    <sup>8</sup>He who made the Pleiades and Orion,
24:17; 38:31    and turns deep darkness into the morning,
Amos 4:13;
  8:9; 9:6

---

The third unit is a doxology (vv. 8–9), praising God, creator of the heavens (v. 8: the Pleiades and Orion are two constellations; cf. Job 9:9), and creator of the earth and all that happens in the world (v. 9). Moreover, his "name" is "the Lord" (v. 8). The Greek translates the tetragram of the divine name as "Pantocrator", Pantocrat, Ruler of all, a single word meant to convey

the omnipotence and sovereignty of the revealed God: "In God, power and essence, will and intelligence, wisdom and justice, form one unity, so that there can be nothing in divine power that is not also at the same time in the just will of God or in his wise understanding" (St Thomas Aquinas, *Summa theologiae*, 1, 25, 5, ad 1; cf. *Catechism of the Catholic Church*, 270).

proiecta est in terram suam, / non est qui suscitet eam. / <sup>3</sup>Quia haec dicit Dominus Deus: / «Urbs, de qua egrediebantur mille, / relinquentur in ea centum; / et de qua egrediebantur centum, / relinquentur in ea decem / pro domo Israel». / <sup>4</sup>Quia haec dicit Dominus domui Israel: / «Quaerite me et vivetis; / <sup>5</sup>et nolite quaerere Bethel / et in Galgalam nolite intrare / et in Bersabee nolite transire, / quia Galgala captiva ducetur, / et Bethel erit iniquitas». / <sup>6</sup>Quaerite Dominum et vivite; / ne forte invadat sicut ignis / domum Ioseph, / et devoret, et non sit / qui exstinguat Bethel. / <sup>7</sup>Qui convertunt in absinthium iudicium / et iustitiam in terram deiciunt. / <sup>8</sup>Qui facit stellas Pliadis et Orionem / et convertit in mane

and darkens the day into night,
who calls for the waters of the sea,
and pours them out upon the surface of the earth,
the LORD is his name,
⁹who makes destruction flash forth against the strong,
so that destruction comes upon the fortress.

## Transgressors threatened

¹⁰They hate him who reproves in the gate,
and they abhor him who speaks the truth.
¹¹Therefore because you trample upon the poor
and take from him exactions of wheat,
you have built houses of hewn stone,
but you shall not dwell in them;
you have planted pleasant vineyards,
but you shall not drink their wine.

Deut 28:30–33
Mic 6:15
Zeph 1:13
Hag 1:6
Zech 5:3–4

---

**5:10–17.** Here again the prophet inveighs against Israel—particularly those who sin against justice ("the gates" of the city were where courts sat: vv. 10, 12, 15), those who exploit the poor and the righteous (vv. 11, 12: in Amos the two words are often synonymous) and seek a life of ease for themselves (v. 11).

Hence the prophet's call to conversion (vv. 14–15). He speaks very movingly. A little earlier he urged his listeners to "seek God and live" (cf. 5: 4, 6); now he tells them that that search means seeking what is good (v. 14). But the way to do that involves doing one very specific thing—establishing "justice in the gate" (v. 15). If they in fact do that, the awesome, almighty Lord ("the God of hosts": vv. 14–15) will be their merciful God: "Conversion is accomplished in daily life by gestures of reconciliation, concern for the poor, the exercise and defence of justice and right (Amos 5:24; Is 1:17), by the admission of faults to one's brethren, fraternal correction, revision of life, examination of conscience, spiritual direction, acceptance of suffering, endurance of persecution for the sake of righteousness. Taking up one's cross each day and following Jesus is the surest way of penance (cf. Lk 9:23)" (*Catechism of the Catholic Church*, 1435).

The verses at the end (vv. 16–17) act as an introduction to the theme of "the day of the Lord" which follows.

tenebras / et diem in noctem obscurat; / qui vocat aquas maris / et effundit eas super faciem terrae; / Dominus nomen eius. / ⁹Qui micare facit vastitatem super robustum / et vastitatem super arcem affert. / ¹⁰Odio habuerunt corripientem in porta / et loquentem perfecte abominati sunt. / ¹¹Idcirco, pro eo quod conculcastis pauperem / et portionem frumenti abstulistis ab eo, / domos quadro lapide aedificastis / et non habitabitis in eis, / vineas plantastis amantissimas / et non bibetis vinum earum. /

<sup>12</sup>For I know how many are your transgressions,
  and how great are your sins—
you who afflict the righteous, who take a bribe,
  and turn aside the needy in the gate.

Mic 2:3  <sup>13</sup>Therefore he who is prudent will keep silent in such a time;
  for it is an evil time.

## Exhortation

Ps 34:13–15;
37:27
Amos 5:4

<sup>14</sup>Seek good, and not evil,
  that you may live;
and so the LORD, the God of hosts, will be with you,
  as you have said.

Is 4:3
Rom 12:9

<sup>15</sup>Hate evil, and love good,
  and establish justice in the gate;
it may be that the LORD, the God of hosts,
  will be gracious to the remnant of Joseph.

## Lamentation

<sup>16</sup>Therefore thus says the LORD, the God of hosts, the Lord:
  "In all the squares there shall be wailing;
  and in all the streets they shall say, 'Alas! alas!'
They shall call the farmers to mourning
  and to wailing those who are skilled in lamentation,

Ex 12:12
Amos 4:12
Nahum 1:12
Mal 3:1–2

<sup>17</sup>and in all vineyards there shall be wailing,
  for I will pass through the midst of you," says the LORD.

## The day of the Lord

Is 2:12; Jer 13:16;
14:19; Joel 1:15;
3:4; 4:1; Zeph
1:14–18

<sup>18</sup>Woe to you who desire the day of the LORD!
  Why would you have the day of the LORD?

---

**5:18–20.** The memory of God's actions in favour of Israel gave the people grounds to hope that a "day" would come when the Lord would intervene again to fulfil the promises he made to the patriarchs. From that viewpoint, the day of the Lord was a day of salvation, a day of grace and glory. However, Amos (cf. also 8:9–14), as other prophets do too (cf. Is 2:11; Jer

<sup>12</sup>Quia cognovi multa scelera vestra / et fortia peccata vestra, / opprimentes iustum, accipientes munus / et pauperes deprimentes in porta. / <sup>13</sup>Ideo prudens in tempore illo tacet, / quia tempus malum est. / <sup>14</sup>Quaerite bonum et non malum, / ut vivatis, / ita ut sit Dominus, Deus exercituum, / vobiscum, sicut dixistis. / <sup>15</sup>Odite malum et diligite bonum / et constituite in porta iudicium, / si forte misereatur Dominus, Deus exercituum, / reliquiis Ioseph. / <sup>16</sup>Propterea haec dicit Dominus, / Deus exercituum, dominator: / «In omnibus plateis planctus, / et in cunctis viis dicetur: "Vae, vae!"; / et vocabunt agricolam ad luctum / et ad planctum eos, qui sciunt lamentationem. / <sup>17</sup>Et in omnibus vineis erit luctus, / quia pertransibo in medio tui», / dicit Dominus. / <sup>18</sup>Vae desiderantibus diem Domini! / Ad quid vobis

It is darkness, and not light;

Mal 3:19–23; Jn 8:12

[19]as if a man fled from a lion,
and a bear met him;
or went into the house and leaned with his hand against
the wall, and a serpent bit him.
[20]Is not the day of the LORD darkness, and not light,
and gloom with no brightness in it?

### Formalism in religion condemned
[21]"I hate, I despise your feasts,

Amos 4:4–5

and I take no delight in your solemn assemblies.

---

30:5–24; Joel 1:15; 2:31; 3:1; Zeph 1:14–18; Mal 4:1–4), gives that day an unexpected meaning: the "day of the Lord" will be a day of judgment, a day when sentences are handed down and misfortune strikes. Over the course of prophetical tradition, the notion of the "day of the Lord" gradually became more precise, and richer in content. Its signs and signals became more defined, and people were able to see that it had two sides to it: it spelt punishment for sinners, and salvation for the righteous. The descriptions in our Lord's eschatological discourse in the Synoptic Gospels (cf. Mt 24:29–41 and par.) are very much in line with those here.

The oracle is very vivid. It is aimed at those who imagine that the Lord is going to intervene dramatically on their behalf. Not so, Amos tells them: the day of the Lord will not be a day of salvation and light; it will be a day of darkness, when things will go wrong (vv. 18–20).

**5:21–25.** This passage contains more criticism (cf. 4:4–5) of formalism in

religion. The prophet contrasts the contemporary position with the way things were during the forty years in the wilderness—a time when there were no sacrifices (v. 25) but justice reigned (v. 24). Amos' words are very clear, and what he says here will be echoed elsewhere in the Old and New Testaments. This passage and Hosea 6:6; 8:13 are classic texts on the need for religious rites to be backed by upright living. As St Thomas teaches, "everything that he sacrifices should partake in some way of himself […], because external sacrifice is a sign of the internal disposition by which the person offers himself to God. By making sacrifice, man also offers up himself" (*Summa theologiae*, 3, 82, 4). From this it follows that "the only perfect sacrifice is the one that Christ offered on the cross as a total offering to the Father's love and for our salvation (cf. Heb 9:13–14). By uniting ourselves with his sacrifice we can make our lives a sacrifice to God" (*Catechism of the Catholic Church*, 2100).

---

dies Domini? / Tenebrae et non lux. / [19]Quomodo si fugiat vir a facie leonis, / et occurrat ei ursus; / et ingrediatur domum / et innitatur manu sua super parietem, / et mordeat eum coluber. / [20]Numquid non tenebrae dies Domini et non lux? / Et caligo sine splendore in ea? / [21]«Odi, proieci festivitates vestras

Lev 3:1,6
Is 1:11
Hos 8:13

²²Even though you offer me your burnt offerings and cereal
    offerings,
  I will not accept them,
and the peace offerings of your fatted beasts
  I will not look upon.
²³Take away from me the noise of your songs;
  to the melody of your harps I will not listen.
²⁴But let justice roll down like waters,
  and righteousness like an ever-flowing stream.

Deut 32:17
Ezek 20:13
*Acts 7:42–43*

²⁵"Did you bring to me sacrifices and offerings the forty years
in the wilderness, O house of Israel?

### The prophet threatens punishment

Amos 4:13

²⁶You shall take up Sakkuth your king, and Kaiwan your star-god,
your images,ᵏ which you made for yourselves; ²⁷therefore I will
take you into exile beyond Damascus," says the LORD, whose
name is the God of hosts.

Jer 5:12–13
Lk 6:24

### A life of luxury gives a false sense of security

**6** ¹"Woe to those who are at ease in Zion,
  and to those who feel secure on the mountain of Samaria,

---

**5:26–27.** This passage is still the subject of debate among scholars. It could have something to do with ancient Israelite religious processions of some sort, or be a reference to the introduction into Samaria of foreign cults. Verse 27 contains a threat of exile to somewhere vaguely "beyond Damascus", the capital of Syria; they will make their way there carrying with them their false gods.

**6:1–14.** The third "woe" (v. 1; cf. 5:7, 18) marks the start of the last section of this part of the book. Two distinct fragments can be detected in this passage, but they both attack pleasure-seeking and pride. The first (vv. 1–7) reproaches those who live thoughtlessly (vv. 4–6), be they in Samaria or in Zion (v. 1), putting their trust in the ruling classes of "the first of the nations", that is, the Northern kingdom, Samaria. In describing the country in that way, Amos is being sarcastic. But there is no sarcasm about his threat that those who "anoint themselves with the finest oils" (v. 6)

/ et non delector coetibus vestris. / ²²Quod si obtuleritis mihi holocautomata, / oblationes vestras non suscipiam / et sacrificia pinguium vestrorum non respiciam. / ²³Aufer a me tumultum carminum tuorum, / et canticum lyrarum tuarum non audiam. / ²⁴Et affluat quasi aqua iudicium, / et iustitia quasi torrens perennis. / ²⁵Numquid hostias et oblationes obtulistis mihi in deserto / quadraginta annis, domus Israel? / ²⁶Et portastis Saccut regem vestrum, / et Caivan, imagines vestras, / sidus deorum vestrorum, quae fecistis vobis. / ²⁷Et migrare vos faciam trans Damascum», / dicit Dominus; Deus exercituum nomen eius. **[6]** ¹Vae, qui tranquilli sunt in Sion / et confidunt in monte Samariae; / designati

k. Heb *your images, your star-god*

to whom the house of Israel come!
²Pass over to Calneh, and see;
    and thence go to Hamath the great;
    then go down to Gath of the Philistines.

---

"will be the first of those who go into exile" (v. 7). The main charge laid against them is that of living a life of luxury, heedless of the misfortunes of others, of "the ruin of Joseph" (v. 6). Concern for others is always a religious duty: "Coming down to practical and particularly urgent consequences, this council [Vatican II] lays stress on reverence for man; everyone must consider his every neighbour without exception as another self, taking into account first of all his life and the means necessary to living it with dignity. [...] In our times a special obligation binds us to make ourselves the neighbour of every person without exception and to actively help him when he comes across our path, whether he be an old person abandoned by all, a foreign labourer unjustly looked down upon, a refugee, a child born of an unlawful union and wrongly suffering for a sin he did not commit, or a hungry person who disturbs our conscience by recalling the voice of the Lord, 'As long as you did it for one of these the least of my brethren, you did it for me' (Mt 25:40)" (*Gadium et spes*, 27).

The second fragment (vv. 8–14) announces dire punishment for those who are proud and have turned their backs on the Lord. The passage is very stinging and contains clever analogies. Verse 10 is difficult to decipher: the language is difficult, and it is hard to see why the verse occurs here; but what it seems to be saying is that not even expressions of religious respect will be able to save Israel from its fate. "Lo-debar" (v. 13) is a city of the tribe of Gad in the Transjordan; Jeroboam II, or his father, Joash, conquered it from the Aramaeans; Israel was very proud of it but, according to Amos, had no reason to be. The "entrance of Hamath" and the "Brook of the Arabah" (v. 14) are mentioned elsewhere (cf. Josh 13:1–19) as the northern and southern limits of the land of Israel. What the passage means is clear: Israel, "the first of the nations", is going to be overrun by another; Amos does not say which nation, but here he seems to be referring to Assyria, a nation that is not mentioned by name anywhere in the book.

Saints and spiritual writers have often used turns of phrase from the Bible to get across their message. St Francis de Sales, for example, uses v. 12 in this way: "There are some bitter, sour hearts, debased by sinful nature, which poison and debase everything they touch. As the prophet says, they have *turned justice into poison*; they judge others severely and without clemency. These people need to place themselves in the care of a good spiritual physician" (*Introduction to the Devout Life*, 28).

---

primitiae populorum, / ad quos venit domus Israel! / ²Transite in Chalanne et videte; / et ite inde in Emath magnam / et descendite in Geth Palaestinorum. / Numquid meliores regnis istis vos, / aut latior

Are they better than these kingdoms?
Or is their territory greater than your territory,
³O you who put far away the evil day,
and bring near the seat of violence?

Amos 3:15    ⁴"Woe to those who lie upon beds of ivory,
and stretch themselves upon their couches,
and eat lambs from the flock,
and calves from the midst of the stall;

1 Chron 23:5
2 Chron 29:26
Neh 12:36    ⁵who sing idle songs to the sound of the harp,
and like David invent for themselves instruments of music;
⁶who drink wine in bowls,
and anoint themselves with the finest oils,
but are not grieved over the ruin of Joseph!

Rev 18:14    ⁷Therefore they shall now be the first of those to go into exile,
and the revelry of those who stretch themselves shall
pass away."

## Divine punishment

Is 28:1
Jer 51:53
Ezek 24:21
Amos 4:2    ⁸The Lord GOD has sworn by himself
(says the LORD, the God of hosts):
"I abhor the pride of Jacob,
and hate his strongholds;
and I will deliver up the city and all that is in it."

Amos 2:14–16
Hab 2:20
Zeph 1:7
Zech 2:17    ⁹And if ten men remain in one house, they shall die. ¹⁰And when a man's kinsman, he who burns him,¹ shall take him up to bring the bones out of the house, and shall say to him who is in the innermost parts of the house, "Is there still any one with you?" he shall say, "No"; and he shall say, "Hush! We must not mention the name of the LORD."

---

terminus eorum termino vestro est? / ³Qui removetis diem malum / et appropinquare facitis solium violentiae. / ⁴Qui dormiunt in lectis eburneis, / recumbentes in stratis suis, / comedentes agnos de grege / et vitulos de medio armenti; / ⁵canentes ad vocem psalterii, / sicut David excogitant sibi vasa cantici; / ⁶bibentes vinum in phialis, / optimis unguentis delibuti, / et non sunt contristati super ruina Ioseph. / ⁷Quapropter nunc migrabunt in capite transmigrantium, / et auferetur factio lascivientium. / ⁸Iuravit Dominus Deus in anima sua, / dicit Dominus, Deus exercituum: / «Detestor ego superbiam Iacob / et domos eius odi / et tradam civitatem et plenitudinem eius». / ⁹Quod si reliqui fuerint / decem viri in domo una, / et ipsi morientur; / ¹⁰et tollet eum propinquus suus / et comburet eum, ut efferat ossa de domo, / et dicet ei, qui in penetralibus domus est: / «Numquid adhuc est penes te?». / Et respondebit:

**l.** Or *who makes a burning for him*

[11]For behold, the LORD commands,
and the great house shall be smitten into fragments,
and the little house into bits.
[12]Do horses run upon rocks?
Does one plough the sea with oxen?
But you have turned justice into poison
and the fruit of righteousness into wormwood—
[13]you who rejoice in Lo-debar,[n]
who say, "Have we not by our own strength
taken Karnaim[o] for ourselves?"
[14]"For behold, I will raise up against you a nation,
O house of Israel," says the LORD, the God of hosts;
"and they shall oppress you from the entrance of Hamath
to the Brook of the Arabah."

*Amos 5:7*
*Deut 8:17*
*1 Kings 8:65*
*2 Kings 14:25*

## 3. SERIES OF PROPHETICAL VISIONS*

**First vision: the locusts**
7 [1]Thus the Lord GOD showed me: behold, he was forming locusts in the beginning of the shooting up of the latter growth;

*Deut 28:38*
*Joel 1:4–7; 2:3–9*

---

*7:1–9:10. This section is the third part of the book. It consists of five visions, with a doxology that comes near the end (9:5–6). Mixed in are some interesting details about Amos and his teaching—the account of his call (7:14–15), a dramatic description of the "day of the Lord" (8:9–14), etc. The passage ends with an announcement of punishment (9:7–10) that serves to underscore the optimism of the final oracle, which is about future restoration.

Most of this passage is taken up with the "five visions of Amos"; these are written to a fairly fixed pattern, in a mixture of prose and verse. The visions mean that Amos' ministry includes that of "seer" as well as prophet. The message of the visions is clear: the Lord cannot be appeased by external, schismatic rites that fail to touch men's hearts or move them to conversion.

7:1–6. The first two visions (the locusts, the fire) follow the same pattern: the Lord gives the prophet the vision; the prophet intercedes; and the Lord "repents" and promises not to do

«Non est»; / et dicet ei: «Tace!»; / non est qui recordetur nominis Domini. / [11]Quia ecce Dominus mandat / et percutiet domum maiorem ruinis / et domum minorem scissionibus. / [12]Numquid currunt in petris equi, / aut aratur mare in bobus, / quoniam convertistis in venenum iudicium / et fructum iustitiae in absinthium? / [13]Qui laetantur pro Lodabar, / qui dicunt: «Numquid non in fortitudine nostra / cepimus nobis Carnaim?». / [14]«Ecce enim suscitabo super vos, domus Israel, / dicit Dominus, Deus exercituum, gentem; / et oppriment vos ab introitu Emath / usque ad torrentem Arabae». [7] [1]Haec

**n.** Or *a thing of naught* **o.** Or *horns*

and lo, it was the latter growth after the king's mowings. [2]When they had finished eating the grass of the land, I said,

"O Lord GOD, forgive, I beseech thee!
How can Jacob stand?
He is so small!"

Deut 32:36    [3]The LORD repented concerning this;
Jon 3:10       "It shall not be," said the LORD.

**Second vision: the fire**

[4]Thus the Lord GOD showed me: behold, the Lord GOD was calling for a judgment by fire, and it devoured the great deep and was eating up the land. [5]Then I said,

"O Lord GOD, cease, I beseech thee!
How can Jacob stand?

---

what he had planned. One cannot fail to notice the reason that Amos gives when he pleads for the people (and is successful); it is that Israel "is so small" (vv. 2, 5). This is a reminder of God's regard for little ones (Mt 18:2–10 and par.) and it is the basis for the importance given in Christian tradition to "being little" before the Lord: "Jesus delighted in showing me the one and only way that leads to our eternal home. This way lies in the helplessness of a small child who sleeps without fear in the arms of his father ... 'Let the little one come to me,' says the Holy Spirit from the mouth of Solomon. The Spirit also says that 'the little ones shall be comforted and forgiven.' And, in His name, Isaiah tells us that on the last day 'the Lord will tend his flock like a good shepherd, he will gather the lambs to himself and press them to his breast'.

And as though all these promises were not enough, the same prophet, whose inspired gaze was lost in the depths of eternity, cries out in the name of the Lord: 'As a mother cares for her child, so shall I console you; I will take you in my arms and caress you'" (St Thérèse of the Child Jesus, *Story of a Soul*, chap. 9).

Amos' conversation with the Lord here also helps us see the "origins" of true prayer: "Prayer is an acknowledgment of our limitations and our dependence: we come from God, we are of God, and we return to God. [...] Prayer is a mysterious, but real, dialogue with God, a dialogue of love and trust. [...] Prayer gives us light so that we can see and judge the events in our lives and in history as a whole from the redemptive perspective of God and eternity" (John Paul II, Address, 14 March 1979).

---

ostendit mihi Dominus Deus: et ecce, ipse formabat lo custas in principio, cum germinarent serotinae fruges; et ecce fruges serotinae post fruges demessas regis. [2]Et factum est, cum consummasset comedere herbam terrae, dixi: «Domine Deus, propitius esto, obsecro; quomodo stabit Iacob, quia parvulus est?». [3]Misertus est Dominus super hoc. «Non erit», dixit Dominus Deus. [4]Haec ostendit mihi Dominus Deus: et ecce, vocabat ad iudicium per ignem Dominus Deus, et devoravit abyssum magnam et comedit simul partem. [5]Et dixi: «Domine Deus, quiesce, obsecro; quomodo stabit Iacob, quia

He is so small!"
<sup>6</sup>The LORD repented concerning this;
"This also shall not be," said the Lord GOD.

### Third vision: the plumb line

<sup>7</sup>He showed me: behold, the Lord was standing beside a wall built
with a plumb line, with a plumb line in his hand. <sup>8</sup>And the LORD
said to me, "Amos, what do you see?" And I said, "A plumb line."
Then the Lord said,

"Behold, I am setting a plumb line
in the midst of my people Israel;
I will never again pass by them;
<sup>9</sup>the high places of Isaac shall be made desolate,
and the sanctuaries of Israel shall be laid waste,
and I will rise against the house of Jeroboam with the sword."

Deut 12:2
2 Kings
15:8–10

### Dispute with Amaziah

<sup>10</sup>Then Amaziah the priest of Bethel sent to Jeroboam king of
Israel, saying, "Amos has conspired against you in the midst of the
house of Israel; the land is not able to bear all his words. <sup>11</sup>For
thus Amos has said,

"Jeroboam shall die by the sword,
and Israel must go into exile
away from his land.'"

1 Kings 12:32
Amos 3:14

Amos 5:27;
6:7; 7:9; 9:4

---

**7:7–17.** The vision of the plumb line (vv. 7–9) exposes the rottenness within the people. They are not level, not right; when they are checked, they are found to be askew (v. 7). From now on, the Lord is not going to overlook their infidelities; what is out of line will be destroyed (v. 9). That may be why the prophet no longer intercedes; he simply notes something that will happen inexorably.

The vision is followed by an account of Amos' altercation with Amaziah, the priest of the sanctuary of Bethel (vv. 10–17). Amaziah, a supporter of King Jeroboam, sees in Amos a prophet who is only going to cause trouble in the kingdom: he has no interest in trying to understand Amos' message—which in fact exposes injustices and deceit to which Amaziah is party.

parvulus est?». <sup>6</sup>Misertus est Dominus super hoc. «Sed et istud non erit», dicit Dominus Deus. <sup>7</sup>Haec ostendit mihi Dominus Deus: ecce vir stans super murum litum, et in manu eius trulla caementarii. <sup>8</sup>Et dixit Dominus ad me: «Quid tu vides, Amos?». Et dixi: «Trullam caementarii». Et dixit Dominus: «Ecce ego ponam trullam in medio populi mei Israel; non adiciam ultra ignoscere ei. <sup>9</sup>Et demolientur excelsa Isaac, et sanctuaria Israel desolabuntur, et consurgam super domum Ieroboam in gladio». <sup>10</sup>Et misit Amasias sacerdos Bethel ad Ieroboam regem Israel dicens: «Conspiravit contra te Amos in medio domus Israel; non poterit terra sustinere universos sermones eius. <sup>11</sup>Haec enim dicit Amos: "In gladio

2 Sam 24:11
1 Kings 12:29
Amos 2:12

1 Sam 10:10–
13; 19:20–24

Amos 2:12

Deut 28:30–33
2 Kings 17:24
Hos 9:3

<sup>12</sup>And Amaziah said to Amos, "O seer, go, flee away to the land of Judah, and eat bread there, and prophesy there; <sup>13</sup>but never again prophesy at Bethel, for it is the king's sanctuary, and it is a temple of the kingdom."

<sup>14</sup>Then Amos answered Amaziah, "I am no prophet, nor a prophet's son;<sup>p</sup> but I am a herdsman, and a dresser of sycamore trees, <sup>15</sup>and the LORD took me from following the flock, and the LORD said to me, "Go, prophesy to my people Israel.'

<sup>16</sup>"Now therefore hear the word of the LORD.

You say, "Do not prophesy against Israel,
    and do not preach against the house of Isaac.'
<sup>17</sup>Therefore thus says the LORD:

Amaziah calls Amos a "seer" (a translation of one of the Hebrew terms used to designate a prophet). But Amos does not regard himself as a prophet in the normal sense, a "son of a prophet" (v. 14), that is, a member of a group or fraternity of prophets, of which there were many in Israel, at least from the time of King Saul onwards (cf. 1 Sam 10:10–13; 19:20–24), nor is he an "official" prophet, a member of the staff of the royal household. Amos' reply is clear: he is a herdsman and a dresser of sycamores. But the Lord sent him to "prophesy" to Israel (v. 15). Amos, then, was an ordinary man (not a prophet, not a priest) who was commissioned by the Lord, out of the blue, to proclaim a message. A call from God is something so imperative that no one should refuse it (cf. 3:8), but at the same time it gives

meaning and strength to the person's life: it confers on him a sense of authority even over institutions such as temple and king. He therefore has the last word (v. 17): "God's calling gives us a mission: it invites us to share in the unique task of the Church, to bear witness to Christ before our fellow men and so draw all things toward God. Our calling discloses to us the meaning of our existence. It means being convinced, through faith, of the reason for our life on earth. Our life—present, past and future—acquires a new dimension, a depth we did not perceive before. All happenings and events now fall within their true perspective: we understand where God is leading us, and we feel ourselves borne along by this task entrusted to us" (St Josemaría Escrivá, *Christ Is Passing By*, 45).

morietur Ieroboam, et Israel captivus migrabit de terra sua"». <sup>12</sup>Et dixit Amasias ad Amos: «Qui vides, gradere. Fuge in terram Iudae et comede ibi panem et prophetabis ibi; <sup>13</sup>et in Bethel non adicies ultra ut prophetes, quia sanctuarium regis est, et domus regni est». <sup>14</sup>Responditque Amos et dixit ad Amasiam: «Non sum propheta / et non sum filius prophetae; / sed armentarius ego sum, vellicans sycomoros. / <sup>15</sup>Et tulit me Dominus, / cum sequerer gregem, / et dixit Dominus ad me: / "Vade, propheta ad populum meum Israel". <sup>16</sup>Et nunc audi verbum Domini. Tu dicis: "Non prophetabis super Israel et non stillabis verba super domum Isaac". <sup>17</sup>Propter hoc haec dicit Dominus: "Uxor tua in civitate fornicabitur, et filii tui et filiae tuae in gladio cadent, et humus tua funiculo metietur; et tu in

**p.** Or *one of the sons of the prophets*

"Your wife shall be a harlot in the city,
and your sons and your daughters shall fall by the sword,
and your land shall be parcelled out by line;
you yourself shall die in an unclean land,
and Israel shall surely go into exile away from its land.'"

**Fourth vision: the basket of fruit**

8 [1]Thus the Lord GOD showed me: behold, a basket of summer fruit.[q] [2]And he said, "Amos, what do you see?" And I said, "A basket of summer fruit."[q] Then the LORD said to me,

Amos 7:7–9
Rev 14:15–18

---

**8:1–14.** The fourth vision, that of the ripe fruit (vv. 13), introduces a denunciation of injustices (vv. 4–8) and a further description of the "day of the Lord" (vv. 9–14). The three things are interconnected. In the vision, the prophet plays with the words (v. 2) "summer fruit", *qayits*, and "end", *qets* (see notes **q** and **r**). In this way he is saying that Israel's rottenness has run its course (vv. 4–8); nothing can be done about it now—nothing but wait for the day of the Lord's judgment (vv. 9–14).

In his denunciation of injustices, Amos mentions, specifically, fraud (v. 5) and exploitation of others when they are suffering need (v. 6). Church catechesis uses this and other passages (cf. Deut 24:14–15; 25:13–16; Jas 5:4) to spell out what the virtue of justice involves: "We should not dedicate our lives to the accumulation of money and wealth when there are so many others who struggle to survive in abject poverty; thus shall we heed the warning contained in the words of the prophet Amos: *Hear this, you who trample upon the needy, and bring the poor of the land to an end, saying, 'When will the new moon be over, that we may sell grain? And the sabbath, that we may offer wheat for sale'*" (St Gregory Nazianzen, *De pauperum amore* [*Oratio*, 14], 24).

The end of the passage (vv. 9–14) contains the second description of the "day of the Lord" (cf. 5:18–20). The darkness motif in the earlier oracle is developed here by reference to an eclipse (v. 9), but the prophet also brings in other themes—lamentation and pain (v. 10), weakness in those who should be strong (v. 13), and, particularly, the fruitless search for the word of God (vv. 11–12). It will be a terrible day, when no one can draw benefit from the word of God. Maybe for this reason, the fourth petition of the Our Father ("Give us this day our daily bread") includes a reference to the bread of the Word of God: "There is a famine on earth, 'not a famine of bread, nor a thirst for water, but of hearing the words of the Lord' (Amos 8:11). For this reason the specifically Christian sense of this fourth petition concerns

---

terra polluta morieris, et Israel captivus migrabit de terra sua"». **[8]** [1]Haec ostendit mihi Dominus Deus: / et ecce canistrum pomorum. / [2]Et dixit: «Quid tu vides, Amos?». / Et dixi: «Canistrum

**q.** Heb *qayits*

> "The end[r] has come upon my people Israel;
> I will never again pass by them.

Amos 6:10    [3]The songs of the temple[s] shall become wailings in that day,"
> says the Lord GOD;
> "the dead bodies shall be many;
> in every place they shall be cast out in silence."[t]

### Exploiters denounced

Amos 2:6–8;    [4]Hear this, you who trample upon the needy,
4:1      and bring the poor of the land to an end,

Deut 25:13    [5]saying, "When will the new moon be over,

---

the Bread of Life—the Word of God accepted in faith, the Body of Christ received in the Eucharist (cf. Jn 6:26–58)" (*Catechism of the Catholic Church*, 2835).

Following the example of Jesus and the apostles, the Fathers often try to find in the prophetical writings of the Old Testament things that are later borne out in the life of Christ. Verses 9–10, it has been suggested, prophesy the death of Jesus and the destruction of Jerusalem that he foretold (cf. Mt 24:2 and par.): "Some prophesied that there would come to Jerusalem a man, scorned and without glory and acquainted with suffering (cf. Is 53:3), seated on the colt of an ass (cf. Zech 9:9); he would offer his back to the lash and his cheeks to their blows, and be led like a lamb to the slaughter (cf. Is 53:7). They would give him gall and vineger to drink (cf. Ps 68:21); all his friends and allies would forsake him; and he would spread out his hands all the day (cf. Is

65:2), and be jeered and mocked by the crowd, who divide out his clothes among themselves and for his vestments cast lots; he would be crushed into the dust of death (cf. Ps 21:6–7). Thus was it foretold: how He was made flesh, and journeyed to Jerusalem, and suffered his passion, crucified and subjected to the cruellest tortures that men could devise (…). But Amos' words, *'And on that day,' says the Lord God, 'I will make the sun go down at noon, and darken the earth in broad daylight. I will turn your feasts into mourning, and all your songs into lamentation'* (Amos 8:9–10), is a clear prophecy of two things: the setting of the sun in the sixth hour, when the Lord was hanging from the cross; and that the feast days the people celebrate according to the Law and the songs they sang would become days of lamentation and mourning dirges when they are handed over to the Gentiles" (St Irenaeus, *Adversus haereses*, 4, 33, 12).

---

pomorum». / Et dixit Dominus ad me: / «Venit finis super populum meum Israel; / non adiciam ultra ignoscere ei. / [3]Et lugent cantatrices palatii in die illa, / dicit Dominus Deus; / multa erunt cadavera, / in omni loco proicientur: silentium. / [4]Audite hoc, qui conteritis pauperem / et deficere facitis egenos terrae, / [5]dicentes: "Quando transibit neomenia, / et venumdabimus merces? / Et sabbatum, et

**r.** Heb *qets*   **s.** Or *palace*   **t.** Or *be silent!*

that we may sell grain?
And the sabbath,
   that we may offer wheat for sale,
that we may make the ephah small and the shekel great,
   and deal deceitfully with false balances,
⁶that we may buy the poor for silver
   and the needy for a pair of sandals,
   and sell the refuse of the wheat?"

Ezek 45:10
Mic 6:10–11
Hos 12:8

Amos 2:6

⁷The LORD has sworn by the pride of Jacob:
"Surely I will never forget any of their deeds.
⁸Shall not the land tremble on this account,
   and every one mourn who dwells in it,
and all of it rise like the Nile,
   and be tossed about and sink again, like the Nile of Egypt?"

Amos 1:1; 9:5

## A day of judgment

⁹"And on that day," says the Lord GOD,
   "I will make the sun go down at noon,
   and darken the earth in broad daylight.
¹⁰I will turn your feasts into mourning,
   and all your songs into lamentation;
I will bring sackcloth upon all loins,
   and baldness on every head;
I will make it like the mourning for an only son,
   and the end of it like a bitter day.

Is 60:20; Jer 15:9
Mic 3:6; Mt 24:29;
27:45; Mk 15:33
Lk 23:44

Tob 2:6; Is 3:24
Jer 6:26
Hos 2:13
Zech 12:10

¹¹"Behold, the days are coming," says the Lord GOD,
   "when I will send a famine on the land;
not a famine of bread, nor a thirst for water,
   but of hearing the words of the LORD.
¹²They shall wander from sea to sea,
   and from north to east;
they shall run to and fro, to seek the word of the LORD,
   but they shall not find it.

Deut 8:3
Amos 4:2
Mt 5:6

Hos 5:6

---

aperiemus frumentum, / ut imminuamus mensuram et augeamus siclum / et supponamus stateras dolosas, / ⁶ut possideamus in argento egenos / et pauperem pro calceamentis / et quisquilias frumenti vendamus?"». / ⁷Iuravit Dominus in superbia Iacob: / «Non obliviscar in perpetuum omnia opera eorum. / ⁸Numquid super isto non commovebitur terra, / et lugebit omnis habitator eius, / et ascendet quasi fluvius universa, / fervebit et decrescet quasi flumen Aegypti? / ⁹Et erit: in die illa, / dicit Dominus Deus, / occidere faciam solem in meridie / et tenebrescere faciam terram in die luminis / ¹⁰et convertam festivitates vestras in luctum / et omnia cantica vestra in planctum; / et inducam super omnes lumbos saccum / et super omne caput calvitium; / et ponam eam quasi luctum unigeniti / et novissima eius quasi diem amarum. / ¹¹Ecce dies veniunt, / dicit Dominus, / et mittam famem in terram; / non famem panis neque sitim aquae, / sed audiendi verbum Domini». / ¹²Et fugient a mari usque ad mare; / et ab

Zech 9:17 <sup>13</sup>"In that day the fair virgins and the young men
shall faint for thirst.
Deut 9:21 <sup>14</sup>Those who swear by Ashimah of Samaria,
1 Kings 12:29–30
Hos 10:7–8    and say, 'As thy god lives, O Dan,'
Amos 5:5    and, 'As the way of Beer-sheba lives,'
they shall fall, and never rise again."

## Fifth vision: the fall of the sanctuary

Amos 2:13–16;
9:9–10
Is 9:13–14

**9** <sup>1</sup>I saw the LORD standing beside<sup>u</sup> the altar, and he said:
"Smite the capitals until the thresholds shake,
and shatter them on the heads of all the people;<sup>v</sup>
and what are left of them I will slay with the sword;
not one of them shall flee away,
not one of them shall escape.

Ps 139:7–12
Jer 23:23–24

<sup>2</sup>"Though they dig into Sheol,
from there shall my hand take them;
though they climb up to heaven,
from there I will bring them down.

Job 3:8; 7:12
Ps 135:6

<sup>3</sup>Though they hide themselves on the top of Carmel,
from there I will search out and take them;
and though they hide from my sight at the bottom of the sea,
there I will command the serpent, and it shall bite them.

Jer 21:10 <sup>4</sup>And though they go into captivity before their enemies,
there I will command the sword, and it shall slay them;

---

**9:1–6.** The fifth and last vision is different from the others. God does not show the vision to the prophet: instead, the prophet actually sees the Lord, who orders him to destroy the sanctuary (probably the sanctuary at Bethel is meant) and the whole nation of Israel. It is all very frightening: no one will escape, no matter where they manage to hide themselves.

In keeping with this punishment, the third and last doxology describes God the Creator and Lord of the universe (vv. 5–6). There is nowhere, however distant, however deep (v. 3), however lofty (v. 2), that falls outside his rule.

aquilone usque ad orientem circuibunt, / quaerentes verbum Domini, / et non invenient. / <sup>13</sup>In die illa deficient virgines pulchrae / et adulescentes in siti. / <sup>14</sup>Qui iurant in delicto Samariae / et dicunt: «Vivit Deus tuus, Dan!» / et «Vivit via, Bersabee!», / et cadent et non resurgent ultra. **[9]** <sup>1</sup>Vidi Dominum / stantem super altare, / et dixit: «Percute capitellum, / et commoveantur superliminaria; / frange eos in capite omnes, / et novissimum eorum in gladio interficiam; / non fugiet ex eis fugitivus, / et non salvabitur superstes eis. / <sup>2</sup>Si descenderint usque ad infernum, / inde manus mea educet eos; / et si ascenderint usque in caelum, / inde detraham eos. / <sup>3</sup>Et si absconditi fuerint in vertice Carmeli, / inde quaeram et auferam eos; / et si celaverint se ab oculis meis / in profundo maris, / ibi mandabo serpenti, et mordebit eos; / <sup>4</sup>et si abierint in captivitatem / coram inimicis suis, / ibi mandabo gladio, et occidet

**u.** Or *upon*  **v.** Heb *all of them*

142

and I will set my eyes upon them
   for evil and not for good."

## Doxology

[5]The Lord, GOD of hosts,
  he who touches the earth and it melts,
    and all who dwell in it mourn,
  and all of it rises like the Nile,
    and sinks again, like the Nile of Egypt;
[6]who builds his upper chambers in the heavens,
    and founds his vault upon the earth;
  who calls for the waters of the sea,
    and pours them out upon the surface of the earth—
  the LORD is his name.

Amos 4:13;
5:8; 8:8

Amos 4:13;
5:8

## Punishment awaits sinners

[7]"Are you not like the Ethiopians to me,
  O people of Israel?" says the LORD.
"Did I not bring up Israel from the land of Egypt,
  and the Philistines from Caphtor and the Syrians from Kir?
[8]Behold, the eyes of the Lord GOD are upon the sinful kingdom,

Amos 8:8
Mt 3:9
Rom 2:25

Amos 3:12
Is 4:3

---

**9:7–10.** Two questions in the style of sapiential writing (v. 7), placed on the lips of God, puncture the pride of Israel: they are just another people in the Lord's eyes—like the Ethiopians, the Philistines or the Syrians. Amos' listeners must have found these words quite shocking: what about all of Israel's privileges? Still, this extremely negative vision of Amos' must be read alongside the verses that follow, which say that any nation that sins will be punished but "I will not utterly destroy the house of Jacob" (v. 8). The Lord is the judge of nations and will give each

its deserts (vv. 9–10); he will punish sinners, Israelites included, especially those who think they are safe because they belong to the chosen people; however, he then speaks a message of hope about a restoration of Israel's fortunes (vv. 11–15).

With Christ, the words of v. 7 came true, for he removed all privileges; everyone shares equally in the same, exalted destiny: "There is neither Jew nor Greek, there is neither slave nor free, there is neither male nor female; for you are all one in Christ Jesus" (Gal 3:28; cf. Rom 2:11; 10:12–13).

---

eos, / et ponam oculos meos super eos / in malum et non in bonum». / [5]Et Dominus, Deus exercituum, / qui tangit terram, et tabescet. / Et lugebunt omnes habitantes in ea; / et ascendet sicut fluvius ea omnis / et decrescet sicut flumen Aegypti. / [6]Qui aedificat in caelo ascensus suos / et cameram suam super terram fundat, / qui vocat aquas maris / et effundit eas super faciem terrae; / Dominus nomen eius. / [7]«Numquid non ut filii Aethiopum / vos estis mihi, filii Israel?, / ait Dominus. / Numquid non Israel ascendere feci / de terra Aegypti / et Philisthim de Caphtor / et Syros de Cir? / [8]Ecce oculi Domini Dei

Jer 30:11
Obad 17

and I will destroy it from the surface of the ground;
except that I will not utterly destroy the house of Jacob,"
    says the LORD.

⁹"For lo, I will command,
    and shake the house of Israel among all the nations
  as one shakes with a sieve,
    but no pebble shall fall upon the earth.

Is 28:15
Jer 5:12

¹⁰All the sinners of my people shall die by the sword,
    who say, 'Evil shall not overtake or meet us.'

## 4. CONCLUSION: MESSIANIC RESTORATION

Is 2:11
*Acts 15:16–17*

¹¹"In that day I will raise up
    the booth of David that is fallen
  and repair its breaches,

---

**9:11–15.** This oracle of benediction contrasts with the recriminations that have been the main feature of the book. It begins by referring to "that day", the day of the Lord, but it focuses on its positive side—the salvation of the righteous. The oracle could be a later addition, for what it says implies that the kingdom of Judah and the city of Jerusalem have collapsed—the "fallen booth" of David, which the Lord promises to restore (v. 11) in the sight of "Edom and all the nations" (v. 12). The features of the restored Israel are: the fruitfulness of the land (vv. 13–14), the return of those sent into exile (v. 14), and the promise that they shall never again be uprooted (v. 15).

Although the oracle announces an era of well-being, one that is in some way definitive, there is no mention here of a messiah as such. However, the apostles read this passage as an announcement of the universal scope of salvation. This is what St James says at the council of Jerusalem: "After they finished speaking, James replied, 'Brethren, listen to me. Symeon has related how God first visited the Gentiles, to take out of them a people for his name. And with this the words of the prophets agree, as it is written, "After this I will return, and I will rebuild the dwelling of David, which has fallen; I will rebuild its ruins, and I will set it up, that the rest of men may seek the Lord, and all the Gentiles who are called by my name, says the Lord, who has made these things known from of old." Therefore my judgment is that

/ super regnum peccans, / et conteram illud / a facie terrae; / verumtamen conterens non conteram / domum Iacob, / dicit Dominus. / ⁹Ecce enim mandabo ego / et concutiam in omnibus gentibus domum Israel, / sicut concutitur triticum in cribro, / et non cadet lapillus super terram. / ¹⁰In gladio morientur omnes peccatores populi mei, / qui dicunt: "Non appropinquabit et non veniet / super nos malum". / ¹¹In die illa suscitabo / tabernaculum David, quod cecidit, / et reaedificabo rupturas eius; / et ea, quae

and raise up its ruins,
and rebuild it as in the days of old;
<sup>12</sup>that they may possess the remnant of Edom
and all the nations who are called by my name,"
says the LORD who does this.

Gen 22:17
Num 24:18

<sup>13</sup>"Behold, the days are coming," says the LORD,
"when the ploughman shall overtake the reaper
and the treader of grapes him who sows the seed;
the mountains shall drip sweet wine,
and all the hills shall flow with it.

Lev 26:5
Amos 5:11

<sup>14</sup>I will restore the fortunes of my people Israel,
and they shall rebuild the ruined cities and inhabit them;
they shall plant vineyards and drink their wine,
and they shall make gardens and eat their fruit.
<sup>15</sup>I will plant them upon their land,
and they shall never again be plucked up
out of the land which I have given them," says the LORD
your God.

Is 61:4;
65:21–22
Jer 30:3;
31:4–5
Ezek
36:10,33–36
Hos 14:8
Joel 4:18
Zech 8:7

---

we should not trouble those of the Gentiles who turn to God [...]'" (Acts 15:13–19). In James' remarks, the Fathers found continuity between the New Testament and the promises contained in the Old: "It is clear that they do not proclaim [the existence of] another Father; rather, they announce the New Covenant of freedom to those who return to their belief in God through the power of the Holy Spirit" (St Irenaeus, *Adversus haereses*, 3, 12, 14).

corruerant, instaurabo / et reaedificabo illud sicut diebus antiquis, / <sup>12</sup>ut possideant / reliquias Edom / et omnes nationes, / super quas invocatum est nomen meum, / dicit Dominus, qui faciet haec. / <sup>13</sup>Ecce dies veniunt, / dicit Dominus, / et comprehendet arator messorem, / et calcator uvae mittentem semen; et stillabunt montes mustum, / et omnes colles liquefient. / <sup>14</sup>Et convertam captivitatem populi mei Israel; / et aedificabunt civitates vastatas et inhabitabunt / et plantabunt vineas et bibent vinum earum / et facient hortos et comedent fructus eorum. / <sup>15</sup>Et plantabo eos super humum suam, / et non evellentur ultra / de terra sua, quam dedi eis», / dicit Dominus Deus tuus.

# OBADIAH

# Introduction

The book of Obadiah, with only 21 verses, is the shortest book of the Old Testament. It comes after Amos in the collection of the minor prophets, and before Jonah. A (late) Jewish tradition identifies Obadiah with the man who was in charge of the palace of King Ahab of Israel (1 Kings 18:3–16); but there is no historical basis for this identification. The traditional form of the name in Latin is Abdias, the Hebrew being '*Obad-yah*, "servant or worshipper of the Lord". Scholars wonder whether the attribution of the text to a prophet is not just a pious invention to bring to twelve the number of minor prophets. No one can say for certain. But there is no doubt about the book's being among the minor prophets in the Jewish canon of Scripture, and it was included without question in the Christian canon.

## 1. STRUCTURE AND CONTENT

From ancient times this has always been seen as a difficult book to interpret.[1] Interpreters dispute both its unity and its literary form. As regards its structure, we can say that there are three parts to it:

1. ORACLE AGAINST EDOM (vv. 5–7), giving God's judgment against that nation (vv. 1–4) and announcing its ruin (vv. 5–7).

2. CHARGES LAID AGAINST EDOM (vv. 8–14). Edom's fault is to have gloated over the fate of Judah and taken advantage of it. The penalty will be Edom's obliteration.

3. THE DAY OF THE LORD (vv. 15–21). An announcement of divine judgment on all nations (vv. 15–16), victory for the chosen people (vv. 17–18), and the definitive restoration of Israel, the kingdom of the Lord (vv. 19–21).

Not only is the book very short: its focus is very narrow and it needs to be read in the context of the other eleven minor prophets. Obadiah deals with only three subjects—a) Edom, a country that symbolizes nations hostile to the

---

1. For example, St Jerome had this to say: "This prophet is a minor prophet because of the small number of verses he has written; he cannot be called 'minor' in the number of ideas he raises. The same applies here as applies in the case of the three books of Solomon: as short as the *Song of Songs* is, it is exceptionally difficult to interpret" (*Commentarii in Abdiam*, 1)

chosen people, will be punished; b) the day of the Lord is a time of divine judgment, when the remnant of Jacob will be rehabilitated after being so grievously persecuted by the nations; c) at the End, the kingdom of God will be established on Mount Zion.

## 2. COMPOSITION AND HISTORICAL BACKGROUND

Obadiah contains no specific references to historical events. But its prophecy against Edom seems to refer to something that happened in the past—treachery by the Edomites towards the Hebrews (their distant kinsmen) during the Babylonian campaign against Jerusalem and in its aftermath (587 BC). We know that after the fall of Jerusalem, the Edomites, descendants of Esau, the twin brother of Jacob (cf. Gen 32:4), took advantage of "their brothers" to plunder and abuse them and take over southern and eastern Judah, where they stayed until at least the early years of the Persian era.

The dating of the book is complicated by the fact that is so fragmentary. It is possible that to the oracle against Edom were added later some verses contained in the second and third parts of the book (vv. 15a and 16–21). The book seems to be built around an oracle from the time of the return from exile, towards the end of the sixth century BC, which was later touched upon and filled out with other prophetical pieces, some of which could date from as late as the start of the fourth century. Hence the difficulty of establishing the dates of the earliest and latest parts of the book. A large part of the text parallels or corresponds to passages in other prophetical books (particularly Jeremiah 49) and in the Psalms.

Except for the last three verses and v. 15, the Hebrew text of Obadiah seems to be well-conserved. There are no significant variants between it and the early Greek and Latin versions.

## 3. MESSAGE

Obadiah comes down very severely on Edom for its behaviour during the time of Judah's misfortune. Edom is a symbol of those nations that oppressed the chosen people. The latter can be sure that God will set things right; this will happen at the End, on the "day of the Lord", when the wicked will be punished and the Kingdom of God will be restored (a prospect completely at odds with the political and social circumstances of Judah, a people without autonomy at the time when this book was composed). Like all the prophetical books, Obadiah exhorts people to trust in the power and justice of God, and not in the precarious strength of men. Given the brevity of the book, it is not surprising that it does not contain material on other important themes associated with the prophets.

## 4. THE BOOK OF OBADIAH IN THE LIGHT OF
## THE NEW TESTAMENT

The only passage of Obadiah that is echoed in the New Testament is the last phrase in the book: "the kingdom shall be the Lord's" (Obad 21): cf. Revelation 11:15 ("The Kingdom of the world has become the kingdom of Our Lord and of his Christ"). The liturgy of the Western Church has made little use of the book. Eastern and Western Fathers and writers have commented on it only in the context of the minor prophets as a whole; they see Edom as a symbol of the enemies of the people of God, and read the book's prophetical threats as expressing God's justified anger towards the hardened sinner. St Augustine brings the open spirit of the Gospel to bear on Obadiah and goes further than that: for him, Esau, the Edomites, stand for the Gentiles in need of salvation; the preaching of the Gospel has turned them from enemies into friends.[2] This must surely be the way that Christians should read the book of Obadiah—with openness of spirit to all peoples and all religions.

**2.** Cf. *De civitate Dei*, 18, 31.

## Title
[1]The vision of Obadiah.

**1–7.** The first part of the book consists of three short sections—the title (v. 1a), God's decree against Edom on account of its pride (vv. 1b–4), and a depiction of the fall of the Edomites (vv. 5–7).

The title mentions a vision (*hazōn*), a term that is used for a prophetical vision that includes hearing the words of God (cf. Is 1:1; Nah 1:1). Therefore, this sort of "vision" is broadly speaking a prophetical message. St Jerome explains it as follows: "If the words that were said, and the shapes those words formed in the mind's eye as they were heard, were added after the word 'vision' in the title, it is clear why the prophet, who was known as a seer in those days, would refer to his experience as a 'vision'" (*Commentarii in Abdiam*, 1).

The sentence against Edom follows (vv. 1b–4). The words of the oracle are almost exactly the same as those in Jeremiah 49:14–16, though here they are more vividly expressed. The oracle consists of two parts—the Lord's message to the nations (v. 1b), which will find fulfilment later (vv. 5–7), and what is said to Edom (vv. 2–4). In the oracle, the prophet plays with words and ideas to give his message more effect. The play on words is the phrase "you who live in the clefts of the rock" (v. 3; see note **a**), which seems to be in reference to Sela, or Petra, the capital of Edom. The Edomites think that they are important, but in fact they are insignificant (v. 2). They think they are safe because they live high up, in rocky

fortresses (v. 3) and can see what is happening down below to others (Judah, presumably: cf. v. 11) and ignore it or not be affected by it (v. 4). But they are wrong; they fail to see that only the Lord is great and he is the only one that truly lives on high. Compared with him, everything else is small, low, impermanent. The Edomites' pride has led them astray (v. 3). The oracle carries a message for anyone who fails to see that he has a duty to address the needs of others: "You cast down the proud, and undo the ambitions of whole nations; you raise the lowly, and humble the arrogant. You give riches and cause poverty; you bring death and give life. You are the one who does good for all souls, you are the God of all bodies; you can search into the deepest depths and see all the works of men; you are a help to those in danger, the saviour of those who have despaired, the creator and protector of every heart. [...] We beseech you, Lord, to be our help and protection: save the oppressed, console the lowly, lift up those who have fallen, show your goodness to all those in need, restore the sick to health, grant the grace of conversion to those who have wandered from your people, feed the hungry, straighten those who are bent over, strengthen the weak" (St Clement of Rome, *Ad Corinthios*, 59, 3–4).

Verses 5–7 (cf. Jer 49:9–10) paint the scene of the fall of Esau (= Edom). The prophet uses vivid images to show that the attack will come from an

[1]Visio Abdiae. Haec dicit Dominus Deus ad Edom. / Auditum audivimus a Domino, / et legatus ad

# 1. ORACLE AGAINST EDOM

## Divine judgment pronounced on Edom

Thus says the Lord GOD concerning Edom:

We have heard tidings from the LORD,

and a messenger has been sent among the nations:

"Rise up! let us rise against her for battle!"

[2]Behold, I will make you small among the nations,

you shall be utterly despised.

[3]The pride of your heart has deceived you,

you who live in the clefts of the rock,[a]

whose dwelling is high,

who say in your heart,

"Who will bring me down to the ground?"

[4]Though you soar aloft like the eagle,

though your nest is set among the stars,

thence I will bring you down, says the LORD.

Num 20:23
Jer 49:14–16
Ezek 25:12; 35:2
Joel 4:19

Jer 49:15–16

Is 14:13

Hab 2:9

## The ruin of Edom foretold

[5]If thieves came to you,

if plunderers by night—

how you have been destroyed!—

would they not steal only enough for themselves?

If grape gatherers came to you,

would they not leave gleanings?

[6]How Esau has been pillaged,

his treasures sought out!

[7]All your allies have deceived you,

they have driven you to the border;

Jer 49:9

Jer 49:10

Jer 38:22; 49:7
Ps 41:10

---

unlikely quarter (old allies who turn against them because they say that there is no wisdom left in Edom) and at a time when it is least expected, like thieves in the night: v. 5. Finally, the prophet warns that Edom's defeat will be total (v. 6): not even gleanings will be left, that is, not even those small pieces not worth the bother of picking up (v. 5).

gentes missus est: / «Surgite, et consurgamus / adversus eum in proelium!». / [2]«Ecce parvulum te dabo in gentibus, / contemptibilis tu es valde. / [3]Superbia cordis tui decepit te / habitantem in scissuris petrae, / exaltantem solium suum; / qui dicit in corde suo: / "Quis detrahet me in terram?". / [4]Si exaltatus fueris ut aquila / et si inter sidera posueris nidum tuum, / inde detraham te», / dicit Dominus. / [5]Si fures introissent ad te, / si latrones per noctem, / quomodo periisses! / Nonne furati essent sufficientia sibi? / Si vindemiatores introissent ad te, / nonne racemos tantum reliquissent? / [6]Quomodo scrutati sunt Esau? / Investigaverunt abscondita eius. / [7]Usque ad terminum eiecerunt te, / omnes viri foederis tui

**a.** Or *Sela*

> your confederates have prevailed against you;
> your trusted friends have set a trap under you—
> there is no understanding of it.

## 2. CHARGES LAID AGAINST EDOM

Gen 36:9  $^8$Will I not on that day, says the LORD,
Jer 8:8–9; 49:7     destroy the wise men out of Edom,
          and understanding out of Mount Esau?

---

**8–14.** The Edomites were under the control of Judah for more than 150 years —from the time of David (cf. 2 Sam 8:13–14) to that of Joram (2 Kings 8:20 –22). The enmity between the Edomites and the Israelites was proverbial, and there were blood ties between them, for Edom was descended from Esau, the son of Isaac (cf. Gen 25:19–34); oracles against Edom are to be found throughout the prophetical books (cf. Is 34:1–17; Ezek 25:12–14; Amos 1:11–12; etc.). However, what the prophet says here refers to a particular historical moment when the Babylonians conquered Jerusalem, and the Edomites joined forces with them and managed to establish themselves in Judah (cf. Ezek 35:10).

There are two parts to the oracle: the first announces the punishment that will befall Edom (vv. 8–10), and the second lists what Edom has done wrong (vv. 11–14). The two parts are linked by the reference to "the day": on the day of the Lord (v. 8) Edom will be punished because on the day of Judah's misfortune (vv. 11–14) Edom failed to come to her aid.

The first part (vv. 8–10) ridicules the wisdom of the Edomites (they have a reputation for wisdom in the Bible: cf. Jer 49:7; Bar 3:22–23; Job 2:11) and their valour, too. (Teman was a warrior chief, a nephew of Esau: Gen 36:15.) Their shrewdness and cleverness, says the prophet, led them to join forces with Nebuchadnezzar against Israel; they used their strength to plunder their brothers (the people of Judah). But the Lord will not ignore forever the misfortunes of his people; therefore, Edom can expect shame as a reward for its opportunism, and it will suffer death for the violence it has done (v. 10).

The second part (vv. 11–14) is a catalogue of errors, a list (in ascending order) of the faults committed by the Edomites on the day of Judah's distress: they remained aloof (v. 11); worse still, they gloated over their brothers' misfortune (v. 12) and even took advantage of it to plunder Judah (v. 13); worse still, they betrayed the Jews and caused their deaths (v. 14). There seems to be a progression in the crimes of which Edom is accused. First they kept their distance, then they rejoiced at Judah's distresss, and eventually they plundered her. Thus, the passage is a lesson about the importance that should be given to

deceperunt te, / invaluerunt adversum te viri pacis tuae; / qui comedunt tecum, ponent insidias subter te. / Non est prudentia in eo. / $^8$«Numquid non in die illa, / dicit Dominus, / perdam sapientes de Edom

154

[9]And your mighty men shall be dismayed, O Teman,
  so that every man from Mount Esau will be cut off by
    slaughter.

Jer 49:22
Bar 3:22–23

[10]For the violence done to your brother Jacob,
  shame shall cover you,
  and you shall be cut off for ever.

Gen 27:41; Ps 137:7
Ezek 35:5; Joel 4:19
Amos 1:11–12

[11]On the day that you stood aloof,
  on the day that strangers carried off his wealth,
  and foreigners entered his gates
  and cast lots for Jerusalem,
  you were like one of them.

Ps 137:7

[12]But you should not have gloated over the day of your
  brother in the day of his misfortune;
  you should not have rejoiced over the people of Judah
    in the day of their ruin;
  you should not have boasted
    in the day of distress.

[13]You should not have entered the gate of my people
    in the day of his calamity;
  you should not have gloated over his disaster
    in the day of his calamity;
  you should not have looted his goods
    in the day of his calamity.

[14]You should not have stood at the parting of the ways
    to cut off his fugitives;
  you should not have delivered up his survivors
    in the day of distress.

---

small things. Serious sins are preceded by carelessness in apparently trivial matters: "While he is in the flesh, man cannot help but have at least some light sins. But do not despise these sins which we call 'light': if you take them for light when you weigh them, tremble when you count them. A number of light objects makes a great mass; a number of drops fills a river; a number of grains makes a heap. What then is our hope? Above all, confession ..." (*Catechism of the Catholic Church,* 1863).

/ et prudentiam de monte Esau? / [9]Et timebunt fortes tui Theman, / ut intereat omnis vir de monte Esau. / [10]Propter interfectionem / et propter iniquitatem / in fratrem tuum Iacob / operiet te confusio, / et peribis in aeternum. / [11]In die cum stares ex adverso, / quando capiebant alieni exercitum eius, / et extranei ingrediebantur portas eius / et super Ierusalem mittebant sortem, / tu quoque eras quasi unus ex eis». / [12]Et non respicies diem fratris tui, / diem calamitatis eius; / et non laetaberis super filios Iudae / in die perditionis eorum; / et non magnificabis os tuum / in die angustiae. / [13]Neque ingredieris portam populi mei / in die ruinae eorum; / neque respicies et tu malum eius / in die vastitatis illius / et non mittes manum in opes eius / in die vastitatis illius; / [14]neque stabis in exitibus, / ut interficias eos, qui

## 3. THE DAY OF THE LORD

**Divine judgment**

Jer 50:29<br>Ezek 30:3; 35:15<br>Joel 3:4; Hab 2:8

¹⁵For the day of the LORD is near upon all the nations.
As you have done, it shall be done to you,
    your deeds shall return on your own head.

Jer 25:28; 49:12<br>Lam 4:21<br>Nahum 3:11

¹⁶For as you have drunk upon my holy mountain,
    all the nations round about shall drink;
they shall drink, and stagger,[b]
and shall be as though they had not been.

---

**15–21.** The third part of the book announces the "day of the Lord for all the nations" (v. 15). The oracle operates on two levels: vv. 15–16 (cf. vv. 18–19) focus on the fate of the Edomites, and vv. 17–21 look ahead to the restoration of Israel.

The announcement of the punishment of Edom seems to be in line with the law of vengeance/retaliation (vv. 15–16). As in similar passages in the Bible, the spirit of vengeance that imbues the poem needs to be set alongside the fact that the passage shows the justice and power of God, who takes the side of the innocent victim against the oppressor.

The second and third parts of the oracle are more instructive. Here, the prophet touches on a number of things: there will be those who escape and find shelter on Zion (v. 17; cf. Joel 2:32); the house of Jacob (the kingdom of Israel) will be restored (v. 18); Esau will be punished (v. 18); and the chosen people will spread through the promised land and the surrounding territories (vv. 19–21). The place-names in vv. 19–20 vary from one manuscript to another;

some (such as "Sepharad") mean nothing to us. However, the general meaning of the two verses is clear: the Israelites of the north will expand to occupy the areas round about; and those in the south will similarly expand. The oracle is thus building towards v. 21, which envisages a united kingdom of Israel and Judah, with Mount Zion at its centre—the way things were in the times of David and Solomon. St Augustine, who reads Obadiah with the universalist approach of the Gospel, says: "The kingdom will have come when the saved of Mount Zion, that is, those in Judah who believe in Christ, the apostles and disciples, go up to rule Mount Esau. They will rule it by the preaching of the gospel, saving all those who believe, freeing them from the power of darkness and leading them into the kingdom of God. This is expressed clearly in the verse: *the kingdom shall be the Lord's*. Mount Zion stands for Judah, where it was foretold that the future salvation would come (…); Mount Esau is Idumea, and stands for the church of all the Gentiles,

---

fugerint, / et non trades reliquos eius / in die tribulationis. / ¹⁵Quoniam iuxta est dies Domini / super omnes gentes: / sicut fecisti, fiet tibi, / retributio tua convertetur in caput tuum. / ¹⁶Quomodo enim

**b.** Cn: Heb *swallow*

### The remnant that shall escape

<sup>17</sup>But in Mount Zion there shall be those that escape,
 and it shall be holy;
and the house of Jacob shall possess their own possessions.
<sup>18</sup>The house of Jacob shall be a fire,
 and the house of Joseph a flame,
 and the house of Esau stubble;
they shall burn them and consume them,
 and there shall be no survivor to the house of Esau;
for the LORD has spoken.

Joel 2:32; 3:5

Is 10:17
Zech 12:6

### Eschatological restoration of the kingdom of God

<sup>19</sup>Those of the Negeb shall possess Mount Esau,
 and those of the Shephelah the land of the Philistines;
they shall possess the land of Ephraim and the land of Samaria
 and Benjamin shall possess Gilead.
<sup>20</sup>The exiles in Halah<sup>c</sup> who are of the people of Israel
 shall possess<sup>d</sup> Phoenicia as far as Zarephath;
and the exiles of Jerusalem who are in Sepharad
 shall possess the cities of the Negeb.
<sup>21</sup>Saviours shall go up to Mount Zion
 to rule Mount Esau;
 and the kingdom shall be the LORD'S.

Ezek 35:15
Amos 9:12
Zeph 2:5–7

Ps 22:29
Mic 4:7
Rev 11:15;
14:1; 19:6

---

who will be ruled and protected as has already been explained" (*De civitate Dei*, 18, 31). For St Augustine, then, Esau stands for the Gentiles in need of salvation: the preaching of the Gospel turns them from enemies into brothers, which was what they were in the beginning.

If one goes along with the idea that Obadiah was written against the background of the post-exile situation, when Judah was a place of no importance and led a precarious existence, one can understand why the territorial aspirations mentioned at the end of the book should be so modest. The victory chant at the end of the book looks beyond a narrow, earthbound horizon to an End of the history of Israel and of man, when "the kingdom shall be the Lord's".

bibistis super montem sanctum meum, / bibent omnes gentes iugiter; / et bibent et absorbebunt / et erunt quasi non fuerint. / <sup>17</sup>Et in monte Sion erit salvatio, / et erit sanctum; / et possidebit domus Iacob / eos, qui se possederant. / <sup>18</sup>Et erit domus Iacob ignis, / et domus Ioseph flamma, / et domus Esau stipula; / et succendentur in eis, et devorabunt eos, / et non erunt reliquiae domus Esau, / quia Dominus locutus est. / <sup>19</sup>Et hereditabunt austrum, / montem Esau, / et Sephelam Philisthim; / et possidebunt regionem Ephraim / et regionem Samariae, / et Beniamin possidebit Galaad; / <sup>20</sup>et transmigratio prima filiorum Israel / possidebit terram Chananaeorum usque ad Sareptam; / et transmigratio Ierusalem, quae in Sapharad est, / possidebit civitates austri. / <sup>21</sup>Et ascendent salvatores in montem Sion / iudicare montem Esau, / et erit Domino regnum.

**c.** Cn: Heb *this army*  **d.** Cn: Heb *which*

JONAH

# Introduction

The restoration of Israel, which featured at the end of the book of Obadiah, is a theme that is developed in the book of Jonah, the fifth of the minor prophets. What comes across in this book is the idea that God plans to restore his people because they have a mission that encompasses the whole world.

The book of Jonah is noticeably different from the other prophetical books. It is, for one thing, very short (it deals with only two episodes in the prophet's life) and the prophet's preaching recorded in it amounts to just one sentence: "Yet forty days, and Nineveh shall be overthrown" (3:4). In fact the message of the book lies not in the prophet's preaching but in the narrative—the adventures and stories it relates and its account of Jonah's conversations with God. As in other books, like those by Ruth and Job, the historicity (or otherwise) of the story is not particularly important: the lessons implied in the story are what matters.

There are all sorts of nuances in the book. It very subtly blends together a broad-minded catholic outlook and a narrow Israelite mentality. Jonah is not a very edifying prophet; he behaves in ways that the reader finds puzzling. Yet he is the only character in the whole story who knows who the true God is.

The book of Jonah has had considerable resonance in both Jewish and Christian tradition. It had little or no difficulty in being accepted into the canon of Scripture. In the Jewish liturgy it is read out on the feast of Yom-Kippur, the great day of Atonement; and in the Christian liturgy it is used at the start of Lent. Jonah is one of the most widely depicted figures in early Christian art, probably because he is a symbol of the burial and resurrection of Christ (cf. Mt 12:40).

## 1. STRUCTURE AND CONTENT

The story-line is very simple. The Lord tells Jonah to go to preach in Nineveh (1:2), but the prophet disobeys and sets sail for Tarshish, that is, as far as one could go in the opposite direction. But this poses no problem for God. By means of a storm and a huge fish (1:17) he brings about the conversion of Jonah's travelling companions and causes the prophet to be returned to dry land. Then the Lord repeats his command to preach against Nineveh (3:2), and this time Jonah obeys. Quite surprisingly, the people of Nineveh, when they hear Jonah's message, set about doing penance, and God forgives them their sins. This is not what the prophet expected would happen, and he becomes very angry with God (4:1–3). In the conversations between Jonah and God at the end of the book the reader learns why God acted in the way he did.

The book divides into two parts, dealing with Jonah's first and second missions. Each part has a narrative section followed by a more discursive section. The narrative sections are very similar to one another: the first one ends with the conversion of the sailors, the captain at their head; the second, with the conversion of the people of Nineveh, the king at their head. So, the structure could be:

1. GOD GIVES JONAH A MISSION (1:1–2:10). This contains a narrative account of Jonah's disobedience and the sailors' conversion (1:1–16), and then a discourse in the form of Jonah's psalm of thanksgiving from the belly of the great fish (2:1–10).

2. JONAH IN NINEVEH (3:1–4:11). The narrative section here is about Jonah's preaching in Nineveh and the conversion of the Ninevites (3:1–10); this is followed by a discursive section justifying God's mercy (4:1–11).

As was pointed out earlier, the book's teaching lies in the narrative. Therefore, although the structure of the work is perfectly symmetrical, the entire account builds up to the last section, which contains the conversation between the Lord and Jonah, in which God justifies his way of acting, which Jonah could not fathom. If we follow the story, we are probably not too surprised when Jonah refuses to obey God's first command (1:1–3). Nineveh is the epitome of wickedness, and the reader simply presumes that Jonah is not a prophet of the same calibre as Elijah or Jeremiah, who were given equally challenging assignments (cf. 1 Kings 19:1–8; Jer 36), but showed no such cowardice. There is nothing surprising, either, about the subsequent course of events (1:4–17): God is almighty, and he is perfectly capable of commandeering the sea and fish to advance his designs. Moreover, the Lord responds where false gods do not: hence the sailors' conversion. This conversion anticipates, in a way, that of the Ninevites which is recounted in the third chapter (3:5–10). If the book were to end with chapter 3, we would not be surprised. What we would have is a story, somewhat ironic in time and meaning, about the tribulations of a disobedient prophet who does not want to do the will of God but who ends up doing it despite himself and all his efforts.

However, the fourth chapter opens with an unexpected change of direction: Jonah gets annoyed with the Lord, for he never expected the people of Nineveh to have a change of heart, and certainly never believed that God would forgive them. We are led to understand at this point that Jonah's first disobedience was not due to cowardice, but to his suspicion that God, being clement and merciful, would end up pardoning the Ninevites, thereby causing Jonah's oracle to fail (cf. Jn 3:4). Then comes the conversation between God and Jonah, but the prophet will not listen to reason. In fact, God's line of argument seems to be meant more for the reader than for Jonah himself. We readers should be the ones who answer the question put by God at the very end of the book: "And should I not pity Nineveh, that great city, in which there are more than a hundred and twenty thousand persons who do not know their right hand from their left, and also much cattle?" (4:11). Each of us should realize what Jonah (and probably any other Israelite in the period when the book was written) did not realize—that God is gentle and compassionate towards all, and if many of the oracles against the nations uttered by the prophets were not in fact fulfilled, it was because the people concerned did mend their ways. The story of Jonah bears out what is said in one of Jeremiah's oracles: "If at any time I declare concerning a nation or a kingdom, that I will pluck up and break down and destroy it, and if that nation, concerning which I have spoken, turns from its evil, I will repent of the evil that I intended to do to it" (Jer 18:7–8).

## 2. COMPOSITION AND HISTORICAL BACKGROUND

From what we have seen, this book does not have the same historical features to be found in most of the prophetical books. It is true that the prophet's name, "Jonah the son of Amittai", is exactly the same as that of a prophet of the Northern kingdom in the time of Jeroboam II (cf. 2 Kings 14:25–27), but there the coincidence stops. The Jonah of the book of Kings was an old-style prophet who preached God's mercy on Israel and the restoration of the nation's borders; the prophet of this book is a man disobedient towards God, cowed by the prospect of danger, entrenched in his views, and narrow-minded. In fact, in the story, with the exception of Jonah, everyone involved is quite pleasant— the sailors, the Ninevites, even the fish ... They are closer to caricatures or idealizations than they are to real people. Other things in the book are standard motifs: in prophetical tradition, Nineveh is the classic example, the symbol, of the corrupt city (cf. Nah 3:1–4), and Tarshish stands for the end of the earth (Is 23:6; 66:19). The book contains no verifiable information about places or dates, and it is perfectly happy to exaggerate and say things that really are not true—for example, that it took three days to cross the city of Nineveh (3:3), or the whole story about the fish (1:17–2:10), or the plant that suddenly grows over Jonah and then dies overnight (4:6–8). For these and other reasons, this should not be read as a book about real events. It is true that its message—a call to conversion—is in line with that of the other prophetical books (which is why the book was long regarded as historical, as they are); but the literary genre of Jonah is different: it is a wisdom narrative in the style of Judith, Job or Ruth. One probable reason why Jonah was at one time considered to be historical is that Jesus refers to the sign of Jonah (cf. Mt 12:39–41; Lk 11:29–32), though he was speaking in a general sense; even many early commentators (St Gregory Nazianzen, St Jerome, Theophylact, etc.) expressed serious doubts about the book's historicity.

So, if the Jonah of this book and the Jonah of 2 Kings share their name on the basis of literary considerations rather than historical fact, there is no reason to date the book to the time of Jeroboam II (eighth century BC). Taking account of the fact that the narrator has a good Hebrew style and uses Aramaic expressions or ones that do not appear in earlier texts (God of heaven, 1:9; Word of the Lord, 3:3; nobles, in RSV, 3:7 etc.) it would seem to make more sense to date the book to after the exile, around the fifth or fourth century BC. That date would also be consistent with the message of the book: it was a time when, against the narrowness of some Jews (to be seen in many passages of the books of Ezra and Joel), there were those, such as the author of this book, or the author of Ruth, who liked to show that salvation was possible for many upright pagans because of their probity and God's magnanimity.


## 3. MESSAGE

Even though this is a very short book and takes the straightforward form of a narrative, it carries a more complex message than might at first appear; its teaching is based on the idea of "God's dominion" over all nations. Just as he can punish any nation (not only Israel), so he can have compassion on any nation and forgive its sins. We are only a step away from the catholicity of salvation that is taught in the New Testament (cf. Rom 9:6–8, 29–30).

At least three things follow from this message, and they, too, are to be found in the book. Firstly, the narrative is an explanation as to why some prophetical oracles against the nations never came true: because those nations did penance. This is what happened to Jonah: his oracle ("Yet forty days ...") came to nothing because the Ninevites were converted and because God is kind and merciful. Therefore, when God threatens, he does so, not out of wrath, but in order to teach people a lesson. In this sense, the book is reminiscent of many passages in Jeremiah. Secondly, the narrative (like many passages in the third part of the book of Isaiah) teaches that God's activity, his blessing, extends to all peoples; this was something that not all Jews yet realized, because they were inward-looking and forgetful of their mission to be the Lord's witnesses to the world at large. The depiction of Jonah in the book pokes fun at such people; they are so attached to their views that they refuse to listen to God. Finally, like most of the prophetical books, the book of Jonah is a call to conversion and penance. It preaches a theology of forgiveness, a forgiveness that is conditional on a change of heart.

## 4. THE BOOK OF JONAH IN THE LIGHT OF THE NEW TESTAMENT

In the words of Jesus' recorded in the Gospels, we find Jonah being explicitly referred to as a figure of Christ, in two different ways—as a sign or symbol of penance and as a sign of Christ's burial and resurrection. At one point, when trying to catch him out, the Pharisees ask Jesus for a sign and he replies by saying, "An evil and adulterous generation seeks for a sign; but no sign shall be given to it except the sign of the prophet Jonah. For as Jonah was three days and three nights in the belly of a whale, so will the Son of man be three days and three nights in the heart of the earth. The men of Nineveh will arise at the judgment with this generation and condemn it; for they repented at the preaching of Jonah, and behold, something greater than Jonah is here" (Mt 12:39–41; cf. Lk 11:29–32).

There are echoes of the message of the book of Jonah in many passages of the New Testament. Scholars have pointed to the similarity between this book and the parable of the prodigal son, since both lay stress on the mercy of God, the conversion of those who have strayed, and the incomprehension shown by someone who took pride in his own election as if it were a privilege that could never be available to others.

# 1. GOD GIVES JONAH A MISSION*

**The prophet is charged with a mission and takes flight**

Mt 12:39
2 Kings 19:36
Nahum 3:1–4
1 ¹Now the word of the LORD came to Jonah the son of Amittai, saying, ²"Arise, go to Nineveh, that great city, and cry against

---

***1:1–2:10.** The first part of the book acts as an introduction to the second, which is where the main message is developed. The first two chapters contain the main storyline and introduce the main characters. As regards the story, they show that when God proposes to do something it will inevitably be done: Jonah does not want to carry out God's command, but he does so despite himself (he is as stubborn and awkward at the end—cf. 3:1–2—as he was at the start—cf. 1:1–2); in addition, some sailors learn to invoke the Lord, the only God.

But the main function of these chapters is to introduce the characters of the story—God, the pagans and Jonah. The Lord God of Israel, as Jonah well knows, is "the God of heaven, who made the sea and dry land" (1:9) and he is also the Just One who never accuses an innocent person, and who acts as he pleases (1:14). His dominion over the animal (1:17; 2:10) and inanimate (1:4, 15) world and over the destinies of men (1:7) goes to show that he has this power.

The sailors, who are pagans, are religious men and well-disposed towards others (cf. the note on 1:4–16).

Jonah is the character around whom the story is built. At first he does not make a very good impression—certainly not, if you focus on his disobedience to

the Lord (1:3). However, the text does have positive things to say about the prophet: Jonah does not hesitate to say that he worships the Lord, the God of heaven and earth, and he is ready to prove his faith by deeds (1:9, 12). He is also a devout person: when he is in the belly of the fish, he prays to the Lord (2:1) in the style of a grateful Israelite (2:1–9). Even so, the sacred writer regards Jonah as an inconsistent man: one moment (1:9) he is saying that God is Lord of sea and earth, and yet he tries to hide from him; and later on, he will acknowledge God to be merciful (4:2), and yet ask him to punish the Ninevites rather than have mercy on them.

There is also another feature that defines Jonah. Despite his disobedience to God's command, Jonah has something that the pagan sailors do not have: he knows the true God and therefore only he knows how to resolve the situation when they are plunged into danger (1:12, 15). If we bear in mind that the name Jonah means "dove" (a name given elsewhere in the Bible to Israel: cf. Hos 7:11; 11:11; etc.), we could say that, if the sailors symbolize pagans in general, Jonah in some way represents Israel. In this sense the book of Jonah is about the role of Israel in the world. In this connexion St Jerome says: "The twelve minor prophets, gathered together in a single volume,

---

[1] ¹Et factum est verbum Domini ad Ionam filium Amathi dicens: ²«Surge et vade in Nineven

it; for their wickedness has come up before me." ³But Jonah rose to flee to Tarshish from the presence of the LORD. He went down to Joppa and found a ship going to Tarshish; so he paid the fare, and went on board, to go with them to Tarshish, away from the presence of the LORD.

Gen 4:13,16
Josh 19:46
1 Kings 10:22
Is 23:6; 66:19

## The storm

⁴But the LORD hurled a great wind upon the sea, and there was a mighty tempest on the sea, so that the ship threatened to break up.

Ps 107:23–30
Mt 8:24
Mk 4:37

---

foretell more and greater ideas and events than can be gleaned from a literal interpretation [...]. Jonah, the most beautiful dove, prefigures the passion of the Lord; he calls the world to conversion and, in his mission to Nineveh, proclaims salvation to the Gentiles" (*Epistulae*, 53).

**1:1–3.** The book begins with the failed attempt to send Jonah on a mission. The place-names and the whole scene are less real than symbolic: Jonah is sent to Nineveh (a most wicked city: cf. v. 2—its reputation in biblical tradition: cf. Nah 3:1–4), but he goes off in the very opposite direction, to Tarshish. This could mean Tartessos, a Phoenician colony in southern Spain, but it could also mean some distant place in the west (cf. the note on Is 23:1–18). If Nineveh is to the east of Jerusalem, Tarshish is to the west, but the main thing about it is that it is "[away] from the presence of the Lord" (v. 3).

Jonah disobeys the Lord and he does so blatantly. However, the sacred writer

is more subtle: he describes Jonah's actions in such a way that they come across as the very opposite of those of Jeremiah, the prophet of the nations (cf. Jer 1:4ff); indeed, Jonah acts more in the style of Cain: like Cain, Jonah flees "from the presence of the Lord" (v. 3; cf. Gen 4:13, 16) and like him he gets very annoyed with God (cf. 4:1–4; Gen 4:4–7), although in the end God protects them both (cf. 2:1–2; Gen 4:15): "The flight of the prophet can be read as a general metaphor for the way that man runs away from the presence of God and immerses himself in the things of this world when he has broken His commandments; but the storms of misfortune and the doom of shipwreck prompt him to remember God's presence and to journey back to the One from whom he sought to flee" (St Jerome, *Commentarii in Ionam*, 1, 4).

**1:4–16.** The story of Jonah's adventure at sea is designed to show two things— that the Lord can also be the God of the pagans; and that even people who do

civitatem grandem et praedica in ea, quia ascendit malitia eius coram me». ³Et surrexit Ionas, ut fugeret in Tharsis a facie Domini; et descendit Ioppen et invenit navem euntem in Tharsis et dedit naulum eius et descendit in eam, ut iret cum eis in Tharsis a facie Domini. ⁴Dominus autem misit ventum magnum in mare, et facta est tempestas magna in mari, et navis periclitabatur conteri. ⁵Et timuerunt nautae et clamaverunt unusquisque ad deum suum et miserunt vasa, quae erant in navi, in mare, ut alleviaretur ab eis. Ionas autem descenderat ad interiora navis et, cum recubuisset, dormiebat sopore gravi. ⁶Et

Ps 107:28
Acts 27:18,19 ⁵Then the mariners were afraid, and each cried to his god; and they threw the wares that were in the ship into the sea, to lighten it for them. But Jonah had gone down into the inner part of the ship and had lain down, and was fast asleep. ⁶So the captain came and said to him, "What do you mean, you sleeper? Arise, call upon your god! Perhaps the god will give a thought to us, that we do not perish."

⁷And they said to one another, "Come, let us cast lots, that we may know on whose account this evil has come upon us." So they Josh 7:19 cast lots, and the lot fell upon Jonah. ⁸Then they said to him, "Tell us, on whose account this evil has come upon us? What is your occupation? And whence do you come? What is your country? And of what people are you?" ⁹And he said to them, "I am a Hebrew; and I fear the LORD, the God of heaven, who made the sea and the dry land." ¹⁰Then the men were exceedingly afraid, and said to him, "What is this that you have done!" For the men knew that he was fleeing from the presence of the LORD, because he had told them.

---

not know God can have many virtues. The episode depicts the sailors as religious men: when shipwreck threatens, they do not just lighten the boat's load, but they pray to their gods. This natural religious feeling of theirs is full of imperfections; however, it is the route they take to discover the true God: each invokes his own god (vv. 5, 6) and they cast lots to find out who is the guilty one, the cause of their misfortune (v. 7). In the writings of some pagan authors (Horace and Cicero, for example), we find evidence of this belief that if someone guilty of sin was on a boat he was a risk to the rest of those on board (cf. v. 10). But the sailors were not only men of faith: they were also kind people: when Jonah suggests that they throw him overboard to quell the storm (cf. v. 12), they don't take him up on it; they try to reach the shore by rowing (v. 13). Only as a last resort do they throw Jonah overboard (v. 15), and not before calling on the Lord not to hold it against them (v. 14): "How great is the faith of these sailors! They find themselves in terrible danger, and plead for the life of another: they know that the spiritual death of sin is worse than physical death" (St Jerome, *Commentarii in Ionam*, 1, 14).

---

accessit ad eum gubernator et dixit ei: «Quid? Tu sopore deprimeris? Surge, invoca Deum tuum, si forte recogitet Deus de nobis, et non pereamus». ⁷Et dixit unusquisque ad collegam suum: «Venite, et mittamus sortes, ut sciamus quare hoc malum sit nobis». Et miserunt sortes, et cecidit sors super Ionam. ⁸Et dixerunt ad eum: «Indica nobis cuius causa malum istud sit nobis. Quod est opus tuum, et unde venis? Quae terra tua, et ex quo populo es tu?». ⁹Et dixit ad eos: «Hebraeus ego sum et Dominum, Deum caeli, ego timeo, qui fecit mare et aridam» ¹⁰Et timuerunt viri timore magno et dixerunt ad eum: «Quid hoc fecisti?». Cognoverant enim viri quod a facie Domini fugeret, quia indicaverat eis.

¹¹Then they said to him, "What shall we do to you, that the sea may quiet down for us?" For the sea grew more and more tempestuous. ¹²He said to them, "Take me up and throw me into the sea; then the sea will quiet down for you; for I know it is because of me that this great tempest has come upon you." ¹³Nevertheless the men rowed hard to bring the ship back to land, but they could not, for the sea grew more and more tempestuous against them. ¹⁴Therefore they cried to the LORD, "We beseech thee, O LORD, let us not perish for this man's life, and lay not on us innocent blood; for thou, O LORD, hast done as it pleased thee." ¹⁵So they took up Jonah and threw him into the sea; and the sea ceased from its raging. ¹⁶Then the men feared the LORD exceedingly, and they offered a sacrifice to the LORD and made vows.

¹⁷ᵃAnd the LORD appointed a great fish to swallow up Jonah; and Jonah was in the belly of the fish three days and three nights.

*Jn 11:50*

*Deut 21:22*
*Jer 26:15*

*Mt 12:40; 16:4*
*Lk 11:30*

**Jonah in the belly of the fish**

2 ¹Then Jonah prayed to the LORD his God from the belly of the fish, ²saying,

*Ps 120:1; 130:1*
*Lam 3:55;*
*Job 7:9*

---

The result of these adventures is that the sailors are converted to the God of Israel, so, instead of each calling on "his god" (vv. 5, 6), they call on the Lord (vv. 14–16). Also, they end up making vows to the Lord and offering sacrifice to him (v. 16); that is, they do exactly what Jonah promises to do once he is saved (cf. 2:9). It is easy to see where all this is leading to—to a situation where salvation, quite plainly, is open to everyone: all who are upright can attain God's salvation; not only in the temple but even on a ship it is possible to offer sacrifice to the Lord.

**1:17–2:10.** Chapter 1 has shown God's providence at work in all sorts of ways. Now that providence focuses on Jonah, saving him from the sea and bringing him onto dry land. Being swallowed by the big fish (1:17) is not a punishment for Jonah, but a salvation (2:2, 6, 9). In biblical tradition, the sea is depicted as a place of elements hostile to man— things that only God can control (cf.

¹¹Et dixerunt ad eum: «Quid faciemus tibi, ut conticescat mare a nobis?». Mare enim magis ac magis intumescebat. ¹²Et dixit ad eos: «Tollite me et mittite in mare, et cessabit mare a vobis; scio enim ego quoniam propter me tempestas haec grandis super vos». ¹³Et remigabant viri, ut reverterentur ad aridam; et non valebant, quia mare magis intumescebat super eos. ¹⁴Et clamaverunt ad Dominum et dixerunt: «Quaesumus, Domine, ne pereamus in anima viri istius, et ne des super nos sanguinem innocentem; quia tu, Domine, sicut voluisti, fecisti». ¹⁵Et tulerunt Ionam et miserunt in mare; et stetit mare a fervore suo. ¹⁶Et timuerunt viri timore magno Dominum et immolaverunt hostias Domino et voverunt vota. **[2]** ¹Et praeparavit Dominus piscem grandem, ut deglutiret Ionam; et erat Ionas in ventre piscis tribus / diebus et tribus noctibus. / ²Et oravit Ionas ad Dominum Deum suum de ventre piscis / ³et

**a.** Ch 2.1 in Heb

### Jonah's psalm of thanksgiving

"I called to the LORD, out of my distress,
and he answered me;
out of the belly of Sheol I cried,
and thou didst hear my voice.

---

Job 7:12; Ps 104:9; etc.), which is why, on occasions, it is likened to Sheol (v. 2; cf. Job 7:9), the domain of death from which none can return (v. 6). If one bears in mind that sense of the word, Jesus' use of the sign of Jonah (Mt 12:40) to explain his own death and resurrection is much less artificial than might appear at first sight: Sheol, the kingdom of death, cannot hold Christ in its grip for more than three days. Also, the role of water in the Jonah story may explain why the text is used in baptismal liturgy. The Christian is immersed, buried, in the water of Baptism and reborn to a new form of life in Christ: "To enter into perfect life, we must imitate the example of Christ, and not only the examples of meekness, patience and humility that he gave us in life, but also the example of his death [...]. We re-live his death in our lives by being buried with him in baptism. What type of tomb is this, and what good does it do us to enter into death of Christ? A clean break with everything in our past lives is necessary, and this is possible only through the new birth of which the Lord spoke: re-birth, as the word itself suggests, marks the beginning of new life [...]. How can we follow Christ when he descends among the dead? We follow him into the tomb by our baptism. The bodies of those who are baptised are, in a certain sense, buried in the waters of baptism. In a mysterious way, baptism strips the body of its past sins" (St Basil, *De Spiritu Sancto*, 15, 35).

Jonah's prayer in the belly of the fish (vv. 2–9) is a mosaic of passages borrowed (not exactly verbatim) from the Psalms. What we have here is a typical thanksgiving psalm—past afflictions recalled, an account of how the person was rescued from them, a promise to offer sacrifices and to keep one's vows. It may seem a little strange that this prayer is proclaimed here: it would, one might think, fit better after v. 10, when Jonah has been saved. Still, the thrust of the prayer is perfectly compatible with the context. Therefore, Origen comments, "Who can tell what evil in our day is represented by the great beast that swallowed Jonah? [...]. Because he was unfaithful, Jonah woke in the body of the whale; when he repented, he was spat out again. Back on dry land, he obeyed the commandments of the Lord and became [...] the herald of salvation to all Ninevites, including those of today, who live under the threat of death. Rejoicing in the mercy of God, Jonah did not want to see God's justice and punishment carried out on the sinful" (*De oratione*, 13, 4).

**b.** Heb *qiqayon*, probably *the castor oil plant*

³For thou didst cast me into the deep,
    into the heart of the seas,
    and the flood was round about me;
all thy waves and thy billows
    passed over me.
⁴Then I said, 'I am cast out
    from thy presence;
how shall I again look
    upon thy holy temple?'
⁵The waters closed in over me,
    the deep was round about me;
weeds were wrapped about my head
⁶at the roots of the mountains.
I went down to the land
    whose bars closed upon me for ever;
yet thou didst bring up my life from the Pit,
    O Lᴏʀᴅ my God.
⁷When my soul fainted within me,
    I remembered the Lᴏʀᴅ;
and my prayer came to thee,
    into thy holy temple.
⁸Those who pay regard to vain idols
    forsake their true loyalty.
⁹But I with the voice of thanksgiving
    will sacrifice to thee;
what I have vowed I will pay.
    Deliverance belongs to the Lᴏʀᴅ!"
¹⁰And the Lᴏʀᴅ spoke to the fish, and it vomited out Jonah upon the dry land.

Job 7:12
Ps 42:8; 104:6

Ps 5:8; 31:23

Ps 69:3

Ps 16:10; 30:4

Ps 18:7; 107:5

Ps 3:9; 22:26;
50:14,23;
116:17,18

---

dixit: «Clamavi de tribulatione mea ad Dominum, / et respondit mihi; / de ventre inferi clamavi, / et exaudisti vocem meam. / ⁴Et proiecisti me in profundum in corde maris, / et flumen circumdedit me; / omnes gurgites tui et fluctus tui / super me transierunt. / ⁵Et ego dixi: "Abiectus sum / a conspectu oculorum tuorum; / verumtamen rursus videbo / templum sanctum tuum". / ⁶Circumdederunt me aquae usque ad guttur, / abyssus vallavit me, / iuncus alligatus est capiti meo. / ⁷Ad extrema montium descendi, / terrae vectes concluserunt me in aeternum, / sed eduxisti de fovea vitam meam, / Domine Deus meus. / ⁸Cum angustiaretur in me anima mea, / Domini recordatus sum, / et venit ad te oratio mea, / ad templum sanctum tuum. / ⁹Qui colunt idola vana, / pietatem suam derelinquunt; / ¹⁰ego autem in voce laudis / immolabo tibi, / quaecumque vovi, reddam; / salus Domini est». ¹¹Et dixit Dominus pisci, et evomuit Ionam in aridam.

## 2. JONAH IN NINEVEH*

**Jonah preaches repentance in Nineveh**

3 ¹Then the word of the LORD came to Jonah the second time, saying, ²"Arise, go to Nineveh, that great city, and proclaim to it the message that I tell you." ³So Jonah arose and went to Nineveh, according to the word of the LORD. Now Nineveh was an exceedingly great city, three days' journey in breadth. ⁴Jonah began to go into the city, going a day's journey. And he cried, "Yet forty days, and Nineveh shall be overthrown!"

Ezek 26:16
Mt 11:21;
12:41; Lk
10:13; 11:30:32 **The people of Nineveh do penance**

⁵And the people of Nineveh believed God; they proclaimed a fast, and put on sackcloth, from the greatest of them to the least of them.

---

*3:1–4:11. The second part of the book has a similar structure to the first—God and Jonah (3:1–3; cf. 1:1–3); Jonah and Gentiles (3:4–10; cf. 1:4–16); Jonah and God (4:1–11; cf. 1:17–2:10). However, the reader is now psychologically prepared for what will happen: Jonah's preaching will produce the desired result and the Ninevites will be converted. So, the story is geared to the last chapter which poses and solves the question that chapter 3 provokes. The episode described in this second part is therefore a practical illustration of the scope of God's mercy. It was used as such in the debate with the Gnostics who argued that there was a difference between the good God (the God revealed in the New Testament) and the God revealed in the Old Testament: "See how the stress is laid on the greatest name and quality of God, his Mercy; that is, God is patient with evildoers, and rich in mercy and

compassion for those who recognize their faults and repent them, as the Ninevites did. If such a Being as he is so good, you [...] have to admit that he can do no evil for, as Marcion himself once said, a good tree cannot bear bad fruit" (Tertullian, *Adversus Marcionem*, 2, 24).

3:1–4. God renews his command to Jonah. And this time Jonah obeys. Maybe the vows he promised to fulfil in 2:9 had to do with this—going to preach in Nineveh. Anyway, the success of his mission is assured, because it depends not on Jonah but on the Lord: it would take three days to cross Nineveh (v. 3), but he has only gone one day in his journey and the people convert (cf. 3:5).

3:5–10. The account of the conversion of the Ninevites looks like a straight copy from other biblical passages, particularly from the prophet Jeremiah:

[3] ¹Et factum est verbum Domini ad Ionam secundo dicens: ²«Surge, vade in Nineven civitatem magnam et praedica in ea praedicationem, quam ego loquor ad te». ³Et surrexit Ionas et abiit in Nineven iuxta verbum Domini. Et Nineve erat civitas magna coram Deo, itinere trium dierum. ⁴Et coepit Ionas introire in civitatem itinere diei unius; et clamavit et dixit: «Adhuc quadraginta dies, et Nineve subvertetur». ⁵Et crediderunt viri Ninevitae in Deo; et praedicaverunt ieiunium et vestiti sunt

⁶Then tidings reached the king of Nineveh, and he arose from his throne, removed his robe, and covered himself with sackcloth, and sat in ashes. ⁷And he made proclamation and published

Is 58:5
Lk 10:13

Ezek 27:30–31

---

Jeremiah is the "prophet to the nations" (Jer 1:5), and Jonah is sent to the archetypal Gentile city. There are many little things in this passage that are reminiscent of Jeremiah: in the book of Jeremiah, Jerusalem is called the "great city", which is what Nineveh is called here (1:2; 3:2; cf. Jer 22:8–9), and both books have similar turns of phrase such as "let every one turn from his evil way", "man and beast", "from the greatest to the least" (3:5, 8; cf. Jer 6:13; 8:10; 36:3, 7), etc. This passage is particularly reminiscent of the call for a fast made by Jeremiah in the time of King Jehoiakim; in Jeremiah 36 we are told how the prophet warned of misfortunes to come and proclaimed a fast for conversion (Jer 36:9), but the king refused to listen. Jonah, too, announces the destruction of Nineveh, but it is the Ninevites themselves who proclaim a general fast, as if God were speaking through them. Their own king establishes what the fast will involve, and he issues a decree that sounds just like something a prophet would have said (vv. 7–9; cf. Joel 2:12–14). Furthermore, the king of the Ninevites seems to be quite familiar with biblical teaching, for he is well aware (cf. Jer 36:3, 9) that displays of penance will not automatically stay God's hand; the king has a genuine change of heart and is ready to submit to God (v. 9), and when God sees that

these people are ready to mend their ways, he revokes his decision to punish them (v. 10). The episode bears out Jeremiah's teaching about repentance (cf. Jer 18:7–8).

The difference between the Ninevites and the Israelites can be seen in the use that Jesus makes of this passage when he compares his Jewish contemporaries with their ancestors: "The men of Nineveh will arise at the judgment with this generation and condemn it; for they repented at the preaching of Jonah, and behold, something greater than Jonah is here" (Mt 12:41). It is not surprising, then, that in Christian tradition, the Ninevites are referred to as a model of repentance: "Let us cast our minds back over the history of men, and see how the Lord, in one generation after another, granted a time of penance to those who desired to be converted to him. Noah preached salvation, and those who listened to him were saved. Jonah told the Ninevites that their city would be destroyed, and they repented of their sins and asked God for forgiveness and were saved by the power of their pleading, even though they were not part of the chosen people" (St Clement of Rome, *Ad Corinthios*, 7, 5–7).

And another text by a great Father of the Eastern Church says: "Do not dwell on how little time you have, but on the love of the Master. The inhabitants of

---

saccis a maiore usque ad minorem. ⁶Et pervenit verbum ad regem Nineve; et surrexit de solio suo et abiecit pallium suum a se et indutus est sacco et sedit in cinere. ⁷Et clamavit et dixit in Nineve decreto regis et principum eius dicens: «Homines et iumenta et boves et pecora non gustent quidquam nec

through Nineveh, "By the decree of the king and his nobles: Let neither man nor beast, herd nor flock, taste anything; let them not feed, or drink water, <sup>8</sup>but let man and beast be covered with sackcloth, and let them cry mightily to God; yea, let every one turn from his evil way and from the violence which is in his hands. <sup>9</sup>Who knows, God may yet repent and turn from his fierce anger, so that we perish not?"

<sup>10</sup>When God saw what they did, how they turned from their evil way, God repented of the evil which he had said he would do to them; and he did not do it.

*Jer 6:13; 8:10; 36:3,7*

*2 Sam 12:22*

*Gen 6:6*
*Jer 26:3*

### Jonah's sense of grievance

*Ex 34:6–7*
*Joel 2:13*
*Jn 1:3*
*Lk 15:28*

**4** <sup>1</sup>But it displeased Jonah exceedingly, and he was angry. <sup>2</sup>And he prayed to the LORD and said, "I pray thee, LORD, is not this

---

Nineveh cooled God's wrath in three days. They did not despair at how little time was left to them; their troubled souls won over the goodness of the Master, and he brought about their salvation" (St John Chrysostom, *De incomprehensibile Dei natura*, 6).

**4:1–11.** The Ninevites repent, and God refrains from pursuing his course of action. The book could end here, if its message were simply that God's salvation extends to the Gentiles as well. However, the dialogue that now takes place between Jonah and the Lord gives an unexpected twist to the story and enriches it from the doctrinal point of view: it shows the full extent of God's mercy; it tells us why some prophetical oracles did not come true, even though they were the utterances of genuine prophets; and it explains, in a definitive way, the reasons behind God's actions.

As in the rest of the book, the message lies in the characters themselves, particularly Jonah. He preached in Nineveh, but all the indications are that he did not expect to have any effect. Indeed, even though he has seen that God has decided to forgive Nineveh, deep down he may feel that that will not last: the Ninevites will go back to their old ways, or God has simply delayed punishing them. So, he takes up a position outside the city "to see what would become of (it)" (v. 5). At first sight, Jonah's anger (vv. 1–4, 8–9) seems almost grotesque; but there is justification for it. To distinguish true from false prophecy, Deuteronomy gave the following criterion: "when a prophet speaks in the name of the Lord, if the word does not come to pass or come true, that is a word which the Lord has not spoken; the prophet has spoken it presumptuously, you need not

---

pascantur et aquam non bibant; <sup>8</sup>et operiantur saccis homines et iumenta et clament ad Deum in fortitudine, et convertatur vir a via sua mala et a violentia, quae est in manibus eorum. <sup>9</sup>Quis scit si convertatur et ignoscat Deus et revertatur a furore irae suae, et non peribimus?». <sup>10</sup>Et vidit Deus opera eorum, quia conversi sunt de via sua mala; et misertus est Deus super malum, quod locutus fuerat ut faceret eis, et non fecit. **[4]** <sup>1</sup>Et afflictus est Ionas afflictione magna et iratus est; <sup>2</sup>et oravit ad

what I said when I was yet in my country? That is why I made haste to flee to Tarshish; for I knew that thou art a gracious God and merciful, slow to anger, and abounding in steadfast love, and repentest of evil. [3]Therefore now, O LORD, take my life from me, I beseech thee, for it is better for me to die than to live." [4]And the LORD said, "Do you do well to be angry?" [5]Then Jonah went out of the city and sat to the east of the city, and made a booth for himself there. He sat under it in the shade, till he should see what would become of the city.

1 Kings 19:4

---

be afraid of him" (Deut 18:22). Therefore, as Jonah sees things, the Lord's decision to punish Nineveh and then his reversal of it amounted to saying that Jonah was not a true prophet.

The question raised here is a complex one and it deserves more than a superficial reply; hence the text's insistence on the mercy of the Lord. When Jonah earlier fled from God, even though he knew him to be the Lord, who created the sea and the dry land (cf. 1:9), he knew that clemency and compassion were essential traits of the Lord (cf. Ex 34:6–7); and he knows the same now (v. 4), but he is unwilling to experience it in real life. Therefore, God uses this "castor-oil plant" to give him a lesson about his mercy—a practical as well as a theoretical lesson. The plant is, in the first place, an additional proof of God's mercy: it makes Jonah comfortable and soothes his anger (v. 6). But then the episode of the plant becomes a kind of parable. If

Jonah pities the plant which relieved his discomfort (v. 10), why should God not take pity on those Ninevites? One could think (as Jonah did) that enough was enough: a show of penance cannot disguise the fact that Nineveh has always been a wicked city (cf. 1:2). And it is at this point that the Lord gives further justification for his desire to forgive. The fact of the matter is that the Ninevites did evil because they knew no better (they did not know their right hand from their left: cf. Eccles 10:2) and there are more than 120,000 of them (literally, twelve times ten thousand), that is, a symbolic number suggesting that the Ninevites are more like the chosen people than Jonah might think.

In this connexion, apropos the number of Ninevites, St John Chrysostom comments: "This great number is mentioned for a particular reason: every prayer, when it is offered in the company of many voices, has enormous power" (*De incomprehensibile Dei natura*, 3).

---

Dominum et dixit: «Obsecro, Domine, numquid non hoc est verbum meum, cum adhuc essem in terra mea? Propter hoc praeoccupavi ut fugerem in Tharsis. Sciebam enim quia tu Deus clemens et misericors es, longanimis et multae miserationis et ignoscens super malitia. [3]Et nunc, Domine, tolle, quaeso, animam meam a me, quia melior est mihi mors quam vita». [4]Et dixit Dominus: «Putasne bene irasceris tu?». [5]Et egressus est Ionas de civitate et sedit contra orientem civitatis et fecit sibimet umbraculum ibi et sedebat subter illud in umbra, donec videret quid accideret in civitate.

⁶And the LORD God appointed a plant,[b] and made it come up over Jonah, that it might be a shade over his head, to save him from his discomfort. So Jonah was exceedingly glad because of the plant.[b] ⁷But when dawn came up the next day, God appointed a worm which attacked the plant,[b] so that it withered. ⁸When the sun rose, God appointed a sultry east wind, and the sun beat upon the head of Jonah so that he was faint; and he asked that he might die, and said, "It is better for me to die than to live."

### God corrects Jonah and justifies his taking pity on Nineveh

⁹But God said to Jonah, "Do you do well to be angry for the plant?"[b] And he said, "I do well to be angry, angry enough to die." ¹⁰And the LORD said, "You pity the plant,[b] for which you did not labour, nor did you make it grow, which came into being in a

Eccles 10:2  night, and perished in a night. ¹¹And should not I pity Nineveh, that great city, in which there are more than a hundred and twenty thousand persons who do not know their right hand from their left, and also much cattle?"

---

⁶Et praeparavit Dominus Deus hederam, et ascendit super Ionam, ut esset umbra super caput eius et protegeret eum ab afflictione sua. Et laetatus est Ionas super hedera laetitia magna. ⁷Et paravit Deus vermem, cum surgeret aurora in crastinum, et percussit hederam, quae exaruit. ⁸Et, cum ortus fuisset sol, praecepit Deus vento orientali calido; et percussit sol super caput Ionae, et elanguit; et petivit animae suae, ut moreretur, et dixit: «Melius est mihi mori quam vivere». ⁹Et dixit Deus ad Ionam: «Putasne bene irasceris tu super hedera?». Et dixit: «Bene irascor ego usque ad mortem». ¹⁰Et dixit Dominus: «Tu doles super hederam, in qua non laborasti neque fecisti, ut cresceret, quae sub una nocte nata est et sub una nocte periit. ¹¹Et ego non parcam Nineve civitati magnae, in qua sunt plus quam centum viginti milia hominum, qui nesciunt quid sit inter dexteram et sinistram suam, et iumenta multa?».

---

**b.** Heb *qiqayon*, probably *the castor oil plant*

# MICAH

# Introduction

The book of Micah comes sixth in the collection of the minor prophets, although the Greek version of the Septuagint puts it third (after Amos and before Joel). The heading of the book says that Micah ministered in the days of Jotham (759–743), Ahaz (743–727) and Hezekiah (729–698), kings of Judah. In other words, he was a contemporary of Isaiah, or at least their lives overlapped for a while. However, there is no great similarity or correspondence between the books of Isaiah and Micah. The sort of imagery that Micah uses is more akin to that of Amos, a man with a rural background, than to that of Isaiah, a prophet from Jerusalem. Still, Micah's preaching was important, and other books (cf. Jer 26:18–19) recall that he succeeded in bringing about a change of heart in king and people. Both for reasons of chronology and the call to conversion that underlies Micah's condemnatory oracles, it is quite appropriate that he should come immediately after Jonah in the canon (Jonah having succeeded in moving the Ninevites to repentance).

## 1. STRUCTURE AND CONTENT

A first reading of Micah shows it to have the classical variety found in other prophetical books—oracles threatening condemnation and others promising deliverance. Thus we find: threats (1:2–2:11); and promises (2:12–13); threats (3:1–12); and more promises (4:1–5:15); threats and reproaches (6:1–7:7), followed by promises and messages of hope (7:8–20). That is how the book is laid out, but some scholars think that 2:12–13 is written in irony, poking fun at the prophecies spoken by false prophets who sought to ingratiate themselves by raising false hopes. Also, the last part of the book (7:8–20) is seen as being more in the genre of "liturgical text", inserted here as a colophon to the book.

There is nothing necessarily artificial about this alternating of reproaches and promises. When one reads the book, one sees that Micah is not a prophet of doom; he is God's spokesman calling the people to conversion. He is utterly convinced that God is faithful, and therefore the message he preaches is always inflected by hope of future salvation.

The book can be said to have the following structure:

1. DIVINE JUDGMENT; SINS CONDEMNED (1:2–3:12). The prophet proclaims the fall of Samaria on account of its sins. He goes on to denounce the

sins of Judah: they are so like those of the Northern kingdom that its fate must be similar.

2. HOPE AND THE RESTORATION OF ZION (4:1–5:15). The sentences in the previous part are now followed by optimistic oracles in which the prophet discerns the future glory of a restored Israel; at its centre is the Messiah who will be born in Bethlehem.

3. FURTHER DIVINE JUDGMENT AND PUNISHMENT OF JERUSALEM (6:1–7:7). More charges are laid here. The prophet denounces religious observance that is not backed up by justice and charity. Corruption is so pervasive that law and order break down.

4. HOPE AND PRAYER FOR THE FUTURE (7:8–20). This part presupposes that Israel has been punished for its sins; it looks forward to a time when God's people will be restored, for the Lord is faithful and he does not go back on his promises.

The book could also be divided into just two parts (chapters 1–5 and 6–7) on the theory that the first part is largely composed of material original to the prophet Micah, with a few later additions, while the second part is more problematic as regards dating, because it contains passages that seem to date from the years after the return from exile in Babylon (537 BC). Still, it must be said that there is considerable unity to the book: the final redactor must be credited with having worked all the various oracles together well; thus the fall of Samaria, caused by that kingdom's sins, is seen as a sign to Jerusalem that it must mend its ways or else it will suffer as a similar fate.

From the point of view of literary genre, the editor has managed to integrate warnings, oracles about future calamity, reproaches in the style of charges in a court case (*rîb*), promises of the salvation and restoration of Zion, and entreaties.

## 2. COMPOSITION AND HISTORICAL BACKGROUND

Micah was born in Moresheth, a small town about 35 km. (22 miles) south-west of Jerusalem, in the Sephalah, the coastal area of Judah. His name *Mî-kâh*, an abbreviation of *Mî-kâ-yâhû* ("Who-is-like-Yahweh"), was not an uncommon one in his time: there was another prophet, Micaiah, the son of Imlah, who lived in the reign of Ahab of Israel (873–852 BC; cf. 1 Kings 22:1–28).

Micah must have begun his prophetical ministry around 727, a few years before the fall of Samaria (cf. 1:5–7), and continued in it until around the year 700. This means that his ministry ran parallel in time with the greater part of Isaiah's (Is 1–39). Both prophets witnessed the same events and suffered in the

# Introduction

same situation. At the time, all the countries of the eastern Mediterranean were under threat from or were invaded by the Assyrian empire. Micah was affected by events in the Northern kingdom of Israel (Samaria) for a number of years prior to its fall to Assyria and then right up to when Sennacherib laid siege to Jerusalem (701); and his oracles concern both the Northern and Southern kingdoms.

However, unlike Isaiah, Micah does not seem to have been personally involved in affairs of state; he seems to have had much less influence than Isaiah did on the social and political life of the kingdoms. Micah's bravery in denouncing social injustice in Israel and Judah is reminiscent of that of Amos. Many passages in his book show almost the same verve and insight of Isaiah.[1] Micah speaks in a direct, forthright way and has a talent for play on words; but taking the book as a whole it must be said that it never reaches the energy and poetic perfection of Isaiah.

When one examines the text carefully, it becomes clear that the process of its formation was complex. The first three chapters are probably original Micah material—except for a few passages involving later editorial additions or refinements such as the title (1:1) or some sapiential reflections (1:13; 3:8). Chapters 4 and 5 would seem to consist substantially of original Micah pieces to which were added, later, passages sapiential in tone (4:5) and earlier oracles applied to the times (4:1–5), which have their parallels in Isaiah (cf. Is 1:20; 2:2–4). The important oracle about the birth of the Messiah in Bethlehem shows every sign of being originally by Micah. The passage 6:1–7:6 must be largely by Micah. The final passage (7:8–20) seems to imply that the fall of Jerusalem has already taken place, and therefore it should be dated to a later period. In other words, the history of the text is quite complicated, though much less so than that of Isaiah. The evidence is that a redactor did a skilful job of shaping some Micah texts into a coherent book which has found its way into Hebrew tradition and the canon of Scripture.

## 3. MESSAGE

Micah is deeply conscious of the sins of the people, of both Israel and Judah; they have led God to distance himself for a while, and to chastise them. Micah's message consists in denouncing sin, preaching repentance, and promising salvation. He is very quick to expose the false sense of security that he finds in the people and their rulers. They say, "Is not the Lord in the midst of us? No evil shall come upon us" (3:11), hoping to be able to combine a life of sin with external religious formalities. They do not see that true religion consists in "doing justice, and living kindness and walking humbly with God"

1. Cf. Mic 1:2–16 and Is 1:2; 26:21; 20:2–4; and Mic 2:1–5 and Is 5:8–9.

(cf. 6:8). Rulers and merchants exploit and steal from those who cannot fend for themselves (3:1–4), and from women and children (2:9). False prophets lead the people astray, telling them what they want to hear (3:5–12). If Samaria fell on account of its sins, Judah will suffer likewise unless it repents (1:2–3:12). The Lord will judge and punish Jerusalem for its many sins (6:1–7:6).

However, although there are denunciations aplenty in Micah, there is also a lot of encouragement. His message of hope is concentrated mainly in the middle of the book (4:1–5:15) when he extols the "mountain of the house of the Lord" (4:1–2) and speaks of the nations flocking to Zion (4:6–8), of a "ruler" who will be born in Bethlehem of Judah (5:2–4), of deliverance from Assyrian oppression (5:5–6) and of salvation for a "remnant of Jacob" (5:7–9). The end of the book is all about blessing (7:8–20).

There are similarities between Micah and other prophetical books—particularly Amos (they both denounce social injustice) and Isaiah, who speaks of a Messiah to be born from the line of David and who, like Micah, is very much aware of divine providence guiding the affairs of all mankind.

## 4. THE BOOK OF MICAH IN THE LIGHT OF THE NEW TESTAMENT

At least two passages from Micah are quoted in the New Testament—Micah 5:1 in Matthew 2:6 (on the birth of the Messiah in Bethlehem), and Micah 7:6 in Matthew 10:35–36 (about man's foes being those of his own household). But quite a number of other passages are referred to more or less directly—as many as fifteen (Mic 7:20 in Lk 1:73; Mic 6:8 in Mt 23:23; etc.), a considerable number, given the fact that Micah is a short book.

In the early centuries of the Church considerable attention was paid to the book of Micah. On grounds of quality and length, St Jerome's commentary on the book stands out. But generally the ecclesiastical writers, the Fathers, and authors of books on theology and spirituality tend not to use the book very much, the reason being that most of what Micah has to say can be found in the more important prophetical books such as Isaiah, Jeremiah, Ezekiel, Amos and Hosea.

Christians are aware of Micah mainly because of the oracle about the Messiah being born in Bethlehem of Judah, and through the use of Micah 6:3–4 in the Reproaches sung during the Adoration of the Cross in the liturgy of Good Friday. It is also significant that the last words of the book are remarkably similar to parts of the Benedictus in chapter 1 of Luke: both passages have the same firm hope in God's fidelity to the promises that he made to the patriarchs; in the case of Micah, hope in a future event; in the canticle of Zechariah, joy that it has come to pass. This agreement between Micah and Luke is an important indication of the unity of Old and New Testament Revelation, and of the common faith shared by the old people of God and the new.

**Title**

1 ¹The word of the LORD that came to Micah of Moresheth in the
days of Jotham, Ahaz, and Hezekiah, kings of Judah, which he
saw concerning Samaria and Jerusalem.

Is 1:1
Jer 26:12

## 1. DIVINE JUDGMENT; SINS CONDEMNED*

**Theophany and indictment of Israel and Judah**
²Hear, you peoples, all of you;
hearken, O earth, and all that is in it;

Is 28:1–4
Ps 49:2

---

**1:1.** The prophet is introduced very much in the same way as Amos is in the book of Amos. We are not told the name of Micah's father (which is what happens in the case of most other prophets) but, rather, where he came from, Moresheth, one of the towns at risk from Assyrian invasion (cf. 1:14). Like Amos (cf. Amos 7:14), he does not seem to have come from a family with a prophetical tradition (he will later inveigh against venal professional prophets: cf. 3:5, 11); rather, he seems to have received a special call from God to denounce injustice and immorality. The text says that he lived in the times of Jotham, Ahaz and Hezekiah. It is not possible to date any oracle in the book specifically to the reign of Jotham. However, Jeremiah 26:18–19 records that Micah preached successfully during Hezekiah's reign and converted the hearts of the people.

*1:2–3:12. These chapters form the first part of the book. Micah ministered as a prophet at a time when Assyria was pursuing an expansionist policy and was gradually taking over the countries that ran along the east coast of the Mediterranean; it was also a time when the (Northern) kingdom of Israel (or Samaria) was economically prosperous. It had increased its trade with the kingdoms of Tyre, Sidon and Damascus; but these contacts allowed inroads to be made in Israel by the religions of those neighbours. Also, material prosperity had brought a more casual approach to religion and a corruption of public morality. The result of this was widespread social injustice, already denounced some years earlier by Amos and Hosea. In his early years as a prophet Micah speaks in much the same vein as Amos. He complains loudly about the people's sins (especially the sins committed by their rulers and the sins of false prophets who uttered prophecies tailored to what people wanted to hear) and he threatens divine judgment: the Lord is sovereign lord of all the earth and he will punish iniquity. But Micah is not only speaking against Samaria: the kingdom of Judah, too, has turned away from the Lord. Therefore, the last verse in this

---

[1] ¹Verbum Domini, quod factum est ad Michaeam Morasthiten in diebus Ioatham, Achaz, Ezechiae

and let the Lord GOD be a witness against you,
the Lord from his holy temple.

Is 26:21
Amos 4:13

[3]For behold, the LORD is coming forth out of his place,
and will come down and tread upon the high places of the earth.

Judg 5:5
Ps 97:5; Is 64:2
Hab 3:6,10
Zech 14:4

[4]And the mountains will melt under him
and the valleys will be cleft,
like wax before the fire,
like waters poured down a steep place.
[5]All this is for the transgression of Jacob
and for the sins of the house of Israel.
What is the transgression of Jacob?
Is it not Samaria?
And what is the sin of the house[a] of Judah?
Is it not Jerusalem?

---

passage (3:12) seems to sum up what has gone before it, and acts as an end-piece: Samaria became a heap of ruins (cf. 1:6–7) and that, too, will be the fate of Jerusalem.

**1:2–5.** The prophet solemnly describes the theophany or "visitation" (cf. Amos 3:14; Hos 12:2; Is 13:11; Jer 44:13) of the Lord who will come down from heaven to punish Israel and Judah for their sins. He underscores the power of the Lord, the fact that he is Judge over all and that his dominion extends over all the earth and over all who live there (vv. 3–5). St Jerome comments: *"The Lord is coming forth out of his place:* because of your sin, He who is kind and good must wear a mask of cruelty that is not his [...]. The mountains and the valleys stand for the leaders and the people [...]. All of this came about because of the sins of the ten tribes, called

Israel and Judah, and the transgressions of Judah, for Samaria was the the city of the ten tribes, and Jerusalem, in the kingdom of Judah, was where high altars were raised to idols" (*Commentarii in Michaeam*, 1, 3–5).

God's visitation has to do with the sins of Israel and Judah. Israel's sin is the fact that Samaria (v. 5) has become idolatrous, as Micah will go on to explain (cf. 1:6–7). This seems to mean that it still has "high places" (v. 5, note **a**) where worship was offered to the gods of Canaan (cf. 2 Kings 15:35; 16:4). Later on, the prophet will inveigh against Israel for sins of injustice and immorality, but here he seems to be talking only of idolatry. In any case, in his preaching, idolatry and moral faults go hand in hand: it is very difficult to lead an upright life if one does not believe in the Lord, and, if one truly believes, then one will lead a good life.

regum Iudae, quod vidit super Samariam et Ierusalem. [2]Audite, populi omnes, / et attendat terra et plenitudo eius; / et sit Dominus Deus vobis in testem, / Dominus de templo sancto suo. / [3]Quia ecce Dominus egreditur de loco suo / et descendet et calcabit / super excelsa terrae; / [4]et liquescent montes

**a.** Gk Tg Compare Syr: Heb *what are the high places*

### Oracle on the downfall of Samaria

⁶Therefore I will make Samaria a heap in the open country,    Mic 3:12
   a place for planting vineyards;
and I will pour down her stones into the valley,
   and uncover her foundations.
⁷All her images shall be beaten to pieces,    Hos 2:5,12
   all her hires shall be burned with fire,
   and all her idols I will lay waste;
for from the hire of a harlot she gathered them,
   and to the hire of a harlot they shall return.

### Lament for the cities of Israel and Judah

⁸For this I will lament and wail;    2 Sam 15:30
   I will go stripped and naked;    2 Kings
I will make lamentation like the jackals,    18:13–19, 37
   and mourning like the ostriches.    Is 20:2–4
       Ezek 24:17–23

---

**1:6–7.** This short oracle points to two consequences of the fall of Samaria—material devastation and spiritual ruin. These words found fulfilment in the destruction of Samaria when the capital was besieged and taken (in 722 BC) by the Assyrian forces of Shalmaneser V and his son Sargon II. The country suffered grievously; it was ethnically cleansed: there were mass deportations, and the land was planted with people from elsewhere. The Northern kingdom was, essentially, dismantled. The part of the population that remained would soon flee to the South and become integrated there as best they could: "The order of punishment corresponds to the order of sin. Samaria sinned first, by making idols and worshipping golden calves instead of the

Lord, and was punished first. It was destroyed by the Assyrians who reduced it to a pile of rubble and stones" (St Jerome, *Commentarii in Michaeam*, 1, 6–7).

**1:8–16.** This is a difficult passage to interpret because the manuscript saw many changes over the course of its composition and because there are a number of plays on words involving the names of the cities (which are sometimes difficult to identify) and the actions that are lamented. For example, in v. 10: "Tell it not (*tgd*) in Gath (*gt*)"; "in Beth-le-aphrah [that is, in the "House of dust"] roll yourselves in the dust."

However, the general tone of the passage is clear enough. The prophet is

subtus eum, / et valles scindentur / sicut cera a facie ignis, / sicut aquae, quae decurrunt in praeceps. / ⁵In scelere Iacob omne istud / et in peccatis domus Israel. / Quod scelus Iacob? / Nonne Samaria? / Et quae excelsa Iudae? / Nonne Ierusalem? / ⁶Et ponam Samariam in acervum lapidum, / in agrum, ubi plantatur vinea; / et detraham in vallem lapides eius / et fundamenta eius revelabo. / ⁷Et omnia sculptilia eius concidentur, / et omnes mercedes eius comburentur igne, / et omnia idola eius ponam in perditionem, / quia de mercedibus meretricis congregata sunt / et usque ad mercedem meretricis revertentur. / ⁸Super hoc plangam et ululabo; / vadam spoliatus et nudus, / faciam planctum velut thoum

Is 8:7,8;
10:28–32
<sup>9</sup>For her wound<sup>b</sup> is incurable;
    and it has come to Judah,
it has reached to the gate of my people,
    to Jerusalem.

2 Sam 1:20
Jer 25:34
<sup>10</sup>Tell it not in Gath,
    weep not at all;
in Beth-le-aphrah
    roll yourselves in the dust.

Josh 15:37
<sup>11</sup>Pass on your way,
    inhabitants of Shaphir,
    in nakedness and shame;
the inhabitants of Zaanan
    do not come forth;
the wailing of Beth-ezel
    shall take away from you its standing place.

---

probably referring to the Assyrian campaigns—Sargon's Palestine campaign around 710 BC, and Sennacherib's later campaign of 701 when he besieged Jerusalem (although he eventually had to raise the siege suddenly: cf. 2 Kings 18:13–19:37). The prophet sees the fall of the Northern kingdom as a wound (v. 9) for the chosen people. Therefore, he laments it and appeals for penance to be done (v. 16) and for the rejection of sin, which is what has caused the collapse of Samaria (1:6–7) and contaminated the daughter of Zion (v. 13). As is clear in so many other biblical passages, when the Lord sends affliction he does so to provoke conversion. That was how Origen interpreted the passage: "It is said that the Lord punishes in order to bring about the conversion of those who are in need of repentance; this argument is neither flawed nor false. *Evil has come down from the Lord to the gate of Jerusalem* (v. 12): that evil is the disgrace brought about by the sufferings inflicted on them by their enemies, and leads to the conversion of the people of the city" (*Contra Celsum*, 6, 56).

However, although the disaster threatened by the prophet did not happen until more than a hundred years later, happen it did, when Jerusalem fell to the forces of Nebuchadnezzar: "That same evil, the punishment of sin that razed Samaria to the ground, will come to Judah, to the very gates of my city, Jerusalem. Samaria was destroyed by the Assyrians; Jerusalem will be destroyed by the Babylonians" (St Jerome, *Commentarii in Michaeam*, 1, 6–9).

/ et luctum quasi struthionum, / <sup>9</sup>quia desperata est plaga eius, / quia venit usque ad Iudam, / tetigit portam populi mei / usque ad Ierusalem. / <sup>10</sup>In Geth nolite annuntiare, / lacrimis ne ploretis, / in Bethleaphra in pulvere volutamini. / <sup>11</sup>Et transite vobis, habitatores Saphir, / confusi ignominia; / non

**b.** Gk Syr Vg: Heb *wounds*

<sup>12</sup>For the inhabitants of Maroth
    wait anxiously for good,
because evil has come down from the L<small>ORD</small>
    to the gate of Jerusalem.
<sup>13</sup>Harness the steeds to the chariots,
    inhabitants of Lachish;
you were<sup>c</sup> the beginning of sin
    to the daughter of Zion,
for in you were found
    the transgressions of Israel.
<sup>14</sup>Therefore you shall give parting gifts
    to Moresheth-gath;
the houses of Achzib shall be a deceitful thing
    to the kings of Israel.
<sup>15</sup>I will again bring a conqueror upon you,
    inhabitants of Mareshah;
the glory of Israel
    shall come to Adullam.
<sup>16</sup>Make yourselves bald and cut off your hair,
    for the children of your delight;
make yourselves as bald as the eagle,
    for they shall go from you into exile.

Ruth 1:20

Josh 15:39
2 Kings 14:19

Josh 15:44

Josh 15:44
1 Sam 22:1
2 Sam 23:13

Is 22:12
Jer 7:29

### The prophet denounces social injustice

**2** <sup>1</sup>Woe to those who devise wickedness
  and work evil upon their beds!

Ps 36:5

**2:1–5.** This is an oracle beginning with "Woe!", and it is directed against the social injustice perpetuated by the well-to-do who take advantage of the poorer members of society. Micah speaks very clearly in this denunciation. The people with power seem to spend all their time coveting, robbing and cheating: they spend their nights making their plans, and their days carrying them out (vv. 1–2). The odd thing is that these men seem to be men of faith, for the words that the prophet puts on their lips (v. 4) are an acknowledgment that the Lord

sunt egressi habitatores Saanan. / Planctus Bethesel / auferet a vobis mansionem suam. / <sup>12</sup>Profecto trement de bono / habitatores Maroth, / quia descendit malum a Domino / in portam Ierusalem. / <sup>13</sup>Iungite quadrigae equos, habitatores Lachis; / principium peccati est filiae Sion, / quia in te inventa sunt scelera Israel. / <sup>14</sup>Propterea dabis dimissionem / super Moresethgeth. / Domus Achzib in deceptionem / regibus Israel. / <sup>15</sup>Adhuc expugnatorem adducam tibi, / quae habitas in Maresa; / usque Odollam veniet / gloria Israel. / <sup>16</sup>Decalvare et tondere / super filios deliciarum tuarum; / dilata calvitium tuum sicut aquila, quoniam captivi ducti sunt ex te. **[2]** <sup>1</sup>Vae, qui cogitant iniquitatem / et

c. Cn: Heb *it was*

187

When the morning dawns, they perform it,
because it is in the power of their hand.

Is 5:8 [2]They covet fields, and seize them;
and houses, and take them away;
they oppress a man and his house,
a man and his inheritance.

Jer 8:2
Amos 3:2; 5:13 [3]Therefore thus says the LORD:
Behold, against this family I am devising evil,
from which you cannot remove your necks;
and you shall not walk haughtily,
for it will be an evil time.

Num 21:27
Deut 28:30–33
Is 14:4
Hab 2:6 [4]In that day they shall take up a taunt song against you,
and wail with bitter lamentation,
and say, "We are utterly ruined;
he changes the portion of my people;
how he removes it from me!
Among our captors[d] he divides our fields."

Deut 32:8
Ps 16:6,7 [5]Therefore you will have none to cast the line by lot
in the assembly of the LORD.

Is 30:13
Amos 2:12 ### Abuses and evil counsel
[6]"Do not preach"—thus they preach—

---

giveth and the Lord taketh away. Micah's teachings are practical applications of the fifth and tenth commandments which prohibit respectively "violence and injustice" and "coveting the goods of another, as the root of theft, robbery and fraud, which the seventh commandment forbids. 'Lust of the eyes' leads to the violence and injustice forbidden by the fifth commandment" (*Catechism of the Catholic Church*, 2534).

The Lord tells what punishment will apply to such sins—the oppression in exile (v. 3), and confiscation of property (v. 4). It seems to be a veiled example of the application of the law of vengeance, though to the Christian reader it sounds somewhat like our Lord's warning: "the measure you give will be measure you get" (Mt 7:2).

**2:6–11.** These verses expand on the previous ones. The people in question

operantur malum in cubilibus suis! / In luce matutina faciunt illud, / quoniam est in potestate manus eorum. / [2]Concupiscunt agros, et violenter tollunt, / domos, et rapiunt. / Et opprimunt virum et domum eius, / hominem et hereditatem eius. / [3]Idcirco haec dicit Dominus: / «Ecce ego cogito / super familiam istam malum, / unde non auferetis / colla vestra; / et non ambulabitis erecti, / quoniam tempus pessimum est. / [4]In die illa / sumetur super vos parabola, / et assumetur lamentum dicentium: "Depopulatione vastati sumus; / pars populi mei commutatur, / quam nemo ei restituet; / infideli regiones nostrae dividuntur". / [5]Propter hoc non erit tibi / mittens funiculum sortis / in coetu Domini». / [6]«Ne vaticinemini!». «Vaticinentur, / non vaticinentur de his, / non cedet confusio!». / [7]Numquid

**d.** Cn: Heb *the rebellious*

"one should not preach of such things;
   disgrace will not overtake us."
⁷Should this be said, O house of Jacob?
   Is the Spirit of the LORD impatient?
   Are these his doings?
 Do not my words do good
   to him who walks uprightly?
⁸But you rise against my people^e as an enemy;          Deut 24:12–13
   you strip the robe from the peaceful,^f
 from those who pass by trustingly
   with no thought of war.
⁹The women of my people you drive out               2 Kings 4:1
   from their pleasant houses;
 from their young children you take away
   my glory for ever.

---

know the power of prophetical preaching; so they tell the prophet to keep quiet (v. 6), not to prophesy, for fear that what he does prophesy might come to pass. The prophet replies in four different ways: he tells them that the patience of the Lord has not diminished, that the Lord has not forgotten the people and that his spirit is speaking through him (Micah); he also tells them that he is not a false prophet who utters what people want to hear (v. 11; cf. Lk 6:26), and that if his words annoy them, then it is because they themselves are not upright—and not because what he is saying is untrue (v. 7); finally (vv. 8–10), he cites three instances of their injustice that are so blatant that there is nothing more to be said. St Jerome comments as follows: "Do not be deceived, house of Jacob, and tell one another, to console yourselves: God is good; the captivity we fear will not come about, because his mercy is great and his spirit clement: shall he who is openhearted and generous to all be strict and severe with us?" (*Commentarii in Michaeam*, 2, 6–8).

But Micah is not a prophet of misfortune: his message is one of conversion. In the midst of all this gloom, he manages to provide a glimpse of salvation. This explains the questions asked in v. 7; given what is said in the whole passage, one can see that the Spirit of the Lord is as strong as ever and the prophet's message is taken on board by those who "walk uprightly"; so, he is also saying that the house of Jacob is not accursed. The Lord is committed to his people, as the next oracle will show.

maledicta est domus Iacob? / Numquid abbreviatus est spiritus Domini, / aut tales sunt actiones eius? / Nonne verba eius bona sunt / cum eo, qui recte graditur? / ⁸Vos autem contra populum meum / ut adversarium consurgitis. / Desuper tunica pallium tollitis ei; / qui transibant fiducialiter, / fiunt quasi bello capti. / ⁹Mulieres populi mei eicitis / de domo deliciarum suarum; a parvulis earum aufertis /

e. Cn: Heb *yesterday my people rose*  f. Cn: Heb *from before a garment*

189

Ex 22:25   <sup>10</sup>Arise and go,
    for this is no place to rest;
    because of uncleanness that destroys
        with a grievous destruction.
Jer 5:31   <sup>11</sup>If a man should go about and utter wind and lies,
Lk 6:26        saying, "I will preach to you of wine and strong drink,"
        he would be the preacher for this people!

**Promise of restoration**

1 Chron 2:1   <sup>12</sup>I will surely gather all of you, O Jacob,
Jer 31:10        I will gather the remnant of Israel;
Ezek 34:1;   I will set them together
37:15–28        like sheep in a fold,
    like a flock in its pasture,
        a noisy multitude of men.
Is 52:12   <sup>13</sup>He who opens the breach will go up before them;
Hos 3:5        they will break through and pass the gate,
Jn 10:4        going out by it.
    Their king will pass on before them,
        the LORD at their head.

---

**2:12–13.** Here, out of the blue, comes a perfectly clear promise that all the people of Israel are going to be restored, re-established. There is no doubt about what the words mean, but in the context of the book they can have two interpretations. Given that this first part of the book is a series of denunciations, it is possible that these words (vv. 12–13) are being spoken by Micah's hearers, to whom the prophet will reply by making further negative predictions (cf. 3:1ff). However, Micah is also a prophet of salvation: the house of Judah is not accursed (cf. 2:7) and, to prove it, he proclaims a future restoration in very much the same terms as one finds elsewhere in the Bible—depicting the Lord as a shepherd who looks after his flock (7:14–17; cf. Ps 23:1; Is 40:11; Ezek 34:23; etc.). Certainly, it seems clear enough that Jesus saw this promise of restoration (extended to include the Gentiles) as being fulfilled in himself, for he called himself the "Good Shepherd": "I am the door of the sheep. [...] I am the good shepherd. The good shepherd lays down his life for the sheep. [...] And I have other sheep, that are not of this fold; I must bring them also, and they will heed my voice. So there shall be one flock, one shepherd" (Jn 10:7, 11, 16).

decorem meum in perpetuum. / <sup>10</sup>«Surgite et ite, / quia non habetis hic requiem!». / Propter immunditiam peribitis / perditione pessima. / <sup>11</sup>Si esset vir vento excitatus / et mendacium loqueretur: / «Vaticinabor tibi de vino et sicera», / hic esset vates populi istius. / <sup>12</sup>Congregatione congregabo, Iacob, totum te; / in unum conducam reliquias Israel, / pariter ponam illum quasi gregem in ovili, / quasi pecus in medio pascuae; / et tumultuabuntur a multitudine hominum. / <sup>13</sup>Ascendet enim pandens iter ante eos; / erumpent et transibunt portam, egredientur per eam. / Et transibit rex eorum coram eis,

**Against rulers who oppress the people**

3 ¹And I said:
   Hear, you heads of Jacob
      and rulers of the house of Israel!
   Is it not for you to know justice?—
   ² you who hate the good and love the evil,
      who tear the skin from off my people,
         and their flesh from off their bones;
   ³who eat the flesh of my people,
      and flay their skin from off them,
   and break their bones in pieces,
      and chop them up like meat^g in a kettle,
         like flesh in a cauldron.

Jer 5:5

Is 5:20,3

Ps 14:5
Ezek 11:3,7;
34:3

---

**3:1–12.** There is a general theme running through these verses which is summed up in vv. 11–12 (indeed, they sum up the whole book so far). Verse 11 lists the sins of the rulers (princes, priests) and prophets; v. 12 spells out their sentence: Samaria will be reduced to rubble (cf. 1:6), and the same will happen to Jerusalem.

The rulers are accused of taking bribes (v. 11; cf. v. 1) and of being unjust towards the poor (they see them as people to be exploited: vv. 2–4). The lesson is clear, then and now (v. 4): there is no way they can see God. Devotion to God is not possible if one is unjust towards others.

Micah criticizes prophets for preaching a false message. They hold their hands out to accept money and they lead people astray (vv. 5, 11). Micah tells them that they will be put to shame (v. 7), for, with no vision or revelation from God to guide them, they will have nothing to say: their life will make no

sense. St Gregory the Great sees in v. 5 an accurate description of bad shepherds who are *"prophets who lead my people astray* [...], like those bad preachers whose teachings confound all who listen to them: they *cry 'Peace' when they have something to eat.* Because of their avarice, they accept the wages of sin given to them in this life, and at the same time they preach the mercy and indulgence of God"* (In librum primum Regum,* 1, 25).

Although in the two reproaches of rulers and prophets one can still discern a note of salvation (the Lord continues to act now, for he hides his face from evildoers, and his revelation from venal prophets), his action is more easily seen in the prophet himself, whom he has filled with his spirit to proclaim justice and denounce sin (cf. v. 8). Thus, the theme of the second part of the book is signalled here—the idea that the Lord never forsakes his people.

---

/ et Dominus in capite eorum. **[3]** ¹Et dixi: «Audite, principes Iacob / et duces domus Israel: / Numquid non vestrum est scire iudicium?». / ²Sed odio habetis bonum et diligitis malum. / Violenter tollitis pelles eorum desuper eos / et carnem eorum desuper ossibus eorum. / ³Qui comedunt carnem

**g.** Gk: Heb *as*

Deut 31:17
Jer 11:11
⁴Then they will cry to the LORD,
> but he will not answer them;
he will hide his face from them at that time,
> because they have made their deeds evil.

### Against corrupt prophets

Is 9:14,15
Jer 23:13
Mic 2:1
⁵Thus says the LORD concerning the prophets
> who lead my people astray,
who cry "Peace"
> when they have something to eat,
but declare war against him
> who puts nothing into their mouths.

Is 8:20,22
Amos 8:9
⁶Therefore it shall be night to you, without vision,
> and darkness to you, without divination.
The sun shall go down upon the prophets,
> and the day shall be black over them;
⁷the seers shall be disgraced,
> and the diviners put to shame;
they shall all cover their lips,
> for there is no answer from God.

### The ruin of Zion foretold

⁸But as for me, I am filled with power,
> with the Spirit of the LORD,
> and with justice and might,
to declare to Jacob his transgression
and to Israel his sin.

Amos 5:7
⁹Hear this, you heads of the house of Jacob
> and rulers of the house of Israel,
who abhor justice
> and pervert all equity,

---

populi mei / et pellem eorum desuper excoriant; et ossa eorum confringunt / et secant sicut carnem assam in lebete / et quasi carnem in medio ollae. / ⁴Tunc clamabunt ad Dominum, / et non exaudiet eos / et abscondet faciem suam ab eis / in tempore illo, / sicut pessima fecerunt opera sua. / ⁵Haec dicit Dominus super prophetas, / qui seducunt populum meum, / qui cum habent, quid mordeant dentibus suis, / praedicant pacem; / et, si quis non dederit in ore eorum quippiam, / sanctificant super eum proelium. / ⁶Propterea nox vobis sine visione erit, / et tenebrae vobis sine divinatione; et occumbet sol super prophetas, / et obtenebrabitur super eos dies. / ⁷Et confundentur videntes, / et confundentur divini, / et operient labia sua omnes, / quia non est responsum Dei. / ⁸Verumtamen ego repletus sum / fortitudine spiritus Domini, / iudicio et virtute, / ut annuntiem Iacob scelus suum / et Israel peccatum suum. / ⁹Audite hoc, principes domus Iacob / et iudices domus Israel, / qui abominamini iudicium /

<sup>10</sup>who build Zion with blood
  and Jerusalem with wrong.
<sup>11</sup>Its heads give judgment for a bribe,
  its priests teach for hire,
  its prophets divine for money;
 yet they lean upon the LORD and say,
  "Is not the LORD in the midst of us?
  No evil shall come upon us."
<sup>12</sup>Therefore because of you
  Zion shall be ploughed as a field;
 Jerusalem shall become a heap of ruins,
  and the mountain of the house a wooded height.

Hab 2:12

1 Sam 9:7
Is 1:23
Jer 6:13; 7:3–4
Ezek 22:12
Rom 2:17

Jer 26:18
Mic 1:6

## 2. HOPE AND RESTORATION OF ZION*

**The nations will come to the mountain of the Lord's temple**

4 <sup>1</sup>It shall come to pass in the latter days
  that the mountain of the house of the LORD

Is 2:2–4
Zech 8:20–22

---

*4:1–5:15. These two chapters form the core of the book. The focus is different to what it was previously. The main theme running through this part is one of consolation and hope of restoration in a messianic age. Some interpreters link the optimism in these oracles to the time of King Hezekiah of Judah's great reforms (761–686 BC). The text is made up of a series of short, linked units: the nations will come to Mount Zion (4:1–5); the Lord will assemble his scattered flock of Israel on Zion (4:6–8); Judah, too, will be put to the test, but she will be redeemed (4:9–5:1); the Messiah is announced, the Saviour to be born in Bethlehem (5:2–4); the Messiah will

free the people from the Assyrian yoke, and peace will prevail (5:5–6); the "remnant" of Jacob in the midst of the nations will be a strong people (5:7–9); and, finally, purification and punishment for sin (5:10–15).

Most of the oracles open with references to time—"in the latter days" (4:1); "in that day" (4:6; 5:10); "then" (5:7)—which project the oracles into an eschatological future; or else they speak of "now" (4:9–14), that is, describe future salvation as something already present.

**4:1–5.** The first verses are almost exactly the same as Isaiah 2:2–4, and quite like Zechariah 8:20–22. The passage as

et omnia recta pervertitis, / <sup>10</sup>qui aedificatis Sion in sanguinibus / et Ierusalem in iniquitate. / <sup>11</sup>Principes eius in muneribus iudicant, / et sacerdotes eius in mercede docent, / et prophetae eius in pecunia divinant; / et super Dominum requiescunt dicentes: / «Numquid non Dominus in medio nostrum? / Non venient super nos mala». / <sup>12</sup>Propter hoc causa vestri / Sion quasi ager arabitur, / et Ierusalem quasi acervus lapidum erit, / et mons templi in excelsa silvarum. **[4]** <sup>1</sup>Et erit in novissimis diebus: / Erit mons domus Domini / praeparatus in vertice montium / et sublimis super colles; / et fluent ad eum populi. /

shall be established as the highest of the mountains,
and shall be raised up above the hills;
and peoples shall flow to it,

---

a whole depicts the scene at the end of time ("in the latter days": v. 1) when God will renew everything. The "action" probably starts in v. 5: if the people walk in the commandments of the Lord, Jerusalem and in particular the temple will be the centrepoint to which the whole world flocks (v. 1); all the nations will make their way to Israel to be taught the Law and the word of the Lord (v. 2). When that happens, one will be able to say that the messianic peace has begun: the Lord will be the only Judge, acknowledged by all; there will be no more wars, and therefore no need for weapons of war (swords and spears, v. 3, will be sent back to the forge and turned into farm implements). Everyone will enjoy peace and tranquillity, in his own home, with no need to look over his shoulder (v. 4).

This description of the messianic era is echoed elsewhere in the Old Testament and in a special way in the New Testament. For example, the ideas of v. 2 recur in Jesus' conversation with the Samaritan woman, when he reminds her that "salvation is from the Jews" (Jn 4:22). Micah's vision speaks of the central role of the temple and of Jerusalem, and Jesus called himself the new temple (cf. Jn 2:18–22). For this reason (and because of many other things said in the New Testament), the Fathers saw this oracle's promises as finding their fulfilment in Jesus and in the Church. Melito of Sardis says, for example: "The Law has become the Word, and

the old is made new; both come forth from Zion and Jerusalem. The commandments are turned into grace, and what was a figure is made real" (*De Pascha*, 45). And St Jerome comments: "What was once hidden, what Moses and the prophets spoke of in the mountains and at the very summits of mountains about Him [Christ], is now revealed. Though what they wrote was holy, they communicated in signs and images, and prophesied the coming of the Lord, a message before which all were made humble and could not climb to the peaks of the mountains. The prophet says: *The mountain of the house of the Lord shall be established as the highest of the mountains, and shall be raised up above the hills* [...] (v. 1). The highest of the mountains, or the mountain that is raised up above the hills, will bear down, or, as it is written in Hebrew, will flow through all the nations like a river, and unite all the people. All shall be made new and equal, Parthians and Medes and Elamites and the citizens of Mesopotamia, Judea and Cappadocia, Pontus and Asia, Phrygia and Pamphylia, Egypt and the parts of Lybia belonging to Cyrene, and visitors from Rome, both Jews and proselytes, Cretans and Arabians (cf. Acts 2:9–10) [...]. *Come, let us go up to the mountain of the Lord* (v. 2): one must ascend the heights to Christ, *to the house of the God of Jacob*, to the Church, which is the house of God, pillar and foundation of the truth" (*Commentarii in Michaeam*, 4, 1–5).

[Jn 4:22]

²and many nations shall come, and say:
"Come, let us go up to the mountain of the LORD,
  to the house of the God of Jacob;
that he may teach us his ways
  and we may walk in his paths."
For out of Zion shall go forth the law,
  and the word of the LORD from Jerusalem.

³He shall judge between many peoples,
  and shall decide for strong nations afar off;
and they shall beat their swords into ploughshares,
  and their spears into pruning hooks;
nation shall not lift up sword against nation,
  neither shall they learn war any more;

[Ps 110:6]
[Joel 4:10]

⁴but they shall sit every man under his vine and under his fig tree,
  and none shall make them afraid;
for the mouth of the LORD of hosts has spoken.

[Is 1:20]
[Zech 3:10]

⁵For all the peoples walk
  each in the name of its god,
but we will walk in the name of the LORD our God
  for ever and ever.

[Is 2:5]

### The gathering of the scattered flock on Zion

⁶In that day, says the LORD,

[Ezek 34:1]
[Zeph 3:19]

---

**4:6–8.** We are still in the context of the messianic times, as the opening words "In that day" imply. The prophet seems to have in mind the sad circumstances of the Babylonian exiles, which he will go on to predict (cf. 4:9–13). From among the people (depicted as ill-treated, lame sheep, a flock gone astray and scattered: vv. 6–7), the Lord, like a good shepherd, will rescue a remnant, and from that remnant make a strong nation. That nation will regain its former glory with a king in Jerusalem.

"Tower of the flock" (v. 8) does not refer to a specific building; it is an affectionate name used by Micah for Mount Zion. Thus, the messianic honor (later promised to Bethlehem: cf. 5:2–4) is promised here to Jerusalem.

²Et properabunt gentes multae et dicent: / «Venite, ascendamus ad montem Domini / et ad domum Dei Iacob, / et docebit nos de viis suis, / et ibimus in semitis eius»; / quia de Sion egredietur lex, / et verbum Domini de Ierusalem. / ³Et iudicabit inter populos multos / et decernet gentibus fortibus usque in longinquum; / et concident gladios suos in vomeres / et hastas suas in falces; / non sumet gens adversus gentem gladium, / et non discent ultra belligerare. / ⁴Et sedebit unusquisque subtus vitem suam / et subtus ficum suam, / et non erit qui deterreat; / quia os Domini exercituum locutum est. / ⁵Quia omnes populi ambulabunt / unusquisque in nomine dei sui; / nos autem ambulabimus in nomine Domini / Dei nostri in aeternum et ultra. / ⁶«In die illa, dicit Dominus, / congregabo claudicantem, / et eam, quam

I will assemble the lame
and gather those who have been driven away,
and those whom I have afflicted;

Is 4:3; 24:23    [7]and the lame I will make the remnant;
Lk 1:33          and those who were cast off, a strong nation;
and the LORD will reign over them in Mount Zion
from this time forth and for evermore.

[8]And you, O tower of the flock,
hill of the daughter of Zion,
to you shall it come,
the former dominion shall come,
the kingdom of the daughter of Jerusalem.

### Testing and redemption

Is 13:8          [9]Now why do you cry aloud?
Jer 6:24; 8:19   Is there no king in you?
Has your counsellor perished,
that pangs have seized you like a woman in travail?

---

**4:9–5:1.** This prophecy distinguishes between the anguish of the present ("now": vv. 9–11, 14) and the future times of salvation and restoration (vv. 12–13). The trials mentioned here seem to refer to three aspects of the collapse of the kingdom of Judah and the exile that followed—the fall of the king (v. 9; he is probably also the "ruler of Israel" in 5:1), the trek to Babylon (v. 10), and the assembly of the nations that jeers at Judah (v. 11).

The consolation of a future restoration is grounded in the fact that the God of Israel is "the Lord of the whole earth" (v. 13). The Lord who takes his people's side is the same Lord as allowed them to be defeated. The identification of the Church as the new, restored, Israel allowed this passage to be read in a spiritual sense: "Many wicked peoples, possessed by demons, unite to inveigh against the daughter of Zion, the Church [...]; they mock her and rejoice at the death of her children, because they are ignorant of God's reasons, nor do they understand his providential plans [...]. He will gather them together again, like sheaves to the threshing floor, to toss with his horn and trample with his hooves everything in them that is thorny or sour, hollow or chaff, and will make an offering of the good, pure grain to the Lord" (St Jerome, *Commentarii in Michaeam*, 4, 11–13).

eieceram, colligam / et quam afflixeram; / [7]et ponam claudicantem in reliquias / et eam, quae laboraverat, in gentem robustam». / Et regnabit Dominus super eos in monte Sion / ex hoc nunc et usque in aeternum. / [8]Et tu, turris gregis, / collis filiae Sion, / usque ad te veniet et perveniet / potestas prima, / regnum filiae Ierusalem. / [9]Nunc quare clamas clamore magno? / Numquid rex non est in te,

[10]Writhe and groan,[h] O daughter of Zion,
 like a woman in travail;
for now you shall go forth from the city
 and dwell in the open country;
 you shall go to Babylon.
There you shall be rescued,
 there the LORD will redeem you
 from the hand of your enemies.

Lk 1:74
Rev 12:2

[11]Now many nations
 are assembled against you,
saying, "Let her be profaned,
 and let our eyes gaze upon Zion."
[12]But they do not know
 the thoughts of the LORD,
they do not understand his plan,
 that he has gathered them as sheaves to the threshing floor.
[13]Arise and thresh,
 O daughter of Zion,
for I will make your horn iron
 and your hoofs bronze;
you shall beat in pieces many peoples,
 and shall[i] devote their gain to the LORD,
 their wealth to the Lord of the whole earth.

Zech 12:8

Is 55:8–9

Lev 27:28
Deut 7:26

**5**[j] [1]Now you are walled about with a wall;[k]
 siege is laid against us;
with a rod they strike upon the cheek
 the ruler of Israel.[l]

Mt 26:67

---

/ aut consiliarius tuus periit, / quia comprehendit te dolor sicut parturientem? / [10]Dole et satage, / filia Sion, quasi parturiens; / quia nunc egredieris de civitate / et habitabis in campo / et venies usque ad Babylonem; / ibi liberaberis, / ibi redimet te Dominus / de manu inimicorum tuorum. / [11]Nunc autem congregatae sunt super te / gentes multae, / quae dicunt: «Profanetur, / et aspiciat in Sion oculus noster». / [12]Ipsi autem non cognoverunt / cogitationes Domini / et non intellexerunt consilium eius, / quia congregavit eos quasi manipulos in area. / [13]Surge et tritura, filia Sion, / quia cornu tuum ponam ferreum / et ungulas tuas ponam aereas, / et comminues populos multos / et vovebis Domino rapinas eorum / et divitias eorum Domino universae terrae. / [14]Nunc incide te, filia incisionis! / Obsidionem posuerunt super nos; / in virga percutiunt / maxillam iudicis Israel. **[5]** [1]Sed tu, Bethlehem Ephratha,

---

**h.** Heb uncertain **i.** Gk Syr Tg: Heb *I will* **j.** Ch 4.14 in Heb **k.** Cn Compare Gk: Heb obscure
**l.** Ch 5.1 in Heb

Josh 15:59
Ruth 4:11
Mt 2:6; Jn 7:42

**The Messiah, the saviour who will be born in Bethlehem**

2 *¹*But you, O Bethlehem Ephrathah,
   who are little to be among the clans of Judah,

---

**5:2–4.** The scenario, darkened for a moment in the previous three verses (4:9–5:1), becomes bright again with the announcement of a "ruler" or governor in Israel, who will be born ("come forth from") Bethlehem, the city of David, a city in the region of "Ephrath" (Gen 35:16). The region is often distinguished from its leading city (cf. 1 Sam 17:12), but in some passages the region and the city are treated as one and the same (Gen 35:19).

There are many contrasts here, a typical feature of salvation oracles: the future king will have humble origins, for he will be born in a small town ("you … who are little" in v. 2 could also be translated as "you … who are least"); still, Bethlehem is not without honour, for it was the birthplace of David and is therefore the place that guaranteed one's belonging to the line of David; this ruler comes from an ancient line, but to perceive his presence one must wait until "she who is in travail has brought forth" (v. 3); all he will do is tend his flock, yet the benefits of his rule will extend to the ends of the earth (v. 4). No contemporary king could match this description; the prophet is referring to the future Messiah-king. There are many elements in this passage that link it to the messianic passages in Isaiah (Is 7:14; 9:5–6; 11:1–4) and to passages about the future offspring of David (2 Sam 7:12–16; Ps 89:3).

Jewish tradition read this passage as a messianic prophecy, as can be seen from passages in the Talmud (*Pesahim*, 51, 1 and *Nedarim*, 39, 2). The New Testament contains clear references to it: for example, the verses in the Gospel of St John that report the opinion of Jesus' contemporaries as to where the Messiah would come from: "Is the Christ to come from Galilee? Has not the scripture said that the Christ is descended from David, and comes from Bethlehem, the village where David was?" (Jn 7:40–42); but Matthew 2:4–6 is the main text that applies the prophecy to Jesus: the evangelist subtly ennobles the city of David (he says: "And you, O Bethlehem, in the land of Judah are *by no means least* among the rulers of Judah", instead of Micah's "who are little" or "least"—in order to enhance the figure of Jesus, the Messiah).

Going along with this interpretation in St Matthew, Christian tradition has seen the Micah passage as an announcement of Jesus' birth in Bethlehem. The Fathers developed many arguments to try to convince Jews that Jesus was the expected Messiah. For example, Tertullian wrote: "Since the children of Israel accuse us of grave error because we believe in Christ, who has come, let us show them from the Scriptures that the Christ who was foretold has come […]. He was born in Bethlehem in

---

*¹* parvulus in milibus Iudae, / ex te mihi egredietur, / qui sit dominator in Israel; / et egressus eius a temporibus antiquis, / a diebus aeternitatis. / *²*Propter hoc dabit eos / usque ad tempus, in quo parturiens

from you shall come forth for me
    one who is to be ruler in Israel,
whose origin is from of old,
    from ancient days.
[3]Therefore he shall give them up until the time        Ps 90:2
    when she who is in travail has brought forth;     Is 7:14
then the rest of his brethren shall return          Hos 6:3
    to the people of Israel.
[4]And he shall stand and feed his flock in the strength of the LORD,
    in the majesty of the name of the LORD his God.
And they shall dwell secure, for now he shall be great
    to the ends of the earth.

## Assyria repulsed

[5]And this shall be peace,                   Amos 1:3
    when the Assyrian comes into our land    Zech 9:10
    and treads upon our soil,[m]            Eph 2:13–14
that we will raise against him seven shepherds
    and eight princes of men;
[6]they shall rule the land of Assyria with the sword,     Ps 2:9

---

Judah, as the prophet foretold: *But you, O Bethlehem, are by no means least … (v. 2)*" (*Adversus Iudaeos*, 13). And St Irenaeus said: "In his day, the prophet Micah told us of the place where the Christ would be born: Bethlehem, in Judah. *O Bethlehem …, who are little to be among the clans of Judah, from you shall come forth for me one who is to be ruler of Israel.* Bethlehem is also in the homeland of David, and Christ comes from the line of David, not only because he was born of the Virgin, but because he was born in Bethlehem" (*Demonstratio praedicationis apostolicae*, 63).

**5:5–6** "This [the Messiah who will be born in Bethlehem] shall be peace" (v. 5). In the same way as "Egypt" was synonymous with "bondage", now Assyria has come to symbolize the oppressive nation. This oracle, then, comes prior to the appearance of Babylon on the horizon of the chosen people. A Christian reading of the passage sees in it a description of any crisis experienced by the people of God or by a sincere believer, who looks to his Lord for peace. Ephesians 2:13–14 echoes 5:4: "But now in Christ Jesus you who once were far off have been brought near in the blood

pariet; / et reliquiae fratrum eius / convertentur ad filios Israel. / [3]Et stabit et pascet in fortitudine Domini, / in sublimitate nominis Domini Dei sui; / et habitabunt secure, quia nunc magnus erit / usque ad terminos terrae, / [4]et erit iste pax. / Assyrius cum venerit in terram nostram / et quando calcaverit in domibus nostris, / suscitabimus super eum septem pastores / et octo primates hominum. / [5]Et pascent terram Assyriae in gladio et terram Nemrod in lanceis; / et liberabit ab Assyrio, / cum venerit in terram nostram / et cum calcaverit in finibus nostris. / [6]Et erunt reliquiae Iacob / in medio populorum

**m.** Gk: *Heb in our palaces*

and the land of Nimrod with the drawn sword;[n]
and they[o] shall deliver us from the Assyrian
when he comes into our land
and treads within our border.

### The "remnant" of Jacob

Is 4:3
Hos 14:6

[7]Then the remnant of Jacob shall be
in the midst of many peoples
like dew from the LORD,
like showers upon the grass,
which tarry not for men
nor wait for the sons of men.
[8]And the remnant of Jacob shall be among the nations,
in the midst of many peoples,
like a lion among the beasts of the forest,
like a young lion among the flocks of sheep,
which, when it goes through, treads down
and tears in pieces, and there is none to deliver.
[9]Your hand shall be lifted up over your adversaries,
and all your enemies shall be cut off.

### Purification. Destruction of the causes of evil

Hos 14:4
Zech 9:10

[10]And in that day, says the LORD,
I will cut off your horses from among you
and will destroy your chariots;

---

of Christ. For he is our peace, who has made us both one, and has broken down the dividing wall of hostility."

**5:7–9.** This is another oracle about the "remnant of Jacob in the midst of the nations" (v. 8). The prophet attributes to this remnant of Israel qualities which are very like those of the Lord himself. The "remnant" will be a blessing (v. 7: "dew" and rain are divine gifts) for

those who welcome it; and they are a threat (the "lion" among beasts, the "young lion" among sheep: v. 8) to their enemies, from whose oppression they will be released.

**5:10–15.** Further things are revealed here about "that day" that will mark the start of the End time: first, resources and weapons of war will be destroyed (vv. 10–11; cf. 4:3; 5:4); secondly, all

---

multorum / quasi ros a Domino / et quasi imbres super herbam, / quae non exspectat virum / et non praestolatur filios hominum. / [7]Et erunt reliquiae Iacob in gentibus, / in medio populorum multorum, / quasi leo in iumentis silvarum / et quasi catulus leonis in gregibus pecorum; / qui cum transierit et conculcaverit et ceperit, / non est qui eruat. / [8]Exaltabitur manus tua super hostes tuos, / et omnes inimici tui interibunt. / [9]«Et erit in die illa, / dicit Dominus, / auferam equos tuos de medio tui / et disperdam quadrigas tuas / [10]et perdam civitates terrae tuae / et destruam omnes munitiones tuas. /

**n.** Cn: Heb *in its entrances*     **o.** Heb *he*

200

<sup>11</sup>and I will cut off the cities of your land
  and throw down all your strongholds;
<sup>12</sup>and I will cut off sorceries from your hand,
  and you shall have no more soothsayers;
<sup>13</sup>and I will cut off your images
  and your pillars from among you,
  and you shall bow down no more
  to the work of your hands;
<sup>14</sup>and I will root out your Asherim from among you
  and destroy your cities.
<sup>15</sup>And in anger and wrath I will execute vengeance
  upon the nations that did not obey.

Hag 2:22

Rev 9:20

Ex 23:24
2 Kings 9:22
Is 47:9
Nahum 3:4

## 3. FURTHER DIVINE JUDGMENT AND PUNISHMENT OF JERUSALEM*

**The Lord hands down his sentence**

**6** <sup>1</sup>Hear what the LORD says:
  Arise, plead your case before the mountains,
  and let the hills hear your voice.
<sup>2</sup>Hear, you mountains, the controversy of the LORD,
  and you enduring foundations of the earth;

Is 5:3–4,13–15;
43:26
Hos 4:1–5

---

traces of idolatry and superstition will be removed—magic and divination (v. 12); images of gods (*pesilîm*) and posts or steles (*masseboth*), which the pagan Canaanites used to set up in open spaces (v. 13); *Asherim*, glades used for fertility rites in honour of the goddess Astarte (v. 14). Finally, God will punish those nations that refuse to obey him (v. 15): the restoration of Israel is beginning to extend to the whole world.

**\*6:1–7:7.** This is the third part of the book. As we have seen, the book oscillates between reproaches and messages of encouragement. This part is of the former type. The book began by taking Israel and Judah to task and by announcing their sentence (1:2–3:12); then came an augury of an eschatological restoration of the kingdom of God, with the coming of the Messiah and the salvation of the "remnant" (4:1–5:15). Now (6:1–7:7) the people are again condemned for their unjust and immoral behaviour. But the last verse (7:7) shows us that the prophet trusts in God and is confident that he

<sup>11</sup>Et auferam veneficia de manu tua, / et divini non erunt in te. / <sup>12</sup>Et perire faciam sculptilia tua / et lapides tuos de medio tui, / et non adorabis ultra / opera manuum tuarum; / <sup>13</sup>et evellam palos tuos de medio tui / et conteram idola tua. / <sup>14</sup>Et faciam in furore / et in indignatione ultionem / in omnibus gentibus, / quae non audierunt». **[6]** <sup>1</sup>Audite, quae Dominus loquitur: / «Surge, contende iudicio coram montibus, / et audiant colles vocem tuam». / <sup>2</sup>Audite, montes, iudicium Domini, / et auscultate,

for the LORD has a controversy with his people,
and he will contend with Israel.

---

will be heard. As in 4:1–5, this confidence on Micah's part is an earnest of what is said in the final verses of the book (7:8–20), where one sees fulfilled all the hopes placed in the future.

The faults for which the prophet criticizes the people are infidelity and ingratitude towards the Lord (6:1–15) and a lack of virtue (6:6–8), particularly injustice (6:9–16), which has led to despair and betrayal (7:1–6).

**6:1–5.** Here begins the arraignment of Israel in the style of a court case (*rîb*) in which the Lord and Israel speak. The *rîb* is a literary form found quite frequently in prophetical writings (cf. Is 3:13–15; 5:3–7; Hos 4:1–3; etc.) It depicts a public trial or debate in which the Lord is the plaintiff (v. 2) and the world around (hills, mountains) is the witness (vv. 1–2). The drama of the scene lies in the fact that the people being addressed are at one and the same time the defendants (v. 2) and those who are expected to give judgment. Given the case made in the oracle, anyone present must agree with the prophet that the thing to do is to try to know the "saving acts of the Lord" (v. 5). The points made by God through the prophet involve basically an appeal to the very origin of the people of Israel and what the Lord did for them: he appeals to the basic elements of Israelite faith (cf. Deut 5:15). Similar arguments should also impress the Christian: "Christian soul, always remember your dignity, and having been invited to partake of the divine nature, do not fall back by your behaviour into your past sinfulness. Be mindful of what head and body you are a member. Remember that you were freed from darkness and led into the light of the kingdom of God" (St Leo the Great, *Sermones*, 21, 3).

This message (especially vv. 3–4) is very familiar to Christians because it is used in the Reproaches sung during the Adoration of the Cross on Good Friday. That chant combines the Micah text with short paragraphs taken from the Trisagium (an ancient liturgical hymn in honour of the Blessed Trinity), from Isaiah 5:1–5, and from events connected with the exodus from Egypt (updated in the liturgy by linking them to episodes in the passion of our Lord). That part of the Good Friday liturgy serves to remind Christians and people in general of their ingratitude towards God (as shown by their sins)—God whose love and generosity are unbounded. It invites us to acknowledge our sins and helps to get us ready (collectively and personally) for conversion. When a Christian kisses the cross of Christ, he can apply the prophet's words to himself—as if Jesus were speaking them to him, for, as St Francis of Assisi says, "The demons alone did not crucify him; you helped them to crucify him, and to crucify him still, by falling into error and sin" (*Admonitiones*, 5, 3; cf. *Catechism of the Catholic Church*, 598). The liturgy of the Adoration of the Cross is an excellent way of taking to heart Micah's oracle.

fundamenta terrae; / quia iudicium Domini cum populo suo, / et cum Israel iudicio contendit. /

3"O my people, what have I done to you?
In what have I wearied you? Answer me!
4For I brought you up from the land of Egypt,
and redeemed you from the house of bondage;
and I sent before you Moses,
Aaron, and Miriam.
5O my people, remember what Balak king of Moab devised,
and what Balaam the son of Beor answered him,
and what happened from Shittim to Gilgal,
that you may know the saving acts of the LORD."

Deut 5:6
1 Sam 12:6

Num 22–24; 25:1

## Formal religion is not enough

6"With what shall I come before the LORD,
and bow myself before God on high?
Shall I come before him with burnt offerings,
with calves a year old?
7Will the LORD be pleased with thousands of rams,
with ten thousands of rivers of oil?
Shall I give my first-born for my transgression,
the fruit of my body for the sin of my soul?"
8He has showed you, O man, what is good;
and what does the LORD require of you

Lev 18:21
1 Sam 15:22
2 Kings 3:27; 16:3

Is 7:9; 30:15; Hos
2:21; Amos 5:21,24
Mt 23:23

**6:6–8.** These verses are a kind of summary of what true religion is; it is not only a matter of formal religious worship: it involves obedience towards God which in turn means practising justice and charity towards one's neighbour (v. 8).

Verse 7 alludes to the abominable Canaanite practice of sacrificing children to the God Moloch and to the Baals—a practice roundly condemned elsewhere in the Bible: "In his days Hiel of Bethel built Jericho; he laid its foundation at the cost of Abiram his first-born, and set up its gates at the cost of his youngest son Segub" (1 Kings 16:34; cf. Lev 20:2; Deut 12:31; etc.). It could be that these sins from the Northern kingdom were finding their way into Judah (cf. 6:16), as 2 Kings 16:3 suggests and as Jeremiah asserts: "[the kings of Judah] have filled this place with the blood of innocents, and have built the high places of Baal to burn their sons in the fire as burnt offerings to Baal" (Jer 19:4–5).

3«Popule meus, quid feci tibi / et quid molestus fui tibi? / Responde mihi. / 4Ego eduxi te de terra Aegypti / et de domo servientium liberavi te / et misi ante faciem tuam Moysen / et Aaron et Mariam. / 5Popule meus, memento, quaeso, / quid cogitaverit Balac rex Moab, / et quid responderit ei Balaam filius Beor, / de Settim usque ad Galgalam, / ut cognoscas iustitias Domini». / 6«Quid dignum offeram Domino, / dum curvo genu Deo excelso? / Numquid offeram ei holocautomata / et vitulos anniculos? / 7Numquid placebunt Domino milia arietum, / multa milia torrentium olei? / Numquid dabo primogenitum meum pro scelere meo, / fructus ventris mei pro peccato animae meae?». / 8Indicatum

but to do justice, and to love kindness,[p]
and to walk humbly with your God?

**Jerusalem is punished for her sins**
⁹The voice of the LORD cries to the city—
and it is sound wisdom to fear thy name:
"Hear, O tribe and assembly of the city![q]

Amos 8:5    ¹⁰Can I forget[r] the treasures of wickedness in the house of
the wicked,
and the scant measure that is accursed?
¹¹Shall I acquit the man with wicked scales
and with a bag of deceitful weights?
¹²Your rich[s] men are full of violence;
your inhabitants speak lies,
and their tongue is deceitful in their mouth.
¹³Therefore I have begun[t] to smite you,
making you desolate because of your sins.

Lev 26:26    ¹⁴You shall eat, but not be satisfied,
Hos 4:10    and there shall be hunger in your inward parts;
you shall put away, but not save,
and what you save I will give to the sword.

---

**6:9–16.** In this passage God spells out the sins being committed in Jerusalem. Among those underlined are injustice and forms of cheating (vv. 10–11); the Hebrew of v. 10 refers to a *bath* (a liquid measure of almost 21 litres or 5 gallons) and an *ephad*, a grain measure of similar size (cf. Ezek 45:11).

But just as virtue breeds virtue, so sin breeds sin: the injustice of the well-to-do leads them to violence and deceit (v. 12). The Lord spells out the penalty

for this—effort that produces no fruit (vv. 13–15). But he senses that even that will not manage to change their hearts. Therefore, by way of a conclusion to the whole passage, we get v. 16. Jerusalem's sins have become like those of Israel (Omri, 885–874 BC, and Ahab, 874–853 BC, kings of Israel, were well known for their transgressions against the Law of the Lord: cf. 1 Kings 16:23–24), and Jerusalem's fate cannot be much different—destruction, desolation, deportation.

---

est tibi, o homo, quid sit bonum, / et quid Dominus quaerat a te: / utique facere iudicium et diligere caritatem / et sollicitum ambulare cum Deo tuo. / ⁹Vox Domini ad civitatem clamat / —et sapientia est timere nomen tuum—: / «Audite, tribus et coetus civitatis! / ¹⁰Numquid tolerabo batum iniquum / et ephi minus maledictum? / ¹¹Numquid iustificabo stateram impiam / et sacelli pondera dolosa? / ¹²Quia divites eius repleti sunt iniquitate, / et habitantes in ea loquebantur mendacium, / et lingua eorum fraudulenta in ore eorum. / ¹³Ego ergo coepi percutere te / perditione super peccatis tuis. / ¹⁴Tu comedes et non saturaberis, / et sordes tuae in medio tui. / Tu removebis et non salvabis; / et, quos salvaveris, in

**p.** Or *steadfast love*   **q.** Cn Compare Gk: Heb *and who has appointed it yet*   **r.** Cn: Heb uncertain
**s.** Heb *whose*   **t.** Gk Syr Vg: Heb *have made sick*

[15]You shall sow, but not reap;
    you shall tread olives, but not anoint yourselves with oil;
    you shall tread grapes, but not drink wine.
[16]For you have kept the statutes of Omri,[u]
    and all the works of the house of Ahab;
    and you have walked in their counsels;
that I may make you a desolation, and your[v] inhabitants a hissing;
    so you shall bear the scorn of the peoples."[w]

Deut 28:30–33
38–40
Amos 5:11
Zeph 1:13
Hag 1:6
1 Kings 16:16,25;
30–33

## Lament about general corruption

7 [1]Woe is me! For I have become
    as when the summer fruit has been gathered,
    as when the vintage has been gleaned:
there is no cluster to eat,
    no first-ripe fig which my soul desires.
[2]The godly man has perished from the earth,
    and there is none upright among men;
they all lie in wait for blood,
    and each hunts his brother with a net.
[3]Their hands are upon what is evil, to do it diligently;
    the prince and the judge ask for a bribe,

Amos 8:1
Hos 9:10

Ps 14:1–3
Jer 5:1

Jer 4:22
Hos 4:18
Mic 3:11

---

**7:1–6.** This passage seems to describe a situation that is the reverse of the messianic plenty heralded in 4:1–5. There the oracle promised peace, tranquillity and fruitfulness (4:3–4), and here war, distrust and fruitlessness, are denounced (vv. 1–3); there people walked in the name of the Lord (4:5), and here dishonesty and confusion abound (vv. 3–4). For that reason, the prophet sees a "day" of punishment coming (v. 4; cf. 1:2–5). Verses 5–6 are difficult to interpret. They may be a continuation of what was said earlier (vv. 1–3), mentioning another aspect of general corruption—distrust reaching such a pitch that even close friends and family members are wary of each other. However, the passage could also be interpreted as instancing the confusion that this "day" will bring. That is how it seems to be taken in the New Testament, when our Lord quotes v. 6 (cf. Mt 10:35; Lk 12:53), as one of the signs of what happens when he comes into the world—bringing confusion (cf. v. 4) but also salvation.

gladium dabo. / [15]Tu seminabis et non metes, / tu calcabis olivam et non ungeris oleo, / mustum et non bibes vinum. / [16]Custodisti praecepta Amri / et omne opus domus Achab; / et ambulasti in voluntatibus eorum, / ut darem te in perditionem / et habitantes tuos in sibilum: / et opprobrium populorum portabitis».   **[7]** [1]Vae mihi, quia factum est mihi / sicut congregata messe, / sicut collecta vindemia! / Non est botrus ad comedendum, / nec praecoqua ficus, quam desideravit anima mea. / [2]Periit pius de terra, / et rectus in hominibus non est; / omnes in sanguine insidiantur, / vir fratrem suum rete venatur. / [3]Ad malum manus eorum paratae sunt; / princeps postulat, / et iudex est pro mercede, / et magnus

**u.** Gk Syr Vg Tg; Heb *the statues of Omri are kept*   **v.** Heb *its*   **w.** Gk: Heb *my people*

and the great man utters the evil desire of his soul;
thus they weave it together.
⁴The best of them is like a brier,
the most upright of them a thorn hedge.
The day of their<sup>x</sup> watchmen, of their<sup>x</sup> punishment, has come;
now their confusion is at hand.

Jer 9:4  ⁵Put no trust in a neighbour,
have no confidence in a friend;
guard the doors of your mouth
from her who lies in your bosom;

Mt 10:21,35–36  ⁶for the son treats the father with contempt,
Lk 12:53   the daughter rises up against her mother,
the daughter-in-law against her mother-in-law;
a man's enemies are the men of his own house.

**The prophet's attitude**
⁷But as for me, I will look to the LORD,
I will wait for the God of my salvation;
my God will hear me.

## 4. HOPE AND PRAYER FOR THE FUTURE*

**Zion looks forward to the future**
Ps 107:10;  ⁸Rejoice not over me, O my enemy;
27:2; 37:5–7   when I fall, I shall rise;
when I sit in darkness,
the LORD will be a light to me.

---

**7:7.** The book of Micah contains denunciations and threats, but it is above all a book that announces salvation. The censures in the third part end with this verse, which not only expresses the prophet's devout and hopeful attitude but also asserts his conviction that the Lord will listen to his prayer.

***7:8–20.** The book ends with some beautiful oracles in which the prophet sees his hopes of restoration fulfilled.

manifestat desiderium animae suae; / vae eis, qui pervertunt illud! / ⁴Qui optimus in eis, est quasi paliurus, / et, qui rectus, quasi spina de saepe; dies speculatorum tuorum, visitatio tua venit: / nunc erit confusio eorum. / ⁵Nolite credere amico, / nolite confidere in proximo; / ab ea, quae dormit in sinu tuo, / custodi claustra oris tui; / ⁶quia filius contumeliam facit patri, / filia consurgit adversus matrem suam, / nurus adversus socrum suam: / inimici hominis domestici eius. / ⁷Ego autem ad Dominum aspiciam, / exspectabo Deum salvatorem meum; audiet me Deus meus. / ⁸Ne laeteris, inimica mea, super me /

**x.** Heb *your*

[9]I will bear the indignation of the LORD
    because I have sinned against him,
until he pleads my cause
    and executes judgment for me.
He will bring me forth to the light;
    I shall behold his deliverance.
[10]Then my enemy will see,                                    Ps 42:3,4,11
    and shame will cover her who said to me,
    "Where is the LORD your God?"
My eyes will gloat over her;
    now she will be trodden down
    like the mire of the streets.

---

The content of these verses reminds us of other prophetical passages such as chapters 33 and 40–55 in the book of Isaiah. The poem begins by focusing on Jerusalem. Fallen and afflicted, she expresses her conviction that the Lord will raise her (vv. 8–10). Then the Lord promises that he will build her anew and that her reputation will increase until she is the boast of the world (vv. 11–13). From this point on, the oracle takes the form of a prayer—first, to ask the Lord to be the people's shepherd (vv. 14–17), and then to thank him for his steadfast love, because he is forgiving and forgets past faults (vv. 18–20).

**7:8–10.** These verses should probably be dated to the time of the exile: Jerusalem has fallen and is under the control of her enemies. But the true Israelite, who is a believer, knows that that fall happened on account of sin, and that the Lord will raise her up again when those sins have been purged (v. 9). The Lord will not forever overlook the plight of his chosen ones; he will always be just (vv. 9–10); Jerusalem has hope, "for the Lord will be a light for me" (v. 8).

The vengeful feelings against enemies here are difficult to square with Christ's commandment of love. So, bearing in mind the fact that the New Testament calls the devil and death enemies of man (cf. 1 Cor 15:26), this oracle can be read in an allegorical sense as meaning the Lord's triumph over those enemies: "Although he died at our hands, he rose from the dead, routed the enemy, stole their victory and removed forever the sting of death. We are heavily weighed down in this world, and the enemy rejoices at our sorrow and bitterness of heart; on the day of resurrection, however, we will destroy his joy, as Micah says: *Rejoice not over me, O my enemy; when I fall, I shall rise.* The resurrection will break the chains of the enemy, and his triumph will encompass the whole world" (St Ambrose, *Enarrationes in xii psalmos,* 40, 34, 2).

quia cecidi: consurgam; / cum sedeo in tenebris, / Dominus lux mea est. / [9]Iram Domini porto, / quoniam peccavi ei, / donec iudicet causam meam / et faciat iudicium meum; / educet me in lucem, / videbo iustitiam eius. / [10]Et aspiciet inimica mea / et operietur confusione, / quae dicit ad me: / «Ubi

**Warning to the nations**

[11]A day for the building of your walls!
   In that day the boundary shall be far extended.
[12]In that day they will come to you,
   from Assyria to[y] Egypt,
   and from Egypt to the River,
   from sea to sea and from mountain to mountain.
[13]But the earth will be desolate
   because of its inhabitants,
   for the fruit of their doings.

**Prayer for Jerusalem**

Ex 34:1    [14]Shepherd thy people with thy staff,
Ps 23:1–2; 95:7        the flock of thy inheritance,
   who dwell alone in a forest
   in the midst of a garden land;
   let them feed in Bashan and Gilead
   as in the days of old.

---

**7:11–13.** The restoration of Israel brings with it three things—the rebuilding of the walls of Jerusalem and the extension of the country's borders far beyond the narrow confines of the kingdom of Judah prior to its fall (v. 11); honour and glory for Jerusalem, which will be where the whole world comes, to learn from the chosen people (v. 12; cf. 4:1–2); finally, desolation for those places where the Law of the Lord is not respected (v. 13). While it is true that some of the things said here are quite harsh, these verses do express the highest hope of all creation. As St Paul says, "When all things are subjected to him, then the Son himself will also be subjected to him who put all things under him, that God may be everything to everyone" (1 Cor 15:28).

**7:14–17.** These verses also deal with hope in the future restoration, but it is now expressed in the form of a prayer to the Lord. He is asked for a return to the way things were in the early days of the chosen people—a repetition of wondrous works that will astound the Gentiles (vv. 16–17) and convince them of the power of the Lord (v. 16). The prayer also desires the Lord to be the only shepherd of his people (v. 14; cf. 5:3), who now occupy the whole of Palestine again, a land that is most

est Dominus Deus tuus?». / Oculi mei videbunt in eam; / nunc erit in conculcationem / ut lutum platearum. / [11]Dies veniet ut aedificentur maceriae tuae; / in die illa dilatabuntur fines tui. / [12]In die illa usque ad te venient / habitantes ab Assyria usque ad Aegyptum / et ab Aegypto usque ad flumen / et a mari usque ad mare / et a monte usque ad montem. / [13]Terra autem erit in desolationem / propter habitatores suos / et propter fructum operum eorum. / [14]Pasce populum tuum in virga tua, / gregem hereditatis tuae, / habitantes solos in saltu, / in medio hortorum; / pascantur Basan et Galaad / iuxta dies

**y.** Cn: Heb *and cities of*

$^{15}$As in the days when you came out of the land of Egypt
    I will show them$^z$ marvellous things.
$^{16}$The nations shall see and be ashamed
    of all their might; Is 26:11
they shall lay their hands on their mouths;
    their ears shall be deaf;
$^{17}$they shall lick the dust like a serpent, Gen 3:15
    like the crawling things of the earth; Ps 72:9
they shall come trembling out of their strongholds,
    they shall turn in dread to the LORD our God,
    and they shall fear because of thee.

### Hymn to the Lord

$^{18}$Who is a God like thee, pardoning iniquity Ex 15:11; 34:6–7
    and passing over transgression Ps 103:9
    for the remnant of his inheritance? Jer 31:34; 50:20
He does not retain his anger for ever
    because he delights in steadfast love.

---

fertile. Bashan and Gilead, on the eastern banks and highlands of the Jordan, were areas renowned for rich pasture-land.

**7:18–20.** The last three verses of the book, in a liturgical tone, celebrate the Lord's steadfast love. Witnessing the works of the Lord (his pardoning of sins, and putting them out of his mind: vv. 18–19; his faithfulness to his promises, no matter what: v. 20), all that the believer can do is be grateful and live in awe: "Who is a God like thee?" (v. 18). Many of the terms used in this short hymn (remnant, inheritance, faithfulness, etc.) have come up earlier in the book and are being rehearsed again

here. But we can appreciate their importance more if we remember the way Micah is echoed in the Benedictus of Zechariah in the New Testament. That hymn sums up very well the hope in the Messiah harboured by generation upon generation of the people of God, and when we reread it, it will help to revive our own hope in the definitive (second) coming of the Lord: "Blessed be the Lord God of Israel, for he has visited and redeemed his people, and has raised up a horn of salvation for us in the house of his servant David, as he spoke by the mouth of his holy prophets from of old" (Lk 1:68–70).

antiquos. / $^{15}$Secundum dies egressionis tuae de terra Aegypti / ostende nobis mirabilia. / $^{16}$Videbunt gentes et confundentur / super omni fortitudine sua, / ponent manum super os, / aures eorum surdae erunt; / $^{17}$lingent pulverem sicut serpens, / velut reptilia terrae. / Trementes exibunt de aedibus suis «ad Dominum Deum nostrum» / formidabunt et timebunt te. / $^{18}$Quis Deus similis tui, / qui aufers iniquitatem / et transis peccatum / reliquiarum hereditatis tuae? / Non servat in aeternum furorem suum,

**z.** Heb *him*

Rom 6:14

¹⁹He will again have compassion upon us,
 he will tread our iniquities under foot.
 Thou wilt[a] cast all our sins
  into the depths of the sea.

Gen 22:16–18;
28:13–15
Lk 1:73
Rom 15:8

²⁰Thou wilt show faithfulness to Jacob
 and steadfast love to Abraham,
 as thou hast sworn to our fathers
  from the days of old.

---

/ quoniam volens misericordiam est. / ¹⁹Revertetur et miserebitur nostri, / calcabit iniquitates nostras / et proiciet in profundum maris / omnia peccata nostra. / ²⁰Dabis veritatem Iacob, / misericordiam Abraham, / quae iurasti patribus nostris / a diebus antiquis.

**a.** Gk Syr Vg Tg: Heb *their*

# NAHUM

# Introduction

The book of Nahum comes seventh in the codex of the minor prophets, in both the Hebrew and the Greek manuscripts. The fact that it always appears in the same place, after Micah, is in line with a very ancient tradition, according to which Nahum is the first in the list of the later books that deal with a single theme only—usually to do with the judgment of God. The entire book revolves around the fall of the Assyrian capital, Nineveh, to the Babylonians (612 BC). The title is unusual: "An oracle concerning Nineveh. The book of the vision of Nahum of Elkosh"; it does not say (as Hosea, Joel, Amos and Micah do) "The word of the Lord that came to …". The person responsible for writing the title probably regarded this book as an oracle against Nineveh, written in a sapiential style.

The name Nahum comes from *naham* (to console), a root also found in other biblical names such as Menahem or Nehemiah. There is no one else called Nahum in the Bible, and we know nothing more about this person other than that he came from Elkosh, which must have been a town somewhere in Judah. From the context of the book one can take it that Nahum was active during the long reign of Manasseh (698–642 BC).

Some commentators have suggested that Nahum was a prophet attached to the temple—on the grounds that this book (along with that of Habakkuk) contains various elements that suggest it may have been used in a liturgical service to celebrate the fall of Nineveh. However, neither the tone of the book nor even the opening poem has features of the psalms or other texts designed for the temple. The book seems to be, rather, a prophetical reflection on the destruction of Nineveh—an event that allowed the writer to underscore God's sovereignty over the impious, to strike a note of warning for the chosen people, and to thank the Lord for ridding Israel of an enemy.

## 1. STRUCTURE AND CONTENT

The book of Nahum belongs to a particular prophetical-sapiential literary genre (*rîb*) which might be called "prophetical disputation". This consists in the sacred author taking it upon himself to dispel doubts and objections raised in connexion with a specific theme. The theme in the case of the book of Nahum is the sovereign power of God—something that is being called into question both by Jews, who cannot see how it is compatible with the splendour of Nineveh, and by the Ninevites, who seem to mock the power of God for they sin with impunity. Nahum replies in no uncertain terms: the great city is going to fall very soon; its collapse will be the work of God alone and it will be something that Nineveh justly deserves; it will be annihilated, and the chosen people will be saved.

The book, as we now have it, falls into three parts, excluding the heading, which is clearly a later addition:

1. HYMN TO GOD, THE MIGHTY JUDGE (1:2–8). This is a theophany celebrating God's power over his enemies.

2. THE FALL OF NINEVEH FORETOLD (1:9–15). This is a sapiential reflection for the benefit of Judah's ears: when the people see the fall of Nineveh, they should acknowledge that it is entirely the work of the Lord, and they should rejoice at their own election.

3. NINEVEH ATTACKED AND OVERTHROWN (2:1–3:19). This, too, is a sapiential reflection, this time for the benefit of the Ninevites: when their city is attacked and destroyed, they too should confess that it is all the Lord's doing.

## 2. COMPOSITION AND HISTORICAL BACKGROUND

There is still much debate among scholars as to the process of formation of the text. Many are of the opinion that the opening hymn celebrating the power and sovereignty of God (1:2–8) was written later than the rest of the book because it is a carefully worked alphabetical psalm designed to explain the book's theology.

The majority view among scholars is that the poems about Nineveh date from the seventh century BC, between 663 and 612, that is, after the destruction of the Egyptian city of Thebes (No-amon, referred to in 3:8) and before Nineveh fell to the Babylonians. That they were written before that event is suggested by the vividness of the account of the assault on Nineveh (2:8–10) and by the description of the cruelty of the invaders (3:1–3) which indicate that the author shares the anti-Assyrian feelings that were widespread in the years leading up to the fall of Nineveh. Also, three years after the collapse of the city, King Josiah died at the hands of the Egyptians (609 BC) and at that time the great enemy was Babylon, so it would not have made much sense to celebrate the fall of Nineveh. Therefore, there is a good case for dating the oracle to c.630, when the death of the Assyrian king Ashurbanipal fanned the flames of Jewish nationalism. In fact, one could argue that these poems, highly charged as they are with patriotic sentiments and praise for Israelite values (especially the Israelite belief in God as the Lord of all), may have made a significant contribution to the religious and political reforms carried out around the year 622.

Once the substantial core of the book was written, a Deuteronomic author probably tinkered with the text after the return from exile, updating the old oracles against Nineveh to apply them to Babylon. The alphabetical hymn at the start of the book gives it a wider range of reference by making the point that the judgment of God will come down on any power that attempts to oppress the chosen people.

The book is very impressive from the literary point of view. In its description of the fall of Nineveh, one scene follows another in a build-up of tension: it begins with the siege and assault on the city (2:3–10): here the author manages to convey all the noise, chaos and mayhem of the events. This is followed by a tongue-in-cheek lamentation about the capital of Assyria, which is described as a "lion" (2:12) and by a threat (also tongue-in-cheek) against the city noted for its immorality and corruption (3:1–7). The reference to Thebes, which had been destroyed by Assyria, underlines the fact that Nineveh's fate will be a similar one, only more violent and bloody (3:8–11). Once again the author uses irony to poke fun at the city's formidable defence works: everything will be consumed by fire (3:12–15a). The inhabitants, even though they are many in number, will scurry away like insects on a cold day (3:15b–17). The book ends with a sarcastic funeral poem celebrating the death of the Assyrian king and proclaiming the joy felt by all nations at the fall of the great king (3:18–19).

### 3. MESSAGE

Scholars have noted with some surprise that the prophet does not denounce even one defect of Judah or predict that any punishment will befall her. The book reads like a patriotic anthem, celebrating with delight the downfall of the oppressor; but two important themes underline Nahum's impassioned poems —God's sovereignty over all peoples, and his special providence towards the chosen people.

a) *The sovereignty of God.* God dominates the created world and the affairs of mankind and there is no one who can successfully challenge him (1:8). This key idea in the alphabetical poem that begins the book is applied to the destruction of Nineveh: the very worst sorts of sins have been committed in Assyria—idolatry, magic-making, tyranny (2:10–13; 3:4–7)—but the whole place will be burned up: "Desolate! Desolation and ruin!" (2:10). In this way, the prophet uses religion as the key to explain history: God is behind the splendour of Nineveh, and God is behind its fall; God bestows dominion on the Assyrians, but he also metes out severe punishment to transgressors. The destruction of Nineveh is described in typical "day of the Lord" language (although that exact phrase is not used). We can see this by comparing turns of phrase in Nahum with those used by earlier prophets to describe the judgment of God—for example, Nahum 2:10 with Isaiah 2:7; Nahum 2:11 with Isaiah 13:7 and Jeremiah 30:5; and Nahum 3:10 with Isaiah 13:16.

b) *God's providence towards the chosen people*. The book celebrates the favours God has done for his people, contrasting them with Nineveh's misfortunes: it is true that God has made his people pay for their sins over a number of years, but there will be an end to their trials (1:12–13). God announces a new era of peace (1:15), which will begin with the destruction of its most cruel enemy, Assyria, and the capital of that great power. Empires come and go, but the people of God remain forever.

## 4. THE BOOK OF NAHUM IN THE LIGHT OF THE NEW TESTAMENT

The Old Testament itself contains some passages that refer to the book of Nahum: for example, so close is the connexion between Nahum 1:15 and Is 52:1–7 that scholars have often wondered which of the two was written first. All the indications are that Nahum was, because it contains some rare expressions that do not seem to fit an author of the late period. For example, the description of the messenger is much more sober in Nahum than it is in Isaiah. The New Testament references to this passage (Rom 10:15 and Mk 16:15–16) derive more from Isaiah than from Nahum. The reference to the locusts in Joel 1:4 and its later application (cf. Joel 2:4–9) may have some connexion with Nahum 3:15. (Tob 14:12–15). The book of Nahum also seems to have influenced the book of Tobit, which rejoices over the fall of Nineveh, thus alluding to the fulfilment of the prophecies about the Assyrian city.

In Jewish literature the book of Nahum tends to be interpreted in nationalistic terms. Flavius Josephus, who dated Nahum to the eighth century (during the reign of Jotham), comments ironically in his *Antiquitates Judaicae* (9, 2, 3): "All the predictions about Nineveh found fulfilment 150 years later."

Some fragments of a commentary on Nahum (4QpNah) came to light in Qumran. These, too, interpret the book in nationalistic terms and they apply it to the Jews' struggle against the Seleucids. There is even a mention of Dionysius III Eukairos and his war against Alexander Jannaeus around the year 88 BC.

We find this nationalistic interpretation of the book still maintained by great medieval authors such as David Kimchi (d. 1235).

In the New Testament the book of Nahum is not quoted explicitly, perhaps because of the excessively nationalistic tone of contemporary commentaries. Nor is it used in Christian liturgy. In the writings of the Fathers, the book of Nahum, and those of Haggai and Obadiah are the prophetical books that receive least attention, and any references there are interpret it as praise of the power and justice of God; in other words, they do not give it a nationalistic interpretation. St Jerome comments that the book carries a message of comfort ("*Nahum* is interpreted as *comforter*"), because it shows that divine justice applies to all: "Every word that is spoken against Nineveh should be interpreted, in a figurative way, as applying to the whole world."[1] A later commentary by St Julian, bishop of Toledo (sixth century) applies to Nahum the four medieval senses of Scripture: this prophecy, he says, "speaks, in a historical sense, of Nineveh; in an allegorical sense, of the destruction of the world on the last day; in a mystical sense, of the redemption of all mankind by Christ; in a moral sense, of man's return to his original state of dignity and innocence"[2] And, later still, Theophylact (eleventh century), who wrote an *Expositio* on Nahum, interpreting it as a text about the universality of divine justice, points out: "The book teaches that because God is just, no man lives beyond the reach of his Providence: each will be rewarded or punished according to his deeds."[3]

---

1. *Commentarium in Nahum*, prologue.  2. *Commentarium in Nahum prophetam*, 1, 1.  3. *Expositio super Nahum*, 1.

Jer 30:2
Hab 1:1
Zech 9:1; 12:1

## Title

**1** ¹An oracle concerning Nineveh. The book of the vision of Nahum of Elkosh.

# 1. HYMN TO GOD, THE MIGHTY JUDGE*

Ex 20:5–6; 34:6–7
Deut 4:24

²The LORD is a jealous God and avenging,
the LORD is avenging and wrathful;

**1:1.** This is an unusual sort of title, not found in any of the other prophetical books. The only one similar to it is that of the book of Habakkuk (1:1), which is probably an indication that the two books share a similar outlook and perhaps even the same origin. "Oracle" (in Hebrew, *massā'*) is a term used to introduce the oracles against the nations (cf. Is 13:1; 15:1; Zech 9:1), and it means not so much an announcement of punishment as a lesson—to the effect that the Lord's judgment extends to all nations, and that the downfall of the pagan nations carries a message for Israel: God in his love will deliver her from them. "Vision" is a word used for a poetic description, with eschatological connotations, prefiguring God's last judgment of his enemies. What is being described here is the fall of Nineveh, the capital of Assyria from the time of Sennacherib onwards. "Book of the vision" means that, even if everything was foretold previously, writing it down guarantees that what the seer sees will indeed come to pass (cf. Jer 30:2).

"Elkosh". It is difficult to say exactly where this was. No Northern town with this name is known, nor any that shares a similar etymology. Nor does it seem likely that Nahum was among the people from the Northern kingdom deported by Sennacherib. It is more likely that he came from Judah, though one can say nothing more than that.

**\*1:2–8.** This is an alphabetical poem, but it runs to only eleven verses, that is, the first half of the alphabet. It is a typical hymn or psalm in praise of God, in which the adjectives describe the person of the Lord (vv. 2a, 3b) and the verbs his astounding actions (vv. 3b–4). In this way, descriptive praise is filled out with narrative praise. The poem contains three sections which are in some way concentric: the first depicts the Lord as "jealous and avenging" (v. 2–3a); the second describes an impressive theophany in which God is revealed in the elements of whirlwind, storm and clouds (vv. 3b–6; cf. Ex 19:16–25; Is 6:1–10); the third (like the first) extols divine attributes—this time, goodness, protectiveness and mercy (vv. 7–8a). And the final verse underscores God's power to judge and punish his enemies (v. 8b).

[1] ¹Oraculum Nineve. Liber visionis Nahum Elcesaei. ²Deus aemulator et ulciscens Dominus, / ulciscens Dominus et habens furorem, / ulciscens Dominus in hostes suos / et servans iram inimicis

the LORD takes vengeance on his adversaries
and keeps wrath for his enemies.
³The LORD is slow to anger and of great might,
and the LORD will by no means clear the guilty.

Ex 34:5–7
Num 14:18
Ps 86:15; 103:8; 145:8

His way is in whirlwind and storm,
and the clouds are the dust of his feet.
⁴He rebukes the sea and makes it dry,
he dries up all the rivers;

Ex 14:16,21; Ps 106:9
Is 50:2

---

**1:2–3.** "A jealous God and avenging". God is often described as jealous (cf. Ex 20:5–6; 34:6–7, 14; etc.) to underscore the fact that justice is as central to God's judgment as mercy. In Nahum's hymn the stress is laid more on the rigour of God's judgment, in a way that sounds shocking to the modern ear. But one needs to remember that the Hebrew root-word translated as "avenging, vengeance etc.", and often applied to the Lord (Ps 58:10; Is 34:8; 61:2), should not be interpreted as meaning the same as when it is applied to human behaviour. To say that God "takes vengeance on his adversaries" means that he "rights a wrong", "asserts a right": he judges fairly, though when he passes sentence his decision is irrevocable.

"Slow to anger": this graphic way of describing God's tenderness occurs often in the books of the Pentateuch and in the Psalms (cf. Ex 34:6; Num 14:18; Ps 86:15; 103:8; 145:8) but not in the prophets. Nahum probably resorts to more traditional expressions in order to make it clear that Nineveh's severe punishment is not at odds with divine mercy. As the great theologians have put it, all qualities combine perfectly in God: "In God, power and essence, will and intelligence, wisdom and justice, form one unity, so that there can be nothing in divine power that is not also at the same time in the just will of God or in his wise understanding" (St Thomas Aquinas, *Summa theologiae*, 1, 25, 5, ad 1).

"His way is in whirlwind": the prophet reaffirms the awe-inspiring presence of the Lord by borrowing words from the Sinai theophany (cf. Ex 19:16). It is a way of acknowledging God's sovereignty over all creation.

**1:4–5.** This additional allusion to the Exodus (v. 4; cf. Ex 14:16, 21) celebrates God's initiative in liberating his people; and the earthquake (v. 5) illustrates his power over all creation. The prophets interpret negative natural phenomena (droughts, earthquakes, etc.) as being signs of divine judgment (cf. Jer 14:3–7) and a proof that God cannot abide injustice and crime and, therefore, always prevails over them. "The Last Judgment will reveal that God's justice triumphs over all the injustices committed by his creatures" (*Catechism of the Catholic Church*, 1040).

suis. / ³Dominus patiens et magnus fortitudine, / nullumque impunitum derelinquet Dominus. / In tempestate et turbine via eius, / et nubes pulvis pedum eius. / ⁴Increpans mare et exsiccans illud / et

Bashan and Carmel wither,
the bloom of Lebanon fades.

Jer 4:24 ⁵The mountains quake before him,
the hills melt;
the earth is laid waste before him,
the world and all that dwell therein.

Rev 6:17 ⁶Who can stand before his indignation?
Who can endure the heat of his anger?
His wrath is poured out like fire,
and the rocks are broken asunder by him.

1 Chron 16:34 ⁷The LORD is good,
Ps 100:5; a stronghold in the day of trouble;
135:3; 145:9 he knows those who take refuge in him.
Jer 33:11 ⁸But with an overflowing flood
Lam 3:25 he will make a full end of his adversaries,ᵃ
and will pursue his enemies into darkness.

## 2. THE FALL OF NINEVEH FORETOLD*

1 Sam 2:6 ⁹What do you plot against the LORD?
He will make a full end;

---

**1:7–8.** God's goodness is a quality that the Psalms link to mercy (cf. Ps 100:5; 135:3; 145:9) and celebrate in liturgical hymns (Ps 34:9). Nahum, too, extols the goodness of God, which is seen in the way that He protects those who trust in him, and destroys enemies. This use of contrasts, a feature of Semitic languages, is designed to stress the Lord's predilection for those who stay loyal to him.

*1:9–2:1.* This section is made up of heterogeneous elements that may have suffered when they were being brought together. Some commentators describe it as a dialogue that the prophet had with Israelites and Assyrians: some verses would be addressed to the Israelites and the Assyrians together (1:9–10), some just to the Assyrians (1:11, 14) and some just to the Israelites (1:12, 13, 15). But that sort of literary artifice would be too

omnia flumina ad desertum deducens. / Elanguit Basan et Carmelus, / et flos Libani elanguit. / ⁵Montes commoti sunt ab eo, / et colles conturbati; / et contremuit terra a facie eius / et orbis et omnes habitantes in eo. / ⁶Ante faciem indignationis eius quis stabit, / et quis resistet in aestu furoris eius? Indignatio eius effusa est ut ignis, / et petrae dissolutae sunt ab eo. / ⁷Bonus Dominus, / refugium in die tribulationis / et sciens sperantes in se / ⁸et in diluvio transeunte; / consummationem faciet adversariorum suorum, / et inimicos eius persequentur tenebrae. / ⁹Quid cogitatis contra Dominum? / Consummationem ipse

**a.** Gk: Heb *her place*

he will not take vengeance[b] twice on his foes.[c]
[10]Like entangled thorns they are consumed,[d]
    like dry stubble.
[11]Did one not[e] come out from you,

Deut 13:14
Ps 18:5

    who plotted evil against the LORD,
    and counselled villainy?

[12]Thus says the LORD,

2 Kings
19:35–36

    "Though they be strong and many,[f]
    they will be cut off and pass away.
Though I have afflicted you,
    I will afflict you no more.
[13]And now I will break his yoke from off you

Is 9:3

    and will burst your bonds asunder."

[14]The LORD has given commandment about you:

Is 14:19–21
Jer 8:1–2

    "No more shall your name be perpetuated;

---

sophisticated for a seventh-century author. It seems more likely that the only speakers here are the inhabitants of Judah and Jerusalem, whom the fall of Nineveh would move to acknowledge the sovereign power of God and the special love he has for his people. In any event, the first verses (1:9–10) are introductory, and the rest are an announcement and an interpretation in prophetical language of the fall of Nineveh which the text will go on to describe.

**1:9–10.** This introduction is a sapiential consideration which is underpinned by the "legal pleading style" (*rîb*) used in

prophetical writing. The rhetorical question, "What do you [plural] plot against the Lord?" and the explanation that follows are addressed to those who interpreted God's inactivity as a sign of powerlessness and a proof that he had forsaken his people. The reply leaves no room for doubt: the Assyrian capital will be assailed and destroyed. The imagery of thorns and drunken people (v. 10 and note **d**) illustrates the state of decadence into which Nineveh has fallen, and its imminent collapse.

**1:11–14.** "Did one not come out from you", that is, did the invader not march

---

faciet; / non consurget duplex tribulatio. / [10]Sicut spinae condensae se invicem complectentes / et sicut potatores inebriati / consumentur quasi stipula omnino arida. / [11]Ex te exivit cogitans contra Dominum malitiam, / mente pertractans praevaricationem. / [12]Haec dicit Dominus: / «Et si incolumes fuerint et numerosi, / sic quoque attondentur et pertransibunt; / afflixi te et non affligam te ultra. / [13]Et nunc conteram virgam eius de dorso tuo / et vincula tua disrumpam». / [14]Et praecipiet super te Dominus: / «Non seminabitur ex nomine tuo amplius. / De domo dei tui disperdam sculptile et conflatile; / ponam

**b.** Gk: Heb *rise up*   **c.** Cn: Heb *distress*   **d.** Heb *are consumed, drunken as with their drink*
**e.** Cn: Heb *fully*   **f.** Heb uncertain

> from the house of your gods I will cut off
> the graven image and the molten image.
> I will make your grave, for you are vile."

<sup>15g</sup>Behold, on the mountains the feet of him
    who brings good tidings,
    who proclaims peace!
Keep your feasts, O Judah,
    fulfil your vows,
for never again shall the wicked come against you,
    he is utterly cut off.

*2 Sam 18:26*
*Is 41:27;*
*52: 7–10*
*Nahum 1:11*
*Acts 10:36*
*Rom 10:15*

---

away, never to return—the invader who had come bent on no good. It is probably a reference to the Assyrian king Sennacherib who, as 2 Kings 18:13–19:37 reports, invaded many cities of Judah in 701 BC, but miraculously failed to take Jerusalem. He would have been the one who "plotted evil … and counselled villainy" (v. 11). Literally, this is "counsellor of Belial", a "lawless" personage, the enemy of God (cf. Neh 1:11; 2:1) and the personification of wickedness (cf. Deut 13:14 and note). The change from plural (v. 9) to singular (v. 11) occurs frequently in prophetical writing: the city is sometimes personified (singular) and sometimes taken as the sum of its inhabitants (plural).

**1:14.** This announcement is addressed to a male individual (the king of Assyria). Here it is presented as being spoken by the Lord so that the Jews will learn from the fate of their arch-enemy and be more faithful in their worship of the Lord by having nothing to do with graven images.

**1:15.** In the context of warfare the messenger is the one who comes from the battlefield bearing good news (cf. 2 Sam 18:26; Is 41:27). The book of Isaiah uses the same words as here in a more catholic context, in a hymn celebrating the kingdom of God (Is 52:7); there, the messenger is a spokesman of the Lord; here, his presence is metaphorical. As well as being the end of war, peace stands for all the good things that God gives his people. Hence the call to celebrate a great feast, probably to hold a pilgrimage to Jerusalem, to celebrate the fact that the dreaded Sennacherib has met his end. This announcement sounds very harsh, but in the background one can glimpse the rehabilitation of justice when the Kingdom of God is established definitively at the End, "a kingdom of justice, love, and peace" (*Roman Missal*, Preface of Christ the King).

---

sepulcrum tuum, / quia inhonoratus es». **[2]** <sup>1</sup>Ecce super montes pedes evangelizantis / et annuntiantis pacem. / Celebra, Iuda, festivitates tuas / et redde vota tua, / quia non adiciet ultra ut pertranseat in te

**g.** Ch. 2.1 in Heb

# 3. NINEVEH ASSAULTED AND OVERTHROWN*

**The fall of Nineveh interpreted**

2 ¹The shatterer has come up against you.
Man the ramparts;
    watch the road;
gird your loins;
    collect all your strength.

²(For the LORD is restoring the majesty of Jacob
    as the majesty of Israel,
for plunderers have stripped them
    and ruined their branches.)

³The shield of his mighty men is red,
    his soldiers are clothed in scarlet.

Is 5:26–30; 10:12
Jer 5:15–17;
6:22–30

Is 5:1–7

---

**\*2:1–3:19.** A brief introduction explaining the significance of the fall of Nineveh (2:1–2), is followed by a very powerful poem about the assault on and destruction of the Assyrian capital (2:3–3:19); it is interwoven with feelings of joy at the fall of the hated city; astonishment at the scale and nature of the violence; and acknowledgment that there is no appeal against God's sentence. The poem is very carefully constructed, and follows the logical course of an invasion—the assault on the city (2:3–13), a description of the crimes that warranted God's sentence (3:1–7), a comparison with the fate of Thebes (3:8–11), the weakness of Nineveh (its army as well as its fortresses: 3:12–17), and finally an "elegy" for the king of Nineveh (3:18–19).

Nineveh, which boasted of being the greatest of all cities, is brought about with a view to the restoration of Israel, which will obtain the majesty and honour that are its right as God's chosen people. The poem applies to Judah the great names of the ancient patriarch ("Jacob", "Israel") now that the Northern kingdom, Israel, is no more. This clarification should help the reader to interpret the more brutal aspects of the description of the fall of Nineveh as a way of stressing (by contrast) God's predilection for his faithful, as the psalmist says: "for not by their own sword did they win the land, nor did their own arm give them victory; but thy right hand, and thy arm, and the light of thy countenance; for thou didst delight in them" (Ps 44:3).

**2:2.** The "majesty of Jacob": the prophet is saying that the destruction of

**2:3–4.** It is very difficult to capture in translation the full impact of the

Belial: / totus interiit. / ²Ascendit, qui dispergat, contra te. / «Custodi munitionem, / contemplare viam, conforta lumbos, robora virtutem valde». / ³Quia restituet Dominus magnificentiam Iacob / sicut magnificentiam Israel, / quia praedones praedati sunt eos / et propagines eorum corruperunt. / ⁴Clipeus

The chariots flash like flame[h]
  when mustered in array;
  the chargers[i] prance.
[4]The chariots rage in the streets,
  they rush to and fro through the squares;
they gleam like torches,
  they dart like lightning.
[5]The officers are summoned,
  they stumble as they go,
they hasten to the wall,
  the mantelet is set up.
[6]The river gates are opened,
  the palace is in dismay;
[7]its mistress[j] is stripped, she is carried off,
  her maidens lamenting,
moaning like doves,
  and beating their breasts.
[8]Nineveh is like a pool
  whose waters[k] run away.
"Halt! Halt!" they cry;
  but none turns back.
[9]Plunder the silver,
  plunder the gold!
There is no end of treasure,
  or wealth of every precious thing.

---

Hebrew original. The prophet manages to convey the sheer terror and anguish of the Ninevites as the Babylonian army pours through the streets and squares of the great capital of Assyria.

**2:7.** The "mistress", literally "she who stands upright". The original text is not in good condition. The New Vulgate translates it as "the Beautiful" (woman). What is being referred to here apparently is the statue of Ishtar, goddess of love and war, much honoured in Nineveh. On seeing the statue destroyed, her devotees and priestesses would make much lamentation.

fortium eius ruber, / viri exercitus in coccineis; / ignitae laminae ferreae curruum, / quando praeparat bellum, / et equites agitantur. / [5]In viis furibundae currunt quadrigae, / invicem colliduntur in plateis; / aspectus eorum quasi lampades, / quasi fulgura discurrentia. / [6]Recordatur fortium suorum, / ruunt in itineribus suis; / currunt ad murum, / et praeparatur umbraculum. / [7]Portae fluviorum apertae sunt, / palatium tremit. / [8]Et speciosa denudatur, tollitur, / et ancillae eius gemunt ut columbae et percutiunt corda sua. / [9]Et Nineve quasi piscina aquarum, / cuius aquae fugiunt. / «State, state!»; / sed non est qui revertatur. / [10]«Diripite argentum, diripite aurum!». / Et non est finis divitiarum; / thesaurus ex omnibus

**h.** Cn: The meaning of the Hebrew word is uncertain  **i.** Cn Compare Gk Syr: Heb *cypresses*  **j.** The meaning of the Hebrew is uncertain  **k.** Cn Compare Gk: Heb *from the days that she has become, and they*

<sup>10</sup>Desolate! Desolation and ruin!
 Hearts faint and knees tremble,
anguish is on all loins,
 all faces grow pale!
<sup>11</sup>Where is the lions' den,
 the cave<sup>l</sup> of the young lions,
where the lion brought his prey,
 where his cubs were, with none to disturb?
<sup>12</sup>The lion tore enough for his whelps
 and strangled prey for his lionesses;
he filled his caves with prey
 and his dens with torn flesh.

<sup>13</sup>Behold, I am against you, says the LORD of hosts, and I will burn your<sup>m</sup> chariots in smoke, and the sword shall devour your young lions; I will cut off your prey from the earth, and the voice of your messengers shall no more be heard.

Is 13:7
Jer 30:6

Jer 21:13;
50:31; 51:25
Ezek 21:8;
29:10; 35:3;
38:3; 39:1
Nahum 3:5

**Nineveh sentenced for its crimes**

3 <sup>1</sup>Woe to the bloody city,
 all full of lies and booty—

---

**2:11–13.** The image of the lions roving around as they please conveys the power and cruelty of which the Ninevites were guilty—all very different from the smoke and ashes to which the city is reduced, once God's sentence is carried out. "Behold, I am against you": a solemn declaration of divine judgment (repeated in 3:5) is typical of the oracles denouncing Israel or other nations, particularly those in Jeremiah (Jer 21:13; 50:31; 51:25) and Ezekiel (Ezek 21:8; 29:10; 35:3; 38:3; 39:1). The form of words

means that God's sentence is irreversible and will be carried out.

**3:1–7.** These unrestrained verses describe the cruelty of the Assyrians (v. 1), the ferocity of the Babylonians (vv. 2–3), the gravity of Nineveh's idolatry and deceit (v. 4), and finally the judgment handed down by God (vv. 5–7). The severity of Nineveh's sentence prefigures the Last Judgment, of which the *Catechism of the Catholic Church,* 677 says: "God's triumph over

vasis desiderabilibus. / <sup>11</sup>Dissipata et vastata et dilacerata, / et cor tabescens, / et dissolutio geniculorum; / et tremor in cunctis renibus, / et facies omnium eorum candentes. / <sup>12</sup>Ubi est habitaculum leonum, / et spelunca catulorum leonum, / ad quam ivit leo, ut duceret illuc catulum leonis, / et non erat qui exterreret? / <sup>13</sup>Leo cepit sufficienter catulis suis / et necavit leaenis suis; / et implevit praeda speluncas suas / et cubile suum rapina. / <sup>14</sup>«Ecce ego ad te, / dicit Dominus exercituum, / et succendam usque ad fumum quadrigas tuas; / et leunculos tuos comedet gladius, / et exterminabo de terra praedam tuam, / et non audietur ultra vox nuntiorum tuorum». **[3]** <sup>1</sup>Vae, civitas sanguinum, / universa mendacii /

**l.** Cn: Heb *pasture* **m.** Heb *her*

no end to the plunder!

[2]The crack of whip, and rumble of wheel,
galloping horse and bounding chariot!

Ezek 39:11–16   [3]Horsemen charging,
flashing sword and glittering spear,
hosts of slain,
heaps of corpses,
dead bodies without end—
they stumble over the bodies!

Is 47:9:12   [4]And all for the countless harlotries of the harlot,
Rev 9:21; 17:2;
18:23     graceful and of deadly charms,
who betrays nations with her harlotries,
and peoples with her charms.

Jer 13:22   [5]Behold, I am against you,
Hos 2:5     says the LORD of hosts,
Nahum 2:14     and will lift up your skirts over your face;
and I will let nations look on your nakedness
and kingdoms on your shame.
[6]I will throw filth at you
and treat you with contempt,
and make you a gazing-stock.

Is 51:19   [7]And all who look on you will shrink from you and say,
Jer 15:5     Wasted is Nineveh; who will bemoan her?
whence shall I seek comforters for her?[n]

### The destruction of Thebes, an object lesson

Jer 46:25   [8]Are you better than Thebes[o]
that sat by the Nile,

---

the revolt of evil will take the form of the Last Judgement after the final cosmic upheaval of this passing world."

**3:8–11.** Thebes ("No-amon": see note o), the capital of the new Egyptian empire, was located in Upper Egypt. It

---

praeda plena! / Non recedet a te rapina. / [2]Vox flagellorum et vox strepitus rotarum, / equi frementes et quadrigae ferventes, / equites irruentes / [3]et gladii micantes et hastae fulgurantes / et multitudo interfectorum et acervi mortuorum; / nec est finis cadaverum, / et corruunt super corpora. / [4]Hoc propter multitudinem fornicationum meretricis / speciosae et gratae et habentis maleficia, / quae vendidit gentes fornicationibus suis / et nationes maleficiis suis. / [5]«Ecce ego ad te, / dicit Dominus exercituum; / et levabo vestimentum tuum in faciem tuam / et ostendam gentibus nuditatem tuam / et regnis ignominiam tuam. / [6]Et proiciam super te abominationes / et contumeliis te afficiam; / et ponam te in exemplum. / [7]Et erit: omnis, qui viderit te, / resiliet a te et dicet: / "Vastata est Nineve! / Quis dolebit super eam? / Unde quaeram consolatorem tibi?". / [8]Numquid melior es quam Noamon, / quae habitabat

**n.** Gk: Heb *you*   **o.** Heb *No-amon*

with water around her,
>  her rampart a sea,
>  and water her wall?
9Ethiopia was her strength,
>  Egypt too, and that without limit;
>  Put and the Libyans were herᴾ helpers.

Jer 46:9

10Yet she was carried away,
>  she went into captivity;
>  her little ones were dashed in pieces
>  at the head of every street;
for her honoured men lots were cast,
>  and all her great men were bound in chains.
11You also will be drunken,
>  you will be dazed;
you will seek
>  a refuge from the enemy.

Hos 10:14
Joel 4:3
Lk 19:44

### Assyria devoid of power
12All your fortresses are like fig trees
>  with first-ripe figs—
if shaken they fall
>  into the mouth of the eater.

had been sacked and occupied in 663 BC by the Assyrian king, Ashurbanipal. The prophet tauntingly reminds Nineveh, it seems, that the law of "a tooth for a tooth" is being applied to her. Now the conquerors will themselves be conquered, the destroyers themselves destroyed. Just as happened in Thebes, the children of Nineveh will be cruelly put to death—a sign of genocide and a symbol of the unrestrained brutality of the Babylonians.

3:12–17. Nineveh's weakness is witheringly mocked: her fortresses are like fig trees (v. 12), her sturdy soldiers like defenceless women (v. 13), her huge army like swarms of locusts that fly off as easily as they came, without putting up a fight (vv. 15–16). The prophet seems to relish the grotesque picture he has drawn; it shows the immense distance that separates God, almighty sovereign, from created beings that seem to be powerful and really amount to nothing at all.

in fluminibus? / Aquae in circuitu eius: / cuius vallum mare, / aquae muri eius. / 9Chus fuit fortitudo eius / et Aegyptus, cuius non est finis; / Phut et Libyes fuerunt in auxilio eius. / 10Sed et ipsa in transmigrationem ducta est, / ivit in captivitatem. / Parvuli eius elisi sunt / in capite omnium viarum; / et super inclitos eius miserunt sortem, / et omnes optimates eius constricti sunt in compedibus. / 11Et tu ergo inebriaberis, / eris despecta; / et tu quaeres / refugium ab inimico. / 12Omnes munitiones tuae

p. Gk: Heb *your*

Is 19:16
Jer 51:30

13Behold, your troops
    are women in your midst.
The gates of your land
    are wide open to your foes;
    fire has devoured your bars.

14Draw water for the siege,
    strengthen your forts;
go into the clay,
    tread the mortar,
    take hold of the brick mould!
15There will the fire devour you,
    the sword will cut you off.
    It will devour you like the locust.

Multiply yourselves like the locust,
    multiply like the grasshopper!
16You increased your merchants
    more than the stars of the heavens.
    The locust spreads its wings and flies away.
17Your princes are like grasshoppers,
    your scribesq like clouds of locusts
settling on the fences
    in a day of cold—
when the sun rises, they fly away;
    no one knows where they are.

### Death of the king of Assyria

1 Kings 22:17

18Your shepherds are asleep,

---

**3:18–19.** This lament over the death of the king of Assyria has nothing in common with the sincere elegies customarily spoken on the death of an important person—such as David's elegy for Jonathan (cf. 2 Sam 1:19–27). It is more in the

---

sicut ficus / cum ficis praecocibus: / si concussae fuerint, / cadent in os comedentis. / 13Ecce populus tuus, / mulieres in medio tui; / inimicis tuis late patebunt / portae terrae tuae; / devorabit ignis vectes tuos. / 14Aquam propter obsidionem hauri tibi, / firma munitiones tuas; / intra in lutum et calca argillam, / tene typum laterum. / 15Ibi comedet te ignis, / peribis gladio, / devorabit te ut bruchus. / Augere ut bruchus, / multiplicare ut locusta. / 16Plures fecisti negotiatores tuos / quam stellae sint caeli; / bruchus exuit pellem / et avolavit. / 17Custodes tui quasi locustae, / et scribae tui quasi agmen locustarum, / quae considunt in saepibus / in die frigoris; / sol ortus est, / et avolaverunt, / non est cognitus locus earum, / ubi fuerint. / 18Dormiunt pastores tui, rex Assyriae, / requiescunt principes tui; / dispersus est populus

q. Or *marshals*

228

O king of Assyria;
    your nobles slumber.
Your people are scattered on the mountains
    with none to gather them.
[19]There is no assuaging your hurt,
    your wound is grievous.
All who hear the news of you
    clap their hands over you.
For upon whom has not come
    your unceasing evil?

Ps 76:5
Jer 50:18
Ezek 31:3

Is 37:18–20
Jer 10:22

---

nature of a satirical poem, short but very cutting: the Assyrian king, in despair, forsaken by his people, is derided by his enemies. His fate serves as a lesson for Israel, and a reminder that God is her protector. Only he can set her free from her enemies.

tuus in montibus, / et non est qui congreget. / [19]Non est remedium fracturae tuae, / insanabilis est plaga tua; / omnes, qui audierint auditionem tuam, / plaudent manibus super te, / quia super quem non transiit / malitia tua semper?».

# HABAKKUK

# Introduction

The book of Habakkuk formed part of the Hebrew collection of the minor prophets from the very start; and it had no difficulty, therefore, in being received into the Christian canon of Old Testament books, where it comes eighth, after Nahum. In the oracle at the start of the book, the Chaldeans (who took over from the Assyrians) are depicted as weapons wielded by God against Israel's oppressors. In this sense there is a direct link between this book and the oracles against Assyria which formed the primary theme of the previous book (Nahum). In terms of content, Habakkuk has similarities with Isaiah, Jeremiah and Micah, and with some Psalms and the book of Job.

All that we know about Habakkuk himself is what can be deduced from the text. He describes himself as a watchman listening for the Lord's message (2:1). The prayer at the end of the book (3:1–19) could lead one to think that he is a Levite or at least someone familiar with the liturgy. References in the text indicate that Habakkuk must have exercised his prophetical ministry at the time when the neo-Babylonian empire was beginning to expand (625–612 BC). A later Jewish tradition, found in the appendices to the book of Daniel (Dan 14:33–43), says that an angel lifted the prophet Habakkuk by the hair of his head and brought him from Judah to Babylon to help Daniel when he was in the lions' den.

## 1. STRUCTURE AND CONTENT

There are clearly two different parts to this book, in two different literary genres—a collection of oracles, and a psalm. The oracles give the book its title: "The oracle [massah] of God which Habakkuk the prophet saw" (1:1); and the second part is headed "A prayer [tephillah] of Habakkuk the prophet" (3:1). The oracles that make up the first two chapters can themselves be divided into two distinct sections. The first (1:1–2:4) is a dialogue between God and the prophet in which the latter asks the Lord to explain why he is so inactive in the face of injustice and, further, why his reply is so difficult to understand. Only the Lord's last word lets in a ray of hope: salvation may be long in coming and seem difficult to attain, but "the righteous shall live by his faith" (2:4). The second section of this first part (2:5–20) is made up of five imprecations or "woes" against the oppressor, in which the prophet complains about the wickedness of the people's enemies (presumably Babylon). The second part of the book (3:1–19) is an epic-style psalm, which contains elements reminiscent of the theophany on Mount Sinai; the descriptions of the divine self-revelation involve natural phenomena and symbols of God as a mighty warrior, again in the style of certain epic psalms. However, the content of this psalm is very closely connected with what was said in the foregoing oracles, for the psalm celebrates God's response that had been so long awaited.

This carefully constructed book can be said to have the following structure:

1. DIALOGUE BETWEEN HABAKKUK AND GOD (1:2–2:4). The prophet complains to the Lord about the injustices suffered by Israel (1:1–4) and the Lord's reply is a paradoxical one, for it depicts the oppressive nation, the Chaldeans, as a weapon wielded by God (1:5–11). The prophet finds this all the more surprising, given that the people selected by God to carry out this purification are hardly a model of virtue (1:12–2:1). Then God gives him an answer he can understand: there is a time for everything; the prophet, like the righteous man, should be patient and lead a faithful life (2:2–4).

2. CURSES ON OPPRESSORS (2:5–20). This is an expansion of God's reply to the prophet's complaint. It begins with an introduction and then come five imprecations against the wickedness of enemies; they are all in the same literary form, beginning with "Woe to him ...". The prophet often uses irony when describing the oppressors' might.

3. THE PSALM OF HABAKKUK (3:1–19). This is clearly designed to act as the conclusion to what has gone before. The prophet recalls the protection that the Lord has afforded his people; he asks God to intervene once more, and rejoices that God does so. After recalling the attributes (3:1) and power of the Lord, as evidenced in the history of the chosen people (3:2–15), the prophet renews his faith in the God of Israel (3:16–19). In this way, the prophet's words, possibly spoken at different times, have been drawn together to form a canticle of hope and a profession of faith in the Lord who never forsakes his people.

## 2. COMPOSITION AND HISTORICAL BACKGROUND

It seems reasonable to suppose that the opening verses of the book (1:1–4) refer to the situation of Israel reflected in other prophetical writings such as those by Micah and Isaiah, that is, the period of Assyrian domination; in which case, the verses that follow (1:5–11) refer to the Chaldeans (the neo-Babylonian empire) who were beginning to make their mark. Therefore, the prophecy of Habakkuk must be dated to around the time of the fall of Nineveh (612 BC) or else to that of the battle of Carchemish (605 BC), which made Nebuchadnezzar of Babylon master of the Near East. Given that the text makes no reference to the siege of Jerusalem (597 BC) or the deportation to Babylon (587 BC), it makes sense to date the oracles in the book towards the end of the seventh century BC (cf. 2 Kings 24:1–7). However, since its references to the "wicked" oppressor are generic (except for the mention of the "Chaldeans" in 1:6), it is possible that the oracles may have been re-read or updated to take account of later invasions.

The book is close in language and style to Isaiah, Jeremiah and Micah. It is a clearly and vividly written body of poetry that easily rises to the quality of epic verse. The third part of the book is an example of an epic psalm, which follows in the tradition of other psalms of the genre.

## 3. MESSAGE

Although this is a short book, it is a profound one. A man steeped in the Israelite faith, Habakkuk firmly believes that God, the sovereign Lord, rules the destinies of nations and takes particular care of his chosen people (1:17; 2:5–20). As Lord of heaven and earth, he rules the elements and is supremely holy and just; he is the only God, the living God; idols are merely man-made objects (2:18–19). Habakkuk is a man who ponders on the truths of Revelation, on current events and on the past fortunes of Israel. And yet, there is something that he cannot work out: If God takes special care of his people, how can it be that he treats them so harshly? Why did God use the Chaldeans to scourge Israel, when they are a proud and cruel people, greater sinners than the Israelites? How can God's holiness and omnipotence be compatible with the existence of injustice and violence between nations, and within the very heart of God's own people?

To find an answer to this difficult question, the prophet engages in conversation with God (this takes up the first two chapters of the book). The Lord's replies are designed to make Habakkuk see that the wrongs committed by the nations, and the sins of Israel, too, are grievous offences against the sovereignty of God, and must be righted and punished. Every wicked oppressor (Habakkuk deals for the most part on the general level of nations) will be punished by the Lord of all; and the righteous man will be saved, provided he perseveres in his fidelity to God (2:4). This is Habakkuk's key message. All the rest of the book is a development of this idea.

In the stage of Revelation when the prophet lived, this was probably the best answer available. When Revelation reaches its height with the coming of Jesus Christ, the question as to why evil exists in the world will be fully answered. The book of Job posed the same question as Habakkuk does, but on the level of the individual person: Why does the just man suffer and the sinner sometimes prosper? Habakkuk puts forward an answer on the collective level of the chosen people and other nations.

## 4. THE BOOK OF HABAKKUK IN THE LIGHT
## OF THE NEW TESTAMENT

Despite its brevity, Habakkuk has had some influence in both Jewish and Christian traditions. We have already mentioned the echo of the book in Daniel 14:33–42 and the fact that the first two chapters were the subject of a commentary by the Jews of Qumran. In the Talmudic period (fourth to sixth century AD), Rabbi Simlay observed that Habakkuk 2:4 was a compendium of the 613 precepts of the Law of Moses.

That same verse is one of the texts St Paul uses in his exposition of the "doctrine of justification by faith" (cf. Rom 1:17; Gal 3:11; Heb 10:38–39), although he gives it a deeper meaning than it has in the prophet: he shows that divine justice in man begins and is perfected by faith, without any need for works of the Law. St Paul also quotes Habakkuk 1:5 in his address in Antioch (Acts 13:41), applying it to the incarnation and ministry of Christ.

Some Fathers deal with the book of Habakkuk in the context of commenting on the minor prophets—most notably St Jerome, St Hesychius of Jerusalem and St Cyril of Alexandria. There are also some commentaries on the Psalm (chapter 3)—for example, that of St Bede—but for the most part the only references made are to Habakkuk 2:4 quoted by St Paul or to the story about how the prophet was brought to Babylon to help Daniel in the lions' den.

**Title**

1 <sup>1</sup>The oracle of God which Habakkuk the prophet saw.

## 1. DIALOGUE BETWEEN HABAKKUK AND GOD

**The prophet's first complaint**

<sup>2</sup>O LORD, how long shall I cry for help,
and thou wilt not hear?
Or cry to thee "Violence!"
and thou wilt not save?
<sup>3</sup>Why dost thou make me see wrongs
and look upon trouble?
Destruction and violence are before me;
strife and contention arise.

Ps 55:10–12
Jer 6:7; 9:2
Amos 3:9–10

---

*1:2–2:4. The message and historical references contained in the book are concentrated in these verses. They appear to be a conversation between the Lord and Habakkuk. The prophet has recourse to the Lord for his help to right grievous wrongs (1:1–4). God's reply is a surprising one, for he tells the prophet that he is going to raise up a people, violent and cruel, "whose own might is their god" (1:5–11). This disconcerts the prophet: How can it be that, to purify his elect, the Lord should use such an irreligious and pitiless nation (1:12–17)? Still, the prophet does not despair; he decides to remain attentive to the voice of the Lord (2:1)—and the Lord does indeed respond to him by telling him in words what he previously told him by gestures: there is a time for everything; obstacles will overthrow the one whose soul is not upright, but he who is righteous shall live (2:1–4).

1:2–4. In his complaint to God, the prophet lists all the things that have gone wrong for the people—wickedness, violence, neglect of the Law, injustices etc. (vv. 3–4). However, what the prophet finds worst of all is the fact that the Lord does nothing about it (v. 2). The vigour of Habakkuk's words probably lies in the fact that he is not just bemoaning the people's lot; he is actually praying—and prayer should never be contrived; it should come straight from the heart: "I say to God simply what I want to say to Him, without using sweet words or beautiful phrases, and He always hears and understands me. [...] For me, in times of suffering and times of joy, prayer is an impulse of the heart, a glance up to heaven, an expression of gratitude and love" (St Thérèse of the Child Jesus, *Autobiographical Writings*, 25).

---

[1] <sup>1</sup>Oraculum, quod vidit Habacuc propheta. <sup>2</sup>Usquequo, Domine, clamabo, / et non exaudis? / Vociferabor ad te: «Violentia!», / et non salvas? / <sup>3</sup>Quare ostendisti mihi iniquitatem / et malitiam

Ps 22:12
Is 59:14
Mic 7:2–3

⁴So the law is slacked
  and justice never goes forth.
For the wicked surround the righteous,
  so justice goes forth perverted.

### God's reply—the Chaldeans are God's scourge

Is 10:13
Acts 13:41

⁵Look among the nations, and see;
  wonder and be astounded.
For I am doing a work in your days
  that you would not believe if told.
⁶For lo, I am rousing the Chaldeans,
  that bitter and hasty nation,
who march through the breadth of the earth,
  to seize habitations not their own.
⁷Dread and terrible are they;
  their justice and dignity proceed from themselves.

Zeph 3:3
Mt 24:28

⁸Their horses are swifter than leopards,
  more fierce than the evening wolves;

---

**1:5–11.** The Lord responds to the prophet by simply saying that He does act: all the prophet has to do is look around (v. 5). If he does so, he will see the mighty Chaldeans, a nation that the Lord himself has raised up (v. 6). The cruelty of the Chaldeans is underscored, as is their success at war (vv. 6–9), their power (v. 10) and their pride (v. 11). Subsequent events will prove that the Chaldeans did destroy Judah and proceeded to deport large numbers of the population to Babylon in 587 BC. This passage does not make it clear whether the Chaldeans come as God's instruments to right wrongs or whether they are simply being used by him to

punish sins and cleanse the people. The prophet (cf. 1:12–2:1) does not seem to think that this first response from God really answers the question; but from v. 5 on it is clear for all to see that the Lord determines the course of human affairs. This is the meaning that St Paul took from the passage in his preaching in Pisidian Antioch (cf. Acts 13:41) when he warned his listeners not to underestimate the grace that was being offered to them, for the Lord had done something unheard of (raised Jesus Christ from the dead and thereby ushered in justification), and had done so in a way no one could have imagined—through Jesus' ignominious death.

vides? / Et vastitas et violentia est coram me, / et facta est contentio, et iurgium exoritur. / ⁴Propter hoc languet lex, / et non pervenit usque ad finem iudicium. / Quia impius praevalet adversus iustum, / propterea egreditur iudicium perversum. / ⁵«Aspicite in gentibus et videte, / admiramini et obstupescite, / quia opus facio in diebus vestris, / quod nemo credet, cum narrabitur. / ⁶Quia ecce ego suscitabo Chaldaeos, / gentem amaram et velocem, / ambulantem super latitudinem terrae, / ut possideat tabernacula non sua. / ⁷Horribilis et terribilis est, / ex semetipsa iudicium eius / et maiestas eius egredietur. / ⁸Leviores pardis equi eius / et saeviores lupis deserti; / et accurrunt equites eius: / equites

their horsemen press proudly on.
Yea, their horsemen come from afar;
    they fly like an eagle swift to devour.
[9]They all come for violence;
    terror[a] of them goes before them.
    They gather captives like sand.
[10]At kings they scoff,
    and of rulers they make sport.
They laugh at every fortress,
    for they heap up earth and take it.
[11]Then they sweep by like the wind and go on,    Is 10:13
    guilty men, whose own might is their god!    Hab 1:7

## The prophet's second complaint

[12]Art thou not from everlasting,           Lev 17:1
    O LORD my God, my Holy One?       Deut 33:27
    We shall not die.                   Ps 90:1–2; 118:17
                                    Is 10:5–7

---

**1:12–2:1.** Here the prophet gives full expression to his confusion. He admits that God is the sovereign Lord who has raised up the Chaldeans "as a judgment" and "for chastisement" (1:12). The chastisement is valid, but what he does not understand is the method God uses: How is it possible for the Lord, who is the immortal Holy One (1:12), to choose a treacherous and unbelieving nation to carry out the punishment (1:13)? And he then goes on to explain in what this treachery and faithlessness consists. He describes the treachery by using the analogy of fishing: men, the righteous (cf. 1:13), are like fish that are living in their natural habitat, the sea, and the invader is like the fisherman who catches them with his hook, net and seine (1:15) and then kills them. But this treachery turns into irreligion; for the invader delights in what he does; worse still, he adores what gives him power (1:16–17; cf. 1:11). There may be a reference here to some Eastern peoples who had the custom of offering an annual sacrifice to their sword, taking it as a symbol of their god of war (Herodotus, *History*, 4, 62), but in biblical tradition the seduction of power is often likened to or described as idolatry: "Idolatry not only refers to false pagan worship. It remains a constant temptation to faith.

namque eius de longe venient, / volabunt quasi aquila / festinans ad comedendum. / [9]Omnes, ut violentiam faciant, venient, / omnes facies eorum ventus urens; / et congregabunt quasi arenam captivos. / [10]Et ipsa reges subsannabit, / tyrannis illudet; / ipsa super omnem munitionem ridebit / et comportabit aggerem et capiet eam. / [11]Tunc ultra progrediens quasi ventus pertransibit / et constituet fortitudinem suam deum suum». / [12]Numquid non tu a principio, Domine, / Deus meus, sanctus meus, / qui non morieris? / Domine, ad iudicium posuisti eam; petra mea, ad corripiendum fundasti eam. /

**a.** Cn: Heb uncertain

239

O LORD, thou hast ordained them as a judgment;
and thou, O Rock, hast established them for chastisement.

Ps 5:5–6   <sup>13</sup>Thou who art of purer eyes than to behold evil
Hab 1:3      and canst not look on wrong,
why dost thou look on faithless men,
and art silent when the wicked swallows up
the man more righteous than he?

Jer 16:16   <sup>14</sup>For thou makest men like the fish of the sea,
Ezek 12:13;    like crawling things that have no ruler.
17:20; 29:4;
32:3; Mt 13:47   <sup>15</sup>He brings all of them up with a hook,
he drags them out with his net,
he gathers them in his seine;
so he rejoices and exults.

<sup>16</sup>Therefore he sacrifices to his net
and burns incense to his seine;
for by them he lives in luxury,[b]
and his food is rich.

<sup>17</sup>Is he then to keep on emptying his net,
and mercilessly slaying nations for ever?

---

Idolatry consists in divinizing what is not God. Man commits idolatry whenever he honours and reveres a creature in place of God, whether this be gods or demons (for example, satanism), power, pleasure, race, ancestors, the state, money, etc. Jesus says, 'You cannot serve God and mammon' (Mt 6:24). Many martyrs died for not adoring 'the Beast', refusing even to simulate such worship. Idolatry rejects the unique Lordship of God; it is therefore incompatible with communion with God" (*Catechism of the Catholic Church*, 2113).

But the prophet is a man of faith; even though he does not understand what God is telling him, he continues to listen carefully, because he knows that God will not fail him: "Listen to the words of Habakkuk: *I will take my stand to watch, and station myself on the tower, and look forth to see what he will say to me, and what I will answer concerning my complaint.* We too, my beloved brothers, should be watchmen, for the day of battle has come. Let us enter into the depths of our hearts, where Christ lives and awaits us. May we refine our spirits and be prudent, never trusting to our own strengths, but concentrating on keeping our watch and weak guard" (St Bernard, *Sermones de diversis*, 5, 4).

<sup>13</sup>Mundi sunt oculi tui, ne videas malum; / et respicere ad iniquitatem non poteris. / Quare respicis super inique agentes et taces, devorante impio iustiorem se? / <sup>14</sup>Fecisti homines quasi pisces maris, / quasi reptile non habens principem super se. / <sup>15</sup>Omnes in hamo sublevat, / trahit eos in sagena sua / et congregat in rete suo; / super hoc laetatur et exsultat. / <sup>16</sup>Propterea immolat sagenae suae / et sacrificat reti suo, / quia in ipsis incrassata est portio eius, / et cibus eius pinguis. / <sup>17</sup>Propter hoc ergo evaginabit gladium suum semper, / ut interficiat gentes sine misericordia?

**b.** Heb *his portion is fat*

2 ¹I will take my stand to watch,
and station myself on the tower,
and look forth to see what he will say to me,
and what I will answer concerning my complaint.

### God's reply

²And the LORD answered me:
"Write the vision;
make it plain upon tablets,
so he may run who reads it.

---

**2:2–4.** As if admitting that the prophet is right, God answers his questions. The first point he makes clear is that when he promises something, it will happen: time may pass, but his word will not pass away unfulfilled (vv. 2–3). And this delay is a test of people's faithfulness (v. 4).

The last verse here ("Behold ... the righteous shall live by his faith") is important in both the Jewish and Christian biblical traditions. Some rabbis saw it as a summary of all 613 commandments of the Law; the writers of the Qumran commentary understood it to mean that he who kept the Law would escape the Judgment; and in the New Testament it is quoted on a number of occasions in connexion with the power of faith and the need for fortitude.

However, the verse is difficult to translate; this can be seen in various translations and even in the way the text is quoted in the New Testament. The Letter to the Hebrews 10:38 quotes this passage, working from the Greek translation, to exhort Christians to persevere in the faith they have received: "My righteous one shall live by faith, and if he shrinks back, my soul has no pleasure in him." Although the author of Hebrews inverts the order of the original, the meaning is unchanged.

Similarly, "faith" ("faithfulness": note **d**) translates a very common word (*'emunah*) which means stability, faithfulness, faith. It is a quality of God (Deut 32:4) and also of those who honour him (2 Chron 19:9) and who are righteous in his eyes (Prov 12:22). In Romans 1:17 and Galatians 3:11, St Paul quotes the second part of the Habakkuk verse ("the righteous shall live by his faith") applied to the individual, to ground his teaching on justification by faith rather than by the works of the Law. St Paul's use of the verse means that it is very important from a Christian point of view.

St Jerome's interpretation takes account of both the original audience and the Christian readership: "If your faith is weak and you begin to doubt that what was promised will come about, you will cause my soul great displeasure. But the just man, who believes in my word and never doubts the promises I make, will receive eternal life as his reward [...]. It is clear

---

[2] ¹Super custodiam meam stabo / et consistam super speculam / et contemplabor, ut videam quid dicat mihi / et quid respondeat ad querelam meam. / ²Et respondit mihi Dominus et dixit: / «Scribe

2 Pet 3:4–10
Num 23:29
Heb 10:37
2 Pet 3:9

Rom 1:17
Gal 3:11
Heb 10:38

³For still the vision awaits its time;
  it hastens to the end—it will not lie.
If it seem slow, wait for it;
  it will surely come, it will not delay.
⁴Behold, he whose soul is not upright in him shall fail,ᶜ
  but the righteous shall live by his faith.ᵈ

## 2. CURSES ON OPPRESSORS*

### Greed

Prov 27:20
Is 5:14

⁵Moreover, wine is treacherous;
  the arrogant man shall not abide.ᵉ

---

that these words contain a prophecy of the coming of Christ. The problem they contain will be resolved by him: sin will triumph and punishment be never-ending until He comes" (*Commentarii in Abacuc*, 2, 4). The verse is similar in style to a proverb (or maxim), and can be readily applied to the Christian life. For example, just as the New Testament says of St Joseph that he was a just man (cf. Mt 1:19), the Habakkuk passage can be applied to him as a sign that justice implies faith: "To be just is not simply a matter of obeying rules. Goodness should grow from the inside; it should be deep and vital—for 'the just man lives by faith' (Hab 2:4). These words, which later became a frequent subject of St Paul's meditation, really did apply in the case of St Joseph. He didn't fulfill the will of God in a routine or perfunctory way; he did it spontaneously

and wholeheartedly. For him, the law which every practising Jew lived by was not a code or a cold list of precepts, but an expression of the will of the living God. So he knew how to recognize the Lord's voice when it came to him so unexpectedly and so surprisingly" (St Josemaría Escrivá, *Christ Is Passing By*, 41).

*2:5–20. These verses seem to provide the content of Habakkuk's vision (cf. 2:2–3). They form a well-constructed group of oracles in which, after an introduction (vv. 5–6), five "imprecations" are uttered against the guilty one. Each of these takes this form: an initial "Woe" is followed by a description of the person cursed and, usually, the reason why he is being punished. At the end of the piece, by way of contrast, comes a proclamation of the holiness of

---

visum / et explana eum super tabulas, / ut percurrat, qui legerit eum. / ³Quia adhuc visus ad tempus constitutum, / sed anhelat in finem et non mentietur; / si moram fecerit, exspecta illum, / quia veniens veniet et non tardabit. / ⁴Ecce languidus, in quo non est anima recta; / iustus autem in fide sua vivet». / ⁵Et profecto divitiae decipiunt virum superbum, / et non perveniet ad finem; / qui dilatat quasi infernus fauces suas / et ipse quasi mors et non adimpletur: / et congregat ad se omnes gentes / et coacervat ad

**c.** Cn: Heb *is puffed up* **d.** Or *faithfulness* **e.** The Hebrew of these two lines is obscure

His greed is as wide as Sheol;
    like death he has never enough.
He gathers for himself all nations,
    and collects as his own all peoples."
    ⁶Shall not all these take up their taunt against him, in scoffing derision of him, and say,

Is 5:8; 14:4
Mic 2:4
Rev 8:13

### First imprecation

"Woe to him who heaps up what is not his own—
    for how long?—
    and loads himself with pledges!"
⁷Will not your debtors suddenly arise,
    and those awake who will make you tremble?
    Then you will be booty for them.

---

the Lord, who presides over the earth and all that happens there.

The sins condemned (theft, violence and idolatry) are moral faults of persons, but the context seems to refer to the actions of the invading nation, the Chaldeans. Hence, the difficulty of working out whom the oracle is directed against: is it the invader, or wicked Jews, starting with the king? The text does not make it clear, but despite this ambiguity it is saying that the sins of nations are always the moral faults of persons as well. St Jerome makes that point: "Everything we say about Babylon and Nebuchadnezzar could be said about the whole world, or about the devil who is arrogant and proud, and believes himself to be powerful though he can bring nothing to its proper end" (*Commentarii in Abacuc*, 2, 5).

**2:5–11.** The first imprecation (vv. 6–8) may have as its background the tribute exacted by Nebuchadnezzar from subject peoples, including Judah (cf. 2 Kings 24:1). And in vv. 9–11 are some words of Jeremiah's (cf. Jer 22:13–17), uttered against King Jehoiakim of Judah. Anyway, the theme running right through this first section is expressed in the first verse. Where the RSV has "wine" in line with the Masoretic Text, there is a variant found in a Qumran text which reads "wealth" and more recent translations use that. Thus, the passage is saying that avarice leads to theft (v. 7) and unjust gain (cf. v. 9). Indeed, it does worse: it leads to idolatry (cf. 2:18–20). Christian catechesis is conscious of all this: "We exhort you to disdain all love for riches, to be chaste and true. Scorn all evil. If a man cannot control himself in these earthly things, how can he be a teacher to others? He who yields to his avarice and greed will also be tainted by idolatry; he will be counted among the pagans who do not understand the justice and the judgment of the Lord" (St Polycarp, *Ad Philippenses*, 10).

se omnes populos. / ⁶Numquid non omnes isti super eum parabolam sument / et loquelam aenigmatum dicentes: / «Vae ei, qui multiplicat non sua —usquequo?— / et aggravat pignora super se!». / ⁷Numquid

Is 33:1
Hab 2:17

⁸Because you have plundered many nations,
all the remnant of the peoples shall plunder you,
for the blood of men and violence to the earth,
to cities and all who dwell therein.

### Second imprecation

Is 14:13
Jer 22:13–17;
49:16; Obad 4

⁹Woe to him who gets evil gain for his house,
to set his nest on high,
to be safe from the reach of harm!

Is 14:20
Hab 1:17

¹⁰You have devised shame to your house
by cutting off many peoples;
you have forfeited your life.
¹¹For the stone will cry out from the wall,
and the beam from the woodwork respond.

### Third imprecation

Jer 22:13
Mic 3:10

¹²Woe to him who builds a town with blood,
and founds a city on iniquity!

Jer 51:58
Mic 3:10

¹³Behold, is it not from the LORD of hosts

---

**2:12–20.** The third and fourth imprecations (vv. 12–14 and 15–18) concern violence. Since they follow on from those to do with greed, the reader will conclude that greed goes hand in hand with violence. But, as before, the oracle is not only a denunciation of an evil but an assertion (found in all the prophets) of God's sovereignty over all things: nothing happens that he does not know about (v. 13: cf. Jer 51:58; v. 14: cf. Is 11:9); there is no wrong that he will not right (v. 16).

Verse 18, at the end of the fourth diatribe, seems to be an introduction to the fifth (vv. 19–20), which deals with idolatry. The guarantee that things will change and that what the prophet says will happen lies in the fact that those people, who are wicked to the core, worship little idols, which are only pieces of wood or metal and have no life in them. The Lord, on the other hand, is the lord of all the earth; he will impose justice and none can gainsay him.

Verse 20 acts as the conclusion to the five "woes". It is very like Zechariah 2:17 and there is an echo of it in Revelation 8:1. Silence is a mark of respect and sometimes precedes the word of God (cf. Ps 76:8; Wis 18:14; Is 41:1; Lam 3:26; Zeph 1:7).

---

non repente consurgent, qui mordeant te, / et evigilabunt agitantes te, / et eris in rapinam eis? / ⁸Quia tu spoliasti gentes multas, / spoliabunt te omnes, qui reliqui fuerint de populis; / propter sanguinem hominum et oppressionem terrae, / civitatum et omnium habitantium in eis. / ⁹Vae, qui congregat lucrum iniustum in malum domui suae, / ut ponat in excelso nidum suum / et salvet se de manu mali! / ¹⁰Consilium cepisti in confusionem domui tuae / concidendi populos multos / et peccasti in animam tuam. / ¹¹Quia lapis de pariete clamabit, / et trabes de contignatione respondebit ei. / ¹²Vae, qui aedificat civitatem in sanguinibus / et condit urbem in iniquitate! / ¹³Numquid non haec a Domino sunt

that peoples labour only for fire,
and nations weary themselves for nought?

[14]For the earth will be filled
with the knowledge of the glory of the LORD,
as the waters cover the sea.

Num 14:21
Is 11:9

## Fourth imprecation

[15]Woe to him who makes his neighbours drink
of the cup of his wrath,[f] and makes them drunk,
to gaze on their shame!

Gen 9:20–21

[16]You will be sated with contempt instead of glory.
Drink, yourself, and stagger![g]
The cup in the LORD's right hand
will come around to you,
and shame will come upon your glory!

Ps 75:9
Is 55:17
Lam 4:21

[17]The violence done to Lebanon will overwhelm you;
the destruction of the beasts will terrify you,[h]
for the blood of men and violence to the earth,
to cities and all who dwell therein.

Is 14:8
Jer 22:23
Hab 2:8

[18]What profit is an idol
when its maker has shaped it,
a metal image, a teacher of lies?
For the workman trusts in his own creation
when he makes dumb idols!

Is 44:20; 49:9
Hos 3:4
Zech 10:2

## Fifth imprecation

[19]Woe to him who says to a wooden thing, Awake;
to a dumb stone, Arise!
Can this give revelation?
Behold, it is overlaid with gold and silver,
and there is no breath at all in it.

---

exercituum, / ut laborent populi pro igne, / et gentes in vacuum fatigentur? / [14]Quia replebitur terra cognitione gloriae Domini, / sicut aquae operiunt mare. / [15]Vae, qui potum dat amico suo / mittens venenum suum et inebrians eum, / ut aspiciat nuditatem eius! / [16]Repleris ignominia pro gloria; / bibe tu quoque et denudare! / Transibit ad te calix dexterae Domini, / et veniet ignominia super gloriam tuam. / [17]Quia vastitas Libani operiet te, / et miseria animalium deterrebit te / propter sanguinem hominum et oppressionem terrae, / civitatum et omnium habitantium in eis. / [18]Quid prodest sculptile, / quia sculpsit illud fictor suus; / conflatile et oraculum mendax, / quia speravit in figmento fictor eius, ut faceret simulacra muta? / [19]Vae, qui dicit ligno: «Expergiscere!», «Surge!» lapidi tacenti! / Numquid ipse docere poterit? / Ecce iste coopertus est auro et argento, / et omnis spiritus non est in visceribus

---

**f.** Cn: Heb *joining to your wrath*   **g.** Cn Compare Gk Syr: Heb *be uncircumcised*   **h.** Gk Syr: Heb *them*

Ps 11:4
Wis 18:14;
Is 41:1; Lam
3:26; Zeph 1:7;
Zech 2:7;
*Rev 8:1*

²⁰But the LORD is in his holy temple;
let all the earth keep silence before him.

## 3. THE PSALM OF HABAKKUK*

**Prayer**

3 ¹A prayer of Habakkuk the prophet, according to Shigionoth.

Deut 2:25
Ps 8:2,10;
76:2,4

²O LORD, I have heard the report of thee,
and thy work, O LORD, do I fear.
In the midst of the years renew it;
in the midst of the years make it known;
in wrath remember mercy.

Num 14:21
Deut 33:2
Judg 5:4

**Epic psalm: Theophany**
³God came from Teman,

---

*3:1–19. Two musical instructions, at start and finish, and the three marked pauses (*Selah*: vv. 3, 9, 13) draw our attention to the fact that this passage belongs to a different literary genre: it is a prayer, but one which is like a psalm. It begins with a verse in which the prophet praises the Lord's attributes (v. 2); then it describes a theophany in which God appears in majesty above the earth (vv. 3–15); and finally the prophet tells of his reaction, and reasserts his trust in the Lord (vv. 16–19).

3:1–2. An editorial verse (v. 1) and a short preface (v. 2) come before the epic Psalm of Habakkuk. Verse 2 itself provides a description of the majesty of God, a God mighty in deeds and words, one who must be feared. Powerful though he is, he is a merciful God; therefore, the prophet asks him to manifest

himself once more on his people's behalf. Such a declaration of the Lord's majesty could not pass unnoticed by tradition. St Bede, when commenting on this psalm (*Expositio in canticum Abacuc prophetae*) is in awe at the greatness of God that is to be seen in the incarnation of his Son. St Augustine quotes the Latin translation of the passage to describe man's sense of awe at the cosmos, the work of God: "If we try to comprehend everything that is, to contemplate it in one panoramic glance, what the prophet foretold will befall us too: *thy work, O Lord, do I fear*" (*Enarrationes in Psalmos*, 118, 27, 1).

3:3–15. This is, as we have said, a psalm in epic style, and the musical instructions (cf. vv. 1, 3, 9, 13) indicate that it was used in Old Testament liturgy. The theophany is described in

---

eius. / ²⁰Dominus autem in templo sancto suo; sileat a facie eius omnis terra. [3] ¹Oratio Habacuc prophetae. Secundum melodiam lamentationum. ²Domine, audivi auditionem tuam / et timui, Domine, opus tuum. / In medio annorum vivifica illud, / in medio annorum notum facies. / Cum iratus fueris, misericordiae recordaberis. / ³Deus a Theman veniet, / et Sanctus de monte Pharan. — Selah. / Operit

and the Holy One from Mount Paran.
His glory covered the heavens,
and the earth was full of his praise.

*Selah*

[4]His brightness was like the light,
rays flashed from his hand;
and there he veiled his power.
[5]Before him went pestilence,
and plague followed close behind.
[6]He stood and measured the earth;
he looked and shook the nations;
then the eternal mountains were scattered,
the everlasting hills sank low.
His ways were as of old.

Ex 15:14–16
Nahum 1:5

**The Lord, a powerful warrior**
[7]I saw the tents of Cushan in affliction;
the curtains of the land of Midian did tremble.

Judg 3:9–11;
7:1–25

---

the sort of epic language used in accounts of the exodus, the Sinai years and the conquest of the promised land. However, it is difficult to discern a chronological order in the episodes mentioned. "Teman" and "Paran" (v. 3) refer, respectively, to a region in Edom and a mountain in the Sinai (cf. Deut 33:2). "Cushan" and "Midian" (v. 7) were to the north-west of Arabia; the judges Othni-el and Gideon conquered those peoples (Judg 3:9–11; 7:1–25). When the psalm talks about "trampling the sea" (v. 15) or the sun and moon standing still (v. 11), etc. it is obviously recalling actions whereby God "saved" (v. 13) his people, that is, delivered them from bondage and made them masters of the promised land. However, all these historical references are subservient to the theophany which manifests God as a mighty warrior who shapes human history, and as sovereign lord of the cosmos and the elements. Descriptions of theophanies naturally bring up the whole question of the degree to which we can "explain" God: "Every man, and all the testimony of the prophets, affirms that God, who fills all things with his glory, is all-powerful: *His glory covered the heavens* ... (v. 3). We know that God exists; we know too what is not God; but we cannot know who God is, nor how he is God. But because God is kind and merciful, he has revealed something of himself to us through his many deeds and gifts" (St Jerome, *Commentarii in Isaiam*, 6, 1–7).

caelos gloria eius, / et laudis eius plena est terra. / [4]Splendor eius ut lux erit, / radii ex manibus eius: / ibi abscondita est fortitudo eius. / [5]Ante faciem eius ibit mors, / et egredietur pestis post pedes eius. / [6]Stetit et concussit terram, / aspexit et dissolvit gentes. / Et contriti sunt montes saeculi, / incurvati sunt colles antiqui / ab itineribus aeternitatis eius. / [7]In afflictione vidi tentoria Chusan; / turbantur pelles

Deut 33:26,27

[8]Was thy wrath against the rivers, O Lord?
Was thy anger against the rivers,
  or thy indignation against the sea,
when thou didst ride upon thy horses,
upon thy chariot of victory?
[9]Thou didst strip the sheath from thy bow,
  and put the arrows to the string.[i]

*Selah*

Thou didst cleave the earth with rivers.

Ex 19:16,18
Ps 68:9

[10]The mountains saw thee, and writhed;
  the raging waters swept on;
the deep gave forth its voice,
  it lifted its hands on high.
[11]The sun and moon stood still in their habitation[j]
  at the light of thine arrows as they sped,
  at the flash of thy glittering spear.
[12]Thou didst bestride the earth in fury,
  thou didst trample the nations in anger.

Hab 2:9–11

[13]Thou wentest forth for the salvation of thy people,
  for the salvation of thy anointed.
Thou didst crush the head of the wicked,[k]
  laying him bare from thigh to neck.[l]

*Selah*

Ps 10:7–9
137:7

[14]Thou didst pierce with thy[m] shafts the head of his warriors,[n]
  who came like a whirlwind to scatter me,
  rejoicing as if to devour the poor in secret.

Ps 77:20
Is 43:16–17

[15]Thou didst trample the sea with thy horses,
  the surging of mighty waters.

---

terrae Madian. / [8]Numquid in fluminibus iratus es, Domine, / aut in fluminibus furor tuus / vel in mari indignatio tua? / Quia ascendes super equos tuos, / quadrigas tuas victrices. / [9]Suscitans suscitabis arcum tuum, / sagittis replevisti pharetram tuam. — Selah. / In fluvios scindes terram, / [10]viderunt te et doluerunt montes. / Effuderunt aquas nubes, / dedit abyssus vocem suam, / in altum levavit manus suas. / [11]Sol et luna steterunt in habitaculo suo, / prae luce sagittarum tuarum discedunt, / prae splendore fulgurantis hastae tuae. / [12]In fremitu calcabis terram, / in furore conteres gentes. / [13]Egressus es in salutem populi tui, / in salutem cum christo tuo. / Percussisti caput de domo impii, / denudasti fundamentum usque ad petram. — Selah. / [14]Confodisti iaculis tuis caput bellatorum eius, / venientium ut turbo ad dispergendum me; / exsultatio eorum, sicut eius, qui devorat pauperem in abscondito. / [15]Viam fecisti in mari equis tuis, / in luto aquarum multarum. / [16]Audivi, et conturbatus est venter meus,

---

**i.** Cn: Heb obscure **j.** Heb uncertain **k.** Cn: Heb *head from the house of the wicked* **l.** Heb obscure **m.** Heb *his* **n.** Vg Compare Gk Syr: Heb uncertain

**The prophet trembles but still he trusts in God**

[16]I hear, and my body trembles,
    my lips quiver at the sound;
rottenness enters into my bones,
    my steps totter[o] beneath me.
I will quietly wait for the day of trouble
    to come upon people who invade us.

Jer 4:19

[17]Though the fig tree do not blossom,
    nor fruit be on the vines,
the produce of the olive fail
    and the fields yield no food,
the flock be cut off from the fold
    and there be no herd in the stalls,
[18]yet I will rejoice in the LORD,
    I will joy in the God of my salvation.
[19]GOD, the Lord, is my strength;
    he makes my feet like hinds' feet,
    he makes me tread upon my high places.

To the choirmaster: with stringed[p] instruments.

Jer 5:17
Hos 9:2
Mt 21:19
Lk 13:6

Ps 13:6
Lk 1:47

Deut 32:13
2 Sam 22:18
Ps 18:33,34;
33:20
Is 58:14
1 Cor 1:24

---

**3:16–19.** Verse 16 mentions again (cf. 3:2) the prophet's fearfulness on hearing reports of the Lord; the note of lament in v. 17 changes to verses praising the power of the Lord and the salvation that he brings (vv. 18–19). The true believer never loses hope; he presses on joyfully to the "high places" (v. 19), trusting in God: "This certainty which the faith gives enables us to look at everything in a new light. And everything, while remaining exactly the same, becomes different, because it is an expression of God's love. Our life is turned into a continuous prayer, we find ourselves with good humour and a peace which never ends, and everything we do is an act of thanksgiving running through all our day" (St Josemaría Escrivá, *Christ Is Passing By*, 144).

---

/ ad vocem contremuerunt labia mea. Ingreditur putredo in ossibus meis, et subter me vacillant / gressus mei. / Conquiescam in die tribulationis, / ut ascendat super populum, qui invadit nos. / [17]Ficus enim non florebit, / et non erit fructus in vineis; / mentietur opus olivae, / et arva non afferent cibum; / abscissum est de ovili pecus, / et non est armentum in praesepibus. / [18]Ego autem in Domino gaudebo / et exsultabo in Deo salvatore meo. / [19]Dominus Deus fortitudo mea / et ponet pedes meos quasi cervorum et super excelsa mea deducet me. / Magistro chori. Ad sonitum chordarum.

**o.** Cn Compare Gk: Heb *I tremble because* **p.** Heb *my stringed*

ZEPHANIAH

# Introduction

The book of Zephaniah follows Habakkuk as the ninth of the minor prophets, in both the Hebrew and Christian Bibles. The Psalm at the end of Habakkuk, calling on God to intervene, is replied to by the central subject of the book of Zephaniah—the day of Judgment. We know very little about the prophet other than what can be deduced from the book, for nowhere else in the Bible is he mentioned. His name means "the Lord hides", "the Lord has treasured", although this etymology has nothing particularly to do with the prophet's message. As regards the historical background to the book, all the indications are that Zephaniah ministered in Jerusalem (for which detailed references are given: cf. 1:10–11) in the time of King Josiah (1:1). According to the book of Kings (2 Kings 22:1–23:30), Josiah reigned in Judah for three decades (639–609 BC). He was eight years old when he came to the throne and it was not until long after his minority, that is, in the eighteenth year of his reign (622), that he instituted the Deuteronomic reform. Zephaniah's preaching reflects very well the period prior to the devout king's reform of religion.

## 1. STRUCTURE AND CONTENT

The text follows the familiar pattern of a prophetical book—denunciation oracles (1:2–3:8) followed by oracles of hope and salvation (3:9–20). The oracles fit together well—which indicates that the book is not an arbitrary collection but a crafted text. They have to do mainly with the destiny of Judah but are always conscious of other nations, for these share in the blessings of Judah—and in its afflictions, too.

Although the text could be divided up into smaller units, the following structure seems to do justice to the fact that it deals with both condemnation and salvation, Judah and the nations:

1. JUDGMENT ON JUDAH AND ON ALL CREATION (1:2–2:3). This part includes oracles that denounce Judah for its sins of idolatry (1:4–6) and injustice (1:9–13). They herald the day of wrath, *dies irae*, when the Lord will judge mankind (1:14–18). To escape the wrath of God, a person must be converted and seek righteousness and humility (2:3).

2. ORACLES AGAINST THE NATIONS AND AGAINST JUDAH (2:4–3:8). Oracles against neighbouring countries that made war on Judah (2:4–15) are

followed by an oracle against Jerusalem for failing to learn from the fate of her neighbours (3:1–8); but a note of hope is struck, too: the Lord will save a remnant of his people and will set things right (3:7).

3. PROMISES OF SALVATION (3:9–20). The book ends with oracles of salvation, in which all manner of good things are promised for a time to come in the future. These oracles open on a catholic note (3:9–10) and end by mentioning the qualities of the "remnant" that will be saved (3:11–13); the exiles will be brought home (3:18–20); Israel will exult over the Lord's doings, and the Lord, too, will rejoice (3:14–18).

## 2. COMPOSITION AND HISTORICAL BACKGROUND

The references in the body of the text to historical matters fit in with what the heading says about Zephaniah having lived in the time of King Josiah. However, 2:8–11 would seem to be more in keeping with the period after the exile to Babylon. There is also some debate about the historical background to 3:14–20: the joy of restoration reflected in these verses is in line with the post-exilic period (like so many passages in the third part of Isaiah), but the similarities between 3:14–17 and some pre-exilic psalms (Ps 47; 95; 96; 97) allow that passage to be assigned to the years when Zephaniah was active.

So, most of the text is attributable to Zephaniah himself. In his time, Assyria, which had been the dominant empire for more than a century, entered a period of decline, under pressure from the neo-Babylonian empire; soon afterwards the Babylonians took Nineveh, the Assyrian capital, and that empire was no more (612 BC). More specifically, Zephaniah's oracles seem to come from the early years of Josiah's reign, when the king, who was still a minor, had not yet embarked on his programme of religious reform (622 BC). Those years still bore evidence of the previous reigns of Manasseh (698–642) and Amon (641–640) which had seen the introduction of foreign religions into Judah—Canaanite cults in the coastal cities, the cult of the Ammonite god Molech (Moloch, Milcom), the cult of the "host of the heavens", etc. It was, then, a time of religious syncretism.

From the literary point of view, the book of Zephaniah has features similar to some found in earlier prophets such as Amos and Isaiah and also in later ones (Joel, Ezekiel and Zechariah). The Hebrew text of Zephaniah presents no particular problems, except for a few rather obscure passages such as 1:2, 14; 2:1–2; and 3:17–19. The Greek version of the Septuagint keeps very close to the Hebrew, apart from a few variants due to copyists' doubts or efforts to clarify the meaning where it proved elusive. Some fragments of the Hebrew text came to light in the Qumram *pesharîm*;[1] there is scarcely any difference between these

1. Commentaries: 1 QpZeph 1:18–2:2; 4 QpZeph 1:12–13.

and the Masoretic Text. The same holds true for fragments found at Muraba'at (1:1, 11; 3: 8–20).

## 3. MESSAGE

The prophetical message in this book hinges on Judgment Day, the "day of the Lord", which is described in epic, eschatological language (1:7–18). The Judgment affects Judah and Jerusalem, on the one hand, and the other nations, who have oppressed the people of God, on the other.

Sin is the reason for God's sentence against Judah and Jerusalem. They have been guilty of idolatry (1:4–6), violence, venality, fraud (1:9; 3:3), and religious indifference (1:12). The prophet upbraids rulers who have adopted foreign ways and who exploit the people (1:8; 3:3), unjust judges and officials (3:3), false prophets and priests who have broken the Law (3:4). These sins have their roots in pride, deceit and rebelliousness towards the Lord (3:1, 11, 13). The nations will be punished for plundering and oppressing Israel and Judah (2:8–13) and for their overweening pride (2:15).

As well as issuing these threats, Zephaniah opens the door to hope: the presence of the Lord on Zion will bring about purification and conversion (3:5). Zephaniah has also important things to say about the "remnant" of Israel and Judah. These are the Lord's faithful; they will be purified and they will seek the Lord in righteousness and humility (2:3; 3:12), in poverty and hope (3:12–13). The "remnant" will be given back their land (2:7–9), and the Lord will reign over them (3:15). The sometime oppressors, the other nations, will also be cleansed and converted and will end up worshipping the Lord (3:9–10).

Throughout the book there is a tension between the particular (the chosen people) and the universal focus (the nations round about, and even all mankind and the world which it inhabits: 1:2–3; 3:8). At the root of this tension is Zephaniah's concept of God as the Lord, ruler and judge of all.

## 4. THE BOOK OF ZEPHANIAH IN THE LIGHT OF THE NEW TESTAMENT

Except for its oracle about the "day of the Lord", the book of Zephaniah has had little influence on later Judaism or on Christianity. The vivid imagery and chilling language used in the prophet's description of the Judgment explain why these verses have found their way into preaching about the "last things" and into the famous liturgical hymn, the *Dies irae*. This passage is probably the prophet's greatest contribution to the history of Revelation and to Christian spirituality.

# Zephaniah

The New Testament quotes (almost verbatim) only one phrase from Zephaniah: "nor shall there be found in their mouth a deceitful tongue" (3:13; cf. Rev 14:5). Nevertheless, the tone of the oracles of consolation in the last part of the book (3:9–20) is very much present in the Infancy Gospel of St Luke (Lk 1:5–2:52); the description of the "humble and lowly" remnant (3:13) is reflected in the life of the Virgin Mary and in that of the parents of John the Baptist; and the joy described by the prophet (3:14–18) is very like that announced to Mary by the angel (Lk 1:26–38).

Zephaniah is treated by the Fathers and ecclesiastical writers in the context of their overall commentaries on the minor prophets, the most famous of which are those by St Jerome, St Cyril of Alexandria and Theodoret of Cyrus.

**Title**

1 ¹The word of the LORD which came to Zephaniah the son of Cushi, son of Gedaliah, son of Amariah, son of Hezekiah, in the days of Josiah the son of Amon, king of Judah.

Jer 1:2; 29:29; 52:24
Zech 6:10,14

## 1. JUDGMENT ON JUDAH AND ON ALL CREATION*

**Apocalyptic threat**

²"I will utterly sweep away everything
    from the face of the earth," says the LORD.

---

**1:1.** Zephaniah is a proper name found elsewhere in the Bible (cf. Jer 29:29; 52:24; Zech 6:10, 14). It means "the Lord hides [or treasures]". This title or heading mentions four ancestors (unusual in the prophetical books); this is presumably done to show that Zephaniah was a true Israelite, though his father's name, Cushi, suggests that he was Ethopian, a "Cushite".

**\*1:2–2:3.** The book of Zephaniah oscillates from focusing (narrowly) on Judah to a catholic vision that encompasses all nations. Here, before announcing judgment against Judah (1:4–2:3) it denounces wickedness throughout the world (1:2–3). The same pattern is followed in the rest of the book. The second part (2:4–3:8) begins with oracles against the nations, and is followed by an oracle against Jerusalem. And the concluding passage about future salvation (3:9–20) also begins with a cleansing of the nations (3:9–10) before celebrating the glory of Jerusalem.

This first part is about the "wrath of the Lord" over the wrongs done by mankind. After a warning to all creation (1:2–3), the prophet denounces the sins of Judah—idolatrous rites (1:4 6), wrongs done by the powerful (1:8–9), abuses in the area of commerce (1:10–11), and the insolence of unbelievers (1:12). When taking these various people to task, the prophet at certain points (1:7, 8, 10) reminds them that the day of the Lord is at hand; this he goes on to describe in a most chilling way: it will be a day of wrath, of distress, of ruin and desolation, etc. But Zephaniah is not a prophet of doom: his message is aimed at bringing about people's conversion; he wants them to practise justice, and to be humble: that way, they will be protected from the Lord's anger (2:3).

**1:2–3.** Universal destruction threatens because it is what mankind's sin deserves. This very brief reference to God's sentence parallels in a way the

[1] ¹Verbum Domini, quod factum est ad Sophoniam filium Chusi filii Godoliae filii Amariae filii Ezechiae, in diebus Iosiae filii Amon regis Iudae. ²«Auferens auferam omnia / a facie terrae, / dicit

Hos 4:3
Ezek 7:19

³"I will sweep away man and beast;
I will sweep away the birds of the air
and the fish of the sea.
I will overthrow[a] the wicked;
I will cut off mankind
from the face of the earth," says the LORD.

**Judah's idolatry**

1 Kings 11:5,33
2 Kings 23:4,12
2 Chron 34:3,4
Hos 10:5

⁴"I will stretch out my hand against Judah,
and against all the inhabitants of Jerusalem;

---

account of the lead-up to the flood (Gen 6:5–7:24). Sin robs man of his dominion over other created things (Gen 1:26), and these are somehow associated with his punishment, for "there is a *solidarity among all creatures* arising from the fact that all have the same Creator and are all ordered to his glory" (*Catechism of the Catholic Church*, 344). Through this solidarity, every person's sin impacts on everyone else and on creation as a whole. "[O]ne can speak of a communion of sin, whereby a soul that lowers itself through sin drags down with itself the Church and, in some way, the whole world" (John Paul II, *Reconciliatio et poenitentia*, 16). This fact should encourage us to feel responsible for others, in the communion of saints, "thanks to which it has been possible to say that 'every soul that rises above itself, raises up the world'" (ibid.).

**1:4–6.** The Lord will cause all trace of idolatry to disappear from Judah. Three idolatrous cults are mentioned here. "Baal" is the name of the Canaanite

god, worshipped by the Phoenicians and repeatedly ridiculed in the Bible. The "host of the heavens" is probably a reference to the stars and the heavenly bodies worshipped by the peoples of Mesopotamia; the book of Kings records that the impious King Manasseh built altars "for all the host of heaven" (2 Kings 21:5), which were later dismantled by the reforming King Josiah (2 Kings 23:12–13). Moloch or Milcom was the god of the Ammonites, a people who lived to the east of the Jordan. Neglect of the Lord (v. 6) was also seen as idolatry. This passage would fit in well with the start of Zephaniah's ministry as a prophet (around the year 640), prior to the reform instituted by King Josiah (622), when religious syncretism was rife, thanks to idolatrous cults brought into Judah during the reigns of Manasseh (698–642) and Amon (641–640). But leaving aside the circumstances at the time, the passage clearly shows that human beings have a religious dimension; when they forget the true God, they end up serving idols:

---

Dominus, / ³auferam hominem et pecus, / auferam volatile caeli / et pisces maris. / Et ruinae impiorum erunt; / et disperdam homines a facie terrae, / dicit Dominus. / ⁴Et extendam manum meam super Iudam / et super omnes habitantes Ierusalem; / et disperdam de loco hoc reliquias Baal / et nomina

**a.** Cn: Heb *the stumbling blocks*

258

and I will cut off from this place the remnant of Baal
and the name of the idolatrous priests;[b]
[5]those who bow down on the roofs
to the host of the heavens;
those who bow down and swear to the LORD
and yet swear by Milcom;
[6]those who have turned back from following the LORD,
who do not seek the LORD or inquire of him."

Deut 4:19
1 Kings 11:7,33
2 Kings 21:3–5;
23:13

## The day of the Lord foretold
[7]Be silent before the Lord GOD!
For the day of the LORD is at hand;
the LORD has prepared a sacrifice
and consecrated his guests.

Is 13:6
Ezek 30:3
Hab 2:20
Zech 2:17
Rev 8:1

---

"Very often, deceived by the Evil One, men have become vain in their reasonings, and have exchanged the truth of God for a lie, and served the creature rather than the Creator. Or else, living and dying in this world without God, they are exposed to ulitmate despair" (*Catechism of the Catholic Church*, 844).

**1:7–13.** Silence is called for because "the day of the Lord is at hand" and because "the Lord has prepared a sacrifice" (v. 7); it is a religious silence, because the day of the Lord implies a day of judgment and a liturgical event, and the people should be silent and attentive while sacrifice is being offered. The denunciation of idolatry in the previous verses is now followed by an attack on moral corruption: the first to be warned are the rulers of the people, who mimic foreign customs, even in dress (v. 8); then priests or temple officials who misuse temple funds (v. 9), business people who have become cheats (vv. 10–11), and cynics, *de facto* atheists, who live as though God did not exist (v. 12). The day of judgment will expose the futility of the empty-headed and evil pursuit of money (v. 13). On this general subject, Cardinal John Henry Newman taught that "Good works follow us, bad works follow us, but everything else is worth nothing; everything else is but chaff. The whirl and dance of worldy matters is but like the whirling of chaff or dust, nothing comes of it; it lasts through the day, but it is not to be found in the evening. And yet how many immortal souls spend their lives in nothing better than making themselves giddy with this whirl of politics, of party, or religious opinion, or money getting, of which nothing can ever come. [...] When we come into God's presence, we shall be

---

aedituorum cum sacerdotibus / [5]et eos, qui adorant super tecta / militiam caeli / et adorant et iurant in Domino / et iurant in Melchom, / [6]et qui avertuntur de post tergum Domini, / et qui non quaerunt Dominum nec investigant eum». / [7]Silete a facie Domini Dei, / quia iuxta est dies Domini; / quia

**b.** Compare Gk: Heb *idolatrous priests with the priests*

Ex 3:16
Is 34:6
Ezek 30:3

⁸And on the day of the LORD'S sacrifice—

"I will punish the officials and the king's sons
and all who array themselves in foreign attire.
⁹On that day I will punish
every one who leaps over the threshold,
and those who fill their master's house
with violence and fraud."

Neh 3:3

¹⁰"On that day," says the LORD,
"a cry will be heard from the Fish Gate,
a wail from the Second Quarter,
a loud crash from the hills.
¹¹Wail, O inhabitants of the Mortar!
For all the traders are no more;
all who weigh out silver are cut off.
¹²At that time I will search Jerusalem with lamps,
and I will punish the men
who are thickening upon their lees,
those who say in their hearts,
'The LORD will not do good,
nor will he do ill.'

Deut 28:30–33,39
Ps 10:4; Ps 14:1
Amos 5:11
Mic 6:15; Hag 1:6

¹³Their goods shall be plundered,
and their houses laid waste.
Though they build houses,
they shall not inhabit them;
though they plant vineyards,
they shall not drink wine from them."

**The day of wrath**

Is 42:13; Joel 2:11
Amos 5:18

¹⁴The great day of the LORD is near,

---

asked two things, whether we were in the Church, and whether we worked in the Church. Everything else is worthless" (Sermon, Septuagesima Sunday).

**1:14–18.** These verses paint a very vivid picture. The language here has become more apocalyptic, the vision more catholic. The day of the Lord

praeparavit Dominus hostiam, / sanctificavit vocatos suos. / ⁸«Et erit in die hostiae Domini: / visitabo super principes / et super filios regis / et super omnes, qui induti sunt / veste peregrina; / ⁹et visitabo super omnem, / qui arroganter ingreditur super limen in die illa, / qui complent domum domini sui / iniquitate et dolo. / ¹⁰Et erit in die illa, / dicit Dominus, / vox clamoris a porta Piscium, / et ululatus ab urbe Nova, / et contritio magna a collibus. / ¹¹Ululate, habitatores Pilae, / quia interiit omnis populus Chanaan, / disperierunt omnes involuti argento. / ¹²Et erit in tempore illo: / scrutabor Ierusalem in lucernis / et visitabo super viros / defixos in faecibus suis, / qui dicunt in cordibus suis: / "Non faciet bene Dominus / et non faciet male". / ¹³Et erunt opes eorum in direptionem, / et domus eorum in desertum; / et aedificabunt domos / et non habitabunt, / et plantabunt vineas / et non bibent vinum earum». / ¹⁴Iuxta est

near and hastening fast;
the sound of the day of the LORD is bitter,
    the mighty man cries aloud there.
<sup>15</sup>A day of wrath is that day,
    a day of distress and anguish,
a day of ruin and devastation,
    a day of darkness and gloom,
a day of clouds and thick darkness,
<sup>16</sup>    a day of trumpet blast and battle cry
against the fortified cities
    and against the lofty battlements.

Hab 3:3–4
Rom 2:5
Rev 6:17

Joel 2:2

Joel 2:1
Num 10:5

(v. 14; cf. v. 7) will be a day marked by bitterness, cries, anguish, ruin, darkness and gloom, trumpet blasts etc. (vv. 14–16). The word "day" is mentioned seven times (always in connexion with some form of calamity), as if the prophet wanted to convey that this destruction is wrought by God, the very opposite of his work of creation (Gen 1:3–2:3). In fact, in Genesis 1:31–2:3 God saw that what he had made was good and he blessed it; but here (v. 18) the poem seems to say that God will, in just one day, put an end "to all the inhabitants of the earth". This passage about the Day of Wrath has had an immense impact on the liturgy of the dead in the Western Church. The middle of the thirteenth century saw the composition of the poem *Dies irae*, based on the Latin translation of these verses; the poem (attributed to Thomas of Celano) has been used as a sequence in Masses for the dead ever since the fourteenth century, and it was also used as the final *Libera me, Domine* chant in funeral Masses.

St Jerome sees lots of connexions between 1:15–16 and past history, citing examples from the Bible and elsewhere: "With regard to the day of the Lord, whether we interpret it as the end of the world or the day of our own deaths, Zephaniah makes it clear that the voice of the Lord will be filled with bitterness, violence, wrath and judgment; even the saints, who shall certainly be saved, are redeemed *only as through fire* (1 Cor 3:15). It shall be a day of great trial and calamity, anguish and misery, and they will say: 'Woe are we, who suffer so greatly!' It shall be a day of darkness, *for every one who does evil hates the light, and does not come to the light, lest his deeds should be exposed* (Jn 3:20). It shall be a day of thick fog and hurricane: the storm of the Lord will sweep through the world, and the sound of the trumpet, which the Apostle refers to, will be heard: the sound of the the last trumpet (1 Cor 15:52)" (*Commentarii in Sophoniam*, 1, 15–16).

dies Domini magnus, / iuxta et velox nimis; / vox diei Domini amara, / tribulabitur ibi fortis. / <sup>15</sup>Dies irae dies illa, / dies tribulationis et angustiae, / dies vastitatis et desolationis, / dies tenebrarum et caliginis, / dies nebulae et turbinis, / <sup>16</sup>dies tubae et clangoris / super civitates munitas / et super angulos

Deut 28:28–29
Ps 79:3; Is 59:10
Jer 9:21

<sup>17</sup>I will bring distress on men,
    so that they shall walk like the blind,
    because they have sinned against the LORD;
their blood shall be poured out like dust,
    and their flesh like dung.

Ezek 7:19
Amos 8:9
Heb 10:27

<sup>18</sup>Neither their silver nor their gold
    shall be able to deliver them
    on the day of the wrath of the LORD.
In the fire of his jealous wrath,
    all the earth shall be consumed;
for a full, yea, sudden end
    he will make of all the inhabitants of the earth.

### Call to conversion

Hos 13:3

**2** <sup>1</sup>Come together and hold assembly,
    O shameless nation,
<sup>2</sup>before you are driven away
    like the drifting chaff,<sup>c</sup>
before there comes upon you
    the fierce anger of the LORD,
before there comes upon you
    the day of the wrath of the LORD.

---

**2:1–3.** Condemnation and forewarning of punishment is now followed by a call to conversion. Here the emphasis is on the practice of humility, which is mentioned twice in v. 3. This is the quality that we will later be told belongs to the people that the Lord will save (3:12), and later still Mary will sing its praises, "for he has regarded the low estate of his handmaiden. For behold, henceforth all generations will call me blessed" (Lk 1:48). This passage opens a door to hope, and is reminiscent of other passages of the Bible: "Who knows, God may yet repent and turn from his fierce anger, so that we perish not?" (Jon 3:9). Humility kindles hope: "The humble of the land are those who seek God with humble hearts, to do him the reverence due to a Father from his children; who obey his commandments, confess their sins, and strive not to sin again; who seek to do what is right, and to be humble, scorning the company of the proud and joining with those who do penance" (St Bonaventure, *Sermones dominicales*, 5, 6).

excelsos. / <sup>17</sup>Et tribulabo homines, / et ambulabunt ut caeci, / quia Domino peccaverunt; / et effundetur sanguis eorum sicut humus, / et viscera eorum sicut stercora. / <sup>18</sup>Sed et argentum eorum et aurum eorum / non poterit liberare eos / in die irae Domini; / in igne zeli eius / devorabitur omnis terra, / quia consummationem cum festinatione faciet / cunctis habitantibus terram.   **[2]** <sup>1</sup>Convenite, congregamini, / gens non amabilis, / <sup>2</sup>priusquam dispergamini / quasi pulvis transeuntes, / antequam veniat super vos

**c.** Cn Compare Gk Syr: Heb *before a decree is born; like chaff a day has passed away*

³Seek the LORD, all you humble of the land,
  who do his commands;
seek righteousness, seek humility;
  perhaps you may be hidden
  on the day of the wrath of the LORD.

Is 57:15
Amos 5:4–6; 15

## 2. ORACLES AGAINST THE NATIONS
## AND AGAINST JUDAH*

**Against the peoples to the east**
⁴For Gaza shall be deserted,
  and Ashkelon shall become a desolation;
Ashdod's people shall be driven out at noon,
  and Ekron shall be uprooted.

Josh 13:2
Is 14:28–32
Jer 47
Ezek 25:15–17
Amos 1:6–8

---

*2:4–3:8. Like other prophets, Zephaniah includes some "oracles against the nations". These have affinities with other prophetical texts (Is 13–21; Jer 46–51; Ezek 25–32; Amos 1–2; etc.). Zephaniah mentions different nations who have assaulted the chosen people from every angle—from the west (2:4–7), the cities of the Philistine coast; from the east (2:8–11), Moab and Ammon; from the south (2:12), the Cushites (Ethiopians), who controlled Egypt for a while; and from the north (2:13–15), Assyria. Like Isaiah 10:29–31 and Micah 1:10–15, Zephaniah makes plays on words here between the names of the cities and the disasters that will overtake them. At the end (3:1–8), the oracle is addressed to Jerusalem, a city that refuses to obey the Lord (3:1–5) and has failed to learn from the fate of its neighbours (3:6–8).

2:4–15. The first oracles (vv. 4–11) are against nations that have oppressed Judah in some way or other. Verse 10 sums up the reason for their condemnation. But the Lord looks after his people: it is true that Judah has suffered at the hands of its neighbours on account of its sins, but the Lord will raise up a "remnant" (vv. 7, 9) of his people who will avenge past aggression and recover its territory. In other prophetical books (cf. Is 10:20–22; 11:11; Amos 3:12; 5:13, 15; etc.), the "remnant" of Israel are those who survive the catastrophe of the day of the Lord (which is a purification), because they keep the Lord's commandments and have not been corrupted. In Zephaniah this "remnant" of Israel is described (3:12 –13) as a people humble and lowly— virtues that the New Testament attributes to Jesus (cf. Mt 11:29) and to his Mother (Lk 1:48): "He who is without stain and

/ ira furoris Domini, / antequam veniat super vos / dies furoris Domini. / ³Quaerite Dominum, / omnes mansueti terrae, / qui iudicium eius estis operati; / quaerite iustitiam, quaerite mansuetudinem, / si quomodo abscondamini / in die furoris Domini. / ⁴Quia Gaza deserta erit, / et Ascalon desolata, /

Deut 2:23
Jer 47:4
Amos 9:7

[5]Woe to you inhabitants of the seacoast,
you nation of the Cherethites!
The word of the LORD is against you,
O Canaan, land of the Philistines;
and I will destroy you till no inhabitant is left.

Zech 10:3

[6]And you, O seacoast, shall be pastures,
meadows for shepherds
and folds for flocks.
[7]The seacoast shall become the possession
of the remnant of the house of Judah,
on which they shall pasture,
and in the houses of Ashkelon
they shall lie down at evening.
For the LORD their God will be mindful of them
and restore their fortunes.

**Against the peoples to the west**

Is 15–16
Jer 48:1,27; 49:1,6
Ezek 25:1–11
Amos 1:13–2:3

[8]"I have heard the taunts of Moab
and the revilings of the Ammonites,
how they have taunted my people
and made boasts against their territory.

Gen 19:1
Is 14:2
Zech 2:13

[9]Therefore, as I live," says the LORD of hosts,
the God of Israel,
"Moab shall become like Sodom,
and the Ammonites like Gomorrah,
a land possessed by nettles and salt pits,
and a waste for ever.
The remnant of my people shall plunder them,
and the survivors of my nation shall possess them."

---

was made man to purify others of their sins wished to be born of an immaculate virgin. He wanted to be born of a lowly woman because he is meek and humble of heart; he wanted to be a perfect example of these virtues for the benefit of all" (St Bernard, *Homiliae super Missus est*, 2, 1).

Of the other oracles, the most notable is that against Nineveh. Nineveh's sin (cf. v. 15) was pride, and desolation her punishment. So, that oracle acts as a lead-in to the one against Jerusalem, who is guilty of the same sin.

Azotum in meridie eicient, / et Accaron eradicabitur. / [5]Vae, qui habitatis funiculum maris, gens Cretensium! / Verbum Domini super vos, / Chanaan, terra Philisthinorum: / «Disperdam te, / ita ut non sit inhabitator». / [6]Et erit funiculus maris / requies pastorum et caulae pecorum. / [7]Et erit funiculus maris / reliquiis domus Iudae: / ibi pascentur, / in domibus Ascalonis ad vesperam requiescent, / quia visitabit eos Dominus Deus eorum / et convertet sortem eorum. / [8]«Audivi opprobrium Moab / et blasphemias filiorum Ammon, qui exprobraverunt populo meo / et magnificati sunt super terminos eorum. / [9]Propterea vivo ego, / dicit Dominus exercituum, Deus Israel, / quia Moab ut Sodoma erit, /

<sup>10</sup>This shall be their lot in return for their pride,
because they scoffed and boasted
against the people of the LORD of hosts.

Jer 48:29

<sup>11</sup>The LORD will be terrible against them;
yea, he will famish all the gods of the earth,
and to him shall bow down,
each in its place,
all the lands of the nations.

### Against the peoples to the south and north

<sup>12</sup>You also, O Ethiopians,
shall be slain by my sword.

Is 18:20
Jer 46
Ezek 29–32
Is 10:5
Jon 1:2

<sup>13</sup>And he will stretch out his hand against the north,
and destroy Assyria;
and he will make Nineveh a desolation,
a dry waste like the desert.

<sup>14</sup>Herds shall lie down in the midst of her,
all the beasts of the field;<sup>d</sup>
the vulture<sup>e</sup> and the hedgehog
shall lodge in her capitals;
the owl<sup>f</sup> shall hoot in the window,
the raven<sup>g</sup> croak on the threshold;
for her cedar work will be laid bare.

Is 34:11

<sup>15</sup>This is the exultant city
that dwelt secure,
that said to herself,
"I am and there is none else."
What a desolation she has become,
a lair for wild beasts!
Every one who passes by her
hisses and shakes his fist.

Is 47:8,10
Jer 18:16;
19:8; 49:17

---

et filii Ammon quasi Gomorra, / possessio spinarum et acervi salis / et desertum usque in aeternum; / reliquiae populi mei diripient eos, / et residui gentis meae possidebunt illos». / <sup>10</sup>Hoc eis eveniet pro superbia sua, quia blasphemaverunt et magnificati sunt / super populum Domini exercituum. / <sup>11</sup>Horribilis Dominus super eos, / quia attenuabit omnes deos terrae; / et adorabunt eum, singuli de loco suo, / omnes insulae gentium. / <sup>12</sup>«Sed et vos, Aethiopes, / interfecti gladio meo eritis». / <sup>13</sup>Et extendet manum suam super aquilonem / et perdet Assyriam; / et ponet Nineven in solitudinem / et in aridam, quasi desertum. / <sup>14</sup>Et accubabunt in medio eius greges, / omne genus animalium. / Et onocrotalus et ulula / in capitellis eius morabuntur; / vox cantat in fenestra, / corvus in limine, / quoniam tabulatum cedrinum sublatum est. / <sup>15</sup>Haec est civitas exsultans, / habitans in confidentia, / quae dicebat in corde

---

**d.** Tg Compare Gk: Heb *nation*   **e.** The meaning of the Hebrew word is uncertain   **f.** Cn: Heb *a voice*
**g.** Gk Vg: Heb *desolation*

**Against the leaders of Judah**

Amos 4:6

**3** <sup>1</sup>Woe to her that is rebellious and defiled,
    the oppressing city!
  <sup>2</sup>She listens to no voice,
    she accepts no correction.
  She does not trust in the LORD,
    she does not draw near to her God.

Ezek 22:25–26  <sup>3</sup>Her officials within her
    are roaring lions;
  her judges are evening wolves
    that leave nothing till the morning.

Jer 23:32
Ezek 22:26  <sup>4</sup>Her prophets are wanton,
    faithless men;
  her priests profane what is sacred,
    they do violence to the law.

Deut 32:4
Ps 101:8  <sup>5</sup>The LORD within her is righteous,
    he does no wrong;
  every morning he shows forth his justice,
    each dawn he does not fail;
  but the unjust knows no shame.

**The nations punished**
  <sup>6</sup>"I have cut off nations;

---

**3:1–5.** The oracles against the nations are followed by this one against Jerusalem. It is similar to Amos 1–2, and Isaiah 1:21–26, in the sense that both diatribes are directed against community leaders—officials, judges, prophets and priests (vv. 3–4). Where once Nineveh, the capital of Assyria, was called an "exultant city", a city full of pride, now Jerusalem is accused of being "rebellious", "oppressing", and of having

rejected four graces—not listening to the voice of the Lord, not accepting conversion, not trusting in the Lord, not drawing near to her God (v. 2). But unlike the Nineveh oracle, the one about Jerusalem ends on a note of hope, for in spite of everything, "the Lord within her is righteous" and he will put things right (v. 5)

**3:6–8.** Now it is the Lord who speaks. The punishment inflicted on the nations

suo: / «Ego sum, et extra me non est alia amplius!». / Quomodo facta est in desertum, / cubile bestiae? / Omnis, qui transit per eam, / sibilabit et movebit manum suam.  [3] <sup>1</sup>Vae, provocatrix et inquinata, / civitas violenta! / <sup>2</sup>Non audivit vocem, / non suscepit disciplinam; / in Domino non est confisa, / ad Deum suum non appropiavit. / <sup>3</sup>Principes eius in medio eius / leones rugientes; / iudices eius lupi deserti, / ossa non relinquunt in mane. / <sup>4</sup>Prophetae eius vaniloqui, / viri fallaces; / sacerdotes eius polluerunt sanctum, iniuste egerunt contra legem. / <sup>5</sup>Dominus iustus in medio eius / non faciet iniquitatem; / mane, mane iudicium suum dabit, sicut lucem, quae non deficit; / nescivit autem iniquus confusionem. / <sup>6</sup>«Disperdidi gentes, / dissipati sunt anguli earum; / desertas feci vias eorum, / dum non

their battlements are in ruins;
I have laid waste their streets
   so that none walks in them;
their cities have been made desolate,
   without a man, without an inhabitant.
[7]I said, 'Surely she will fear me,
   she will accept correction;
she will not lose sight[h]
   of all that I have enjoined upon her.'
But all the more they were eager
   to make all their deeds corrupt."

Amos 4:6
Hab 2:8

[8]"Therefore wait for me," says the LORD,
   "for the day when I arise as a witness.
For my decision is to gather nations,
   to assemble kingdoms,

Gen 3:17–18
Rev 16:1

---

should have been warning enough to make Jerusalem mend her ways (vv. 6–7). But she has persisted in evil (v. 7). Her behaviour will bring the wrath of God down upon her; the whole earth will be consumed (v. 8): it parallels in a way the sin of Adam which brought evil and death into the world (Gen 3:17–18). As at the start of the book (1:2–3), there is an underlying idea here about the connexion between what man does and what happens to the rest of creation. The oracle reverts to apocalyptic language to describe God's condemnation of the earth on account of man's sin. Verse 8 is used by St Cyprian to encourage Christians to be patient in times of persecution: "Many people hope that they will soon be avenged for the anguish they suffered in the injuries done to them or the torment they endured in the attacks by those who persecute them. I cannot remain silent in the midst of all the trials and tribulations of this world, the persecutions carried out by the Jews and pagans and heretics: we must wait patiently for the coming of the day of justice and retribution. We should not plead for the punishment of those who inflicted our sufferings upon us, for as it is written: '*Therefore wait for me,*' says the Lord, '*for the day when I arise as a witness. For my decision is to gather nations, to assemble kingdoms, to pour out upon them my indignation, all the heat of my anger*'" (*De bono patientiae,* 21).

est qui transeat; / desolatae sunt civitates eorum, / non remanente viro nec ullo habitatore. / [7]Dixi: Nunc timebis me, / suscipies disciplinam! / Et non evanescent ab oculis eius omnia, in quibus visitavi eam. / Verumtamen acceleraverunt corrumpere / omnes actiones suas. / [8]Quapropter exspecta me, / dicit Dominus, / in die qua surgam ut testis; / quia iudicium meum, ut congregem gentes / et colligam regna,

**h.** Gk Syr: Heb *and her dwelling will not be cut off*

to pour out upon them my indignation,
　　all the heat of my anger;
for in the fire of my jealous wrath
　　all the earth shall be consumed.

# 3. PROMISES OF SALVATION*

**Conversion of the nations**

Gen 11:1–9<br>Zeph 2:3 ⁹"Yea, at that time I will change the speech of the peoples
　　to a pure speech,
that all of them may call on the name of the LORD
　　and serve him with one accord.

Gen 11:8<br>Deut 4:27; 28:64<br>Acts 8:27 ¹⁰From beyond the rivers of Ethiopia
　　my suppliants, the daughter of my dispersed ones,
　　shall bring my offering.

---

**\*3:9–20.** The Lord is still speaking here, but there is a total change of focus—from destruction to salvation, which is the intention behind divine punishment. The opening verses proclaim the purification of the nations (vv. 9–10), in a reversal of what happened to Babel of old (Gen 11:1–9). Those scattered abroad after God confused the language of the sons of men (Gen 11:8–9)—they are called "the daughter of my dispersed ones" in v. 10—will return, bringing offerings with them. Then the text speaks of the purification of Judah (vv. 11–13), of the survival of a "humble" remnant, who will hope in the Lord, will act rightly and will live in peace. As a consequence of the conversion of Judah and Israel, great will be the joy on Zion (vv. 14–18a). The faithful remnant is called "daughter of Zion" and "daughter of Jerusalem" (v. 14), some-

what paralleling the "daughter of my dispersed ones" (v. 10). In v. 14 there are four calls to rejoice—"sing aloud", "shout", "rejoice", "exult". The source of all this joy is the Lord's presence in their midst (v. 17), which brings with it all kinds of advantages (vv. 17–18). At the end of the passage (vv. 18–20), Zion's joy is made complete by the return of the exiles and Israel's prestige among the nations.

**3:9–10.** Throughout the book (1:2–3; 2:11; 3:6–8), the prophet has been pointing out the connexion between Judah and other nations. Now, as the oracles of blessing begin, we read a promise of universal salvation. The Second Vatican Council read in this passage a prophetical announcement of the day when all peoples will invoke the name of the true God: "As Holy

---

/ ut effundam super eas indignationem meam, / omnem iram furoris mei; / in igne enim zeli mei / devorabitur omnis terra. / ⁹Quia tunc reddam populis / labium purum, / ut invocent omnes in nomine Domini / et serviant ei umero uno. / ¹⁰Ultra flumina Aethiopiae, / inde supplices mei, / filii dispersorum

## Salvation of the remnant of Israel

¹¹"On that day you shall not be put to shame
   because of the deeds by which you have rebelled against me;
for then I will remove from your midst
   your proudly exultant ones,
and you shall no longer be haughty
   in my holy mountain.

¹²For I will leave in the midst of you
   a people humble and lowly.
They shall seek refuge in the name of the LORD,

¹³  those who are left in Israel;
they shall do no wrong
   and utter no lies,
nor shall there be found in their mouth
   a deceitful tongue.
For they shall pasture and lie down,
   and none shall make them afraid."

Zech 11:7
Mt 11:29
Lk 1:48

Is 53:9
Jn 1:47
*Rev 14:5*

## Psalms of joy in Zion

¹⁴Sing aloud, O daughter of Zion;
   shout, O Israel!

Is 12:6; 54:1
Zech 2:14
Jn 12:15

---

Scripture testifies, [...] in company with the prophets and the Apostle himself, the Church awaits that day, known to God alone, on which all peoples will address the Lord in a single voice and 'serve him shoulder to shoulder' (Zeph 3:9)" (*Nostra aetate,* 4).

**3:11–13.** The oracle becomes very tender at this point. The prophet is able to see a "remnant" of Israel who will be saved and become the core of the great restoration. Through the prophet, God describes this remnant as "a people humble and lowly", but the catalogue

of their qualities (vv. 12–13) shows that poverty and humility here do not refer to social status but to the people's inner attitude towards God. In fact, these terms ("humble and lowly"), through the Greek of the Septuagint, which translates them as *praiis* (meek) and *tapeinós* (humble), will become part of the vocabulary of Jesus' preaching: "learn from me; for I am gentle and lowly in heart" (Mt 11:29; cf. Mt 5:3, 5; 21:5).

**3:14–18a.** Now the promise becomes a song of jubilation. The Lord, the Saviour, sees to it that all is joy (v. 14), and there

---

meorum / deferent munus mihi. / ¹¹In die illa non confunderis / super cunctis actionibus tuis, / quibus praevaricata es in me; / quia tunc auferam de medio tui / magniloquos superbos tuos, / et non adicies exaltari amplius / in monte sancto meo. / ¹²Et derelinquam in medio tui / populum pauperem et egenum». / Et sperabunt in nomine Domini / reliquiae Israel. / ¹³Non facient iniquitatem / nec loquentur mendacium; / et non invenietur in ore eorum / lingua dolosa, / quoniam ipsi pascentur et accubabunt, / et non erit qui exterreat. / ¹⁴Lauda, filia Sion; / iubilate, Israel! / Laetare et exsulta in omni corde, / filia

Rejoice and exult with all your heart,
O daughter of Jerusalem!

Is 40:2
Mt 27:42
Mk 15:32
Jn 1:49; 12:13

[15]The LORD has taken away the judgments against you,
he has cast out your enemies.
The King of Israel, the LORD, is in your midst;
you shall fear evil no more.
[16]On that day it shall be said to Jerusalem:
"Do not fear, O Zion;
let not your hands grow weak.

Is 62:5
Jer 32:41

[17]The LORD, your God, is in your midst,
warrior who gives victory;
he will rejoice over you with gladness,
he will renew you[i] in his love;
he will exult over you with loud singing
[18]as on a day of festival.[j]

### Return of the exiles

"I will remove disaster[k] from you,
so that you will not bear reproach for it.

---

is no room for fear (v. 16). The Christian, in reading these verses, cannot but be reminded of the scene of the Annunciation: Mary, too, the humble Virgin (Lk 1:48), is invited to rejoice (Lk 1:28) and not to fear (Lk 1:20), because the Lord is with her (Lk 1:28). And indeed, with the Incarnation of the Word, the Lord did come to dwell among his people, and the salvation that was promised came to pass.

**3:18b–20.** The theme of the return reappears here: "I will bring you home," "I gather you together," "when I restore your fortunes" (v. 20); this time they are assembled not for judgment

but for salvation. The purification of the "remnant" will involve Israel receiving "praise and renown in all the earth" (v. 19): it is the mission of the chosen people, by their good example, to attract other nations to the Lord. On the day of the definitive salvation, the joy of having the Lord present among the people, and of bringing all mankind together, will come about through Christ's presence in the midst of his people, the Church: "Rejoice and be glad, Church of God, because you are the one body of Christ. Arm yourself with fortitude and fill your heart with happiness. You sufferings have been turned into joy. Your mourning clothes

---

Ierusalem! / [15]Abstulit Dominus iudicium tuum, / avertit inimicos tuos; / rex Israel, Dominus, in medio tui, / non timebis malum ultra. / [16]In die illa dicetur Ierusalem: / «Noli timere, Sion; / ne dissolvantur manus tuae! / [17]Dominus Deus tuus in medio tui, / fortis ipse salvabit; / gaudebit super te in laetitia, / commotus in dilectione sua; / exsultabit super te in laude / [18]sicut in die conventus». / «Auferam a te

**i.** Gk Syr: Heb *he will be silent*    **j.** Gk Syr: Heb obscure    **k.** Cn: Heb *they were*

<sup>19</sup>Behold, at that time I will deal
  with all your oppressors.
And I will save the lame
  and gather the outcast,
and I will change their shame into praise
  and renown in all the earth.
<sup>20</sup>At that time I will bring you home,
  at the time when I gather you together;
yea, I will make you renowned and praised
  among all the peoples of the earth,
when I restore your fortunes
  before your eyes," says the LORD.

Is 11:11
Mal 4:6

have been changed for robes of joy. Poverty and barrenness lie in the past. By one act you have restored many people and nations to Christ. Great is your Spouse, whose power governs you. He will turn your sufferings into joys, your enemies into friends. Do not weep or be sorrowful because some of your children have been taken from you for a short time. Keep your eye fixed on Christ, your head. Deepen in your faith. The promises of old have been fulfilled. You know now the sweetness of charity and the delights of unity. Preach peace and harmony among the nations. Have no other ambition but the unity of all peoples. Sow nothing but the seeds of peace and love. Rejoice in the Lord, for you have not been deceived in your beliefs. The ice and snow of winter have melted, and everything that was conceived amid your cries and constant prayers is born and comes to light like the flowers in spring" (St Leander, *Homilia in laudem Ecclesiae*).

calamitatem, / ut non ultra habeas super ea opprobrium. / <sup>19</sup>Ecce ego interficiam / omnes, qui afflixerunt te / in tempore illo; / et salvabo claudicantem / et eam, quae eiecta fuerat, congregabo; / et ponam eos in laudem et in nomen in omni terra confusionis eorum, / <sup>20</sup>in tempore illo, quo adducam vos, / et in tempore, quo congregabo vos. Dabo enim vos in nomen et in laudem / omnibus populis terrae, / cum convertero sortem vestram / coram oculis vestris», / dicit Dominus.

# HAGGAI

# Introduction

The book of Haggai is the tenth of the minor prophets in the Hebrew and Christian canons: both place it here on the grounds of chronology. Haggai is the first in a bloc of post-exilic (Persian era) prophets. They all share two features—the precision of the oracles (which are all dated in the text) and the simplicity of the message. *Haggai* in Hebrew means "My feast", a strange name, not borne by anyone else in the Old Testament. The prophet appears twice in the book of Ezra (Ezra 5:1; 6:14), but is mentioned only in passing. Jewish tradition holds him to have been one of the repatriated Babylonian exiles. His ministry may have lasted longer than the three long months covered in this book. Along with Zechariah, Haggai took an active part in the restoration, and according to Jewish tradition both prophets were involved in the start of the Great Assembly, the official Jewish body for the interpretation of the Law.

## 1. STRUCTURE AND CONTENT

Haggai is not a book about profound visions or theological reflections; its message is simple and specific: the people of Judah should put their best efforts into rebuilding the temple of Jerusalem as a first step towards rehabilitating their devastated country. If they obey this wish of the Lord, they will be given everything they need and desire: the earth will produce its crops and all their labours will be fruitful (1:1–15). There are difficulties, not least the dispiritedness among the people, for even the foundations of the building show that the new temple will not be as fine as the temple of Solomon; but the Lord promises that this little temple will have a splendour greater than the former temple ever had (2:1–9).

The text consists of four oracles, all of them carefully dated, along with short accounts of how the rulers and people reacted to them (1:1; 2:1; 2:10; 2:20). The fourth oracle (2:10–19) has two sections to it, which do not marry very well together, and for that reason some scholars see the second part of it (2:15–19) as a continuation of the first oracle (1:1–15). Others divide the section in two, and therefore see the book has having five parts.

If we focus on the dates given in the text, the thing to do, it seems, is to divide the text in line with the prophet's four oracles:

1. REBUILDING OF THE TEMPLE (1:1–15). Here the prophet calls for the rebuilding of the temple (1:1–11), and the authorities and the people respond positively (1:12–15).

2. THE TEMPLE'S GLORY IN THE FUTURE (2:1–9). The prophet promises that the new temple will be more splendid than the first temple, the one built by Solomon.

3. WORTHY OFFERINGS GUARANTEE PROSPERITY (2:10–19). Without the temple, offerings will be unclean (2:10–14); once the temple rebuilding starts, the Lord promises that everything will prosper (2:15–19).

4. MESSIANIC ORACLES FOR ZERUBBABEL (2:20–23). The blessings for the new temple, promised in the second oracle, are bestowed on Zerubbabel, who is a messianic figure.

## 2. COMPOSITION AND HISTORICAL BACKGROUND

Because the oracles etc. are carefully dated (1:1, 15; 2:1, 10, 20) it is quite easy to identify when they were originally spoken. The prophet refers to things that happened to Judah between 29 August 520 BC and 18 December of the same year, that is, a period of little more than three and a half months, during the second year of the reign of Darius I of Persia. At that time Judah was a province of the Persian empire, under the authority of a governor, Zerubbabel, and a high priest, Joshua.

The expeditions of Jews returning from exile in Babylon, which began after Cyrus issued his famous edict in 539 BC, found the land of Judah in ruins; they also discovered serious social problems there. The population that had been left behind after the destruction of Jerusalem in 587 were unskilled and uneducated, and the task of rebuilding the country was beyond them. Moreover, in the countryside, lands abandoned by the deportees had been occupied by folk who were now difficult to dislodge. Agricultural work was at a standstill; towns and their walls, in ruins. The first of the returned exiles, who had come back with Cyrus' permission to rebuild the temple, had set about that task, but they soon lost heart due to the obstacles they encountered. Almost twenty years went by, with very little work to show on the temple project. It was at this point that Haggai received messages from the Lord urging the authorities and the people to press on with the work. The prophet Zechariah, whose book complements that of Haggai, was given a similar vision. The urgency about the rebuilding preached by Haggai could have had a connexion with the prophecy in Jeremiah 25:11–12 and 29:10, which spoke of a restoration happening in seventy years' time. The rebuilding of the temple was a matter of great importance because it would mark the beginning of a new stage in the history of the salvation of the chosen people.

Whenever the prophet is mentioned in the book, it is in the third person. This has led scholars to think that the work was not composed by the prophet himself, but is a later collection of his material made by his disciples. The fact that 2:15–19 seems odd where it is, is easier to understand if the book is a collection of the type just described. Still, that collection could not have been assembled much later than the events referred to, for the book contains no mention of the completion of the building works, which took place five years later and in the absence of Zerubbabel (cf. Ezra 6:13–18). The language of the book is simple and direct; part is in prose and part in verse; the poetry serves the book's purposes, but is of little literary value.

### 3. MESSAGE

The book's message concentrates on two things—the rebuilding of the temple, and messianic/eschatological themes. The temple rebuilding is not just a matter of physical construction: it is a proof of deep faith in the significance of the Lord's Presence among his people and in his absolute sovereignty over the lives of men. Haggai takes the repatriates to task for their meanness towards the Lord: in their eagerness to rebuild their own houses, they have stopped work on the "house of the Lord"; the prophet urges them to be generous, to put their trust in God and set to work immediately; if they do, divine blessing will be theirs, and material well-being, too. In the straitened circumstances of the time, it required profound faith in the "Lord of hosts" to envisage the advent of a messianic era when the promises of salvation made to the house of David would come true. The language of the last verse of the book strikes an eschatological note, raising it above the personal circumstances of the governor, Zerubbabel, to a time in the future, to provide a glimpse of the Messiah.

Prophets of the pre-exilic period tended to put the emphasis on threats of punishment for sins; those of the exile period itself stressed the need for conversion; Haggai and other post-exilic prophets dwell more on physical and spiritual "rebuilding".

### 4. THE BOOK OF HAGGAI IN THE LIGHT OF THE NEW TESTAMENT

The New Testament contains very few echoes of the book of Haggai: the shaking of the heavens and the earth (2:6, 21) appears again in the eschatological discourse in the Synoptic Gospels (Mt 24:29; Lk 21:26), and the shaking of the earth (2:6) is mentioned in Hebrews 12:26. Throughout the

Christian centuries, the verse most quoted is 2:7: on the basis of the Latin translation ("et veniet Desideratus cunctis gentibus": "the Desired of all nations shall come"), that verse was read as a direct prophecy about Jesus, the Messiah; hence its use as an antiphon in some Advent liturgies. Commentaries on Haggai are to be found in the works of those Fathers who comment on the minor prophets—St Cyril of Alexandria, Theodoret of Cyrus, St Jerome, etc.

# 1. REBUILDING OF THE TEMPLE

**1** ¹In the second year of Darius the king, in the sixth month, on the first day of the month, the word of the LORD came by Haggai the prophet to Zerubbabel the son of She-alti-el, governor of Judah, and to Joshua the son of Jehozadak, the high priest, ²"Thus says the LORD of hosts: This people say the time has not yet come to rebuild the house of the LORD." ³Then the word of the

---

**1:1.** The text appears to be following the Persian calendar, which was based on the lunar month, with regular adjustments to keep it in line with the solar year. The date mentioned here would be 29 April 520 BC. References to dates in Haggai can be checked against dates found in Chronicles, Ezra and Zechariah.

The prophecy is addressed to Zerubbabel and Joshua, the two senior administrators, civil and religious (cf. Ezra 3:2, 8; 4:2, 3). Zerubbabel was a grandson of Jehoiachin, the king exiled to Babylon (cf. 1 Chron 3:16–19). St Matthew (cf. Mt 1:12–13) includes him among the ancestors of Jesus.

**1:2–15.** The first oracle includes the message communicated by Haggai (vv. 2–11) and the positive response of his audience (vv. 12–15). The words of the prophet are addressed to the leaders of the people mentioned in 1:1 and also to the "remnant" of the people (v. 14). In his oracle, the prophet plays with three ideas—"the time", the "house" and an invitation to "consider". The whole line of argument is based on what the people are saying: "the time has not

come to rebuild the house of the Lord" (v. 2). The prophet pokes fun at their saying this, given that the time has come for them to build comfortable houses for themselves and leave the temple rebuilding for later (the "House" of the Lord: vv. 2, 4, 8, 9). Therefore, he twice (vv. 5, 9) invites them to consider the matter; they will find that they have worked a lot but nothing has come of it (vv. 6, 9). This leads to the conclusion of the message: the earth withholds its produce because the people have shown such distrust in God; he is the Lord of nature; he can make the land fruitful—or barren.

This rallying of the people to get them to rebuild the temple may seem a minor matter compared with the high moral tone found in the prophetical books generally. However, it derives from a profound faith: the people, whom God "created", will never have a proper sense of their identity unless they can see God in their midst. This idea comes across clearly in the middle of the oracle: "build the house … that I may take pleasure in it and that I may appear in my glory" (v. 8). This should be read in the context of other biblical

---

[1] ¹In anno secundo Darii regis, in mense sexto, in die prima mensis, factum est verbum Domini in manu Aggaei prophetae ad Zorobabel filium Salathiel ducem Iudae et ad Iesua filium Iosedec sacerdotem magnum dicens: ²«Haec ait Dominus exercituum dicens: Populus iste dicit: "Nondum venit

LORD came by Haggai the prophet, [4]"Is it a time for you yourselves to dwell in your panelled houses, while this house lies in
ruins? [5]Now therefore thus says the LORD of hosts: Consider how
you have fared. [6]You have sown much, and harvested little; you
eat, but you never have enough; you drink, but you never have
your fill; you clothe yourselves, but no one is warm; and he who
earns wages earns wages to put them into a bag with holes.

[7]"Thus says the LORD of hosts: Consider how you have fared.
[8]Go up to the hills and bring wood and build the house, that I may
take pleasure in it and that I may appear in my glory, says the
LORD. [9]You have looked for much, and, lo, it came to little; and
when you brought it home, I blew it away. Why? says the LORD of
hosts. Because of my house that lies in ruins, while you busy

Deut 28:38
Is 5:10; Amos
5:11; Mic 6:15;
Hos 4:3

Ps 132:13–14

Lev 26:19–20

---

passages that assert how good God is to
reach down to his people: "For the Lord
has chosen Zion; he has desired it for
his habitation: 'This is my resting place
for ever' " (Ps 132:13–14). A logical
consequence of this is that God should
be offered the best that we can give
him, and that offering should also be
seen in the beauty of church decoration,
for the arts, "by their very nature, are
oriented toward the infinite beauty of
God which they attempt in some way to
portray by the work of human hands;
they achieve their purpose of redounding
to God's praise and glory in proportion
as they are directed the more exclu-
sively to the single aim of turning men's
minds devoutly toward God" (Vatican
II, *Sacrosanctum Concilium*, 122).

Verses 12–15 report the people's
response. The text describes an interest-

ing chain of events: Haggai's listeners
"obeyed" the oracle and were filled
with fear of the Lord (v. 12); God then
hastens to comfort them, assuring them,
as he always did the leaders of Israel, "I
am with you" (v. 13; Gen 26:3; 31:3;
Ex 4:12; Josh 1:5; etc.); and he encourages them to set to work with a will (v.
14). Twenty-four days have passed (v.
15; cf. v. 1) since Haggai first addressed
them, but the Lord has achieved his
objective. Drawing on her great experience of friendship with God, St Teresa
of Avila said something that would fit
in here: "Since he does not want to
force our will, he takes whatever he is
given; but he does not give everything
of himself until he sees that we have
given everything of ourselves to him"
(*Way of Perfection*, 48, 4).

---

tempus domus Domini aedificandae"». [3]Et factum est verbum Domini in manu Aggaei prophetae
dicens: [4]«Numquid tempus vobis est, ut habitetis in domibus laqueatis, et domus ista deserta? [5]Et nunc
haec dicit Dominus exercituum: Ponite corda vestra super vias vestras: [6]seminastis multum et intulistis
parum, comedistis et non estis satiati, bibistis et non estis inebriati, operuistis vos et non estis calefacti,
et, qui pro mercede operatus est, misit eam in sacculum pertusum. [7]Haec dicit Dominus exercituum:
Ponite corda vestra super vias vestras. [8]Ascendite in montem, portate lignum et aedificate domum, et
acceptabilis mihi erit et glorificabor, dicit Dominus. [9]Respexistis ad amplius, et ecce factum est minus;
et intulistis in domum, et exsufflavi illud. Quam ob causam?, dicit Dominus exercituum. Quia domus

yourselves each with his own house. [10]Therefore the heavens above you have withheld the dew, and the earth has withheld its produce. [11]And I have called for a drought upon the land and the hills, upon the grain, the new wine, the oil, upon what the ground brings forth, upon men and cattle, and upon all their labours."

[12]Then Zerubbabel the son of She-alti-el, and Joshua the son of Jehozadak, the high priest, with all the remnant of the people, obeyed the voice of the LORD their God, and the words of Haggai the prophet, as the LORD their God had sent him; and the people feared before the LORD. [13]Then Haggai, the messenger of the LORD, spoke to the people with the LORD'S message, "I am with you, says the LORD." [14]And the LORD stirred up the spirit of Zerubbabel the son of She-alti-el, governor of Judah, and the spirit of Joshua the son of Jehozadak, the high priest, and the spirit of all the remnant of the people; and they came and worked on the house of the LORD of hosts, their God, [15]on the twenty-fourth day of the month, in the sixth month.

*Deut 28:38*
*Is 5:10*
*Mic 6:15*

*Ezra 5:2*

*Gen 26:3;*
*31:3*
*Ex 4:12*
*Josh 1:5*

## 2. THE TEMPLE'S GLORY IN THE FUTURE

2 In the second year of Darius the king, [1]in the seventh month, on the twenty-first day of the month, the word of the LORD

*Lev 23:34:35*

---

**2:1–9.** The dating given in v. 1 (which corresponds to 17 October 520) indicates that this is a different prophetical discourse. Scarcely a month has passed since the date in 1:15, and one gets the impression that the people have been working extremely hard, but the results are somewhat disappointing—at least for the older people, who knew how splendid the temple of Solomon was (v. 3). This fits in with what the book of Ezra has to say: "Many of the priests and Levites and heads of fathers' houses, old men who had seen the first house, wept with a loud voice when they saw the foundation of this house being laid" (Ezra 3:12). But they should not have been surprised; it was one thing to build

mea deserta est, et vos festinatis unusquisque in domum suam. [10]Propter hoc super vos prohibiti sunt caeli, ne darent rorem, et terra prohibita est, ne daret fructum suum. [11]Et vocavi siccitatem super terram et super montes et super triticum et super vinum et super oleum et, quaecumque profert humus, et super homines et super iumenta et super omnem laborem manuum». [12]Et audivit Zorobabel filius Salathiel et Iesua filius Iosedec sacerdos magnus et omnes reliquiae populi vocem Domini Dei sui et verba Aggaei prophetae, sicut misit eum Dominus Deus eorum ad ipsos; et timuit populus a facie Domini. [13]Et dixit Aggaeus nuntius Domini secundum mandatum Domini populo dicens: «Ego vobiscum, dicit Dominus». [14]Et suscitavit Dominus spiritum Zorobabel filii Salathiel ducis Iudae et spiritum Iesua filii Iosedec sacerdotis magni et spiritum reliquorum omnium de populo; et ingressi sunt et faciebant opus in domo Domini exercituum Dei sui. [15]In die vicesima et quarta mensis, in sexto mense, in anno secundo Darii regis. **[2]** [1]In septimo mense, vicesima et prima mensis, factum est verbum Domini in

came by Haggai the prophet, [2]"Speak now to Zerubbabel the son of She-alti-el, governor of Judah, and to Joshua the son of Jehozadak, the high priest, and to all the remnant of the people, and say, [3]'Who is left among you that saw this house in its former glory? How do you see it now? Is it not in your sight as nothing?

Ezra 3:10–13

---

a temple in a period of splendour like Solomon's, when money was no object; it was quite another to do so in a country still in a state of desolation. Hence the encouraging tone of Haggai's oracle: the Lord renews the promises he made at the time of the exodus (vv. 4–5), when he turned a crowd of slaves into a nation; moreover, he promises that the new temple will be richer than the first: Solomon's temple had its glory (v. 3), but the new temple will be filled with splendour (v. 7); it will be more splendid than the first (v. 9); and it will be a source of prosperity (v. 9) and all the nations will flock there (v. 7; cf. Is 60: 7–11). The language of these verses is similar to that of apocalyptic passages in other prophets (cf. e.g. Is 2:2, Amos 5:8, Zeph 1:4). The tone of what Haggai says here allows these verses to be interpreted as a prophecy about Christ and the Church: "The coming of the Lord into this world was like the building of a great temple, glorious beyond imagining; this temple is more perfect and beautiful than that of old, as the worship of Christ according to his Gospel is more perfect than the worship of God according to the law, as the reality is more beautiful than its image [...]. The glory of the new temple, the Church, is much greater than the glory of the old.

Those who give of themselves and work devoutly to build the new temple will receive Christ himself, as their reward from the Saviour and as a gift from heaven; he is our peace, the peace of all mankind, the one through whom we can go to the Father in the one Spirit. He himself said: *and in this place I will give prosperity, says the Lord of hosts*" (St Cyril of Alexandria, *Commentarius in Aggaeum*, 14).

This messianic tone is even more clear in v. 7. In the words, "the treasures of all nations shall come in", the word translated as "treasures" has a wide range of meaning: the Hebrew root to which the noun belongs means to desire, wish, delight in; in Hebrew usage, the noun means "that which is desired", riches, treasures. The phrase was translated by the Latin Vulgate/Douai as "the Desired of all nations shall come" (a 1956 Douai edition gives it in capital letters), implying a direct reference to the Messiah; this led to the phrase entering the Advent liturgy, and to "the Desired" becoming a name for Christ in catechesis: "Open your heart to faith, beloved Virgin, your lips to give consent, your chaste body to the Master. Look, the one who all desire to possess is standing at your gates" (St Bernard, *Homiliae super Missus est*, 4, 8).

---

manu Aggaei prophetae dicens: [2]«Loquere ad Zorobabel filium Salathiel ducem Iudae et ad Iesua filium Iosedec sacerdotem magnum et ad reliquos populi dicens: [3]Quis in vobis est derelictus, qui vidit domum istam in gloria sua prima? Et quid vos videtis eam nunc? Numquid non ita est quasi non sit

⁴Yet now take courage, O Zerubbabel, says the LORD; take courage, Zech 4:7
O Joshua, son of Jehozadak, the high priest; take courage, all you
people of the land, says the LORD; work, for I am with you, says
the LORD of hosts, ⁵according to the promise that I made you Ex 29:45:46
when you came out of Egypt. My Spirit abides among you; fear
not. ⁶For thus says the LORD of hosts: Once again, in a little while, Is 60:7–11<br>Lk 21:26<br>Heb 12:26
I will shake the heavens and the earth and the sea and the dry land;
⁷and I will shake all nations, so that the treasures of all nations Is 5:2;<br>60:7–11<br>Mal 3:1
shall come in, and I will fill this house with splendour, says the
LORD of hosts. ⁸The silver is mine, and the gold is mine, says the
LORD of hosts. ⁹The latter splendour of this house shall be greater Jn 14:27
than the former, says the LORD of hosts; and in this place I will
give prosperity, says the LORD of hosts.'"

## 3. WORTHY OFFERINGS

¹⁰On the twenty-fourth day of the ninth month, in the second year
of Darius, the word of the LORD came by Haggai the prophet,

---

**2:10–19.** Verses 15–19 look as though
they would fit better immediately after
the end of the first oracle (1:15); however, the two parts of this third oracle
(vv. 10–14 and 15–19) are both given
the same date, "the twenty-fourth day
of the ninth month" (vv. 10, 18), that is,
18 December 520.

The oracle begins in a different literary style—an approach or a consultation
with the priests, the guardians of the
Law, particularly in matters to do with
worship and liturgy (cf. Jer 18:18). In
the context of the rebuilding of the

temple, the question as to things
becoming holy or unclean (vv. 11–14)
could be understood in one of two
ways. It is possible that the uncleanness
referred to by Haggai arose because the
people were allowing Samaritans to
help in the reconstruction of the temple
(cf. Ezra 4:1–4)—which would render
the temple unclean. But it is more likely
that the charge has to do with the chosen
people themselves and their lack of
commitment to the temple project: the
prophet would be saying that, unless
the temple is rebuilt, no matter how

---

in oculis vestris? ⁴Sed et nunc confortare, Zorobabel, dicit Dominus, et confortare, Iesua fili Iosedec
sacerdos magne, et confortare, omnis popule terrae, dicit Dominus exercituum; et facite, quoniam ego
vobiscum sum, dicit Dominus exercituum. ⁵Verbum quod pepigi vobiscum, cum egrederemini de terra
Aegypti, et spiritus meus stat in medio vestrum; nolite timere. ⁶Quia haec dicit Dominus exercituum:
Adhuc unum modicum est, et ego commovebo caelum et terram et mare et aridam. ⁷Et movebo omnes
gentes, et venient thesauri cunctarum gentium, et implebo domum istam gloria, dicit Dominus
exercituum. ⁸Meum est argentum et meum est aurum, dicit Dominus exercituum. ⁹Maior erit gloria
domus istius novissima plus quam prima, dicit Dominus exercituum; et in loco isto dabo pacem, dicit
Dominus exercituum». ¹⁰In vicesima et quarta noni mensis, in anno secundo Darii, factum est verbum

Zech 1:1,7 — 11"Thus says the LORD of hosts: Ask the priests to decide this
Lev 10:10 — question, 12'If one carries holy flesh in the skirt of his garment,
2 Chron: 35:3 — and touches with his skirt bread, or pottage, or wine, or oil, or any
Jer 11:15 — kind of food, does it become holy?'" The priests answered, "No."
Lev 22:4–7 — 13Then said Haggai, "If one who is unclean by contact with a dead
body touches any of these, does it become unclean?" The priests
Lev 22:4 — answered, "It does become unclean." 14Then Haggai said, "So is
Num 19:21 — it with this people, and with this nation before me, says the Lord;
and so with every work of their hands; and what they offer there
Amos 4:6 — is unclean. 15Pray now, consider what will come to pass from this
day onward. Before a stone was placed upon a stone in the temple
of the LORD, 16how did you fare?[a] When one came to a heap of
twenty measures, there were but ten; when one came to the
Deut 28:22 — winevat to draw fifty measures, there were but twenty. 17I smote
Amos 4:9 — you and all the products of your toil with blight and mildew and
Ezra 3:10 — hail; yet you did not return to me, says the LORD. 18Consider from
Zech 8:9 — this day onward, from the twenty-fourth day of the ninth month.
Since the day that the foundation of the LORD's temple was laid,
consider: 19Is the seed yet in the barn? Do the vine, the fig tree, the
pomegranate, and the olive tree still yield nothing? From this day
on I will bless you."

---

holy the offerings they make, they are contaminated by the people's apathy and are thereby rendered impure. Obedience to the Lord's orders is what draws down his blessings.

The text implies that the people have in fact obeyed the Lord and set about rebuilding the temple; that is why Haggai considers that day (v. 18) to mark the start of the new era. There is no longer any talk of fruitless work and unproductive land (cf. 1:5–6: 9) but of blessing from God (v. 19).

---

Domini ad Aggaeum prophetam dicens: 11«Haec dicit Dominus exercituum: Interroga sacerdotes legem dicens: 12Si tulerit homo carnem sanctificatam in ora vestimenti sui et tetigerit de summitate eius panem aut pulmentum aut vinum aut oleum aut omnem cibum, numquid sanctificabitur?». Respondentes autem sacerdotes dixerunt: «Non». 13Et dixit Aggaeus: «Si tetigerit pollutus cadavere omnia haec, numquid contaminabuntur?». Et responderunt sacerdotes et dixerunt: «Contaminabuntur». 14Et respondit Aggaeus et dixit: «Sic populus iste et sic gens ista ante faciem meam, dicit Dominus, et sic omne opus manuum eorum et omnia, quae offerunt ibi, contaminata sunt. 15Et nunc ponite corda vestra a die hac et supra: Antequam poneretur lapis super lapidem in templo Domini, 16quid fuistis? Cum accederetis ad acervum viginti modiorum, erant decem; cum intraretis ad torcular, ut hauriretis quinquaginta lagenas, erant viginti. 17Percussi vos ariditate et rubigine et grandine omnia opera manuum vestrarum, et non fuit in vobis qui reverteretur ad me, dicit Dominus. 18Ponite corda vestra ex die ista et in futurum, a die vicesima et quarta noni mensis, a die, qua fundamenta iacta sunt templi Domini, ponite super cor vestrum. 19Numquid adhuc semen in horreo est, et adhuc vinea et ficus et

**a.** Gk: Heb *since they were*

## 4. MESSIANIC ORACLE FOR ZERUBBABEL

²⁰The word of the LORD came a second time to Haggai on the twenty-fourth day of the month, ²¹"Speak to Zerubbabel, governor of Judah, saying, I am about to shake the heavens and the earth, ²²and to overthrow the throne of kingdoms; I am about to destroy the strength of the kingdoms of the nations, and overthrow the chariots and their riders; and the horses and their riders shall go down, every one by the sword of his fellow. ²³On that day, says the LORD of hosts, I will take you, O Zerubbabel my servant, the son of She-alti-el, says the LORD, and make you like a signet ring; for I have chosen you, says the LORD of hosts."

Lk 21:26
Heb 12:26

Dan 2:44
Mic 5:10

Is 42:1
Jer 22:24

**2:20–23.** The messianic oracle for Zerubbabel bears the same date as the previous one. Verses 21–22 are an echo of the previous promise about the future splendour of the temple—the shaking of heaven and earth (v. 21; cf. 2:6), well-being instead of war (v. 22; cf. 2:9), and the fear felt by the nations (v. 22; cf. 2:7); however, here it is all focused on Zerubbabel (v. 23), the "servant", "the chosen one", the "signet ring" of the Lord. The language used here to describe Zerubbabel is the sort of language typically used about the future Messiah, and therefore it can be applied to Jesus Christ: "The message is mystical and refers to the end of the world; therefore, the prophet is instructed to speak only with Zerubbabel, who is an image and figure of Christ. We have already seen how Christ is a descendant of David […]. After the thrones have been destroyed, and those who sat on them cast down, with their chariots and riders and horses, on that day, says the Lord Almighty, I will lift up Zerubbabel, son of Shealtiel, my servant. He is called 'servant' because he was made flesh, and because the Son *will be subjected to him who put all things under him* (cf. 1 Cor 15:28).When all of this has been fulfilled, God will put a mark on his hand: *on him has God the Father set his seal* (Jn 6:27); *he reflects the glory of God and bears the very stamp of his nature* (Heb 1:3). On all who believe in God he shall set his seal" (St Jerome, *Commentarii in Aggaeum*, 2).

malogranatum et lignum olivae non portavit fructum? Ex die hac benedicam». ²⁰Et factum est verbum Domini secundo ad Aggaeum in vicesima et quarta mensis dicens: ²¹«Loquere ad Zorobabel ducem Iudae dicens: Ego movebo caelum pariter et terram ²²et subvertam solium regnorum et conteram fortitudinem regnorum gentium et subvertam quadrigam et ascensores eius; et descendent equi et ascensores eorum, unusquisque percussus gladio fratris sui. ²³In die illo, dicit Dominus exercituum, assumam te, Zorobabel fili Salathiel, serve meus, dicit Dominus, et ponam te quasi signaculum, quia te elegi», dicit Dominus exercituum.

# ZECHARIAH

# Introduction

Zechariah, Haggai and Malachi were prophets who exercised their ministry after the return from exile. Their books close the collection of the twelve minor prophets. It makes perfect sense that Zechariah is positioned after Haggai and before Malachi. Zechariah shares with Haggai the optimism of those who had come back from exile eager to see the temple rebuilt and very hopeful of a national restoration under the leadership of Zerubbabel, a descendant of David (cf. Hag 2:20–23); this is plain to see from the first part of the book. But from chapter 9 onwards the whole focus changes; the book looks away into the future, to a time when the kingdom of God on earth will at last be established—an everlasting kingdom with Jerusalem as its capital, and the temple a place of pilgrimage for all nations (cf. Zech 14). The book of Malachi will take up again the theme of the temple and the duties of its priests, and then go on to proclaim the day of the Lord's coming (Mal 3:13–21). Thus God's promises made through the Old Testament prophets stir up and keep alive people's hope in the establishment of the Kingdom of God, which Jesus will proclaim to be present in his person and in all that he does.

## 2. STRUCTURE AND CONTENT

The book of Zechariah consists of two distinct parts; each carries a different date and the style of editing in each is different. The first part, covering eight chapters, is written in prose and takes place, according to the text itself, in the period 520–518 BC. The second part (chaps. 9–14) is almost entirely in verse and, unlike the first, carries no indication regarding its date. Because this second part is presumed to be later than the first, it is known as "Deutero-Zechariah".

1. ACTIVITY OF THE PROPHET (1:1–8:23). The background to these chapters is the rebuilding of Jerusalem by the returned exiles—and the reconstruction, too, of Jewish institutions and social life. This part begins by specifying the time when the prophet uttered the oracle that follows, an oracle calling for conversion (1:1–6). Then Zechariah himself reports eight visions he had at night, and an interpretation of them which was given to him by an angel. The visions are full of symbols, and their message is, largely, that God has pity on Jerusalem and will undermine her enemies (1:7–17; 1:18–21; 6:1–8): the Lord is coming to dwell in her (2:1–13), the priesthood has been cleansed (3:1–10), Zerubbabel will undertake the rebuilding of the temple

(4:1–13), and there will be no more iniquity or wickedness in the holy land (5:1–8). After these visions comes an oracle about the coronation of the high priest Joshua (6:9–15), and words about the present and future condition of the people—a warning about a false form of fasting (7:1–14), and ten prophecies about the joy and gladness that the Lord will give his people and, through them, other nations once the temple has been built (8:1–23).

2. MESSIANIC ORACLES (9:1–14:21). This part consists of two long oracles, the second of which follows on from the first, although there is a considerable amount of repetition. The first (9:1–11:17), after outlining that Israel's neighbours will submit to her (9:1–8) and describing the arrival of the Messiah in Jerusalem (9:9–10) and the reunification of the nation (9:11–10:12), goes on to utter a lament and describe how a shepherd (a Messiah king) is rejected by the people (11:1–17). The second oracle (12:1–14:21) prophesies that the Lord himself will intervene to make Jerusalem and Judah strong against their enemies (12:1–9), lead the people to conversion and purification (12:9–13:9) and rule the whole world from Jerusalem, his throne (14:1–21).

## 2. COMPOSITION AND HISTORICAL BACKGROUND

Very little is known about the prophet to whom this book is attributed. He must have been born in Babylon and been among the exiles who returned to Judea in the year 537. He belonged to a priestly family and succeeded his grand-father Iddo (mentioned in Nehemiah 12:4) as head of the family (1:1, 7; cf. Neh 12:10–16). He was therefore a contemporary of Haggai (cf. Ezra 5:1; 6:14), but ministered after him. Like Haggai, Zechariah writes his book to encourage the people to trust in the Lord and to help in the rebuilding of the sanctuary (cf. 4:8–10; Hag 1–2); this objective comes across clearly in the first part of the book.

Zechariah is very aware that he is the Lord's prophet, and keen to pass on the revelation that he has received. So he uses the same sort of literary devices used by earlier prophets—spelling out that what he says is the word of the Lord (cf. 1:2; 8:1; etc.), performing symbolic actions full of meaning and accompanied by oracles (cf. 6:9–15); notably, he develops the genre (started by Ezekiel: cf. Ezek 1:4; 40:2) of narrating visions—but with this difference: Zechariah's visions are all set between heaven and earth; they all involve angels and they are about what is happening and what is going to happen on earth (cf. 1:18; 3:1; 4:1; etc.).

The time when Zechariah spoke his oracles and had his visions is provided by an editor who refers to the prophet in the third person (cf. 1:1; 7:1, 8; 8:1). It was during the years 520 and 519, when Jewish repatriates once more set about rebuilding the temple, work having stopped in 530 due to harassment

from the Samaritans and a shortage of materials. It was a time when the people
were led by Zerubbabel, a descendant of David, who was civil governor, and
Joshua, the high priest; these are the two olive trees spoken of in chapter 4.
Zechariah's visions (1:7–6:8) and exhortations (7:1–8:23) may have been
collected at the same time, or the compilation may have been made later on,
when the two oracles of the second part of the book were inserted.

Those two oracles belong to a later historical context: there is no reference
made in them to the rebuilding of the temple (presumably because the work
was completed); there is instead a lament about the fact that the people have
turned their backs on a certain good shepherd (11:1–17), an elegy over one
whom they have slain (12:10). Moreover, in chapter 6, in the prophetical
gesture of the crowning of Joshua (6:9–15), functions and titles are attributed
to Joshua that previously belonged to Zerubbabel, such as his supervision of
the finishing of the temple (4:7–10), and the title of "the Branch" (3:8). All this
suggests that when these oracles were composed Zerubbabel was no longer
around; he may even have met a tragic end. So, it would have been after the
governor's death that the second part of the book was written and the final
collection of oracles done. Because the book of Malachi begins with an
introductory formula that is virtually the same as that for the two oracles in the
second part of Zechariah, it is commonly thought that what we have here are
three anonymous oracles composed after the temple building was completed.
Things have not turned out as well as was expected; if anything, they have
become more stressful; that may be why the hope contained in these oracles is
projected into an eschatological end time.

Some scholars have suggested that the second part of Zechariah is of a
much later date than the first and belongs to the Greek period, around the end
of the fourth century or into the third century. In support of this, they argue that
the sudden toppling of the nations to the north of Israel, described in 9:1–7,
refers to the dramatic conquests made by Alexander the Great in the year 333
BC; moreover, what is called Greece is mentioned in 9:13. However, these
references are not clear enough to date "Deutero-Zechariah" to so late a time.
Other scholars think that the two oracles in the second part of the book should
each be seen as a work in its own right; they speak of a "Trito-Zechariah".
However, the arguments in favour of this theory are by no means open and
shut. The historical background that comes across from the whole book is that
of Zechariah's own time, broadly speaking, that is, before and after the temple
was rebuilt, in the Zerubbabel period and for some time thereafter.

### 3. MESSAGE

The most significant aspect of the book of Zechariah is the fact that God is
giving his people a message of hope at a time when they need encouragement.

The people have come home from exile, and are faced with the task of rebuilding the temple; God assures them that they shall succeed in doing so, because he so wills it and he is almighty; and once it is built he will dwell there and be a source of salvation for all the nations (cf. 8:22). That promise also includes a cleansing of the priesthood and of the people (3:1–10; 5:1–9). The Lord also promises that a Messiah will come, who will bring peace and prosperity to Jerusalem and Zion (9:9–10). Even when the people reject the good shepherd (cf. 11:4–17), God's word still holds: he himself will come, and from Jerusalem he will rule over all the earth (cf. 14:1–21).

When passing on the Lord's message, the sacred writer is also showing the way God works: what the Lord is asking of those whom the prophet is addressing, what the Messiah will be like, and what will happen in the end when the Kingdom of God comes into being. Although the language he uses is quite in line with that of earlier prophets, Zechariah does use new imagery and literary devices which will later be found in other prophetical books such as the book of Daniel or the Revelation to John.

God's actions are in accordance with what he revealed through the prophets (cf. 1:6). Maybe Zechariah's very name, which means "God remembered", contains the key to how God goes about things. God remembered his people; therefore he is going to come to their aid (1:14–17; 8:2–3), and through them he will open a path of salvation for all nations (cf. 8:20–23; 14:16–19; Gen 12:3). The main divine initiative disclosed in this book is God's coming to dwell in the midst of his people in the temple of Jerusalem (1:16; 2:15–16; 8:3; 14:4, 17). To make this possible, he is going to dispose of the people's enemies (cf. 1:15; 2:14–15; 12:1–3; 14:2–4, 12) and will make Jerusalem a city of peace, and Judah a "holy land" (2:5, 12); he will cleanse and re-establish the priesthood (3:1–10; 6:9–15); he will remove sin and iniquity from the land (5:1–9), and idolatry and its adherents, too (13:1–6); he will bring all the exiles home (9:11–17; 10:9–12); he will send rain and plenty of good things (1:17; 8:4–5, 12–13; 14:8–11), and joy and gladness (2:10), feast instead of fast (8:19); he will make a new Covenant (13:9). Angels minister to God; through them he exercises his dominion over all the earth (1:8–11; 1:18–21; 5:9; 6:1–8) —especially through the "angel of the Lord" who intercedes for the people (1:9–16) and defends the high priest Joshua against his accuser, Satan (3:1–2).

The book depicts God's intervention as being a great promise, one whose fulfilment depends on the conversion of the chosen people (1:2–6), their being just towards neighbours and kind towards those in need (7:8–14; 8:14–17). In the first part of the book, where the completion of the temple is in sight, God calls on the people to be strong and to help in the temple project (8:9). In the second part, what he looks for is remorse for having rejected the Messiah (12:10–13); and we are told that the nations will come to Jerusalem to be assured of rain and health (14:16–19).

The messianic promises differ from one part of the book to the other, but there is a progression through them, and they knit together well. In the first part, the high point of the promise (and therefore the focus of hope) is the completion of the temple rebuilding and the protection afforded by God who will dwell there (1:16–17; 2:10; 8:9–12). The second part begins with a prophecy of the arrival of the Messiah in Jerusalem as a king of peace, who will bring salvation and well-being to the chosen people (9:9–10); but then we find the people rejecting the good shepherd (11:1–17). However, the text goes on to announce that God will intervene in person: he will cause Jerusalem and Judah to triumph over their enemies (12:1–9) and will then take possession of them himself; from there he will reign over all the earth (14:5). In that eschatological Kingdom there is no sign of the Messiah.

Taking the book as a whole, and given the way the text is arranged, its message amounts to this: to liberate the chosen people and bring salvation to the nations, the rebuilding of the temple of Jerusalem is not enough; therefore God promises a Messiah, a king of peace, a good shepherd, who will be rejected by the people and put to death; but, later, the people will look on him and they will weep; finally, God himself will establish his Kingdom, and all the Gentile nations will benefit thereby.

## 4. THE BOOK OF ZECHARIAH IN THE LIGHT OF THE NEW TESTAMENT

Some passages of the book of Zechariah are quoted literally in the New Testament as finding fulfilment in Jesus Christ. Thus, when describing Christ's entry into Jerusalem riding on an ass (cf. Mt 21:5; Jn 12:14–15), reference is made to the prophecy in Zechariah 9:9; and the account of Judas' treachery in selling Jesus for thirty pieces of silver quotes 11:12–13, although the evangelist links the episode to a prophecy in Jeremiah (cf. Jer 18:2–3; 32:6–15); finally, in John 19:37 the words "they look on him whom they have pierced" (12:10) are quoted to show the significance of the soldier sticking his lance into our Lord's side when he is on the cross. What these evangelists are saying is that Jesus is the Messiah promised by God in the book of Zechariah, and that in him are fulfilled the rejection and death of the Messiah proclaimed by the prophet in a veiled way.

The style and language of Zechariah found their way into the book of the Apocalypse. There we find much of the imagery used by Zechariah—for example, the horses representing divine emissaries (cf. 1:8; 6:2–3 and Rev 6:2–4; 19:11), the measuring-out of the city (cf. 2:5 and Rev 11:1), and the lampstands and the two olive trees (cf. 4:11 and Rev 11:4). But in the Apocalypse God's triumph has already been attained in the death and resurrection of Christ, and the end that is awaited is his second coming, which will see the glorious establishment of the Kingdom of God and his Messiah over a transformed earth (cf. Rev 21–22).

In line with the application of Zechariah's prophecies to Jesus in the New Testament, the Fathers developed a messianic interpretation of the figures and symbols found in the book of Zechariah—the angel of the Lord, the high priest Joshua, the golden lampstand, the king who comes to Zion, the good shepherd rejected by the people. As early as the *Letter to Barnabas*, *c*.AD 100 (5, 12) the sheep scattered after the shepherd is wounded (cf. 13:6–7) are interpreted as meaning the Jewish people. Later on, many Fathers and ecclesiastical writers commented on passages of the book. The commentary of Didymus the Blind and St Cyril of Alexandria are perhaps the most remarkable.

The Church's liturgy uses the most clearly messianic passages of the book— the passage about the king of peace arriving in Jerusalem (9:9–10), in the Mass of Palm Sunday, and that about the protection that God gives his people (12:7–10), on the 22nd Sunday in Ordinary Time.

# PART ONE

## ACTIVITY OF THE PROPHET*

### INTRODUCTION*

**Call to conversion**

1 ¹In the eighth month, in the second year of Darius, the word of the LORD came to Zechariah the son of Berechiah, son of Iddo, the prophet, saying, ²"The LORD was very angry with your fathers. ³Therefore say to them, Thus says the LORD of hosts: Return to

Neh 12:4,16
Hag 1:12;
2:1,10
Mal 3:7
Jas 4:8

---

*1:1–8:23. These chapters form the first part of the book and record the prophet's preaching. First comes a call to conversion (1:1–6); this is followed by an account of eight visions in which God reveals his purposes to the prophet (1:7–6:15); it concludes with a clarification about the nature of fasting (7:1–14; 8:18–19) and predictions about the salvation of Israel and all nations (8:1–17, 20–23). The focus of attention is the rebuilding of the temple of Jerusalem and the organization of the community under Zerubbabel and Joshua. The prophet seeks to bolster the people's morale by telling them about all the good things God will do for Israel and the nations once he comes to dwell in the temple; people are expected to live upright lives and be considerate towards others.

*1:1–6. This is an oracle meant for the people and is presented in the form of a divine locution to the prophet. It is couched in the sort of language used in earlier prophetical books (cf. Is 1; Jer 1; Ezek 1–3) and, in it, God urges the people to come back to him (v. 3) by reminding them of what happened to their forebears: they failed to listen to the prophets and were punished for that failure by being sent into exile (vv. 4–5); only then did they return to the Lord.

1:1–2. The date indicated here is in November 520 BC; it means that Zechariah was preaching two months after Haggai (cf. Hag 1:1).

1:3. God is always ready to forgive. St Augustine comments: "God does not withdraw, nor does he draw near; he does not change when he chastises, nor is he tainted by this world when he punishes. If he is far from you, it is because you have strayed far from him. It was you who fell away from him, not he who hid himself from you. Now, listen to what he says: *Return to me, says the Lord of hosts, and I will return*

---

[1] ¹In mense octavo, in anno secundo Darii, factum est verbum Domini ad Zachariam filium Barachiae filii Addo prophetam dicens: ²«Iratus est Dominus super patres vestros iracundia. ³Et dices ad eos: Haec dicit Dominus exercituum: Convertimini ad me, ait Dominus exercituum; et convertar ad

me, says the LORD of hosts, and I will return to you, says the LORD
Is 55:7
Lk 15:20
of hosts. [4]Be not like your fathers, to whom the former prophets
cried out, 'Thus says the LORD of hosts, Return from your evil
ways and from your evil deeds.' But they did not hear or heed me,
Jn 8:52
says the LORD. [5]Your fathers, where are they? And the prophets,
Ex 36:31
Jer 3:15
Zech 7:7–14
Rev 10:7
do they live for ever? [6]But my words and my statutes, which I
commanded my servants the prophets, did they not overtake your
fathers? So they repented and said, As the LORD of hosts purposed
to deal with us for our ways and deeds, so has he dealt with us."

## 1. THE BOOK OF THE VISIONS*

### First vision: the horsemen

Zech 6:2–7
Rev 6:2–8
[7]On the twenty-fourth day of the eleventh month which is the
month of Shebat, in the second year of Darius, the word of the

---

to you; in other words: 'I cannot come
to you if you do not return to me.' God
goes towards those who turn back to
him, and illumines the faces of those
who turn to face him again. O fugitive!
Where will you flee from God? [...] He
is your judge; turn to him and you will
meet your father" (*Sermones*, 142, 4).

**1:5–6.** Although the prophets have
passed away, the word of God spoken by
them continues in force. Therefore, these
people's forebears would have seen, in
time, that God did right in punishing
them with exile, for the words of warning uttered by those prophets were
intended for them to hear and heed.

**\*1:7–6:15.** The sacred writer now pro-
ceeds to report Zechariah's prophecy,

and he presents it again as a locution
spoken by the Lord (cf. v. 1); then he
immediately quotes the prophet, who
speaks in the first person. But the
prophet does not relay what the Lord
said to him; instead he recounts eight
visions, attaching to each the interpretation given to him by the angel of
the Lord. In those visions Zechariah
recounts events past, present and future
concerning Israel's enemies, Jerusalem,
and the governor, Zerubbabel, and the
priest, Joshua. The prophet had these
visions around the middle of February
519 and, as he informs us, they all took
place on the same night. This is the
time when, after the return from exile
in 537, the Jews were rebuilding the
temple and re-establishing religious and
civic life under the civil governship of

vos, dicit Dominus exercituum. [4]Ne sitis sicut patres vestri, ad quos clamabant prophetae priores
dicentes: Haec dicit Dominus exercituum: Convertimini de viis vestris malis et de cogitationibus vestris
malis; et non audierunt neque attenderunt ad me, dicit Dominus. [5]Patres vestri ubi sunt? Et prophetae
numquid in sempiternum vivent? [6]Verumtamen verba mea et praecepta mea, quae mandavi servis meis
prophetis, numquid non attigerunt patres vestros? Et conversi sunt et dixerunt: "Sicut cogitavit
Dominus exercituum facere nobis, secundum vias nostras et secundum adinventiones nostras fecit
nobis"». [7]In die vicesima et quarta undecimi mensis, qui est mensis Sabath, in anno secundo Darii,

LORD came to Zechariah the son of Berechiah, son of Iddo, the prophet; and Zechariah said, [8]"I saw in the night, and behold, a man riding upon a red horse! He was standing among the myrtle trees in the glen; and behind him were red, sorrel, and white horses. [9]Then I said, 'What are these, my lord?' The angel who talked with me said to me, 'I will show you what they are.' [10]So

Josh 5:13
Dan 9:21
Rev 6:4

Rev 5:6

---

Zerubbabel, a prince of David's line, and under the leadership of Joshua, a high priest of the Zadok line.

**1:7–17.** This vision has to do with the completion of the temple project and with the general well-being of Jews in Jerusalem and in the cities of Judah. Neither of these objectives have been achieved; as the prophet sees it, God has shown more favour to Judah's neighbours than to his own people. But now things are going to change. God is going to make life difficult for those nations (they felt quite at ease, and they were in fact harassing the Jews: vv.14–15); and he is going to show compassion to the Jews and give them what they desire (vv. 16–17).

When is that going to happen and how does the prophet know that God has made this promise? The answer is: it has already happened, for in his vision the prophet can see God becoming aware of the sad plight of his people and deciding that the temple and Jerusalem will be rebuilt. The prophet receives that revelation through an angel who forms part of the vision— the man riding upon a red horse. It is not clear what the myrtle trees in the

glen mean. The glen could be the abyss or dark chaos that is identified here with the world of the nations that have kept Israel in vassaldom; the myrtles (evergreen shrubs) could symbolize the hope that the Jews in the midst of that world still have. The horses of different colours, or rather their riders, symbolize other angels. These report on the situation to the angel of the Lord (v. 11), who in v. 8 is the man on the red horse, and he intercedes with God on behalf of Jerusalem and Judah (v. 12).

That great angel is charged with the task of revealing God's purposes and interceding with God on behalf of Israel. Some centuries later, in the book of Daniel, those functions will be perceived as belonging to two angels— Gabriel, charged with making known divine revelations (cf. Dan 9:21) and Michael, charged with helping the people of God (cf. Dan 12:1). And we find these two angels with the same functions in the New Testament: Gabriel makes God's plans know to Zechariah and Mary (cf. Lk 1:19, 26); and Michael battles in heaven against the devil in defence of man (Rev 12:7). Horses are also used to symbolize divine messengers in Revelation 6:2–8; 19:11.

---

factum est verbum Domini ad Zachariam filium Barachiae filii Addo prophetam dicens: [8]«Vidi per noctem, et ecce vir sedens super equum rufum et ipse stabat inter myrteta, quae erant in profundo; et post eum equi rufi, fulvi et albi. [9]Et dixi: "Quid sunt isti, domine mi?". Et dixit ad me angelus, qui loquebatur in me: "Ego ostendam tibi quid sint isti". [10]Et respondit vir, qui stabat inter myrteta, et dixit:

the man who was standing among the myrtle trees answered, 'These are they whom the LORD has sent to patrol the earth.' [11]And they answered the angel of the LORD who was standing among the myrtle trees, 'We have patrolled the earth, and behold,

Hab 2:6
Mal 1:4
Rev 6:10

all the earth remains at rest.' [12]Then the angel of the LORD said, 'O LORD of hosts, how long wilt thou have no mercy on Jerusalem and the cities of Judah, against which thou hast had indignation these seventy years?' [13]And the LORD answered gracious and

Zech 8:2

comforting words to the angel who talked with me. [14]So the angel who talked with me said to me, 'Cry out, Thus says the LORD of

Is 47:6

hosts: I am exceedingly jealous for Jerusalem and for Zion. [15]And I am very angry with the nations that are at ease; for while I was

Ezra 6:14,15
Is 54:6–10
Jer 31:39
Zech 2:15;
4:9; 13:9
Rev 11:1

angry but a little they furthered the disaster. [16]Therefore, thus says the LORD, I have returned to Jerusalem with compassion; my house shall be built in it, says the LORD of hosts, and the measuring line shall be stretched out over Jerusalem. [17]Cry again, Thus says the LORD of hosts: My cities shall again overflow with prosperity, and the LORD will again comfort Zion and again choose Jerusalem.'"

### Second vision: the horns and the smiths

Deut 33:17
Dan 7:8

[18a]And I lifted my eyes and saw, and behold, four horns! [19]And I said to the angel who talked with me, "What are these?" And he

---

**1:14.** God's "jealousy" arises from his love for his people. Human feelings are being attributed to God to convey the fact that his love for his people is greater than their sin.

**1:18–21.** For the people of God to enjoy prosperity in Judah after their return from exile, they need to be free from any threat from hostile nations. This vision assures them that they can rest easy. The number four may symbolize the four cardinal points, that is, all nations in whatever direction; or it may mean Egypt, Assyria, Babylon and Persia. The horns symbolize power and

---

"Isti sunt quos misit Dominus, ut perambularent terram". [11]Et responderunt angelo Domini, qui stabat inter myrteta, et dixerunt: "Perambulavimus terram, et ecce omnis terra habitatur et quiescit". [12]Et respondit angelus Domini et dixit: "Domine exercituum, usquequo tu non misereberis Ierusalem et urbium Iudae, quibus iratus es? Iste septuagesimus annus est!". [13]Et respondit Dominus angelo, qui loquebatur in me verba bona, verba consolatoria. [14]Et dixit ad me angelus, qui loquebatur in me: "Clama dicens: Haec dixit Dominus exercituum: Zelatus sum Ierusalem et Sion zelo magno, [15]sed ira magna ego irascor super gentes opulentas, quia ego iratus sum parum, ipsi vero adiuverunt in malum. [16]Propterea haec dicit Dominus: Revertar ad Ierusalem in misericordiis. Domus mea aedificabitur in ea, ait Dominus exercituum, et perpendiculum extendetur super Ierusalem. [17]Adhuc clama dicens: Haec dicit Dominus exercituum: Adhuc affluent civitates meae bonis, et consolabitur adhuc Dominus Sion et eliget adhuc Ierusalem". **[2]** [1]Et levavi oculos meos et vidi, et ecce quattuor cornua; [2]et dixi ad

**a.** Ch 2.1 in Heb

answered me, "These are the horns which have scattered Judah, Israel, and Jerusalem." [20]Then the LORD showed me four smiths. Jer 48:25 [21]And I said, "What are these coming to do?" He answered, "These are the horns which scattered Judah, so that no man raised his head; and these have come to terrify them, to cast down the horns of the nations who lifted up their horns against the land of Judah to scatter it."

### Third vision: the measurer

2[b][1]And I lifted my eyes and saw, and behold, a man with a measuring line in his hand! [2]Then I said, "Where are you Jer 31:38–39<br>Ezek 41:13<br>Rev 11:1;<br>21:15–16

---

strength (cf. Ps 18:2; Rev 17:12). The smiths stand for the defenders of the people—possibly angelic forces, or the Persians who allowed the Jews to make their way home from Babylon. In any event, even if the symbolism is not clear, we can see that in his vision the prophet is given to understand (and passes on the message) that God will free his people from danger.

**2:1–13.** What the prophet now sees and hears concerns the city of Jerusalem. It is going to be remodelled as an open city, without walls; its defence will be provided by God himself and therefore more people will be able to live there. The man with the measuring line is an angel, as are the other two figures mentioned. The idea of measuring the city in order to rebuild it is also found in Ezekiel 40–42 and Jeremiah 31:38–40 and, later, Revelation 11:1.

The vision is followed by an oracle (vv. 6–10) in which the Lord speaks through the angel. He invites the Jews to leave Babylon and return to the holy land. This is a call that is also found in Isaiah and Jeremiah (cf. Is 48:20; Jer 50:8; 51:6). It could be that some were reluctant to move. God promises that in Judah they will be safe from other nations because they are his beloved people, the "apple of his eye" (v. 8), and his angel will defend them. Moreover, he will settle there, and many nations will become his people (vv. 10–11).

Presence of the Lord, security against enemies and a way for the nations to become people of God— these are the features that Judah and Jerusalem will have following the return from exile. In this sense, they prefigure the Church. Commenting on v. 4, St Jerome points out: "Reading in a spiritual sense, all of these things are to be found in the Church, which is *without walls*, or, as the Septuagint puts it, *katákarpos*; that is, filled with an abundance of fruit and a great

angelum, qui loquebatur in me: "Quid sunt haec?". Et dixit ad me: "Haec sunt cornua, quae ventilaverunt Iudam et Israel et Ierusalem". [3]Et ostendit mihi Dominus quattuor fabros; [4]et dixi: "Quid isti veniunt facere?". Qui respondit dicens: "Haec sunt cornua, quae ventilaverunt Iudam per singulos viros, ut nemo eorum levaret caput suum; et venerunt isti deterrere ea, ut deiciant cornua gentium, quae levaverunt cornu super terram Iudae, ut dispergerent eam". [5]Et levavi oculos meos et vidi; et ecce vir,

**b.** Ch 2.5 in Heb

299

going?" And he said to me, "To measure Jerusalem, to see what is its breadth and what is its length." ³And behold, the angel who talked with me came forward, and another angel came forward to meet him, ⁴and said to him, "Run, say to that young man, 'Jerusalem shall be inhabited as villages without walls, because of the multitude of men and cattle in it. ⁵For I will be to her a wall of fire round about, says the LORD, and I will be the glory within her.'"

⁶Ho! ho! Flee from the land of the north, says the LORD; for I have spread you abroad as the four winds of the heavens, says the LORD. ⁷Ho! Escape to Zion, you who dwell with the daughter of Babylon. ⁸For thus said the LORD of hosts, after his glory sent me to the nations who plundered you, for he who touches you touches the apple of his eye: ⁹"Behold, I will shake my hand over them, and they shall become plunder for those who served them. Then you will know that the LORD of hosts has sent me. ¹⁰Sing and

*Is 49:19–20*
*Jer 31:27*
*Rev 21:3; 22:3*
*Is 48:20*
*Jer 50:8; 51:6*
*Rev 7:1*
*Deut 32:10*
*Ps 17:8*
*Is 14:2*
*Zeph 2:9*

---

multitude of men and asses [...]. The men and the asses [cattle, animals] stand for the two peoples, the Jews and the Gentiles; those who came to faith in Christ through the fulfilment of the Law are called men; we, however, who were idolatrous and lived as though in a wilderness, being far from the Law, and alone, because of our distance from the prophets who suffered, are the asses [...]. But these animals hear the voice of the good shepherd, and know him, and they follow him" (*Commentarii in Zachariam*, 2, 4).

**2:10.** This call for rejoicing, similar to that made by the prophet Zephaniah (cf. Zeph 3:14) and one made later (9:9), is repeated in the angel Gabriel's greeting to the Blessed Virgin when he tells her that she is to conceive the Messiah (cf. Lk 1:28). That event will truly bring about what is said here, for Mary is "the mother of him in whom 'the whole fullness of deity dwells bodily' (Col 2:9)" (*Catechism of the Catholic Church*, 722). John Paul II sees Mary, the Mother of the Redeemer, prefigured in the title "daughter of Zion" found here: "Her presence in the midst of Israel—a presence so discreet as to pass almost unnoticed by the eyes of her contemporaries—shone very clearly before the Eternal One, who had associated this hidden 'daughter of Sion' (cf. Zeph. 3:14; Zeph. 2:10) with the plan of salvation embracing the whole history of humanity" (*Redemptoris Mater*, 3).

et in manu eius funiculus mensorum. ⁶Et dixi: "Quo tu vadis?". Et dixit ad me: "Ut metiar Ierusalem et videam, quanta sit latitudo eius et quanta longitudo eius". ⁷Et ecce angelus, qui loquebatur in me, egrediebatur, et angelus alius egrediebatur in occursum eius; ⁸et dixit ad eum: "Curre, loquere ad puerum istum dicens: Absque muris habitabitur Ierusalem prae multitudine hominum et iumentorum in medio eius. ⁹Et ego ero ei, ait Dominus, murus ignis in circuitu et in gloria ero in medio eius. ¹⁰Heu, heu! Fugite de terra aquilonis, dicit Dominus, quoniam in quattuor ventos caeli dispersi vos, dicit Dominus. ¹¹Heu, Sion, fuge, quae habitas apud filiam Babylonis! ¹²Quia haec dicit Dominus exercituum, cuius gloria misit me ad gentes, quae spoliaverunt vos: Qui tetigerit vos, tangit pupillam oculi mei. ¹³Quia ecce ego levo manum meam super eos, et erunt praeda servorum suorum; et

rejoice, O daughter of Zion; for lo, I come and I will dwell in the midst of you, says the LORD. [11]And many nations shall join themselves to the LORD in that day, and shall be my people; and I will dwell in the midst of you, and you shall know that the LORD of hosts has sent me to you. [12]And the LORD will inherit Judah as his portion in the holy land, and will again choose Jerusalem."

Zeph 3:14
Rev 3:11

Is 45:22

Zech 1:17

[13]Be silent, all flesh, before the LORD; for he has roused himself from his holy dwelling.

Zeph 1:7
Hab 2:20

**Fourth vision: the high priest and the "Branch"**

3 [1]Then he showed me Joshua the high priest standing before the angel of the LORD, and Satan standing at his right hand to

Job 1:6
Hag 1:1
Zech 6:11

---

**2:13.** The *Catechism of the Catholic Church*, 2143, interprets this silence as one "of loving adoration". This is the attitude that all will have when they see what God will do for Judah and Jerusalem; for Christians, it is the attitude they will have towards the incarnation, passion, death and resurrection of our Lord and towards what God does for his Church.

**3:1–9.** The Israel that has come back from exile and is beginning to settle down again in Judah and Jerusalem will need a cleansed and reformed priesthood. The prophet sees this cleansing being performed by Joshua the priest, who came back with the repatriates (cf. Ezra 2:2; Neh 7:7). The purification will take the form of a trial in which the Lord chooses to overlook the past sins of the people (symbolized by the "filthy garments" of the priest) and gives orders for Joshua to be dressed in

holiness (symbolized by rich apparel) and to be instituted as high priest (with the high priest's turban). Here, Satan (v. 1) is not the devil, but the accusing angel and enemy of man, as in Job 1:6. Elsewhere it is made clear that he is also the enemy of God (cf. 1 Kings 22:22; Wis 2:24). The New Vulgate, following the Syriac version, translates v. 2 as "The angel of the Lord said to Satan ...".

The priest, now that he has been made holy, must be outstanding in his obedience to the Law of the Lord; this will ensure that he has authority in the temple and can partake of the glory of the angels who minister there (v. 7). The Lord also proclaims that the holiness of the priests is a sign of the coming of the Messiah, called here "the Branch" (v. 8) as in Isaiah 4:2; Jeremiah 23:5; 33:15. The holiness of the priests and people is the guarantee of the nearness of the messianic age

---

cognoscetis quia Dominus exercituum misit me. [14]Iubila et laetare, filia Sion, / quia ecce ego venio / et habitabo in medio tui, / ait Dominus. / [15]Et applicabuntur gentes multae / ad Dominum in die illa / et erunt ei in populum. / Et habitabo in medio tui, / et scies quia Dominus exercituum / misit me ad te. / [16]Et possidebit Dominus Iudam / partem suam super terram sanctam / et eliget adhuc Ierusalem. / [17]Sileat omnis caro a facie Domini, / quia consurrexit de habitaculo sancto suo". [3] [1]Et ostendit mihi Iesua sacerdotem magnum stantem coram angelo Domini; et Satan stabat a dextris eius, ut adversaretur

Amos 4:11
Jude 9

Is 61:10
Ezek 16:10
Jude 23
Rev 19:8

Is 6:7
Jer 31:34
Ezek 36:33
Mal 2:7

accuse him. ²And the LORD said to Satan, "The LORD rebuke you, O Satan! The LORD who has chosen Jerusalem rebuke you! Is not this a brand plucked from the fire?" ³Now Joshua was standing before the angel, clothed with filthy garments. ⁴And the angel said to those who were standing before him, "Remove the filthy garments from him." And to him he said, "Behold, I have taken your iniquity away from you, and I will clothe you with rich apparel." ⁵And I said, "Let them put a clean turban on his head." So they put a clean turban on his head and clothed him with garments; and the angel of the LORD was standing by.

⁶And the angel of the LORD enjoined Joshua, ⁷"Thus says the LORD of hosts: If you will walk in my ways and keep my charge, then you shall rule my house and have charge of my courts, and

which is expected to come through Zerubbabel, David's descendant. That descendant is referred to as the "Branch" (cf. Jer 23:5) and probably also as the "stone" (v. 9) with seven facets, symbolizing the fullness of wisdom and understanding (cf. Ps 118:22–23; Is 8:13–15; 28:16; Dan 2:34), although this stone could also stand for the temple. In any event, an age of peace and happiness is promised, symbolized by neighbours sitting together under the vine and the fig trees (v. 10). The term "branch", however, is translated by the Septuagint as "east", and that is how it appears in the Vulgate: *oriens* (Douai: "I will bring my servant the Orient": v. 8). In the *Benedictus* (cf. Lk 1:78) that title will be given to Jesus, for he is the Messiah of the line of David foretold by the prophets: "He was the Orient,

that is, the Sun of justice. He rose, and shed light on all of us who lived in darkness; moreover, he woke us up to a life of righteousness and made us shine with his grace; we, who lived in the night as though we were asleep, our souls deadened by the things of this world and the eyes of our minds dimmed" (St Cyril of Alexandria, *Commentarii in Zacchariam*, 3, 8–9).

Joshua the priest (whose name in Hebrew is also Jesus), when he was dressed in dirty vestments, was interpreted by the Fathers in an allegorical sense as symbolizing Jesus Christ dressed in our tarnished flesh: "His clothes were stained because he wore my sins; he put on our clothes so that he could dress us in the splendour of immortality" (St Ambrose, *Expositio psalmi CXVII*, 5, 4).

ei. ²Et dixit angelus Domini ad Satan: "Increpet Dominus in te, Satan! Et increpet Dominus in te, qui elegit Ierusalem! Numquid non iste torris est erutus de igne?". ³Et Iesua erat indutus vestibus sordidis et stabat ante faciem angeli. ⁴Qui respondit et ait ad eos, qui stabant coram se, dicens: "Auferte vestimenta sordida ab eo". Et dixit ad eum: "Ecce, abstuli a te iniquitatem tuam; induam te mutatoriis". ⁵Et dixit: "Ponite cidarim mundam super caput eius". Et posuerunt cidarim mundam super caput eius et induerunt eum vestibus; et angelus Domini stabat. ⁶Et contestabatur angelus Domini Iesua dicens: ⁷"Haec dicit Dominus exercituum: Si in viis meis ambulaveris et ministerium meum custodieris, tu quoque iudicabis domum meam et custodies atria mea; et dabo tibi accessum inter eos, qui nunc hic

I will give you the right of access among those who are standing here. ⁸Hear now, O Joshua the high priest, you and your friends who sit before you, for they are men of good omen: behold, I will bring my servant the Branch. ⁹For behold, upon the stone which I have set before Joshua, upon a single stone with seven facets, I will engrave its inscription, says the LORD of hosts, and I will remove the guilt of this land in a single day. ¹⁰In that day, says the LORD of hosts, every one of you will invite his neighbour under his vine and under his fig tree."

Is 8:18; 42:1
Jer 23:5; 33:15
Zech 6:12
Zech 4:10
Rev 5:6; 7:27

**Fifth vision: the lampstand and the two olive trees**

4 ¹And the angel who talked with me came again, and waked me, like a man that is wakened out of his sleep. ²And he said

---

**4:1–14.** In this vision the prophet considers the social and religious structure that God desires the Jewish community to have after the return from exile. The golden lampstand stands for the community; the seven lamps are the splendour of the Lord over them; and the two olive trees, the political and religious authorities respectively—Zerubbabel and Joshua. Zerubbabel will see to the completion of the temple, helped by the Spirit of God and overcoming all obstacles (symbolized by the "great mountain": v. 7). This means that a wonderful era of peace and joy will soon come, despite the fact that they are really starting in a small way, in the sense that they have limited resources for the rebuilding of the Sanctuary. Both Joshua the priest and Zerubbabel the governor will be servants of the people and of the glory of the Lord (v. 11). Both are called, literally, "sons of

the oil", that is, "anointed". This scene as interpreted by the prophet will give rise to expectations of a priest-Messiah and a Davidic Messiah as evidenced in some later Jewish writings that did not not become part of the Bible (cf. the note on 6:9–15). But Jesus' apostles did regard him as the Davidic Messiah and the priest Messiah (albeit a priest of the line of Melchizedek: cf. Heb 5:5–10; 7:1–3). "In Israel those consecrated to God for a mission that he gave were anointed in his name. This was the case for kings (cf. 1 Sam 9:16; 10:1; 16:1, 12–13; 1 Kings 1:39), for priests (cf. Ex 39:7; Lev 8:12) and, in rare instances, for prophets (cf. 1 Kings 19:16). This had to be the case all the more so for the Messiah whom God would send to inaugurate his kingdom definitively (cf. Ps 2:2; Acts 4: 26–27). It was necessary that the Messiah be anointed by the Spirit of the Lord (cf. Is 11:2) at once

---

assistunt. ⁸Audi, Iesua sacerdos magne, tu et amici tui, qui sedent coram te, quia viri portendentes sunt: Ecce enim ego adduco servum meum Germen. ⁹Quia ecce lapis, quem dedi coram Iesua: super lapidem unum septem oculi sunt; ecce ego caelabo sculpturam eius, ait Dominus exercituum, et auferam iniquitatem terrae illius in die una. ¹⁰In die illa, oraculum Domini exercituum, vocabit vir amicum suum subter vitem et subter ficum". **[4]** ¹Et reversus est angelus, qui loquebatur in me, et excitavit me quasi virum, qui excitatur de somno suo. ²Et dixit ad me: "Quid tu vides?". Et dixi: "Vidi: et ecce candelabrum

Ex 25:31–40
Rev 4:5
to me, "What do you see?" I said, "I see, and behold, a lampstand all of gold, with a bowl on the top of it, and seven lamps on it, with seven lips on each of the lamps which are on the top of it.
Rev 11:4
³And there are two olive trees by it, one on the right of the bowl and the other on its left." ⁴And I said to the angel who talked with

---

as king and priest (cf. Zech 4:14; 6:13), and also as prophet (cf. Is 61:1; Lk 4:16–21). Jesus fulfilled the messianic hope of Israel in his threefold office of priest, prophet and king" (*Catechism of the Catholic Church*, 436).

The Fathers interpreted the symbolism of this passage in different ways. For example, Didymus the Blind says of the gold lampstand that its "being made all of gold shows that the lampstand and all the lights that shine from it are spiritual and immaterial ... [and] ... at the top of the lampstand made all of gold is a lamp—the resplendent doctrine of the Trinity", and he adds, "in another sense, the lampstand stands for the soul and body that the Lord assumed when he came. How could it not be made all of gold, since he neither knew nor committed any sin? The seven lamps represent the spirit of wisdom and understanding, the spirit of counsel and power, of knowledge, piety and fear of the Lord". As regards the two olive trees, Didymus suggests that the "study of spiritual things and the charisms of the Holy Spirit is the oil that is collected from the olive tree on the right; the study of nature, its structure and God's providential plan for all the world, is the oil that is collected from the olive tree on

the left. [...] According to another interpretation, the olive tree to the right of the lampstand is the contemplation of the Son of God; and the olive tree on the left is the doctrine of the incarnation. The latter illumines and enlightens as well, but not without the contemplation that comes before it and stands on the right hand side of the lampstand" (*Commentarii in Zachariam*, 277–284). St Cyril of Alexandria, on the other hand, interprets that "the lampstand also represents the Church, honoured throughout the world, her virtue shining brightly, made brilliant by her true knowledge of God. At the top of the lampstand is a lamp, Christ, the one of whom God the Father said: *For Zion's sake I will not keep silent, ... until her vindication goes forth as brightness, and her salvation as a burning torch* (Is 62:1). [...] The two olive trees on either side of the lampstand are the two peoples gathered in a circle around Christ. Some were the fruit of an olive tree that was tended, in the Jewish synagogue; the others are wild fruit, from among the multitude of pagans. Grafted onto the tended olive tree, they draw on the roots of wisdom, as the blessed Paul said (cf. Rom 11:17)" (*Commentarius in Zacchariam*, 4, 1–3).

---

aureum totum, et ampulla super caput ipsius, et septem lucernae eius super illud, et septena infusoria lucernis, quae erant super caput eius. ³Et duae olivae super illud, una a dextris ampullae et una a sinistris eius". ⁴Et respondi et aio ad angelum, qui loquebatur in me, dicens: "Quid sunt haec, domine

me, "What are these, my lord?" [5]Then the angel who talked with me answered me, "Do you not know what these are?" I said, "No, my lord." [6]Then he said to me, "This is the word of the LORD to Zerubbabel: Not by might, nor by power, but by my Spirit, says the LORD of hosts. [7]What are you, O great mountain? Before Zerubbabel you shall become a plain; and he shall bring forward the top stone amid shouts of 'Grace, grace to it!'" [8]Moreover the word of the LORD came to me, saying, [9]"The hands of Zerubbabel have laid the foundation of this house; his hands shall also complete it. Then you will know that the LORD of hosts has sent me to you. [10]For whoever has despised the day of small things shall rejoice, and shall see the plummet in the hand of Zerubbabel.

"These seven are the eyes of the LORD, which range through the whole earth." [11]Then I said to him, "What are these two olive trees on the right and the left of the lampstand?" [12]And a second time I said to him, "What are these two branches of the olive trees, which are beside the two golden pipes from which the oil^c is poured out?" [13]He said to me, "Do you not know what these are?" I said, "No, my lord." [14]Then he said, "These are the two anointed who stand by the Lord of the whole earth."

Hos 1:7

Is 40:4
Jer 51:25

Zech 3:9
Rev 5:6

Rev 11:4

### Sixth vision: the flying scroll

**5** [1]Again I lifted my eyes and saw, and behold, a flying scroll! [2]And he said to me, "What do you see?" I answered, "I see a

Jer 29:18
Ezek 2:9–10
Rev 10:9–11

---

**5:1–4.** The prophet is told of a new feature of that people that is being established on the earth: there will be no sinners among them, for those who commit sin will be uprooted. God desires to have a holy people. That is what this vision means. The scroll, of impossible proportions (for its measurements are those of the vestibule of Solomon's temple: cf. 1 Kings 6:3),

---

mi?". [5]Et respondit angelus, qui loquebatur in me, et dixit ad me: "Numquid nescis quid sunt haec?". Et dixi: "Non, domine mi". [6]Et respondit et ait ad me dicens: "Hoc est verbum Domini ad Zorobabel dicens: Non in exercitu nec in robore sed in spiritu meo, dicit Dominus exercituum. [7]Quis tu, mons magne, coram Zorobabel? Eris in planum. Et educet lapidem primarium inter clamores: Quam venustus! [8]Et factum est verbum Domini ad me dicens: [9]Manus Zorobabel fundaverunt domum istam et manus eius perficient eam, et scietis quia Dominus exercituum misit me ad vos. [10]Quis enim despexit diem initiorum parvorum? Et laetabuntur et videbunt lapidem stanneum in manu Zorobabel. Septem illae oculi sunt Domini, qui discurrunt in universa terra". [11]Et respondi et dixi ad eum: "Quid sunt duae olivae istae ad dexteram candelabri et ad sinistram eius?". [12]Et respondi secundo et dixi ad eum: "Quid sunt duo rami olivarum, qui duabus fistulis aureis effundunt ex se aurum?". [13]Et ait ad me dicens: "Numquid nescis quid sunt haec?". Et dixi: "Non, domine mi". [14]Et dixit: "Isti sunt duo filii olei, qui assistunt Dominatori universae terrae".  **[5]** [1]Et conversus sum et levavi oculos meos et vidi: et ecce volumen volans. [2]Et dixit ad me: "Quid tu vides?". Et dixi: "Ego video volumen volans; longitudo eius

---

c. Cn: Heb *gold*

flying scroll; its length is twenty cubits, and its breadth ten cubits."

Ex 20:7,15 ³Then he said to me, "This is the curse that goes out over the face of the whole land; for every one who steals shall be cut off henceforth according to it, and every one who swears falsely shall be cut off henceforth according to it. ⁴I will send it forth, says the LORD of hosts, and it shall enter the house of the thief, and the house of him who swears falsely by my name; and it shall abide in his house and consume it, both timber and stones."

**Seventh vision: the woman in the ephah**

⁵Then the angel who talked with me came forward and said to me, "Lift your eyes, and see what this is that goes forth." ⁶And I said, "What is it?" He said, "This is the ephah that goes forth." And he said, "This is their iniquity[d] in all the land." ⁷And behold, the

---

contains the curses that will apply to sinners. These sinners are typified in the thief and in the person who swears falsely by the Lord's name (third and eight commandments of the Law), that is, they cover both sin against one's neighbour and failure to reverence the name of God. Theodoret of Cyrus interprets these two sins as encapsulating all sins that transgress the commandment to love God and one's neighbour: "The breaking of an oath is the greatest sin: he who does so will be deprived of the love of God. The thief does evil against his neighbour, for no one who loves his neighbour can do him harm" (*Interpretatio in xii prophetas minores*, 5, 4).

**5:5–11.** The previous vision contained the prophecy that the thief and the perjurer would be destroyed; now the prophet is told that wickedness itself will have no place in the new community in the land of Judah. The "ephah" is a measure, a receptacle that could hold approximately 20 litres (4·5 gallons), used as a measure of dry goods. The size of the ephah is exaggerated here (just as the scroll in the previous vision was extraordinarlily large); the ephah is big enough for a woman to fit in it. The two women with wings stand for angels, and the wind stands for the strength of the Lord. Shinar is Babylon, where Iniquity was venerated as a god. Judah and Jerusalem, which are set free from iniquity, prefigure the Church who waits for the mystery of iniquity to be cast out of her (cf. 2 Thess 2:6–8) so that she can appear holy and radiant with the glory of the Lord (cf. Rev 21–22).

---

viginti cubitorum et latitudo eius decem cubitorum". ³Et dixit ad me: "Haec est maledictio, quae egreditur super faciem omnis terrae; quia omnis fur hinc iuxta illud expurgatur, et omnis periurus illinc iuxta illud expurgatur. ⁴Educo illud, dicit Dominus exercituum, et veniet ad domum furis et ad domum iurantis in nomine meo mendaciter; et commorabitur in medio domus eius, et consumet eam et ligna eius et lapides eius". ⁵Et egressus est angelus, qui loquebatur in me, et dixit ad me: "Leva, quaeso, oculos tuos et vide. Quid est hoc, quod egreditur?". ⁶Et dixi: "Quidnam est?". Et ait: "Haec est epha egrediens". Et dixit: "Hoc est peccatum eorum in universa terra". ⁷Et ecce operculum plumbi elevatum

**d.** Gk Compare Syr: Heb *eye*

leaden cover was lifted, and there was a woman sitting in the ephah! [8]And he said, "This is Wickedness." And he thrust her back into the ephah, and thrust down the leaden weight upon its mouth. [9]Then I lifted my eyes and saw, and behold, two women coming forward! The wind was in their wings; they had wings like the wings of a stork, and they lifted up the ephah between earth and heaven. [10]Then I said to the angel who talked with me, "Where are they taking the ephah?" [11]He said to me, "To the land of Shinar, to build a house for it; and when this is prepared, they will set the ephah down there on its base."

Gen 11:2

### Eighth vision: the four chariots

**6** [1]And again I lifted my eyes and saw, and behold, four chariots came out from between two mountains; and the mountains were mountains of bronze. [2]The first chariot had red horses, the second black horses, [3]the third white horses, and the fourth chariot dappled gray[e] horses. [4]Then I said to the angel who talked with me, "What are these, my lord?" [5]And the angel answered me,

Rev 6:2–8

Zech 1:8
Rev 6:2,4,5

Ps 104:4
Zech 1:8

---

**6:1–8.** The eighth and last vision parallels the first (cf. 1:7–17) so that together they form a sort of literary frame for the sequence of visions. The similarity between them lies in the colours, though the function of the divine emissaries (here chariots; in the first vision, riders) is different: now the emissaries defeat the nations that are oppressing Israel. The two mountains from which the chariots emerge seem to be the Mount of Olives and Mount Zion, although they could stand for the mountains that in Babylonian mythology stood at the entrance to the dwelling-place of the gods. In any case, they are a sign that the emissaries are envoys from God. The north country stands for those nations that were traditionally invaders of Israel—now in fact Babylon; the south stands for Egypt. The angel tells Zechariah that judgment against Babylon has caused God's anger to cease; this must be a reference to Babylon's overthrow by Cyrus the Great (v. 8). It is a way of inviting the Jews who still lived in Babylon to return to Jerusalem and play their part in the rebuilding of the temple.

est, et ecce mulier una sedens in medio ephae. [8]Et dixit: "Haec est impietas". Et proiecit eam in epham et misit massam plumbeam in os eius. [9]Et levavi oculos meos et vidi: et ecce duae mulieres egredientes, et ventus in alis earum, et habebant alas quasi alas milvi; et levaverunt epham inter terram et caelum. [10]Et dixi ad angelum, qui loquebatur in me: "Quo istae deferunt epham?". [11]Et dixit ad me: «Ut aedificetur ei domus in terra Sennaar; et, postquam constructa fuerit, ponetur ibi super basem suam». [6] [1]Et rursus levavi oculos meos et vidi: et ecce quattuor quadrigae egredientes de medio duorum montium; et montes, montes aerei. [2]In quadriga prima equi rufi, et in quadriga secunda equi nigri, [3]et in quadriga tertia equi albi, et in quadriga quarta equi varii. [4]Et respondi et dixi ad angelum, qui loquebatur in me: "Quid sunt haec, domine mi?". [5]Et respondit angelus et ait ad me: "Isti sunt quattuor

**e.** Compare Gk: The meaning of the Hebrew word is uncertain

Heb 1:7,11
Rev 6:2–5 "These are going forth to the four winds of heaven, after present-
ing themselves before the LORD of all the earth. ⁶The chariot with
the black horses goes toward the north country, the white ones go
toward the west country,ᶠ and the dappled ones go toward the
south country." ⁷When the steeds came out, they were impatient to
get off and patrol the earth. And he said, "Go, patrol the earth." So
they patrolled the earth. ⁸Then he cried to me, "Behold, those who
go toward the north country have set my Spirit at rest in the north
country."

## The crowning of Joshua

⁹And the word of the LORD came to me: ¹⁰"Take from the exiles
Heldai, Tobijah, and Jedaiah, who have arrived from Babylon; and

---

**6:9–15.** As a climax to the visions comes a prophetic action by Zechariah (the crowning of Joshua) and an oracle, in the style of the ancient prophets. They link up with the third and fourth visions that dealt with Joshua the priest, and the "Branch" or Davidic Messiah. The prophet has to make a crown from material donated by the leading families that have returned from Babylon (we know no more about them than what is said here), and he must leave the crown in the temple as a memorial to the priest's coronation (v. 14) and as encouragement for Jews still abroad to return (v. 15).

There are aspects of this passage that differ from what was said in the visions: there the "Branch" was Zerubbabel, a descendant of David, and he was entrusted the task of finishing the reconstruction of the temple (cf. 3:8; 4:7–10); but here Joshua is called the "Branch" and he must build the temple. To explain this anomaly, some scholars have suggested that the original text of Zechariah must have been edited and the name "Joshua" (v. 11) inserted in the place of Zerubbabel. That may well have happened, or the text could originally have referred to both Joshua and Zerubbabel and have spoken of there being crowns (plural), which is what the Hebrew says (cf. note **h**). But it is also possible that the prophet himself was given to see things differently later and that, when he wrote this oracle by divine inspiration, he was thinking only of the priest Joshua as the Lord's anointed and as having a civil role as well. We do not know why Zerubbabel is not mentioned in the text here; but the fact of the matter remains that the priest is depicted as the point of reference for messianic expectations.

---

venti caeli, qui egrediuntur, postquam steterunt coram Dominatore omnis terrae". ⁶In qua erant equi nigri, egrediebantur in terram aquilonis, et albi egressi sunt post eos, et varii egressi sunt ad terram austri. ⁷Et equi fortes exierunt et quaerebant ire et discurrere per terram. Et dixit: "Ite, perambulate terram". Et perambulaverunt terram. ⁸Et vocavit me et locutus est ad me dicens: "Ecce, qui egrediuntur in terram aquilonis requiescere fecerunt spiritum meum in terra aquilonis". ⁹Et factum est verbum Domini ad me dicens: ¹⁰"Sume ab his, qui de captivitate sunt, ab Holdai et a Thobia et ab Iedaia, et

**f.** Cn: Heb *after them*

go the same day to the house of Josiah, the son of Zephaniah. [11]Take from them silver and gold, and make a crown,[g] and set it upon the head of Joshua, the son of Jehozadak, the high priest; [12]and say to him, 'Thus says the LORD of hosts, "Behold, the man whose name is the Branch: for he shall grow up in his place, and he shall build the temple of the Lord. [13]It is he who shall build the temple of the LORD, and shall bear royal honour, and shall sit and rule upon his throne. And there shall be a priest by his throne, and peaceful understanding shall be between them both."' [14]And the crown[h] shall be in the temple of the LORD as a reminder to Heldai,[i] Tobijah, Jedaiah, and Josiah[j] the son of Zephaniah.

[15]"And those who are far off shall come and help to build the temple of the LORD; and you shall know that the LORD of hosts has sent me to you. And this shall come to pass, if you will diligently obey the voice of the LORD your God."

*Zech 3:5*
*Rev 19:12*

*Jer 23:5*
*Zech 3:8*

*Ps 110:4; Zech 4:14; Mt 16:18*
*Eph 2:20–22*
*Heb 3:3*

*Rev 2:10*

---

"By his throne" (v. 13): in the Septuagint and the New Vulgate this is "on his right"—which seems to be a later correction introduced at a time post-Zechariah when Jewish thinking had difficulty with the idea of the Anointed (Messiah) being both king and priest, even though in earlier times (cf. Ps 110) that was no problem. We know, for example, that in Qumran two anointed ones (messiahs) were expected —one with kingly functions, a descen- dant of David; the other with priestly functions, a descendant of Aaron. Only in the New Testament will the title of Christ (Anointed) be applied to Jesus as Son of David (cf. Mt 1:1; 9:27; 15:22; Mk 10:47; etc.) and as eternal Priest (cf. Heb 7:17, 21; etc.). St Cyril of Alexandria comments: "He is, at the same time, both king and high priest; therefore, the coming of the one Em- manuel was foretold by two prophets" (*Commentarius in Zacchariam*, 6, 9–15).

venies tu in die illa et intrabis domum Iosiae filii Sophoniae, qui venerunt de Babylone. [11]Et sumes argentum et aurum et facies coronam et pones in capite Iesua filii Iosedec, sacerdotis magni, [12]et loqueris ad eum dicens: Haec ait Dominus exercituum dicens: Ecce vir, Germen nomen eius; et in loco suo aliquid germinabit et aedificabit templum Domini. [13]Et ipse exstruet templum Domini; et ipse portabit gloriam et sedebit et dominabitur super solio suo; et erit sacerdos ad dexteram eius, et consilium pacis erit inter illos duos. [14]Et corona erit Helem et Thobiae et Iedaiae et Hen filio Sophoniae memoriale in templo Domini. [15]Et qui procul sunt, venient et aedificabunt in templo Domini; et scietis quia Dominus exercituum misit me ad vos. Erit autem hoc, si oboedieritis voci Domini Dei vestri"».

**g.** Gk Mss: Heb *crowns*   **h.** Gk: Heb *crowns*   **i.** With verse 10: Heb *Helem*   **j.** With verse 10: Heb *Hen*

## 2. THE BOOK OF THE DISCOURSES*

**On fasting**

Neh 1:1
Zech 1:1,7

7 ¹In the fourth year of King Darius, the word of the LORD came to Zechariah in the fourth day of the ninth month, which is Chislev. ²Now the people of Bethel had sent Sharezer and Regemmelech and their men, to entreat the favour of the LORD, ³and to ask the priests of the house of the LORD of hosts and the prophets, "Should I mourn and fast in the fifth month, as I have done for so many years?" ⁴Then the word of the LORD of hosts came to me:

---

**\*7:1–8:23.** A reference to a new date (corresponding to December 518 BC) introduces a series of passages about Zechariah's teachings—two oracles about fasting (7:2–14, 8:18–19) and ten short prophecies about the messianic age, all but one of which opens with the words "Thus says the Lord of hosts" (8:1–17, 20–23). The medium by which the prophet receives God's revelation now is not visions but locutions, in the style of the ancient prophets. Zechariah receives the word of God and the command to speak to all the people (7:4–5). The situation is the same as that when the prophet received the visions: the people have returned from exile and are engaged in the rebuilding of the temple. But now a new problem is raised: what sort of fasting should be done, and what has the Lord done for his people and what will he do for them? The prophet's teaching in these chapters complements that contained in the visions.

**7:1–3.** The sacred writer puts on record the occasion that gave rise to the prophecies that follow. A delegation was sent from Babylon to enquire of the priests of the temple of Jerusalem, and the prophets too (Zechariah included), as to whether they should continue to observe the fast commemorating the destruction of Jerusalem and the temple in the fifth month of 587 (cf. 2 Kings 25:8–10; Jer 52:12–14) given that the rebuilding work has now begun. (Bethel, here, is a personal name, not the name of the site of the ancient Northern sanctuary.) The prophet's reply to the actual question posed comes at the end of the passage (cf. 8:18–19).

**7:4–14.** Before replying to the messengers from Babylon, Zechariah speaks in the name of the Lord to the people who have come back from exile and to the temple priests. He wants them to see that when God scattered them, he was right to do so, for they had failed to obey him in their treatment of others. In this way the prophet is preparing them to understand what he will tell them in the next chapter—

---

[7] ¹Et factum est in anno quarto Darii regis, factum est verbum Domini ad Zachariam in quarta mensis noni, qui est Casleu. ²Et Bethel miserat Sarasar et Regemmelech et viros, qui erant cum eo, ad deprecandam faciem Domini, ³ut dicerent sacerdotibus domus Domini exercituum et prophetis loquentes: «Numquid flendum est mihi in quinto mense vel ieiunandum, sicut iam feci multis annis?». ⁴Et factum est verbum Domini exercituum ad me dicens: ⁵«Loquere ad omnem populum terrae et ad

[5]"Say to all the people of the land and the priests, When you fasted and mourned in the fifth month and in the seventh, for these seventy years, was it for me that you fasted? [6]And when you eat and when you drink, do you not eat for yourselves and drink for yourselves? [7]When Jerusalem was inhabited and in prosperity, with her cities round about her, and the South and the lowland were inhabited, were not these the words which the LORD proclaimed by the former prophets?"

[8]And the word of the LORD came to Zechariah, saying, [9]"Thus says the LORD of hosts, Render true judgments, show kindness and mercy each to his brother, [10]do not oppress the widow, the fatherless, the sojourner, or the poor; and let none of you devise evil against his brother in your heart." [11]But they refused to hearken, and turned a stubborn shoulder, and stopped their ears that they might not hear. [12]They made their hearts like adamant lest they should hear the law and the words which the LORD of

Is 58:5
Amos 5:21

Is 1:17
Mt 23:23

Ex 22:20–21
Jer 5:28
Mic 6:8

Ex 32:9
Is 48:4
Mic 2:1
Ezek 11:19

---

that God brought about their return from exile and is helping them to rebuild Jerusalem and the temple, and is doing so out of sheer mercy (cf. 8:1–17). He begins here by telling them that their fasting during the exile was insincere, for they served themselves, not God (vv. 5–6). (The fasting in question was done during the seventy years or so of exile—cf. Jer 25:11–12; 29:10—and was designed to lament the destruction of the temple and the city—this was the "fast in the fifth month"—and to commemorate the assassination of Gedaliah—the fast of the seventh month, cf. 2 Kings 25:22–26; Jer 41:1–3.) This is followed by verses in

which God (v. 8) summarizes what he laid down in the Law about the needy (vv. 9–10; cf. Ex 22:20–21), and once more put it on record that the people failed to listen to him or simply disobeyed him (vv. 11–12), and that was why exile befell them (vv. 13–14).

**7:12.** The words of the prophets have authority because they were inspired by the Spirit of God (cf. Neh 9:30; 2 Pet 1:21). St Justin makes the same point: "When you hear the prophets say that they speak in their own person, it is not the holy writers [of Scripture] who say this: the divine Word moves them to say it" (*Apologia*, 1, 36, 1–3).

---

sacerdotes dicens: Cum ieiunaretis et plangeretis in quinto et septimo mense per hos septuaginta annos, numquid revera ieiunastis mihi? [6]Et cum comedistis et bibistis, numquid non vobis comedistis et vobismetipsis bibistis? [7]Numquid non sunt verba, quae locutus est Dominus in manu prophetarum priorum, cum adhuc Ierusalem habitaretur et esset opulenta, ipsa et urbes in circuitu eius, et Nageb habitaretur simul cum Sephela?». [8]Et factum est verbum Domini ad Zachariam dicens: [9]«Haec ait Dominus exercituum dicens: Iudicium verum iudicate et misericordiam et miserationes facite unusquisque cum fratre suo; [10]et viduam et pupillum et advenam et pauperem nolite calumniari, et malum unusquisque contra fratrem suum nolite cogitare in corde vestro. [11]Et noluerunt attendere; et opposuerunt dorsum rebelle et aures suas aggravaverunt, ne audirent. [12]Et cor suum posuerunt adamantem, ne audirent legem et verba, quae misit Dominus exercituum in spiritu suo per manum

hosts had sent by his Spirit through the former prophets. Therefore great wrath came from the LORD of hosts. [13]"As I called, and they would not hear, so they called, and I would not hear," says the LORD of hosts, [14]"and I scattered them with a whirlwind among all the nations which they had not known. Thus the land they left was desolate, so that no one went to and fro, and the pleasant land was made desolate."

Deut 4:27
Zeph 3:6
Zech 9:8

## Ten promises of messianic salvation

8 [1]And the word of the LORD of hosts came to me, saying, [2]"Thus says the LORD of hosts: I am jealous for Zion with great jealousy, and I am jealous for her with great wrath. [3]Thus says the LORD: I will return to Zion, and will dwell in the midst of Jerusalem, and Jerusalem shall be called the faithful city, and the mountain of the LORD of hosts, the holy mountain. [4]Thus says the LORD of hosts: Old men and old women shall again sit in the streets of Jerusalem, each with staff in hand for very age. [5]And the streets of the city shall be full of boys and girls playing in its streets. [6]Thus says the LORD of hosts: If it is marvellous in the sight of the remnant of this people in these days, should it also be

Zech 1:14
Is 1:26

Is 65:20,22

Deut 4:40

Jer 32:27

---

**7:13.** The Lord acted justly, as this verse so eloquently puts it: he behaved towards his people as they behaved towards him.

**8:1–23.** The first five prophecies (8:1–8) have to do with God's love for his people (v. 2) and the fulfilment of his promises to dwell in Jerusalem (v. 3; cf. Is 1:26) and to make it a city perfectly at peace (vv. 4–5), even though to the repatriated exiles that might seem an impossible ideal (v. 6), particularly when it includes

not only the Babylon exiles but all Jews from all over the world, who will form a united people of God (vv. 7–8). The other five prophecies (8:9–23) concern the rebuilding of the temple (vv. 9–13) because the Lord is fully behind the project again (vv. 14–15); the specific norms of behaviour that the people must follow, including fasting (vv. 16–19); and the establishment of that era when Jerusalem and the Jews will eventually be instruments of salvation for all the Gentiles (vv. 20–23).

---

prophetarum priorum, et facta est indignatio magna a Domino exercituum. [13]Et factum est, sicut cum clamaret, et ipsi non audierunt, sic clamabunt, et non exaudiam, dicit Dominus exercituum. [14]Et disperdam eos per omnes gentes, quas nesciunt; et terra desolata est post eos, ita ut non esset transiens et revertens. Et posuerunt terram desiderabilem in desertum». **[8]** [1]Et factum est verbum Domini exercituum dicens: [2]«Haec dicit Dominus exercituum: Zelatus sum Sion zelo magno / et ardore magno zelatus sum eam. [3]Haec dicit Dominus: Reversus sum ad Sion et habitabo in medio Ierusalem; et vocabitur Ierusalem civitas Veritatis, et mons Domini exercituum mons Sanctitatis. [4]Haec dicit Dominus exercituum: Adhuc sedebunt senes et anus in plateis Ierusalem et unusquisque cum baculo suo in manu sua prae multitudine dierum; [5]et plateae civitatis complebuntur pueris et puellis ludentibus in plateis eius. [6]Haec dicit Dominus exercituum: Si videbitur difficile in oculis reliquiarum populi huius

marvellous in my sight, says the LORD of hosts? ⁷Thus says the LORD of hosts: Behold, I will save my people from the east country and from the west country; ⁸and I will bring them to dwell in the midst of Jerusalem; and they shall be my people and I will be their God, in faithfulness and in righteousness."

Jer 31:31
Rev 21:7

⁹Thus says the LORD of hosts: "Let your hands be strong, you who in these days have been hearing these words from the mouth of the prophets, since the day that the foundation of the house of the LORD of hosts was laid, that the temple might be built. ¹⁰For before those days there was no wage for man or any wage for beast, neither was there any safety from the foe for him who went out or came in; for I set every man against his fellow. ¹¹But now I will not deal with the remnant of this people as in the former days, says the LORD of hosts. ¹²For there shall be a sowing of peace; the vine shall yield its fruit, and the ground shall give its increase, and the heavens shall give their dew; and I will cause the remnant of this people to possess all these things. ¹³And as you have been a byword of cursing among the nations, O house of Judah and house of Israel, so will I save you and you shall be a blessing. Fear not, but let your hands be strong."

Hag 1:15

Gen 12:2,3
Ps 72:17
Jer 42:18

---

**8:8.** This verse repeats the wording of the Covenant often used by the ancient prophets: "You shall be my people, and I will be your God" (Jer 30:22; cf. Hos 2:25; etc.). Zechariah updates it by applying it to the Jews assembled in Jerusalem after being brought home from all the countries where they had been scattered.

**8:9–13.** The rebuilding of the temple is going to change the circumstances of the people in the promised land and their relationships with other nations, for, from his sanctuary, God will bestow prosperity, peace among the Jews, fruitfulness to the land, and prestige for Israel among the nations. But, for this to happen, all must play their part and work hard, as Haggai and Zechariah have told them.

---

in diebus illis, numquid etiam in oculis meis difficile erit?, dicit Dominus exercituum. ⁷Haec dicit Dominus exercituum: Ecce ego salvabo populum meum de terra orientis / et de terra occasus solis: / ⁸et adducam eos, / et habitabunt in medio Ierusalem; / et erunt mihi in populum, / et ego ero eis in Deum / in veritate et iustitia. ⁹Haec dicit Dominus exercituum: Confortentur manus vestrae, qui auditis in his diebus sermones istos per os prophetarum in die, qua fundata est domus Domini exercituum, ut templum aedificaretur. ¹⁰Siquidem ante dies istos / merces hominis non erat, / nec merces iumenti erat, / neque introeunti neque exeunti / erat pax prae tribulatione; / et dimisi omnes homines, / unumquemque contra proximum suum. / ¹¹Nunc autem non iuxta dies priores ego sum / reliquiis populi huius, / dicit Dominus exercituum. / ¹²sed semen pacis erit: / vinea dabit fructum suum, / et terra dabit proventum suum, / et possidere faciam / reliquias populi huius / universa haec. ¹³Et erit: sicut eratis maledictio in gentibus, domus Iudae et domus Israel, sic salvabo vos, et eritis benedictio. Nolite timere;

Jer 31:28;
32:42

Mt 5:9
Eph 4:25

Mt 5:33; 9:4

Zech 7:1–3
Is 35:10
Jer 31:13
Mt 9:14–15

¹⁴For thus says the LORD of hosts: "As I purposed to do evil to you, when your fathers provoked me to wrath, and I did not relent, says the LORD of hosts, ¹⁵so again have I purposed in these days to do good to Jerusalem and to the house of Judah; fear not. ¹⁶These are the things that you shall do: Speak the truth to one another, render in your gates judgments that are true and make for peace, ¹⁷do not devise evil in your hearts against one another, and love no false oath, for all these things I hate, says the LORD."

¹⁸And the word of the LORD of hosts came to me, saying, ¹⁹"Thus says the LORD of hosts: The fast of the fourth month, and the fast of the fifth, and the fast of the seventh, and the fast of the tenth, shall be to the house of Judah seasons of joy and gladness, and cheerful feasts; therefore love truth and peace.

²⁰"Thus says the LORD of hosts: Peoples shall yet come, even the inhabitants of many cities; ²¹the inhabitants of one city shall

**8:14–17.** Through the prophet, the Lord sets out the terms of a new agreement with the repatriates, spelling out what he will do (vv. 14–15) and what the people must do (vv. 16–17). What he requires of them is summed up in terms of truthfulness, justice and loyalty towards others. The exhortation in v. 16 is updated in Ephesians 4:25 to underline the duties of Christians towards their neighbour.

**8:19.** The new situation will involve a change in the way celebrations are held as compared with during the exile. Now, they are going to be days of joy and gladness. To the fasts mentioned earlier are added the fast of the fourth

month, to commemorate the breach made in the city wall by Nebuchadnezzar (cf. 2 Kings 25:3–4; Jer 39:2), and that of the tenth month, recalling the start of the siege (2 Kings 25:1; Jer 39:1).

**8:20–22.** The new situation described by the prophet will be marked by efforts on the part of the nations to seek the God of Israel, the one, true God. All will find divine favour in Jerusalem. This will mean the fulfilment of God's promise to Abraham that all the nations of the earth would be blessed in him (cf. Gen 12:3). The picture painted by the prophet is a figure of what will happen with the coming of Christ and the establishment of his Church.

confortentur manus vestrae. ¹⁴Quia haec dicit Dominus exercituum: Sicut cogitavi, ut affligerem vos, cum ad iracundiam provocassent patres vestri me, dicit Dominus exercituum, ¹⁵et non sum misertus, sic conversus cogitavi in diebus istis, ut benefaciam Ierusalem et domui Iudae; nolite timere. ¹⁶Haec sunt ergo, quae facietis: Loquimini veritatem unusquisque cum proximo suo et iudicium pacis iudicate in portis vestris, ¹⁷et unusquisque malum contra amicum suum ne cogitetis in cordibus vestris et iuramentum mendax ne diligatis: omnia enim haec sunt quae odi», dicit Dominus. ¹⁸Et factum est verbum Domini exercituum ad me dicens: ¹⁹«Haec dicit Dominus exercituum: Ieiunium quarti et ieiunium quinti et ieiunium septimi et ieiunium decimi erit domui Iudae in gaudium et laetitiam et in sollemnitates praeclaras; veritatem tantum et pacem diligite. ²⁰Haec dicit Dominus exercituum: Adhuc venient populi et habitatores civitatum magnarum, ²¹et ibunt habitatores unius ad alteram dicentes:

go to another, saying, 'Let us go at once to entreat the favour of the LORD, and to seek the LORD of hosts; I am going.' [22]Many peoples and strong nations shall come to seek the LORD of hosts in Jerusalem, and to entreat the favour of the LORD. [23]Thus says the LORD of hosts: In those days ten men from the nations of every tongue shall take hold of the robe of a Jew, saying, 'Let us go with you, for we have heard that God is with you.'"

Zech 2:11

Is 66:18
1 Cor 14:25
Rev 5:9

# PART TWO

## MESSIANIC ORACLES*

### 1. ORACLE OF THE MESSIAH KING, THE GOOD SHEPHERD*

**Punishment of the nations**

# 9

[1]An Oracle

The word of the LORD is against the land of Hadrach
    and will rest upon Damascus.
For to the LORD belong the cities of Aram,[k]

---

**8:23.** Here the prophet graphically describes the power of intercession with God that the Jews will have, enabling all mankind to find favour with him. The number ten symbolizes completeness, and the name "Jew" here means an inhabitant of Judea after the return from exile (cf. Jer 32:12). "By saying that men of every tongue shall take hold of the robe, it is made abundantly clear that on that day the call to holiness will be heard not only by the Israelites, but by all

men and women everywhere throughout the world" (St Cyril of Alexandria, *Commentarius in Zacchariam*, 8, 23).

**\*9:1–14:21.** The prophecies concerning the new circumstances of Jerusalem and Judah in chapters 7–8 give way now to two long oracles describing how that definitive time will be established by the Messiah (chaps. 9–10), and how the kingdom of God will come about (chaps. 12–14). Worked in among these

---

"Eamus, ut deprecemur faciem Domini et quaeramus Dominum exercituum; vadam etiam ego". [22]Et venient populi multi et gentes robustae ad quaerendum Dominum exercituum in Ierusalem et deprecandam faciem Domini. [23]Haec dicit Dominus exercituum: In diebus illis apprehendent decem homines ex omnibus linguis gentium, apprehendent fimbriam viri Iudaei dicentes: "Ibimus vobiscum; audivimus enim quoniam Deus vobiscum est"». **[9]** [1]Oraculum. «Verbum Domini in terra Hadrach

**k.** Cn: Heb *the eye of Adam* (or *man*)

even as all the tribes of Israel;
[2]Hamath also, which borders thereon,
Tyre and Sidon, though they are very wise.
[3]Tyre has built herself a rampart,
and heaped up silver like dust,
and gold like the dirt of the streets.

Ezek 26:17    [4]But lo, the Lord will strip her of her possessions
and hurl her wealth into the sea,
and she shall be devoured by fire.

[5]Ashkelon shall see it, and be afraid;
Gaza too, and shall writhe in anguish;
Ekron also, because its hopes are confounded.
The king shall perish from Gaza;
Ashkelon shall be uninhabited;
[6]a mongrel people shall dwell in Ashdod;
and I will make an end of the pride of Philistia.

Lev 3:17    [7]I will take away its blood from its mouth,
Is 4:3    and its abominations from between its teeth;
it too shall be a remnant for our God;

---

themes are short prophetical pieces which are apparently anonymous, for there is no mention of Zechariah in them and no dates are given. The two oracles start in the same way: "An oracle. The word of the Lord …" (9:1; 12:1), a formula which is also used at the start of the book of Malachi (Mal 1:1). Because this construction is found on only these three occasions in the Old Testament, the three pieces are thought to come from some third source and to have found their way into the biblical text here—two into the book of Zechariah and one into that of Malachi.

*9:1–11:17. This first oracle includes two prophetical proclamations—one about the advent of the Messiah king (9:1–10:12), and the other about the rejection of the good shepherd who tries to lead the people along the paths of faithfulness and unity (11:1–17). The first one starts with a prophetical description of the victorious progress of the Lord as he makes his way down to Jerusalem from the north (9:1–8); then the city is invited to rejoice at the arrival of its king (9:9–10); and finally the restoration of Israel is proclaimed (9:11–17).

/ et Damasci requiei eius, / quia Domini est oculus Aram / sicut omnes tribus Israel. / [2]Emath quoque in terminis eius / et Tyrus et Sidon, quae sapiens est valde. / [3]Et aedificavit Tyrus munitionem suam / et coacervavit argentum quasi pulverem / et aurum ut lutum platearum. / [4]Ecce Dominus possidebit eam / et percutiet in mari fortitudinem eius; / et haec igni devorabitur. / [5]Videbit Ascalon et timebit, / et Gaza dolore torquetur nimis, / et Accaron, quoniam confusa est spes eius; / et peribit rex de Gaza, / et Ascalon non habitabitur. / [6]Et habitabit spurius in Azoto, / et disperdam superbiam Philisthim. / [7]Et auferam sanguinem eius de ore eius / et abominationes eius de medio dentium eius, / et relinquetur

it shall be like a clan in Judah,
and Ekron shall be like the Jebusites.
⁸Then I will encamp at my house as a guard,
so that none shall march to and fro;
no oppressor shall again overrun them,
for now I see with my own eyes.

### The arrival of the Messiah

⁹Rejoice greatly, O daughter of Zion!
Shout aloud, O daughter of Jerusalem!
Lo, your king comes to you;
triumphant and victorious is he,
humble and riding on an ass,
on a colt the foal of an ass.
¹⁰I will cut off the chariot from Ephraim
and the war horse from Jerusalem;

Is 12:6
Zeph 3:14
*Mt 11:29; 21:5*
Mk 11:2
*Jn 12:15*

Ps 72:8
Is 9:5; 11:6
Hos 1:7; 2:20
Eph 2:14

---

**9:1–8.** Beginning with Syria (vv. 1–2a), and then passing through Phoenicia (v. 2b–4) and the cities of the Philistines (vv. 5–7), the Lord enters the holy land where he encamps and provides his people with protection against any would-be invader (v. 8). Those countries of the north, represented by the cities mentioned, will become the Lord's property. In the case of the Philistines, they will even form part of the holy people once they have been cleansed of their abominable practices— which consist, as far as one can deduce from the text, in eating meat with blood in it (v. 7), a grave sin, as far as the Jews were concerned (cf. Lev 19:26; Deut 12:16).

**9:9–10.** The prophet now speaks directly to Jerusalem ("daughter of Zion") and her citizens ("daughter of

Jerusalem") as representatives of the entire chosen people. An invitation to rejoice and celebrate is often found in the Old Testament in connexion with the arrival of the messianic era (cf. Is 12:6; 54:1; Zeph 3:14); here it is issued because Jerusalem's king is arriving. Although the text does not say so explicitly, it is implied that he is the descendant of David; there is an echo here of 2 Samuel 7:12–16 and Isaiah 7:14. This king is distinguished by what he is and what he does. The word "triumphant" translates the Hebrew *saddiq*, which means "just": he does the will of God perfectly; and the term "victorious" means that he enjoys divine protection and salvation. The Septuagint and the Vulgate, however, read it as meaning that he was the saviour. He is also "humble", that is, he

etiam ipse Deo nostro, / et erit quasi dux in Iuda, / et Accaron quasi Iebusaeus. / ⁸Et circumdabo domum meam ut praesidium / contra euntes et revertentes; / et non transibit super eos ultra exactor, / quia nunc vidi in oculis meis. / ⁹Exsulta satis, filia Sion; / iubila, filia Ierusalem. / Ecce rex tuus venit tibi / iustus et salvator ipse, / pauper et sedens super asinum / et super pullum filium asinae. / ¹⁰Et disperdam currum ex Ephraim / et equum de Ierusalem; / et confringetur arcus belli, / et loquetur

and the battle bow shall be cut off,
> and he shall command peace to the nations;

his dominion shall be from sea to sea,
> and from the River to the ends of the earth.

Ex 24:4–8; Mt
26:28; Mk 14:24
1 Cor 11:25
Heb 10:29; 13:20
Is 49:9; 61:7

**The restoration of Israel**

<sup>11</sup>As for you also, because of the blood of my covenant with you,
I will set your captives free from the waterless pit.

---

is not boastful in the presence of either God or men. He is peaceable—as can be seen from the fact that he rides not on a horse like kings of the time but on an ass, like the princes of ancient times (cf. Gen 49:11; Judg 5:10; 10:4; 12:14). He will cause the weapons of war to disappear from Samaria and Judah (cf. Is 2:4, 7; Mic 5:9), who will form a single, united people; and he will also establish peace among the nations (v. 10). This king has features similar to those of the "servant of the Lord" of whom Isaiah spoke (cf. Is 53:11) and to those of the lowly people whom God found acceptable (cf. Zeph 2:3; 3:12). Our Lord Jesus Christ fulfilled this prophecy when he entered Jerusalem before the Passover and was acclaimed by the crowd as the Messiah, the Son of David (cf. Mt 21:1–5; Jn 12:14). "The 'King of glory' (Ps 24:7–10) enters his City 'riding on an ass' (Zech 9:9). Jesus conquers the Daughter of Zion, a figure of his Church, neither by ruse nor by violence, but by the humility that bears witness to the truth (cf. Jn 18:37)" (*Catechism of the Catholic Church*, 559). In an allegorical reading, Clement of Alexandria takes the young ass of v. 9 to stand for people who are not subject to evil: "It was not enough to say a 'colt';

the sacred writer added, 'the foal of an ass', to emphasize the youth of the humanity of Christ, his eternal youth. The divine groom tends to us and trains us, the youngest, smallest colts" (*Paedagogus*, 1, 15, 1).

**9:11–17.** This prophetical proclamation is also addressed to Jerusalem and Judah, now seen as the people of the Covenant. The "blood" of v. 11 is reminiscent of the sacrifice that sealed the pact of Mount Sinai (cf. Ex 24:8). First the Lord speaks (vv. 11–13); then the prophet (vv. 14–17). But their voices fuse to utter the same promises—the release and the repatriation of the exiles. St Augustine, who sees in v. 11 an announcement of the forgiveness of sins that Christ would bring about, interprets the "waterless pit" as "the waterless and barren pit of human misery, into which the stream of righteousness does not run, where only the mire of sinfulness lies" (*De civitate Dei*, 18, 35). "Greece" here must mean all the people of the eastern Mediterranean, including the Greeks. Their mention here suggests that the second part of the book of Zechariah was written after the conquests of Alexander the Great, king of Macedonia.

pacem gentibus. / Et imperium eius a mari usque ad mare / et a flumine usque ad fines terrae. / <sup>11</sup>Tu quoque: in sanguine testamenti tui / extraho vinctos tuos de lacu, / in quo non est aqua. / <sup>12</sup>Convertimini

¹²Return to your stronghold, O prisoners of hope;
    today I declare that I will restore to you double.
¹³For I have bent Judah as my bow;
    I have made Ephraim its arrow.
 I will brandish your sons, O Zion,
    over your sons, O Greece,
    and wield you like a warrior's sword.

¹⁴Then the LORD will appear over them,
    and his arrow go forth like lightning;
the Lord GOD will sound the trumpet,
    and march forth in the whirlwinds of the south.
¹⁵The LORD of hosts will protect them,
    and they shall devour and tread down the slingers;[l]
and they shall drink their blood[m] like wine,
    and be full like a bowl,
    drenched like the corners of the altar.

¹⁶On that day the LORD their God will save them
    for they are the flock of his people;
for like the jewels of a crown
    they shall shine on his land.
¹⁷Yea, how good and how fair it shall be!
    Grain shall make the young men flourish,
    and new wine the maidens.

Cross references (margin):
Deut 33:2
Ps 18:15
Hab 3:4
Ex 27:2
Is 2:11; 11:10,12; 62:3
Ezek 34:1
Jer 31:12–13

---

ad munitionem, / vincti spei; / hodie quoque annuntians: / Duplicia reddam tibi. / ¹³Nam extendi mihi Iudam quasi arcum, / implevi Ephraim; / et suscitabo filios tuos, Sion, / super filios tuos, Graecia, / et ponam te quasi gladium fortium. / ¹⁴Et Dominus super eos videbitur, / et exibit ut fulgur iaculum eius; / et Dominus Deus in tuba canet / et vadet in procellis austri. / ¹⁵Dominus exercituum proteget eos; / et devorabunt et conculcabunt lapides fundae / et bibent, agitabuntur quasi vino / et replebuntur ut phialae et quasi cornua altaris. / ¹⁶Et salvabit eos Dominus Deus eorum / in die illa / ut gregem populi sui, / quia lapides coronae / fulgebunt super terram eius. / ¹⁷Quid enim bonum eius est, / et quid pulchrum eius! / Frumentum succrescere facit iuvenes, / et mustum virgines.

**l.** Cn: Heb *the slingstones*   **m.** Gk: Heb *be turbulent*

## Faithfulness to the Lord, and restoration of Israel

Deut 11:14
Ps 135:7

10 [1]Ask rain from the LORD
in the season of the spring rain,
from the LORD who makes the storm clouds,
who gives men showers of rain,
to every one the vegetation in the field.

1 Sam 15:22
Jer 23:25; 27:9
Ezek 34:5
Mt 9:36

[2]For the teraphim utter nonsense,
and the diviners see lies;
the dreamers tell false dreams,
and give empty consolation.
Therefore the people wander like sheep;
they are afflicted for want of a shepherd.

Ezek 32:4

[3]"My anger is hot against the shepherds,
and I will punish the leaders;[n]
for the LORD of hosts cares for his flock, the house of Judah,
and will make them like his proud steed in battle.
[4]Out of them shall come the cornerstone,
out of them the tent peg,
out of them the battle bow,

---

**10:1–2.** These verses look like a short insertion advising people that when they pray for rain they should have recourse to the Lord only, and not to magicians. And it tells us why: the Lord is master of the clouds and provident towards all: people who resort to divination, etc. are deceitful; they deceive the people (cf. Jer 27:9; Mic 3:7). On the *teraphim* (idols), see the note on Judges 17:5.

**10:3–12.** Once again the Lord speaks, his voice mingling with that of the prophet. Now he promises that he will be with Judah and Samaria (here called Joseph or Ephraim) and will make them strong. Judah will have pre-eminence (vv. 3–6) and into her will come those from the Northern kingdom who were deported by the Assyrians (cf. 2 Kings 17:5–6; 18:9–12). This return and reunification are described as a new exodus from Egypt. This prophecy when applied to the new situation of the return from exile means that the new community that is formed will include within it all the people of Israel: the differences that existed in the time of the two kingdoms will be completely erased.

[10] [1]Petite a Domino pluviam / in tempore pluviae serotinae. / Dominus facit fulgura / et pluviam imbris dabit eis, / singulis herbam in agro. / [2]Quia teraphim loquuntur inania, / et divini vident mendacium, / et somnia loquuntur vana, / vane consolantur; / idcirco migrant quasi grex, / affliguntur, quia non est eis pastor. / [3]Super pastores iratus est furor meus, / et super hircos visitabo: / certe visitat Dominus exercituum / gregem suum, domum Iudae, / et faciet eos quasi equum gloriae suae / in bello. / [4]Ex ipso angulus, / ex ipso paxillus, / ex ipso arcus proelii, / ex ipso egredietur omnis exactor simul.

**n.** Or *he-goats*

out of them every ruler.
⁵Together they shall be like mighty men in battle,
    trampling the foe in the mud of the streets;
they shall fight because the LORD is with them,
    and they shall confound the riders on horses.

⁶"I will strengthen the house of Judah,                    Is 41:7
    and I will save the house of Joseph.
I will bring them back because I have compassion on them,
    and they shall be as though I had not rejected them;
    for I am the LORD their God and I will answer them.
⁷Then Ephraim shall become like a mighty warrior,        Ps 104:15
    and their hearts shall be glad as with wine.
Their children shall see it and rejoice,
    their hearts shall exult in the LORD.

⁸"I will signal for them and gather them in,
    for I have redeemed them,
    and they shall be as many as of old.
⁹Though I scattered them among the nations,               Deut 30:1–3
    yet in far countries they shall remember me,          Lk 15:1–7
    and with their children they shall live and return.
¹⁰I will bring them home from the land of Egypt,          Is 11:11; 27:13
    and gather them from Assyria;                          Hos 11:11
and I will bring them to the land of Gilead and to Lebanon,
    till there is no room for them.
¹¹They shall pass through the sea of Egypt,ᵒ
    and the waves of the sea shall be smitten,
    and all the depths of the Nile dried up.
The pride of Assyria shall be laid low,
    and the sceptre of Egypt shall depart.
¹²I will make them strong in the LORD                     Mic 4:5
    and they shall gloryᵖ in his name," says the LORD.

---

/ ⁵Et erunt quasi fortes / conculcantes lutum viarum in proelio / et bellabunt, quia Dominus cum eis; et confundentur ascensores equorum. / ⁶Et confortabo domum Iudae / et domum Ioseph salvabo / et reducam eos, quia miserebor eorum; / et erunt, sicut non proiecissem eos: / ego enim Dominus Deus eorum et exaudiam eos. / ⁷Et erunt quasi fortes Ephraim, / et laetabitur cor eorum quasi a vino, / et filii eorum videbunt et laetabuntur, / et exsultabit cor eorum in Domino. / ⁸Sibilabo eis et congregabo illos, / quia redemi eos, / et multi erunt, sicut multi ante fuerant. / ⁹Et seminabo eos in populis, / et de longe recordabuntur mei; / et alent filios suos et revertentur. / ¹⁰Et reducam eos de terra Aegypti / et de Assyria congregabo eos / et ad terram Galaad et Libani adducam eos, / et non invenietur eis locus. / ¹¹Et transibunt per mare angustiae, / et percutiet in mari fluctus, / et exiccabuntur omnia profunda fluminis; / et humiliabitur superbia Assyriae, / et sceptrum Aegypti recedet. / ¹²Confortabo eos in Domino, / et

o. Cn: Heb *distress*    p. Gk: Heb *walk*

**The powerful are brought low***

11 [1]Open your doors, O Lebanon,
that the fire may devour your cedars!
[2]Wail, O cypress, for the cedar has fallen,
for the glorious trees are ruined!
Wail, oaks of Bashan,
for the thick forest has been felled!
[3]Hark, the wail of the shepherds,
for their glory is despoiled!
Hark, the roar of the lions,
or the jungle of the Jordan is laid waste!

---

***11:1–17.** The tone of lamentation in this chapter contrasts sharply with the tone of the previous one (which was so full of promise), and even more so with the first part of the book, which announced the completion of the new temple and an era of peace for a united Israel. The prophet now sees a different situation—that of a divided people who reject their shepherd. It could have to do with events that occurred between the completion of the temple in 515 and the arrival of Nehemiah in 445, when Nehemiah found the community and the city to be in a deplorable state (cf. Neh 2:11–18). It is a period about which the Bible has very little to say except for what can be read in these pages of Zechariah and in the books of Ezra and Nehemiah. In that period, the descendants of the Davidic dynasty, whose last recorded representative is Zerubbabel, disappear completely; and the focus of attention changes to the chief priests, who held the reins of internal government of the community.

**11:1–3.** Because the language of this passage is so metaphorical, it is difficult to say exactly what it means. The trees could mean the nations hostile to Israel, and the shepherds and lions, their kings. But the geographical references (Lebanon, Bashan and the Jordan banks) suggest, rather, that the trees may be Joseph (Samaria) and Judah, whom other prophets also depicted as trees (cf. Amos 5:2; Is 14:4–21). This lament anticipates and summarizes the state of desolation of the country after its rejection of the good shepherd (about which we will soon hear). A Christian interpretation reads the passage as a prophecy of the rejection of Christ, the Good Shepherd and King of the Universe, in accordance with the prophesy in Psalm 2:3: "Let us burst their bonds asunder, and cast their cords from us": "They break the mild yoke, they throw off their burden, a wonderful burden of holiness and justice, of grace and love and peace. Love makes them angry; they laugh at the gentle goodness of a God who will not call his legions of angels to his help. If our Lord would only make a deal, if only he would sacrifice a few innocent people to satisfy a majority of

in nomine eius ambulabunt», / dicit Dominus. **[11]** [1]Aperi, Libane, portas tuas, / et comedat ignis cedros tuas. / [2]Ulula, abies, quia cecidit cedrus, / quoniam magnifici vastati sunt; / ululate, quercus Basan, / quoniam corruit saltus impervius. / [3]Vox ululatus pastorum, / quia vastata est magnificentia

### Allegory of the two shepherds

<sup></sup>⁴Thus said the LORD my God: "Become shepherd of the flock doomed to slaughter. ⁵Those who buy them slay them and go

Jer 12:3
Ezek 34:1
Rom 8:36
Rev 3:17

---

blameworthy people, there might be a chance of arriving at some understanding with him. But that's not the way God thinks" (St Josemaría Escrivá, *Christ Is Passing By*, 185).

**11:4–17.** The Lord commands the prophet to perform a symbolic action that is full of meaning. He dresses himself as the shepherd king of his people, whom their leaders are leading to their deaths ("the flock doomed to slaughter": v. 4). He wants to see divine benevolence reign in the land, when the people will be faithful and the country unified; that grace and union are symbolized by the two staffs used to shepherd the flock. He may manage to expel a succession of leaders who were causing all the discord; but in the end he can do no more, his patience is exhausted and he gives up trying. This is symbolized by his breaking the Grace staff (v. 10), that is, the one which steers the people along paths of faithfulness to the Lord. He is paid a ridiculously low fee for the work he has done—the price of a slave in ancient times (cf. Ex 21:32). The gesture of throwing the money into the treasury of the temple means that the shepherd stood for God and it is God himself who has been rejected (v. 13). Then the Union staff is broken (v. 14) and, also sym-

bolized in the person of the prophet, God raises up a useless shepherd who takes no care of the sheep and is cursed by God for his neglect. The prophet and the good shepherd of the first part of the allegory stand for the lawful king, the Lord's anointed. This prophecy will be fulfilled when Jesus is handed over by Judas for thirty pieces of silver, as the evangelists are not slow to point out (cf. Mt 26:14–15; 27:3–10). The Fathers did not fail to notice this passage from Zechariah. St Gregory Nazianzen uses it in his discussion of the office of the priest: "This is my prayer: May the God of peace who makes us both one (cf. Eph 2:14) and makes a gift of us for others, who sets the king on his throne—*He raises the poor from the dust, and lifts the needy from the ash heap* (Ps 113:7)—who chose David, the last and least of the sons of Jesse, to be his servant while he tended the flocks, and who gives the teachers of the Gospel the word and the power to carry out their mission; may He hold our hand, guide us by his will, take us to himself with honour, tend to the shepherds and guide the guides, so that we will be able to tend to his flock wisely, and not become like *the worthless shepherd, who deserts the flock*" (*Apologetica* [*Oratio*] 2, 117).

---

eorum; / vox rugitus leonum, / quoniam vastata est superbia Iordanis. ⁴Haec dicit Dominus Deus meus: «Pasce pecora occisionis. ⁵Quae, qui emunt, occidunt et non dolent; et, qui vendunt ea, dicunt:

unpunished; and those who sell them say, 'Blessed be the LORD, I have become rich'; and their own shepherds have no pity on them. [6]For I will no longer have pity on the inhabitants of this land, says the LORD. Lo, I will cause men to fall each into the hand of his shepherd, and each into the hand of his king; and they shall crush the earth, and I will deliver none from their hand."

[7]So I became the shepherd of the flock doomed to be slain for those who trafficked in the sheep. And I took two staffs; one I named Grace, the other I named Union. And I tended the sheep. [8]In one month I destroyed the three shepherds. But I became impatient with them, and they also detested me. [9]So I said, "I will not be your shepherd. What is to die, let it die; what is to be destroyed, let it be destroyed; and let those that are left devour the flesh of one another." [10]And I took my staff Grace, and I broke it, annulling the covenant which I had made with all the peoples. [11]So it was annulled on that day, and the traffickers in the sheep, who were watching me, knew that it was the word of the LORD.

Mt 26:15 [12]Then I said to them, "If it seems right to you, give me my wages; but if not, keep them." And they weighed out as my wages Mt 27:3–10 thirty shekels of silver. [13]Then the LORD said to me, "Cast it into the treasury"[q]—the lordly price at which I was paid off by them. So I took the thirty shekels of silver and cast them into the treasury[q] in the house of the LORD. [14]Then I broke my second staff Union, annulling the brotherhood between Judah and Israel.

Ezek 34:2–4
Is 42:3
Jer 23:1
Mt 12:20
Jn 10:12
[15]Then the LORD said to me, "Take once more the implements of a worthless shepherd. [16]For lo, I am raising up in the land a shepherd who does not care for the perishing, or seek the wandering,[r] or heal the maimed, or nourish the sound, but devours

---

"Benedictus Dominus! Dives factus sum". Et pastores eorum non miserentur eorum. [6]Et ego non miserebor ultra super habitantes terram, dicit Dominus; ecce ego tradam homines, unumquemque in manu proximi sui et in manu regis sui; et concident terram, et non eruam de manu eorum». [7]Et ego pavi pecus occisionis pro mercatoribus gregis. Et assumpsi mihi duas virgas: unam vocavi Gratiam et alteram vocavi Funiculum; et pavi gregem. [8]Et succidi tres pastores in mense uno, et taeduit eorum animam meam; siquidem et animam eorum taeduit mei. [9]Et dixi: «Non pascam vos. Quae moritura est, moriatur; et, quae succidenda est, succidatur; et reliquae devorent unaquaeque carnem proximae suae». [10]Et tuli virgam meam, quae vocabatur Gratia, et abscidi eam, ut irritum facerem foedus meum, quod percussi cum omnibus populis. [11]Et irritum factum est in die illa; et cognoverunt mercatores gregis, qui observabant me, quia verbum Domini est. [12]Et dixi ad eos: «Si bonum est in oculis vestris, afferte mercedem meam et, si non, quiescite». Et appenderunt mercedem meam triginta siclos argenteos. [13]Et dixit Dominus ad me: «Proice illud in thesaurum, decorum pretium, quo appretiatus sum ab eis». Et tuli triginta siclos argenteos et proieci illos in domum Domini in thesaurum. [14]Et praecidi virgam meam secundam, quae appellabatur Funiculus, ut dissolverem germanitatem inter Iudam et Israel. [15]Et dixit Dominus ad me: «Adhuc sume tibi vasa pastoris stulti; [16]quia ecce ego suscitabo pastorem in terra, qui perituram ovem non visitabit, / dispersam non quaeret / et contritam non sanabit / et stantem non

**q.** Syr: Heb *to the potter*    **r.** Syr Compare Gk Vg: Heb *the youth*

the flesh of the fat ones, tearing off even their hoofs.

[17]Woe to my worthless shepherd,
  who deserts the flock!
May the sword smite his arm
  and his right eye!
Let his arm be wholly withered,
  his right eye utterly blinded!"

Jn 10:12–13

## 2. ORACLES CONCERNING THE RESTORATION

### Prophecies concerning Jerusalem, Judah and Israel

# 12[1]    An Oracle

Num 16:22
1 Cor 2:4

The word of the LORD concerning Israel: Thus says the LORD, who stretched out the heavens and founded the earth and formed the spirit of man within him: [2]"Lo, I am about to make Jerusalem

Gen 2:7
Is 42:5;
51:17,22

---

*12:1–14:21. This section, which consists of the second great oracle (cf. 9:1), promises the eventual, permanent restoration of Jerusalem and Judah. The prophecies are each prefaced by the phrase "On that day", which occurs nineteen times. It means the day in which God acts definitively, when Israel will fully triumph over her enemies (12:1–9), the people's conversion to God will be complete and irreversible (12:10–13:9), and Jerusalem will be established forever in splendour as the capital of the Kingdom of God on earth (14:1–4).

12:1–9. The reference to God's creation of the world and of man gives a tone of formality to the oracle and underscores the fact that the almighty power of God

will determine the destiny of his people. Here, Israel (v. 1) does not mean the Northern kingdom but the entire people. The main idea running through the passage is the triumph of Jerusalem and Judah over all the nations of the earth that joined forces against them. The oracle speaks first about Jerusalem and then about Judah, as if they were two different entities, sometimes focusing on the city (vv. 3–4), sometimes on the region (vv. 6–7). One can even sense a certain hostility between the two, which may reflect a rivalry between countryfolk and townsmen (cf. v. 7), or a serious confrontation between city and countryside on political and economic matters, after some split had occurred between them. To show that

---

sustinebit / et carnes pinguium comedet / et ungulas earum confringet. / [17]Vae stulto meo pastori / derelinquenti gregem! / Gladius super brachium eius / et super oculum dextrum eius; / brachium eius ariditate siccetur, / et oculus dexter eius tenebrescens obscuretur». [12] [1]Oraculum. Verbum Domini super Israel et super Iudam. Oraculum Domini, qui extendit caelum et fundat terram et fingit spiritum hominis in eo: [2]«Ecce ego pono Ierusalem pateram crapulae omnibus populis in circuitu. Hoc erit in

a cup of reeling to all the peoples round about; it will be against
Judah also in the siege against Jerusalem. ³On that day I will make
Jerusalem a heavy stone for all the peoples; all who lift it shall
grievously hurt themselves. And all the nations of the earth will
come together against it. ⁴On that day, says the LORD, I will strike
every horse with panic, and its rider with madness. But upon the
house of Judah I will open my eyes, when I strike every horse of
the peoples with blindness. ⁵Then the clans of Judah shall say to
themselves, 'The inhabitants of Jerusalem have strength through
the LORD of hosts, their God.'

⁶"On that day I will make the clans of Judah like a blazing pot in
the midst of wood, like a flaming torch among sheaves; and they
shall devour to the right and to the left all the peoples round about,
while Jerusalem shall still be inhabited in its place, in Jerusalem.

⁷"And the LORD will give victory to the tents of Judah first, that
the glory of the house of David and the glory of the inhabitants of
Jerusalem may not be exalted over that of Judah. ⁸On that day the
LORD will put a shield about the inhabitants of Jerusalem so that
the feeblest among them on that day shall be like David, and the
house of David shall be like God, like the angel of the LORD, at
their head. ⁹And on that day I will seek to destroy all the nations
that come against Jerusalem.

*Lk 21:24*
*Rev 11:2*

*Deut 28:28*

*Zech 14:10*

*Zech 14:3*

---

both, Jerusalem and Judah, will cause harm to their enemies, the prophet uses new imagery, such as the "cup of reeling" (v. 2: perhaps a reference to the cup of the wrath of God in Isaiah 51:17), the "heavy stone" that hurts anyone who lifts it (v. 3), the "blazing pot" and the "flaming torch" that burn anyone that goes near them (v. 6). The passage looks forward to the messianic era that will come into being on "that day": it depicts the "house of David" leading the people (v. 8), just as God led them by means of his angel when they were in the wilderness (cf. Ex 14:19; 23:20; etc.).

St Bonaventure drew on v. 6 and Isaiah 31:9 when he wrote: "The fire is God; his furnace, as the prophet tells us, is in Jerusalem; Christ sets it aflame with his passion" (*Itinerarium mentis in Deum*, 7, 6).

obsidione contra Ierusalem. ³Et erit: in die illa ponam Ierusalem lapidem portandum cunctis populis; omnes portantes eam concisione lacerabuntur, et colligentur adversus eam omnes gentes terrae. ⁴In die illa, dicit Dominus, percutiam omnem equum in stuporem et ascensorem eius in amentiam; et super domum Iudae aperiam oculos meos et omnem equum populorum percutiam caecitate. ⁵Et dicent duces Iudae in corde suo: "Robur habitantium Ierusalem est in Domino exercituum, Deo eorum". ⁶In die illa ponam duces Iudae sicut ollam ignis super ligna et sicut facem ignis super fenum; et devorabunt ad dexteram et ad sinistram omnes populos in circuitu, et habitabitur Ierusalem rursus in loco suo. ⁷Et salvabit Dominus prius tabernacula Iudae, ut non elevetur gloria domus David et gloria habitantium Ierusalem contra Iudam. ⁸In die illa proteget Dominus habitatores Ierusalem; et erit, qui offenderit ex eis in die illa quasi David, et domus David quasi Deus, sicut angelus Domini in conspectu eorum. ⁹Et

[10]"And I will pour out on the house of David and the inhabitants of Jerusalem a spirit of compassion and supplication, so that, when they look on him whom they have pierced, they shall mourn for him, as one mourns for an only child, and weep bitterly over him, as one weeps over a first-born. [11]On that day the mourning in Jerusalem will be as great as the mourning for Hadad-rimmon in the plain of Megiddo. [12]The land shall mourn, each family by itself; the family of the house of David by itself, and their wives by themselves; the family of the house of Nathan by itself, and their wives by themselves; [13]the family of the house of Levi by itself, and their wives by themselves; the family of the Shime-ites by itself, and their wives by themselves; [14]and all the families that are left, each by itself, and their wives by themselves.

Amos 8:10
Jn 3:14,16;
*19:37*
Col 1:15,18
*Rev 1:7*

2 Kings 23:29
Mt 24:30

---

**12:10–14.** The End time will be marked by profound repentance and penance in Jerusalem induced by the spirit of God. The reason for this is the fact that a man, much loved by the people, has been put to death. The meaning of the passage is not very clear because it could be read in the sense that the one whom they pierced is God (v. 10); however, it goes on immediately to say that the person who has died is a man for whom the people will mourn. The mysterious death of this person has effects similar to the death of the Servant of the Lord in Isaiah 52:13–53:12, given that an effect of that death will be to atone for Judah's and Jerusalem's sin, and to bring about their complete rejection of idolatry (cf. 13:1–2). It is possible that there is an allusion here to the death of Zerub-babel, the last descendant of David to be mentioned in the Old Testament—a death that was to be followed by the coming of peace. Or perhaps the sacred writer is speaking about a king like Josiah who, though upright and devout, died violently at the hands of his enemies (cf. 2 Kings 23:29). In any event, that much lamented person prefigures Jesus Christ nailed on the cross on whom sinful man will look, as we read in John 19:37. "It is in discovering the greatness of God's love that our heart is shaken by the horror and weight of sin and begins to fear offending God by sin and being separated from him. The human heart is converted by looking upon him whom our sins have peirced (cf. Jn 19:37; Zech 12:10)" (*Catechism of the Catholic Church*, 1432).

---

erit: in die illa quaeram conterere omnes gentes, quae veniunt contra Ierusalem, [10]et effundam super domum David et super habitatores Ierusalem spiritum gratiae et precum; et aspicient ad me. Quem confixerunt, plangent quasi planctu super unigenitum et dolebunt super eum, ut doleri solet super primogenitum. [11]In die illa magnus erit planctus in Ierusalem sicut planctus Adadremmon in campo Mageddo; [12]et planget terra, singulae familiae seorsum: familia domus David seorsum / et mulieres eorum seorsum; / familia domus Nathan seorsum / et mulieres eorum seorsum; / [13]familia domus Levi seorsum / et mulieres eorum seorsum; / familia Semei seorsum / et mulieres eorum seorsum; / [14]omnes reliquae familiae, singulae familiae seorsum / et mulieres eorum seorsum.

**Cleansing of the land**

Jn 7:38; 19:34
Ezek 36:25;
47:1

# 13

¹"On that day there shall be a fountain opened for the house of David and the inhabitants of Jerusalem to cleanse them from sin and uncleanness.

²"And on that day, says the LORD of hosts, I will cut off the names of the idols from the land, so that they shall be remembered no more; and also I will remove from the land the prophets and

Mk 3:21

the unclean spirit. ³And if any one again appears as a prophet, his father and mother who bore him will say to him, 'You shall not live, for you speak lies in the name of the LORD'; and his father and mother who bore him shall pierce him through when he

2 Kings 1:18
Mic 3:6–7

prophesies. ⁴On that day every prophet will be ashamed of his

---

**13:1–6.** Other features of the End time will be the cleansing of the people by means of water from a special fountain set up by God, and the removal of everything to do with false gods. This cleansing from sin and uncleanness is purification of the heart; just as in Leviticus 14:8–9 leprosy was cured by means of water, now the image of the fountain is used for the cleansing that follows on from the New Covenant that God will make with his people (cf. Jer 31:34; Ezek 36:25). Idols will not even be a memory, and the false prophets who ministered to idols ("the unclean spirit") will disappear from the land, for their own parents will kill them if they catch them prophesying (v. 3). And those who set themselves up as prophets will be ashamed of their visions; they will cease to dress as prophets (cf. 2 Kings 1:8, which describes how Elijah dressed), they will

admit that they are not prophets, and they will disguise the scars they obtained in ritual trances. The idea that they should disappear suggests that, in the post-exilic times, there were still false prophets around (cf. Neh 6:12–14); they could have posed a danger to the people by falsely claiming that they spoke on God's account. That is why the prophet depicts the disappearance of the prophetical institution as a feature of the eschatological times.

In Christian tradition, the words of v. 6 have been applied in an allegorical sense to Christ, wounded by our sins. St Josemaría Escrivá, meditating on the passion of our Lord, quoted these words of the prophet and added: "Look at Jesus. Each laceration is a reproach; each lash of the whip, a reason for sorrow for your offences and mine" (*The Way of the Cross*, 1, 5).

---

[13] ¹In die illa erit fons patens domui David et habitantibus Ierusalem pro peccatis et immunditia. ²Et erit in die illa, dicit Dominus exercituum, disperdam nomina idolorum de terra, et non memorabuntur ultra; et pseudoprophetas et spiritum immundum auferam de terra. ³Et erit: cum prophetaverit quispiam ultra, dicent ei pater eius et mater eius, qui genuerunt eum: "Non vives, quia mendacium locutus es in nomine Domini"; et configent eum pater eius et mater eius, qui genuerunt eum, cum prophetaverit. ⁴Et erit: in die illa confundentur prophetae, unusquisque ex visione sua, cum prophetaverit; nec

vision when he prophesies; he will not put on a hairy mantle in
order to deceive, [5]but he will say, 'I am no prophet, I am a tiller of
the soil; for the land has been my possession[t] since my youth.'
[6]And if one asks him, 'What are these wounds on your back?' he
will say, 'The wounds I received in the house of my friends.'"

Mt 3:4; Mk 1:6
Amos 7:14

1 Kings 18:28

## The injured shepherd and the new people

[7]"Awake, O sword, against my shepherd,
against the man who stands next to me," says the LORD of hosts.
"Strike the shepherd, that the sheep may be scattered;
I will turn my hand against the little ones.
[8]In the whole land, says the LORD,
two thirds shall be cut off and perish,
and one third shall be left alive.

Ezek 34:1
*Mt 26:31*
*Mk 14:27*
Jn 10:30,31;
16:32

---

**13:7–9.** This poem seems to interrupt the prophecies about "that day" which began at 12:1 and appear again in the next chapter. It speaks of a wounded shepherd (v. 7), a remnant that is left in the land of Israel (v. 8), and a cleansing and a covenant (v. 9). The person described by the Lord as "my shepherd" (v. 7) contrasts with the "worthless shepherd" of 11:17, and is like the good shepherd of 11:4–16, the Messiah king, and the one who was pierced in 12:10. His violent death causes the people to be scattered. What we have here may be a further allusion to Zerubbabel and his death, but that is only speculation, because the text leaves the identity of this person a mystery. However, Jesus applied the shepherd analogy to himself when he foretold his death (cf. Mt 26:31; Mk 14:27) and the fact that his disciples

would forsake him (cf. Mt 26:56; Mk 14:49–52). "The good shepherd who gives his life for his sheep [...] is struck down by the will of the Father, and the Man who said, *the Father is in me and I am in the Father* (Jn 10:38; 14:11), is united with God. He is nailed to the cross, and says: *Father, into thy hands I commend my spirit!* (Lk 23:46). At that moment, the whole flock of those who believed in Christ was scattered [...]. When the little ones have been tested, the ones whom the Lord has guided and tended with his hand, and when the whole multitude of nations has answered the call to believe in him, then the whole company of believers will call Christ by his name: to him who said, *They are my people, they will respond, The Lord is my God"* (St Jerome, *Commentarii in Zachariam*, 13, 7–9).

operientur pallio saccino, ut mentiantur, [5]sed dicet: "Non sum propheta; homo operans terram ego sum, quoniam terra est possessio mea ab adulescentia mea". [6]Et dicetur ei: "Quid sunt plagae istae in medio manuum tuarum?". Et dicet: "His plagatus sum in domo eorum, qui diligebant me". [7]Framea, suscitare super pastorem meum / et super virum cohaerentem mihi, / dicit Dominus exercituum. / Percute pastorem, et dispergentur oves, / et convertam manum meam contra parvulos. / [8]Et erit in omni terra, /

**t.** Cn: Heb *for man has caused me to possess*

Ps 91:15
Is 1:25; 65:24
Jer 31:31
Hos 2:23
1 Pet 1:7
Rev 8:7

[9] And I will put this third into the fire,
   and refine them as one refines silver,
   and test them as gold is tested.
They will call on my name,
   and I will answer them.
I will say, 'They are my people';
   and they will say, 'The LORD is my God.'"

### The eschatological battle*

Joel 3:2;
4:2,12

**14** [1] Behold, a day of the LORD is coming, when the spoil taken from you will be divided in the midst of you. [2] For I will gather all the nations against Jerusalem to battle, and the city shall be taken and the houses plundered and the women ravished; half of the city shall go into exile, but the rest of the people shall not be cut off from the city. [3] Then the LORD will go forth and fight

Ex 11:29
Joel 3:14

against those nations as when he fights on a day of battle. [4] On that day his feet shall stand on the Mount of Olives which lies before Jerusalem on the east; and the Mount of Olives shall be split in

---

*14:1–21. This passage has to do with the last battle in the eschatological wars of which we heard earlier in 12:1–9; the climax has come, with the intervention of God in person (vv. 1–5), the establishment of a new order in time and in creation (vv. 6–11), the punishment of Israel's enemies (vv. 12–15) and all the nations coming in pilgrimage to the temple (vv. 16–21).

14:1–5. "That day" is now the "day of the Lord", that is, the day on which everything will be resolved by his intervention. He will gather the nations

around Jerusalem to attack her and do her harm (v. 2; cf. Joel 3:9–12) and, like a warrior, he will sally forth to do battle with them (v. 3). An awesome scene is painted in vv. 4–5: first, the Lord strikes terror into the attackers, towering over them like a giant and causing them to flee; then he takes possession of the city, his angels all around him. In the New Testament the fulfilment of these prophecies will be projected on to the second coming of our Lord, when he comes in glory with his angels (cf. Mt 25:31; 1 Thess 3:13; Jude 14; Rev 19:14).

---

dicit Dominus: / partes duae in ea dispergentur et deficient, / et tertia pars relinquetur in ea; / [9] et ducam tertiam partem per ignem / et purgabo eos, sicut purgatur argentum, / et probabo eos, sicut probatur aurum: / ipse vocabit nomen meum, / et ego exaudiam eum. / Dicam: Populus meus est ille; / et ipse dicet: "Dominus est Deus meus". **[14]** [1] Ecce venit dies Domino, et dividentur spolia tua in medio tui, [2] et congregabo omnes gentes ad Ierusalem in proelium, et capietur civitas, et vastabuntur domus, et mulieres violabuntur; et egredietur media pars civitatis in captivitatem, et reliquum populi non auferetur ex urbe. [3] Et egredietur Dominus et proeliabitur contra gentes illas, sicut proeliatus est in die certaminis. [4] Et stabunt pedes eius in die illa super montem Olivarum, qui est contra Ierusalem ad orientem; et scindetur mons Olivarum ex media parte sui ad orientem et ad occidentem, praerupto

two from east to west by a very wide valley; so that one half of the Mount shall withdraw northward, and the other half southward. [5]And the valley of my mountains shall be stopped up, for the valley of the mountains shall touch the side of it; and you shall flee as you fled from the earthquake in the days of Uzziah king of Judah. Then the LORD your[u] God will come, and all the holy ones with him.[v]

Amos 1:1
Mt 16:27
1 Thess 3:13

[6]On that day there shall be neither cold nor frost.[w] [7]And there shall be continuous day (it is known to the LORD), not day and not night, for at evening time there shall be light.

Is 30:26
Rev 21:23

[8]On that day living waters shall flow out from Jerusalem, half of them to the eastern sea and half of them to the western sea; it shall continue in summer as in winter.

Ezek 47:1
Jn 4:1,10
Rev 21:6
Rev 11:15; 19:6

[9]And the LORD will become king over all the earth; on that day the LORD will be one and his name one.

[10]The whole land shall be turned into a plain from Geba to Rimmon south of Jerusalem. But Jerusalem shall remain aloft

Is 40:4
Zech 12:6

---

**14:6–11.** With the coming of the Lord, creation will be transformed. There will be seasons no more, only an eternal spring; there will be no night or darkness, but endless day (v. 6). Jerusalem will be a great fount of waters, and from her the Lord will rule over all the earth; the region of Judah and Jerusalem will be transformed into a huge plain where the people will dwell in peace (vv. 10–11). All this imagery is designed to express hope in the fact that God will at last establish his kingdom in this world, and that creation itself will be wonderfully renewed in the land where the Lord dwells. The "living waters" of v. 8 symbolize fruitfulness and life (cf. Ezek 47:1–12). The Christian economy of salvation helps us to see that "the symbolism of water signifies the Holy Spirit's action in Baptism, since after the invocation of the Holy Spirit it becomes the efficacious sacramental sign of new birth [...]. Thus the Spirit is also personally the living water welling up from Christ crucified (cf. Jn 19:34; 1 Jn 5:8) as its source and welling up in us to eternal life (cf. Jn 4:10–14; 7:38; Ex 17:1–6; Is 55:1; Zech 14:8; 1 Cor 10:4; Rev 21:6; 22:17)" (*Catechism of the Catholic Church*, 694).

---

grandi valde, et separabitur medium montis ad aquilonem et medium eius ad meridiem. [5]Et fugietis ad vallem montium eorum, quoniam vallis montium pertinget usque ad Iasol; et fugietis, sicut fugistis a facie terraemotus in diebus Oziae regis Iudae, et veniet Dominus Deus meus, omnesque sancti cum eo. [6]Erit: in die illa non erit lux sed frigus et gelu; [7]et erit dies una, quae nota est Domino, non dies neque nox; et in tempore vesperi erit lux. [8]Et erit: in die illa exibunt aquae vivae de Ierusalem, medium earum ad mare orientale, et medium earum ad mare occidentale: in aestate et in hieme erunt. [9]Et erit Dominus rex super omnem terram: in die illa erit Dominus unus, et erit nomen eius unum. [10]Et revertetur omnis

---

**u.** Heb *my*   **v.** Gk Syr Vg Tg: Heb *you*   **w.** Compare Gk Syr Vg Tg: Heb uncertain

upon its site from the Gate of Benjamin to the place of the former gate, to the Corner Gate, and from the Tower of Hananel to the king's wine presses. [11]And it shall be inhabited, for there shall be no more curse;[x] Jerusalem shall dwell in security.

Jer 31:30
Rev 22:3

[12]And this shall be the plague with which the Lord will smite all the peoples that wage war against Jerusalem: their flesh shall rot while they are still on their feet, their eyes shall rot in their sockets, and their tongues shall rot in their mouths. [13]And on that day a great panic from the Lord shall fall on them, so that each will lay hold on the hand of his fellow, and the hand of the one will be raised against the hand of the other; [14]even Judah will fight against Jerusalem. And the wealth of all the nations round about shall be collected, gold, silver, and garments in great abundance. [15]And a plague like this plague shall fall on the horses, the mules, the camels, the asses, and whatever beasts may be in those camps.

Is 66:24

Ezek 38:21

[16]Then every one that survives of all the nations that have come against Jerusalem shall go up year after year to worship the King,

Ex 23:14
Lev 23:34
Is 66:23

---

**14:12–15.** Contrasting with the favour enjoyed by Jerusalem and Judah, those who made war on them must now be punished. Their chastisement is described in terms of a plague (cf. Ezek 38:22; 39:17–20) which, in addition to causing death, creates such panic that they fight among themselves and are stripped of all their wealth, which will find its way to Jerusalem (v. 14). It may be that Jerusalem and Judah, too, will fight among themselves or else that both of them will join forces in the last battle. Another plague will strike down animals (v. 15). This description of punishment serves to underscore the dominion that God has over mankind and the animal world: there is none who can escape, even if he or she be far from Jerusalem.

**14:16–21.** The Kingdom of God in this world must be acknowledged by the whole world. In the language of prophecy this means that all the nations, especially Egypt, Israel's traditional

---

terra in desertum, a Gabaa usque ad Remmon ad austrum Ierusalem, quae exaltabitur et habitabitur in loco suo, a porta Beniamin usque ad locum portae Prioris, et usque ad portam Angulorum, et a turre Hananeel usque ad Torcularia regis. [11]Et habitabunt in ea, et anathema non erit amplius; sed habitabitur Ierusalem secura. [12]Et haec erit plaga, qua percutiet Dominus omnes gentes, quae pugnaverunt adversus Ierusalem: tabescet caro uniuscuiusque stantis super pedes suos, et oculi eius contabescent in foraminibus suis, et lingua eius contabescet in ore suo. [13]In die illa erit tumultus Domini magnus in eis, et apprehendet vir manum proximi sui, et elevabitur manus eius super manum proximi sui. [14]Sed et Iudas pugnabit in Ierusalem, et congregabuntur divitiae omnium gentium in circuitu, aurum et argentum et vestes multae nimis. [15]Et sic erit ruina equi, muli, cameli et asini et omnium iumentorum, quae fuerint in castris illis, sicut ruina haec. [16]Et omnes, qui reliqui fuerint de universis gentibus, quae venerunt contra Ierusalem, ascendent ab anno in annum, ut adorent Regem, Dominum exercituum, et

**x.** Or *ban of utter destruction*

the LORD of hosts, and to keep the feast of booths. [17]And if any of the families of the earth do not go up to Jerusalem to worship the King, the LORD of hosts, there will be no rain upon them. [18]And if the family of Egypt do not go up and present themselves, then upon them shall[y] come the plague with which the LORD afflicts the nations that do not go up to keep the feast of booths. [19]This shall be the punishment to Egypt and the punishment to all the nations that do not go up to keep the feast of booths.

[20]And on that day there shall be inscribed on the bells of the horses, "Holy to the LORD." And the pots in the house of the LORD shall be as the bowls before the altar; [21]and every pot in Jerusalem and Judah shall be sacred to the LORD of hosts, so that all who sacrifice may come and take of them and boil the flesh of the sacrifice in them. And there shall no longer be a trader in the house of the LORD of hosts on that day.

Ex 28:36
2 Chron 35:13

Jn 2:16
Mt 21:12

---

enemy, must visit Jerusalem on pilgrimage for the feast of booths, to be assured of rain and to be cured of the plague. In the holy land, everything will be consecrated to the Lord or set aside for use in the liturgy; worship will be pure, with no trace of commerce attaching to it. Thus, God, who "founded the earth and formed the spirit of man" (12:1), establishes his kingdom on earth and draws to himself and to his temple the hearts of all men.

In the New Testament the hope instilled by these prophecies endures; it is grounded on our Lord Jesus Christ and is seen in sharper focus. He brought the Kingdom of God into this world (cf. Mt 4:17:10:7; Lk 10:9; etc.); but it will be at his second coming that the Kingdom will be definitively established; all creation will be transformed (cf. Rom 8:16–30), the powers of evil will be overcome and forever defeated (Rev. 20:10), and he will live for ever in the midst of men (Rev 21:1–5). The image of a new and glorious Jerusalem coming down from heaven as described in Revelation 21–22 rounds off the picture provided by the book of Zechariah.

---

celebrent festivitatem Tabernaculorum. [17]Et erit: qui non ascenderit de familiis terrae ad Ierusalem, ut adoret Regem, Dominum exercituum, non erit super eos imber. [18]Quod et si familia Aegypti non ascenderit et non venerit, super eos erit plaga, qua percutit Dominus gentes, quae non ascenderint ad celebrandam festivitatem Tabernaculorum. [19]Haec erit poena Aegypti, et haec poena omnium gentium, quae non ascenderint ad celebrandam festivitatem Tabernaculorum. [20]In die illa erit super tintinnabula equorum; "Sanctum Domino"; et erunt lebetes in domo Domini quasi phialae coram altari. [21]Et erit omnis lebes in Ierusalem et in Iuda sanctificatus Domino exercituum; et venient omnes immolantes et sument ex eis et coquent in eis, et non erit mercator ultra in domo Domini exercituum in die illo».

**y.** Gk Syr: Heb *shall not*

# MALACHI

# Introduction

The book of Malachi is the last of the books of the minor prophets, and it comes chronologically later than Haggai and Zechariah. We know little about the author; there is no prophet of Israel named Malachi anywhere else in the Bible. Also, the Hebrew expression *Mal'aki* (Mal 1:1 and note **a**) is not a proper name; it simply means "my messenger" (3:1), and most scholars think that the book's title comes from 3:1. Some Jewish commentators, and St Jerome,[1] attributed the book to Ezra. However, the vocabulary of the book and the way certain themes are dealt with are more in line with the Deuteronomic tradition than with the Priestly tradition (to which Ezra belonged). The book is probably a collection of oracles by an anonymous prophet of the mid-fifth century BC, in which he exhorts the returned exiles to have more hope in God and to take their religious duties more seriously.

The Jewish tradition regards Malachi as the last of the prophets, the seal, as it were, of the book of the prophets—as, indeed, the Christian tradition does.

## 1. STRUCTURE AND CONTENT

The book consists of six parts of unequal length, plus an epilogue. Each of the parts has a similar construction and more or less conforms to the literary genre known as the "dispute" (*rîb*): the Lord or his prophet make a statement (normally it includes or alludes to a quotation or precept taken from Deuteronomy), and then takes the people or priests to task for some failure in regard to it; this is disputed by priests or people, usually in the form of a question or questions; finally the original statement is developed in the light of the objection raised.

The suggested structure then is:

1. THE LORD'S LOVE FOR ISRAEL (1:1–5). God loves Israel. This is to be seen in his choice of Israel and in the fact that he protects her—which is not the case with Edom.

2. POLLUTED OFFERINGS AND THE FAULTS OF PRIESTS (1:6–2:9). The prophet reproaches them for their faults in performing ritual sacrifices (1:6–14) and in the way they teach the people (2:1–9). In this context, he proclaims a new, perfect, universal sacrifice (1:11).

1. *Commentarii in Malachiam*, prologue.

3. MIXED MARRIAGE AND DIVORCE (2:10–16). The prophet condemns both these practices, which he sees as a form of infidelity to the Covenant and out of keeping with God's plan as regards how things should be.

4. THE DAY OF THE LORD (2:17–3:5). He announces the coming of the Lord to his temple. He will be preceded by a messenger, for the day of the Lord's coming will be a day of purification (in the area of religious rites) and a day when wrongs are righted.

5. TEMPLE TITHES (3:6–12). People are not obeying the law concerning tithes and first fruits intended for the upkeep of the temple and its Levites (the reason being, apparently, that harvests had not been good). The prophet tells them that the reason for bad harvests is their meanness: if they were generous in giving tithes, they would soon see how generous the Lord is to them.

6. THE RIGHTEOUS ON THE DAY OF THE LORD (3:13–4:3). Some people are puzzled and complain to the Lord about the apparent success of those who do not fear God; the prophet tells them that the Lord is not at all detached from what people do, and he announces a day of judgment which will mean joy for the righteous and downfall for evildoers.

EPILOGUE (4:4–6). These three verses summarize the prophet's teaching: people must be faithful to the Law of Moses (4:4); they must be ever on the look-out for the day of the Lord's revelation, which will be preceded by the appearance of Elijah (4:5); God will use Elijah to re-establish harmony between parents and children (4:6).

The book follows a clear line of argument. It begins by asserting God's love for Israel; this is the subtext of the whole book. In view of that love, the prophet criticizes faults in the area of religious worship, the touchstone of Israelite piety. In reply to objections raised, he builds up the people's hope by announcing the day of the Lord—a fearsome day, yet one of consolation for those who fear God.

Editions of the Hebrew text, and the New Vulgate, divide the book into three, not four, chapters; but the Vulgate and some modern editions make the last six verses a fourth chapter, as does the RSV.

## 2. COMPOSITION AND HISTORICAL BACKGROUND

Although, as we have said, we have no other information about a prophet with the name of Malachi, the contents of the book make it possible to date it fairly confidently to the period after the return from the Babylonian exile. The temple has been rebuilt (1:8; 3:1), but people's initial enthusiasm and zeal have waned. There is apathy in matters to do with religious worship (1:8–14) and obedience to the precepts of the Covenant (2:8; 3:14; etc.), especially in regard to tithes (3:6–10) and marital fidelity (2:14). For their part, the people complain to the Lord: the harvests have not been as good as they would have liked (3:11); God has not delivered on his promises, and his love for his people is open to question (1:2). The reform instituted by Ezra and Nehemiah sought to resolve some of the more serious problems (cf. Ezra 9–10; Neh 10:31–39; 13:23–29). If the rebuilding of the temple ended in 515 BC and Ezra's religious reform took place around 398, Malachi's oracles must have been a little before that reform, perhaps in the last quarter of the fourth century BC.

This is the background to the prophet's appeal to his fellow-citizens for faithfulness to the Covenant. His oracles denounce meanness in the practice of the Law of God. The author is a polemicist and he uses the literary form of the dispute. He is keenly aware of who Israel is and who the God of Israel is. The people of Israel are, above all, beloved of the Lord, and the Lord rules over the affairs of men. If the Israelites stay true to the Covenant, the future will see God manifesting himself to the nations (1:5, 14), and Israel herself will be congratulated by them (3:12). There is a message of hope, here, in the glorious coming of the Lord, the day when he will take action (3:2, 17–18; 4:1).

## 3. MESSAGE

The book deals with specific problems—religious worship, repudiation of wives, tithes, the precepts of the Law—in general terms. This broad outlook draws together the prophet's message with regard to the various problems.

The book's fundamental assumption is the enduring validity of the Covenant that God made with the patriarchs. God loves his people, he is committed to them (1:2–5), and when he determines to do something he does not go back on his word—unlike his people (3:6). They are not in fact responding to him: they do not keep his precepts (3:7), temple sacrifices are not being carried out properly (1:8; 3:10), people complain unjustly against God (2:17; 3:14) etc. The prophet then announces that if the Israelites keep the Covenant—the covenant with Levi (2:4), the covenant with the fathers (2:10), the covenant of marriage (2:14)—they will be filled with blessings (3:10) and will amaze the world (1:5; 3:12).

Looked at from the point of view of the Covenant, the book also has things to say about rewards and punishments. Evildoers (people who do not obey the laws of the Covenant even when things are going well for them) seem to enjoy success; but the prophet declares that on the day when the Lord is revealed everything will be brought out into the open: the righteous will receive justice and consolation (2:5; 3:17; 4:2), and the impious will be like dust and ashes (4:1, 3). But, most importantly of all, reward and punishment are not based on belonging to the people of Israel: what matters is good works and fear of the Lord (3:16).

The prophet's teaching about the messianic times is closely linked to his vision of the day of the Lord. He announces the arrival of the Lord at his temple preceded by a messenger (3:1), the prophet Elijah (3:23). He also announces a new act of worship, a perfect and universal sacrifice (1:11) that far exceeds people's present notion of sacrifice. This oracle is scarcely more than a hint, but in the Synoptic Gospels the messenger announced by Malachi is identified as John the Baptist (11:14).

## 4. THE BOOK OF MALACHI IN THE LIGHT OF THE NEW TESTAMENT

Although it is a very short book, Malachi is quoted a number of times in the New Testament. Sometimes the quotation is not very significant, as in Romans 9:13, where St Paul uses a phrase from 1:2–3 ("I have loved Jacob but I have hated Esau") to make the point that God's choice of people precedes any merit on their part. Most of the New Testament quotations from Malachi are in connexion with the "messenger" (3:1), that is, Elijah (4:5). In Jesus' time (cf. the note on 4:4–6), it was commonly believed that Elijah would appear as a mysterious messenger before the coming of the Lord; this idea is expressed in all four Gospels. Jesus teaches his disciples that the promises in Malachi found fulfilment in him and, therefore, that the prophet Elijah who was supposed to precede him was none other than John the Baptist. This idea is found in the Synoptic Gospels, without significant variation. In St Matthew, it is quite clear: Jesus says, regarding the Baptist, "If you are willing to accept it, he is Elijah who is to come" (Mt 11:14; cf. 17:10–11). In St Mark it is less clear (Mk 9:11–12), although the evangelist does explicitly quote Malachi 3:1 to explain the activity of John the Baptist (Mk 1:2). St Luke clearly identifies John the Baptist with the messenger who is supposed to come in advance of the Lord (Lk 7:24–30; cf. Mal 3:1), although he does not report Jesus' words identifying Elijah with John the Baptist. However, in the announcement to Zechariah, the angel says regarding John that "he will go before him in the spirit and power of Elijah, to turn the hearts of the fathers to the children and the disobedient to the wisdom of the just, to make ready for the Lord a people prepared" (Lk 1:17; cf. Mal 4:5–6).

The early Patristic tradition gave much importance to the announcement in Malachi 1:11 of a new sacrifice, perfect and universal, which they read as a prophecy that finds fulfilment in the Eucharist.

# Title

**1** [1]The oracle of the word of the LORD to Israel by Malachi.[a]

## 1. FIRST EXCHANGE: THE LORD'S LOVE FOR ISRAEL

[2]"I have loved you," says the LORD. But you say, "How hast thou loved us?" "Is not Esau Jacob's brother?" says the LORD. "Yet I have loved Jacob [3]but I have hated Esau; I have laid waste his hill

Deut 4:37; 7:6,7
Is 54:8; Jer 31:3
Ezek 16; Hos
11:1; Gen 25:23
Jer 49:10

---

**1:1.** This verse acts as a title to the work, similar to the titles in the books of Haggai and Zechariah. Unlike what happens in other prophetical books, no surname or family name is given. The word *mal'aki* is not a personal name. The oracle is addressed to Israel instead of to Judah-Israel, which is the name that the book of Deuteronomy usually uses to refer to the chosen people (Deut 1:1, 38; 2:12; etc.). Like the other books of the Old Testament, Malachi has been commented on by the Fathers with reference to Christ. Drawing together the various themes in this prophecy, St Cyril of Alexandria comments: "In the end, he speaks of the coming of our Saviour (cf. 3:1–2): a pure sacrifice will be offered to God (cf. 1:11), which will wipe away the guilt of all and cancel all debts; sin will be cast out, and man made new for a new life" (*Commentarius in Malachiam*, 1, 1, 2–5).

**1:2–5.** God's love for Israel is characteristic of all of Holy Scripture, particularly the book of Deuteronomy (Deut 4:37; 7:7–15; etc.). The opening assertion in

v. 2 is immediately answered by the people: "How hast thou loved us?" Malachi bases what he has to say mainly on God's assertion about his special choice, which had nothing to do with any merit on Jacob's (Israel's) part: "I have loved Jacob but I have hated Esau" (vv. 2–3). He then goes on to argue the point. A clear proof of God's love can be found in events of the recent past, evoked in vv. 3–4. The Edomites, descendants of Esau (Gen 36:1), saw their country devastated by Arab incursions. The rivalry between Edomites and Israelites went a long way back in history. The book of Obadiah, for example, mentions how the Edomites rejoiced over the exile to Babylon. Therefore, from an Israelite point of view, the invasion of the land of Edom was a blessing that augured well for the restoration of Israel. Still, there is much more to come. However much the Edomites strive to re-establish themselves, the Lord is stronger than they are, and (what matters most) he never changes, his love for Israel endures (cf. 3:6). The people will see this, and they will be amazed (v. 5).

---

[1] [1]Oraculum. Verbum Domini ad Israel in manu Malachiae. [2]«Dilexi vos, dicit Dominus, et dixistis: "In quo dilexisti nos?". Nonne frater erat Esau Iacob?, dicit Dominus; et dilexi Iacob, [3]Esau autem odio

**a.** Or *my messenger*

Ezek 25,13;
35,4
Rom 9:13 country and left his heritage to jackals of the desert." ⁴If Edom says, "We are shattered but we will rebuild the ruins," the LORD of hosts says, "They may build, but I will tear down, till they are called the wicked country, the people with whom the LORD is angry for ever." ⁵Your own eyes shall see this, and you shall say, "Great is the LORD, beyond the border of Israel!"

## 2. SECOND EXCHANGE: POLLUTED OFFERINGS AND
## OTHER FAULTS OF PRIESTS

Ex 20:12
Deut 1:31; 32:6
Is 29:3; Mt 6:9 ⁶"A son honours his father, and a servant his master. If then I am a father, where is my honour? And if I am a master, where is my

---

These five verses, therefore, contain the essence of the book. In a context of general apathy among the people, the prophet reminds them that God's love calls for an appropriate response. St Paul (cf. Rom 9:13) will use vv. 2–3 to make the point that God's election precedes any merit on the part of those whom he chooses. St Cyril of Alexandria has this to say about the passage: "[God] chose Jacob, from whom the Jewish people descends, and rejected Esau; but he did not choose on a whim. God is just: he cannot pass an unjust sentence against any man or people. Being God, he could see the lives and beliefs of both peoples in the future, and he chose the better part, the people who would remain closer to him and be more worthy of his love [...]. Paul tells us that we too, justified by our faith, were made holy in the same way" (*Commentarius in Malachiam*, 4).

**1:6–2:9.** The prophet's thesis is based on the fact that the Lord is a father to Israel, yet they do not respect the Lord as a son should respect his father (1:6; cf. Deut 5:16). The priests wonder where they are at fault (1:6–7), and Malachi replies by telling them that they profane the name of the Lord when they transgress ritual precepts (cf. Lev 22:17–25) by offering blemished animals in sacrifice (1:8–10, 13–14). This meanness in offerings even goes against common sense (cf. 1:8); the prophet announces a new, catholic sacrifice that will indeed be pleasing to God (1:11).

Malachi is a prophet of the restoration and one who puts firm emphasis on religious ritual as an expression of fidelity to the Covenant, so it is surprising to hear him speak of a universal sacrifice and one that is pure even though it is offered outside the temple

---

habui et posui montes eius in solitudinem et hereditatem eius thoibus deserti. ⁴Quod si dixerit Edom: "Destructi sumus, sed revertentes aedificabimus, quae destructa sunt", haec dicit Dominus exercituum: Isti aedificabunt, et ego destruam; et vocabuntur 'Termini impietatis' et 'Populus, cui iratus est Dominus usque in aeternum'. ⁵Et oculi vestri videbunt, et vos dicetis: "Magnificatus est Dominus ultra terminos Israel". ⁶Filius honorat patrem, et servus dominum suum. Si ergo pater ego sum, ubi est honor

fear? says the LORD of hosts to you, O priests, who despise my
name. You say, 'How have we despised thy name?' [7]By offering  1 Cor 10:21

---

of Jerusalem. It is difficult to believe
that he could be talking of ritual worship being offered in the Diaspora, and
of course any sort of syncretism or
intermingling of religions would be out
of the question. These expressions, outlining various contrasts, are probably
meant to show the merely relative value
that even the sacrifice in Jerusalem has
in the eyes of the Lord; the oracles
envisage an ideal situation. Therefore,
the early Christian writers read this
announcement as a prophecy of the
sacrifice of the Eucharist: "Gathered
together every Sunday, break bread and
give thanks after you have confessed
your sins, so that your sacrifice will be
pure. No man who is in dispute with his
neighbour should join in the gathering
until they are reconciled to one another,
so that the sacrifice will not be profaned. For this is the sacrifice of which
the Lord said: *From the rising of the
sun to its setting my name is great
among the nations, and in every place
incense is offered to my name, and a
pure offering; for my name is great
among the nations, says the Lord of
hosts*" (*Didaché*, 14, 1–3). This interpretation, which runs through virtually
all the Fathers, found its way into the
teaching of the Magisterium: "This is
the pure offering, which cannot be
defiled no matter how unworthy and
evil those who profane it are; for thus
God told us through the prophet
Malachi, when he said that a pure
offering be made to his Name, the

Name that is great among the nations
(cf. Mal 1:11)" (Council of Trent,
*Doctrine on the sacrifice of the Mass*,
chap 1).

The second part of the oracle (2:1–9)
is an exhortation to priests. The prophet
reproaches them for not honouring the
Lord (2:1; cf. 1:6) and for causing
many to stumble "by your instruction"
(2:8), or "by the Law" (which is another
possible translation), and moreover
they have shown partiality (2:9): it all
means that they are breaking the
covenant that the Lord made with Levi
(2:4–5; cf. Deut 18:1–8; 33:8–11). For
their ministry to be effective (2:2–3),
they should practise the virtues that
Levi had—fear of God, humility, sincerity in speech (2:5–6). This last
aspect is given special emphasis: a
priest does not speak on his own behalf;
he is the Lord's messenger (*mal'ak*),
and his words should have the wisdom
of the Law (2:7). The Second Vatican
Council says something that recalls this
passage, on the subject of the priest's
mission to preach: "The people of God
are joined together primarily by the
word of the living God. And rightfully
they expect this from their priests.
Since no one can be saved who does
not first believe, priests, as co-workers
with their bishops, have the primary
duty of proclaiming the Gospel of God
to all. In this way they fulfill the
command of the Lord … and [they]
establish and build up the people of
God" (*Presbyterorum ordinis*, 4).

meus? Et si Dominus ego sum, ubi est timor meus?, dicit Dominus exercituum ad vos, o sacerdotes,
qui despicitis nomen meum et dicitis: "In quo despeximus nomen tuum?". [7]Offertis super altare meum

polluted food upon my altar. And you say, 'How have we polluted it?' [b]By thinking that the LORD's table may be despised. [8]When you offer blind animals in sacrifice, is that no evil? And when you offer those that are lame or sick, is that no evil? Present that to your governor; will he be pleased with you or show you favour? says the LORD of hosts. [9]And now entreat the favour of God, that he may be gracious to us. With such a gift from your hand, will he show favour to any of you? says the LORD of hosts. [10]Oh, that there were one among you who would shut the doors, that you might not kindle fire upon my altar in vain! I have no pleasure in you, says the LORD of hosts, and I will not accept an offering from your hand.

### Worship of the Lord right across the world

[11]For from the rising of the sun to its setting my name is great among the nations, and in every place incense is offered to my name, and a pure offering; for my name is great among the nations, says the LORD of hosts. [12]But you profane it when you say that the LORD's table is polluted, and the food for it[c] may be despised. [13]'What a weariness this is,' you say, and you sniff at me,[d] says the LORD of hosts. You bring what has been taken by violence or is lame or sick, and this you bring as your offering! Shall I accept that from your hand? says the LORD. [14]Cursed be the cheat who has a male in his flock, and vows it, and yet sacrifices to the Lord what is blemished; for I am a great King, says the LORD of hosts, and my name is feared among the nations.

### Shortcomings of priests

2 [1]"And now, O priests, this command is for you. [2]If you will not listen, if you will not lay it to heart to give glory to my name,

*Margin references:*
Lev 22:18–25
Amos 5:21
Jer 6:20
Ps 113:3
Is 45:6; 56:7; 60:3–5
Zeph 3:9
Jn 4:21
Lev 22:18–25
Ps 102:16
Deut 28:15,20

---

panem pollutum et dicitis: "In quo polluimus te?". In eo quod dicitis: "Mensa Domini contemptibilis est". [8]Si offeratis caecum ad immolandum, nonne malum est? Et si offeratis claudum et languidum, nonne malum est? Offer illud duci tuo, si placuerit ei, aut si susceperit faciem tuam!, dicit Dominus exercituum. [9]Sed nunc deprecamini vultum Dei, ut misereatur vestri! De manu enim vestra factum est hoc. Num suscipiet facies vestras?, dicit Dominus exercituum. [10]Quis est in vobis, qui claudat ostia, ne incendatis altare meum gratuito? Non est mihi voluntas in vobis, dicit Dominus exercituum; et munus non suscipiam de manu vestra. [11]Ab ortu enim solis usque ad occasum magnum est nomen meum in gentibus, et in omni loco sacrificatur et offertur nomini meo oblatio munda, quia magnum nomen meum in gentibus, dicit Dominus exercituum. [12]Vos autem polluistis illud in eo quod dicitis: "Mensa Domini contaminata est, et contemptibilis esca eius". [13]Et dicitis: "Quantus labor!", et despicitis illam, dicit Dominus exercituum. Et infertis de rapinis claudum et languidum et infertis sicut munus. Numquid suscipiam illud de manu vestra?, dicit Dominus. [14]Maledictus dolosus, qui habet in grege suo masculum et votum faciens immolat debile Domino. Quia Rex magnus ego, dicit Dominus exercituum, et nomen meum horribile in gentibus.    [2] [1]Et nunc ad vos mandatum hoc, o sacerdotes. [2]Si nolueritis audi re et si nolueritis ponere super cor, ut detis gloriam nomini meo, ait Dominus exercituum, mittam

**b.** Gk: Heb *thee*    **c.** Heb *its fruit, its food*    **d.** Another reading is *it*

says the LORD of hosts, then I will send the curse upon you and I will curse your blessings; indeed I have already cursed them, because you do not lay it to heart. [3]Behold, I will rebuke your offspring, and spread dung upon your faces, the dung of your offerings, and I will put you out of my presence.[e] [4]So shall you know that I have sent this command to you, that my covenant with Levi may hold, says the LORD of hosts. [5]My covenant with him was a covenant of life and peace, and I gave them to him, that he might fear; and he feared me, he stood in awe of my name. [6]True instruction[f] was in his mouth, and no wrong was found on his lips. He walked with me in peace and uprightness, and he turned many from iniquity. [7]For the lips of a priest should guard knowledge, and men should seek instruction[f] from his mouth, for he is the messenger of the LORD of hosts. [8]But you have turned aside from the way; you have caused many to stumble by your instruction; you have corrupted the covenant of Levi, says the LORD of hosts, [9]and so I make you despised and abased before all the people, inasmuch as you have not kept my ways but have shown partiality in your instruction."[f]

Num 25:12
Deut 18:1–8;
33:8–11

Deut 33:9–10

Lev 10:11
Deut 21:5
Jer 18:18

Mt 23:13:15

## 3. THIRD EXCHANGE: MIXED MARRIAGE
## AND DIVORCE

[10]Have we not all one father? Has not one God created us? Why then are we faithless to one another, profaning the covenant of our

Mt 23:9; Jn 8:41
Eph 4:6
1 Cor 8:6

---

**2:10–16.** The third "dispute" follows on from the previous one (1:6–2:9). There the prophet criticized priests for profaning the Lord and his name (1:7, 12) and for not keeping the covenant of Levi (2:4–5, 8); now he says that all Judah has pro-

faned the sanctuary of the Lord and the covenant made with the patriarchs (vv. 10–12). (In v. 12, where it says "any to witness or answer", other translations read "the son and the grandson" or "he who does it and he who consents to it".)

---

in vos maledictionem et maledicam benedictionibus vestris; et maledicam illis, quoniam non posuistis super cor. [3]Ecce ego abscindam vobis brachium / et dispergam stercus super vultum vestrum, / stercus sollemnitatum vestrarum, / et assumet vos secum; / [4]et scietis quia misi ad vos mandatum istud, / ut esset pactum meum cum Levi, / dicit Dominus exercituum. / [5]Pactum meum fuit cum eo vitae et pacis, / et dedi haec ei simul cum timore, et timuit me / et a facie nominis mei pavebat. / [6]Lex veritatis fuit in ore eius, / et iniquitas non est inventa in labiis eius; / in pace et in aequitate ambulavit mecum / et multos avertit ab iniquitate. / [7]Labia enim sacerdotis custodiunt scientiam, / et legem requirunt ex ore eius, / quia angelus Domini exercituum est. / [8]Vos autem recessistis de via / et scandalizastis plurimos in lege; / irritum fecistis pactum Levi, / dicit Dominus exercituum; / [9]propter quod et ego dedi vos / contemptibiles et humiles omnibus populis, / sicut non servastis vias meas / et accepistis personam in lege. [10]Numquid non pater unus omnium nostrum? Numquid non Deus unus creavit nos? Quare ergo

**e.** Cn Compare Gk Syr: Heb *and he shall bear you to it* **f.** Or *law*

fathers? [11]Judah has been faithless, and abomination has been committed in Israel and in Jerusalem; for Judah has profaned the sanctuary of the LORD, which he loves, and has married the daughter of a foreign god. [12]May the LORD cut off from the tents of Jacob, for the man who does this, any to witness[g] or answer, or to bring an offering to the LORD of hosts!

[13]And this again you do. You cover the LORD's altar with tears, with weeping and groaning because he no longer regards the

---

The two faults being condemned here have to do with marriage in the context of the Convenant. The prophet is against marriage between a Jew and a foreigner (a "daughter of a foreign God": v. 11), probably because of the risk of idolatry that the marriage might give rise to (cf. Deut 7:3). He is similarly outspoken about those who repudiate their wives (v. 16). Although the Law of Moses allowed that to be done in certain circumstances (cf. Deut 24:1ff), the prophet vigorously defends the marriage covenant: just as God is witness to the commitment made by the spouses to each other when they marry (v. 14), he cannot accept offerings made to him by a man who, at the same time, is being unfaithful to his marriage covenant; and the prophet reminds people that the marital union and its fruitfulness (v. 15) derive from God himself.

The Fathers of the Church do not fail to note the strength of Malachi's argument here: "It seems to me that the verse, *Has not the one God made and sustained for us the spirit of life?* (v. 15), means that the man became one, body and soul, with the woman who was given to him according to the Law. As they became one body, so too they became one soul; for love drew them together and bound them by the unity of the divine Law. It is as if the woman became part of the man's spirit, part of his soul, when they became one body in love" (St Cyril of Alexandria, *Commentarius in Malachiam,* 28).

On the question of repudiation and divorce, our Lord uses arguments along more of less the same lines (cf. Mt 19: 1–12). However, it must be said that Malachi's criticism of mixed marriages at times approaches the exclusivity found in some passages of Nehemiah (Neh 13: 23–27) and away from the more sensitive treatment of the subject found in the book of Ruth, which tells the story of a Gentile woman who is converted to the Lord and becomes a member of the chosen people.

---

dolum facit unusquisque nostrum cum fratre suo, violans pactum patrum nostrorum? [11]Dolum fecit Iuda, et abominatio facta est in Israel et in Ierusalem, quia contaminavit Iuda sanctuarium Domini, quod diligit, et accepit uxorem filiam dei alieni. [12]Disperdet Dominus virum, qui fecerit hoc, filium et nepotem, de tabernaculis Iacob et de offerentibus munus Domino exercituum. [13]Et hoc rursum facitis: operitis lacrimis altare Domini, fletu et mugitu, ita ut non respiciam ultra ad sacrificium nec accipiam

**g.** Cn Compare Gk: Heb *arouse*

offering or accepts it with favour at your hand. [14]You ask, "Why does he not?" Because the LORD was witness to the covenant between you and the wife of your youth, to whom you have been faithless, though she is your companion and your wife by covenant. [15]Has not the one God made[h] and sustained for us the spirit of life?[i] And what does he desire? Godly offspring. So take heed to yourselves, and let none be faithless to the wife of his youth. [16] "For I hate[j] divorce, says the LORD the God of Israel, and covering one's garment with violence, says the LORD of hosts. So take heed to yourselves and do not be faithless."

Gen 2:24
Mt 5:31–32
Eph 5:25–32

## 4. FOURTH EXCHANGE: THE DAY OF THE LORD

[17]You have wearied the LORD with your words. Yet you say, "How have we wearied him?" By saying, "Every one who does evil is

Job 21:7–8
Is 43:24
2 Pet 3:4

---

**2:17–3:5.** As at the start of the book, the question raised here is a fairly general one: What is the point of keeping the Law if those who do evil are the ones who have success in life? The question focuses on rewards in this life only (cf. 2:17), but the prophet's reply extends beyond that: he announces a day of judgment when priests and ritual will be purified (3:3–4) and the oppressed will receive justice (3:5); on the day of the Lord, God will set everything right.

However, the force of the oracle lies not so much in the fact of divine judgment as in the mysterious way in which that day is announced (3:1–2). We are told that the Lord of hosts him-

self will come to his temple, and his coming will strike fear into the hearts of men. The passage, in fact, seems to be speaking about three different personages—the messenger who will precede the coming of the Lord and who later on, in the epilogue, is identified as the prophet Elijah (cf. 4:5); the Lord himself; and the angel (literally the "messenger") of the Covenant (3:1). In mentioning the first (the messenger who prepares the way: 3:1) the prophet may have in mind the sort of protocol used by kings who had a herald announce their arrival. This personage's role is similar to that described in Isaiah 40:3ff. However, a little further on there is the "messenger of the covenant". It is

---

placabile quid de manu vestra; [14]et dicitis: "Quam ob causam?". Quia Dominus testificatus est inter te et uxorem adulescentiae tuae, cui tu factus es infidelis; et haec particeps tua et uxor foederis tui. [15]Nonne unitatem fecit carnis et spiritus? Et quid unitas quaerit nisi semen a Deo? Custodite ergo spiritum vestrum; et uxori adulescentiae tuae noli esse infidelis. [16]Si quis odio dimittit, dicit Dominus, Deus Israel, operit iniquitas vestimentum eius, dicit Dominus exercituum. Custodite spiritum vestrum et nolite esse infideles. [17]Laborare facitis Dominum in sermonibus vestris et dicitis: "In quo eum facimus laborare?". In eo quod dicitis: "Omnis, qui facit malum, bonus est in conspectu Domini, et

**h.** Or *has he not made one?* **i.** Cn: Heb *and a remnant of spirit was his* **j.** Cn: Heb *he hates*

good in the sight of the LORD, and he delights in them." Or by asking, "Where is the God of justice?"

Is 40:3; 63:9
Mal 4:5; Hag 2:7
*Mt 11:10; Mk 1:2*
Lk 1:17,76; 7:27
Jn 1:6,26; Rev 22:16
Zeph 1:14; Joel 2:11
Rev 6:17

3 ¹"Behold, I send my messenger to prepare the way before me, and the Lord whom you seek will suddenly come to his temple; the messenger of the covenant in whom you delight, behold, he is coming, says the LORD of hosts. ²But who can endure the day of his coming, and who can stand when he appears?

---

not clear what this means; it could be the Lord himself; a further messenger, whose role is similar to that of Moses, that is, a mediator of the Covenant; or, finally, the messenger mentioned earlier, the herald, who is now being given a new role. No clear interpretation can be established beyond doubt.

The New Testament will resolve this question of interpretation. The Synoptic Gospels (cf. Mk 1:2) and Jesus himself (Mt 11:7–15; cf. Lk 7:24–30) identify the first messenger, the one who prepares the way, with Elijah, and sees his fulfilment in the person of John the Baptist. This makes Jesus the Lord who comes to his temple. The Church reads it that way when the liturgy of the feast of the Presentation of Jesus in the Temple (cf. Lk 2:22–40) includes Malachi 3:1–4 as a first reading. But as can be seen from many passages of the New Testament (for example, the episode of the Transfiguration: Mt 17:1–13 and par.), Jesus is also the mediator of the New Covenant.

In the tradition of the Church, the ambiguity here is seen as a way of indicating the two-fold coming of the Lord—in the humility of the flesh, and in the glory and splendour of the End:

"We proclaim the coming of Christ: he comes not once, but twice, and the second coming will be more glorious than the first. The first was a time of suffering; in the second, however, he will wear the crown of divine kingship. Almost everything in the life our Lord Jesus Christ has two meanings. He was born twice: once, of the Father, from all eternity; and then, of the Virgin, in the fullness of time. He comes twice, too: he came first in silence, like rain falling on wool; and he will come again in glory. First, he was wrapped in swaddling clothes and laid in a manger; when he comes again, he will be robed in light. First, he shouldered the cross, without fear of suffering; when he comes again, he will come in glory, surrounded by the hosts of angels. Let us consider not only the life of the Lord, but also his future coming [...]. Because of his great mercy, he was made man to teach men and persuade them; when he comes again, all men, whether they want to or not, will be made subject to the power and authority of the King. The words of the prophet Malachy refer to both of these events" (St Cyril of Jerusalem, *Catecheses ad illuminandos*, 15, 1–2).

tales ei placent" aut: "Ubi est Deus iudicii?". **[3]** ¹Ecce ego mittam angelum meum, et praeparabit viam ante faciem meam; et statim veniet ad templum suum Dominator, quem vos quaeritis, et angelus testamenti, quem vos vultis. Ecce venit, dicit Dominus exercituum; ²et quis poterit sustinere diem adventus eius, et quis stabit, cum apparebit? Ipse enim quasi ignis conflans et quasi herba fullonum;

"For he is like a refiner's fire and like fullers' soap; ³he will sit    Jer 6:29
as a refiner and purifier of silver, and he will purify the sons of
Levi and refine them like gold and silver, till they present right
offerings to the LORD. ⁴Then the offering of Judah and Jerusalem
will be pleasing to the LORD as in the days of old and as in former
years.

⁵"Then I will draw near to you for judgment; I will be a swift    Ex 22:20–21
witness against the sorcerers, against the adulterers, against those    Lev 19:13
who swear falsely, against those who oppress the hireling in his    Jas 5:4
wages, the widow and the orphan, against those who thrust aside
the sojourner, and do not fear me, says the LORD of hosts.

## 5. FIFTH EXCHANGE: TEMPLE TITHES

⁶"For I the LORD do not change; therefore you, O sons of Jacob,    Num 23:19
are not consumed. ⁷From the days of your fathers you have turned    Zech 1:3
                                                                       Jas 4:8

---

**3:6–12.** According to the Law (cf. Num 18:20ff; Deut 14:22ff), the tenth part of the harvest was supposed to be given to the temple for the upkeep of the Levites. There is a play on words here: the Israelites rob (*'aqab*) the tithe, because they are sons of Jacob (v. 6), the one who deceives (*qaba'*). The prophet berates his fellow-citizens because of their failure to obey the law about tithes, or at least because they do not fully obey it (cf. v. 10).

Perhaps a plague of locusts "devoured" the harvests (cf. v. 11) and the Israelites were simply waiting for more prosperous times before paying in all their tithes. But the prophet, very much in line with what a Deuteronomic writer would do, argues the very opposite: if they keep the Law, the precepts of the Covenant, the Lord will bless them and see to it that the earth becomes most fruitful (cf. vv. 11–12). It is a message that never goes out of date: "Don't fall into a vicious circle. You are thinking: when this is settled one way or another, I'll be very generous with my God. Can't you see that Jesus is waiting for you to be generous without reserve, so that he can settle things far better than you imagine? A firm resolution, as logical consequence: in each moment of each day I will try generously to carry out the will of God" (St Josemaría Escrivá, *The Way*, 776).

³et sedebit conflans et emundans argentum et purgabit filios Levi et colabit eos quasi aurum et quasi argentum, et erunt Domino offerentes sacrificia in iustitia. ⁴Et placebit Domino sacrificium Iudae et Ierusalem sicut diebus pristinis et sicut annis antiquis. ⁵Et accedam ad vos in iudicio; et ero testis velox maleficis et adulteris et periuris et, qui opprimunt mercennarios, viduas et pupillos et flectunt ius peregrinorum nec timuerunt me, dicit Dominus exercituum. ⁶Ego enim Dominus et non mutatus sum; / sed vos, filii Iacob, nondum ad finem pervenistis. / ⁷A diebus enim patrum vestrorum / recessistis a praeceptis legitimis meis et non custodistis ea. / Revertimini ad me, / et revertar ad vos, / dicit Dominus

aside from my statutes and have not kept them. Return to me, and I will return to you, says the LORD of hosts. But you say, 'How shall we return?' [8]Will man rob God? Yet you are robbing me. But you say, 'How are we robbing thee?' In your tithes and offerings.
Deut 28:15 [9]You are cursed with a curse, for you are robbing me; the whole
Prov 3:9–10 nation of you. [10]Bring the full tithes into the storehouse, that there
2 Cor 9:6–8 may be food in my house; and thereby put me to the test, says the LORD of hosts, if I will not open the windows of heaven for you and pour down for you an overflowing blessing. [11]I will rebuke the devourer[k] for you, so that it will not destroy the fruits of your soil; and your vine in the field shall not fail to bear, says the LORD of
Is 61:9 hosts. [12]Then all nations will call you blessed, for you will be a
Lk 1:48 land of delight, says the LORD of hosts.

## 6. SIXTH EXCHANGE: THE RIGHTEOUS ON THE DAY OF THE LORD

[13]"Your words have been stout against me, says the LORD. Yet you
Job 21:14–15 say, 'How have we spoken against thee?' [14]You have said, 'It is
Is 58:3 vain to serve God. What is the good of our keeping his charge or
Jer 12:1 of walking as in mourning before the LORD of hosts? [15]Henceforth
Zeph 1:12 we deem the arrogant blessed; evildoers not only prosper but when they put God to the test they escape.'"

---

**3:13–4:3.** The question posed here is similar to that in the fourth "dispute" (2:17–3:5): if things go well for those who do evil and tempt God (v. 15), why should one obey the Lord's commandments (v. 14)? The prophet's reply is very similar to his previous one (cf. 3:2, 5): he announces a day of judgment when the wicked will be destroyed (4:1, 3). However, Malachi is more explicit than he was earlier as regards the reward of the righteous. The Lord is not unaware of the trials and worries of those who fear him; in fact he is like a great king who records in his annals (cf. Esther 6:1–3) the good deeds of the

exercituum. / Et dicitis: "In quo revertemur?". / [8]Numquid homo potest defraudare Deum? / Sed vos defraudatis me. / Et dicitis: "In quo defraudavimus te?". / In decimis et in primitiis. / [9]Maledictione vos maledicti estis, / quia me vos defraudatis, gens tota. / [10]Inferte omnem decimam in horreum, / et sit cibus in domo mea; / et probate me super hoc, / dicit Dominus exercituum: / si non aperuero vobis cataractas caeli / et effudero vobis benedictionem usque ad abundantiam / [11]et increpabo pro vobis devorantem, / et non corrumpet fructum terrae, / nec erit sterilis vobis vinea in agro, / dicit Dominus exercituum. / [12]Et beatos vos dicent omnes gentes; / eritis enim vos terra desiderabilis, / dicit Dominus exercituum. [13]Invaluerunt super me verba vestra, dicit Dominus; [14]et dicitis: "Quid locuti sumus contra te?". Dicitis: "Vanum est servire Deo; et, quod emolumentum, quia custodivimus praecepta eius et quia ambulavimus tristes coram Domino exercituum? [15]Ergo nunc beatos dicimus arrogantes; siquidem

**k.** Or *devouring locust*

[16]Then those who feared the LORD spoke with one another; the LORD heeded and heard them, and a book of remembrance was written before him of those who feared the LORD and thought on his name. [17]"They shall be mine, says the LORD of hosts, my special possession on the day when I act, and I will spare them as a man spares his son who serves him. [18]Then once more you shall distinguish between the righteous and the wicked, between one who serves God and one who does not serve him.

Dan 7:10
Rev 3:5; 20:20

Ps 103:13
Eph 1:14
1 Pet 2:9

4 [1][l]"For behold, the day comes, burning like an oven, when all the arrogant and all evildoers will be stubble; the day that comes shall burn them up, says the LORD of hosts, so that it will leave them neither root nor branch. [2]But for you who fear my name the sun of righteousness shall rise, with healing in its wings. You shall go forth leaping like calves from the stall. [3]And you shall tread down the wicked, for they will be ashes under the soles of your feet, on the day when I act, says the LORD of hosts.

Amos 5:18
1 Cor 3:13

Lk 1:78
Jn 8:12

## EPILOGUE

[4]"Remember the law of my servant Moses, the statutes and ordinances that I commanded him at Horeb for all Israel.
[5]"Behold, I will send you Elijah the prophet before the great

Mt 17:10–13;
11:14
Mk 9:11–12
Lk 1:17
Jn 1:21

---

just (3:16). Therefore, the day when the Lord reveals himself will be for them a day of splendour and inexpressible joy (4:2), for they enjoy God's special protection (3:17–18).

The expression "sun of righteousness" (4:2), applied to the coming of the Lord, is echoed in the New Testament *Benedictus* or canticle of Zechariah (cf. Lk 1:78). Therefore, it is not surprising that Christian tradition

should apply it to Jesus Christ: "The Lord came in the evening to a world in decline, when the course of life was almost run; but when the *Sun of justice* came, he gave new life and began a new day for those who believed in him" (Origen, *Homiliae in Exodum*, 7, 8).

**4:4–6.** According to biblical tradition, Elijah did not die but was taken up to heaven in a chariot of fire (cf. 2 Kings

---

aedificati sunt facientes impietatem et tentaverunt Deum et salvi facti sunt". [16]Tunc locuti sunt timentes Dominum, unusquisque cum proximo suo. Et attendit Dominus et audivit; et scriptus est liber memorabilium coram eo timentibus Dominum et cogitantibus nomen eius. [17]Erunt mihi, ait Dominus exercituum, in die, qua ego facio in peculium; et parcam eis, sicut parcit vir filio suo servienti sibi. [18]Rursum videbitis quid sit inter iustum et impium, inter servientem Deo et non servientem ei. [19]Ecce enim dies veniet succensa quasi caminus; et erunt omnes superbi et omnes facientes impietatem stipula; et inflammabit eos dies veniens, dicit Dominus exercituum, quae non derelinquet eis radicem et ramum.

l. Ch 4.1–6 are Ch 3.19–24 in the Hebrew

Josh 6:17
Sir 48:10
Lk 1:17

and terrible day of the Lord comes. ⁶And he will turn the hearts of fathers to their children and the hearts of children to their fathers, lest I come and smite the land with a curse."ᵐ

---

2:11). Now (cf. vv. 5–6) Malachi says that Elijah will return before the day of the Lord, for he is "the messenger" (cf. 3:1) who is to prepare his way. This idea occurs in other books of Scripture (cf. Sir 48:10) and it was very much part of common knowledge in Jesus' time. For example, when, after the Transfiguration, the disciples become aware of who Jesus is, they ask him, "Then why do the scribes say that first Elijah must come?" (Mt 17:10). And our Lord's reply shows them that the Elijah who must come is none other that John the Baptist (cf. Mt 17:12–13).

These three verses, which close the "Law and the Prophets", are in fact very important for understanding the episode of the Transfiguration. Moses (v. 4) is the first mediator of the Law;

Elijah stands for the prophets and he will be the last mediator (vv. 5–6). Moreover, both Moses (v. 4; cf. Ex 33: 19–23) and Elijah (cf. 1 Kings 19:1–14) saw God on Mount Horeb. When our Lord is seen transfigured on the mount with "Moses and Elijah, who appeared in glory and spoke of his departure, which he was to accomplish at Jerusalem" (Lk 9:30–31), he is showing that in him the Law and the prophets find fulfilment and that the Covenant which he made in his death and resurrection is the new and everlasting Covenant of God with mankind. Moreover, in the transfigured Jesus the apostles have revealed to them in a glorious manner "the unveiled face of Him whom they sought" (*Catechism of the Catholic Church*, 2583).

---

²⁰Et orietur vobis timentibus nomen meum sol iustitiae et sanitas in pennis eius; et egrediemini et salietis sicut vituli saginati ²¹et calcabitis impios, cum fuerint cinis sub planta pedum vestrorum in die, quam ego facio, dicit Dominus exercituum. ²²Mementote legis Moysi servi mei, / cui mandavi / in Horeb ad omnem Israel / praecepta et iudicia. / ²³Ecce ego mittam vobis / Eliam prophetam, / antequam veniat dies Domini / magnus et horribilis; / ²⁴et convertet cor patrum ad filios / et cor filiorum ad patres eorum, / ne veniam et percutiam / terram anathemate».

**m.** Or *ban of utter destruction*

# Explanatory Notes

These Notes appear in the Revised Standard Version Catholic Edition. An asterisk *in* the biblical text as distinct from the Navarre Bible headings refers the reader to the Notes given here. N.B. In these Notes Vulgate additions are quoted in the Douay Version.

## THE MINOR PROPHETS

These twelve are grouped together both in the Hebrew and in the Greek. The only reason for this seems to be that those books happen to be short. They are not "minor" in any other way; their religious value is great. They do not belong to any one historical period and they range from Amos (eight century BC) to Malachi, Joel, Obadiah and Jonah (fifth to fourth century BC). They are here arranged according to their traditional order in the Hebrew, which is not the same as their historical order. The Latin Vulgate also follows the order of the Hebrew.

## HOSEA

Hosea preached and prophesied during the century—the eighth—that saw the decline and final destruction of the Northern kingdom. It was a period of both moral and material dissolution, and it is this that gives his prophecy its peculiar characteristics. Hosea seems to take occasion of his own unhappy marriage to draw a parallel between it and the relationship between God and his unfaithful spouse Israel. He attacks passionately the moral evils and the injustice of the society in which he lives. Above all, he condemns the idolatry rampant everywhere, as well as the debased Yahweh worship. Israel will be punished, but after repentance the people will be welcomed back by their God.

## JOEL

Joel prophesied about four centuries later than Hosea, during the postexilic period. He foretells a plague of locusts as punishment and speaks threateningly of the "day of the Lord"; but then at once declares the Lord to be merciful and kind to those who repent. Towards the end of chapter 2 the style becomes apocalyptic and he speaks of the outpouring of the Spirit upon the people in the messianic age. This was fulfilled (Acts 2:16–21) at Pentecost.

## AMOS

Amos was a shepherd of Judah called suddenly by God to denounce social corruption and injustice in the Northern kingdom during the reign of Jeroboam II (eighth century BC). It was a time of great material luxury and worldly splendour, and the pastoral origins of the prophet contrasted strongly with the sophisticated decadence which, together with the people's infidelity, he denounced. He foretells the "day of the Lord," a time of punishment for men's sins, but holds out a hope of God's mercy to "the remnant of Joseph" (5:15). Some of the prophecies are probably of a later age.

## OBADIAH

The book of Obadiah is so short that it is difficult to be certain of its date and character. It is a tirade against the people of Edom, who are told not to exult over the misfortune of Jerusalem, for they shall be utterly destroyed, while a remnant from Israel shall survive. It seems to apply to the situation of the postexillic period when the surrounding nations, including Edom, had partly occupied the vacant territory of Judah.

# Explanatory Notes

## JONAH

The story is set in the reign of Jeroboam II (eighth century BC), but the book was probably written long after the Exile. This suggests that it is not meant to be taken historically, although the central figure, Jonah, is mentioned in 2 Kings 14:25 and appears to have been a well-known prophet of the time. In this story the writer, making use of many improbable details, teaches that God is merciful even in his punishments, if only his people will repent; and so far from being the God of Israel alone, he is prepared to extend his mercy to others, provided they possess or acquire the necessary dispositions of heart. Our Lord himself quotes the conversion of the Ninevites and the three days Jonah spent inside the great fish (Mt 12:38–41), but this is not a testimony to its historical character. He is concerned rather with its teaching.

## MICAH

Micah lived and prophesied at about the same time as Isaiah, in the kingdom of Judah. Like his contemporaries, he denounces the evils of his age, which he contrasts dramatically with the requirements of God: "to do justice, and to love kindness, and to walk humbly" with God (6:8). He foretells God's punishments, even the fall of Jerusalem (3:12). At the same time he prophesies, like Isaiah, that a remnant shall be saved (chapters 4–5) and speaks of the Messiah to come (5:2).

## NAHUM

The opening words announce the central theme—the coming destruction of Nineveh, the great oppressor of God's people. The passion with which this lyric poetry is imbued is explained by the tyranny endured for so long by Israel. But the deliverance announced will not, unfortunately, be of long duration. The fall of Nineveh (612 BC) will be followed by the fall of Jerusalem, but that is not part of the prophet's message.

## HABAKKUK

There is not much evidence for the date of the book, but it is likely that the prophet is speaking against the Chaldeans under Neuchadnezzar, who destroyed Jerusalem in 586 BC. The book starts with a dialogue between the prophet and God—the prophet complaining, and the Lord explaining and foretelling the coming destruction of the oppressor. All this took place probably before the fall of Jerusalem. Habakkuk has some originality; he asks God to explain his thought: for example, why does he punish his erring people by a nation more wicked than itself? And hence, why does wickedness seem to triumph? This is the problem found all through the Old Testament.

## ZEPHANIAH

Zephaniah prophesied shortly before the religious reform of Josiah, i.e., about the year 630 BC, and he proclaims in clarion tones the "day of the Lord," when his people will be crushed by their enemies because of their sins; cf. Amos. The words of Zephaniah (1.15) remind one of the *Dies irae*, which seems to have drawn its imagery from here. The prophet foretells punishment not only for Judah but also for the nations round about (2:4–15). Then, after more threats against Jerusalem (3:1–8), he utters consolations (3:9–20): the people will be restored, but chastened and humble. The reform of Josiah was too shortlived to affect the results of these prophecies—the Exile and the return followed within the century.

## HAGGAI

Haggai is the first of the postexilic prophets and differs considerably from the earlier ones. No longer do we read threats of punishment for sin or words of consolation in adversity. The people need to be helped in their work of restoration and encouraged to persevere. Haggai first insists that the temple must be built before they think of anything else. This is to be the focal point of their life, as it was in the past, and they cannot hope for any prosperity without it. In spite of its humble appearance, the Spirit of God will rest upon it and the "latter splendour of this house shall be greater than the former, says the Lord of hosts" (2:9).

# Explanatory Notes

## ZECHARIAH

Zechariah prophesied at the same time as Haggai, about 520 BC, and, like him, exhorted the people to press on with the building of the temple, but he goes on to develop the plans for the national restoration. He speaks in terms of a messianic era in which the priesthood is supreme but the royal prerogatives are possessed by "the branch" (6:12), a messianic term for Zerubbabel. Chapters 1–8 relate a series of visions and are apocalyptic in tone. The second part (chapters 9–14) is quite different, and consists of a collection of prophecies dating from the fourth century and edited later during the Greek period. These are chiefly noteworthy for the messianic passages in them, especially 9:9, fulfilled on Palm Sunday, and 12:10: "when they look on him whom they have pierced, they shall mourn."

## MALACHI

The name Malachi merely means "my messenger," and the book is probably anonymous. Its contents suggest that the historical context is the period of Ezra and Nehemiah. The theme is the love of God for his people in spite of their backsliding. Both priests and people are guilty of not offering a clean sacrifice— and in 1:11 is the prophecy of the universal sacrifice, relating evidently to messianic times. The prophet also denounces marriages with Gentiles and the practice of divorce. He goes on to proclaim the "day of the Lord," "great and terrible.' Like many prophets, he does not distinguish between the first and second coming.

# Sources quoted in the Commentary

## 1. DOCUMENTS OF THE CHURCH

**Second Vatican Council**
*Gaudium et spes*: Pastoral Constitution on the Church in the modern world, 21 November 1964, AAS 57 (1965) 5–71.
*Nostra aetate*: Declaration on the relation of the Church to non-Christian religions, 28 October 1965, AAS 58 (1966) 740–744.
*Presbyterorum ordinis:* Decree on the ministry and life of priests, 7 December 1965, AAS 58 (1966) 991–1024.
*Sacrosanctum Concilium*: Constitution on the Sacred Liturgy, 4 December 1963, AAS 56 (1964) 5–71.
**John Paul II**
*Dives in misercordia*: Encyclical Letter on the mercy of God, 30 November 1980, AAS 72 (1980) 1177–1232.
*Reconciliatio et paenitentia*: Apostolic Exhortation on reconciliation and penance, 2 December 1984, AAS 77 (1985) 185–275.
*Redemptoris Mater*: Encyclical Letter on the mother of the Redeemer, 25 March 1987, AAS 79 (1987) 361–443.

OTHER

*Catechism of the Catholic Church,* Dublin, 1994

## 2. LITURGICAL TEXTS

*Roman Missal*: *Missale Romanum*, editio typica altera, Vatican City, 1975
*Divine Office*: *Liturgia Horarum iuxta Ritum Romanum*, editio typica altera, Vatican City, 1987.

## 3. THE FATHERS, ECCLESIASTICAL WRITERS AND OTER AUTHORS

**Anon.**
*Didaché* in F.X. Funk (ed.), *Patres Apostolici*, vol. 1, Tübingen, 1901.
Letter of Barnabas: *Epistula Barnabae*: in F.X. Funk (ed.), *Patres Apostolici*, vol. 1, Tübingen, 1901.
**Augustine, St**
*De civitate Dei libri XXII*, PL 41, 13–804.
*Enarrationes in Psalmos*, PL 36–37
*Sermones*, PL 38–39.
**Ambrosiaster**
*Commentaria in epistolam ad Ephesios*, PL 17, 372–404.
**Ambrose, St**
*De virginitate liber unus*, PL 16, 279–316.
*In psalmi CXVIII expositionem*, PL 15, 1257–1604.

**Basil, St**
*Homilia de humilitate*, PG 31, 525–540.
*De Spiritu Sancto*, PG 32, 68–217.
**Bede, St**
*Super canticum Abacuc prophetae allegoricae expositio*, PL 91, 1235–1254.
**Bernard, St**
*Homilae super Missus est*, PL 183, 55–88.
*Sermones in Cantica Canticorum*, PL 183, 785–1198.
*Sermones de diversis*, PL 183, 35–56.
**Bonaventure, St**
*Itinerarium mentis in Deum*
*Sermones dominicales.*
**Cyprian, St**
*De bono patientiae*, PL 4, 621–634.
**Cyril of Alexandria, St**

# Sources quoted in the Commentary

*Commentarius in Isaiam prophetam*, PG 70, 9ff.
*In Aggaeum prophetam commentarius*, PG 71,
   1021–1062.
*In Zachariam prophetam commentarius*, PG
   72, 10–276.
*In Malachiam prophetam commentarius*, PG 72,
   276–364.
**Cyril of Jerusalem, St**
*Catecheses ad illuminandos*, PG 33, 331–1180.
**Clement of Rome, St**
*Epistula Clementis ad Corinthios I*: F.X. Funk
   (ed.), *Patres Apostolici*, vol. 1, Tübingen, 1901.
**Didymus the Blind**
*Commentarii in Zachariam*: cf. SC 83–85.
**Francis of Assisi, St**
*Admonitiones*.
**Francis de Sales, St**
*Introduction to the Devout Life*
**Gregory the Great, St**
*In librum primum Regum viarum expositionem*
   *libri VI*, PL 79, 17–468.
**Gregory Nazianzen, St**
*Apologetica (Oratio 2)*, PG 35, 408–513.
*De pauperum amore (Oratio 14)*, PG 35,
   857–909.
**Irenaeus of Lyons, St**
*Adversus haereses*
*Demonstratio praedicationis apostolicae*
**Jerome, St**
*Commentarii in Isaiam*, PL 24, 9–678.
*Commentarium in Nahum*, PL 25, 1231–1272.
*Commentarii in Osee*, PL 25, 815–946.
*Commentarii in Ioelem*, PL 25, 947–988.
*Commentarii in Amos*, PL 25, 989–1096.
*Commentarii in Abdiam*, PL 25, 1097–1118.
*Commentarii in Ionam*, PL 25, 1117–1152.
*Commentarii in Michaeam*, PL 25, 1151–1230.
*Commentarii in Abacuc*, PL 25, 1273–1338.
*Commentarii in Sophoniam*, PL 25, 1337–1388.
*Commentarii in Aggaeum*, PL 25, 1387–1416.
*Commentarii in Zachariam*, PL 25, 1415–1542.

**Jerome, St** (cont.)
*Commentarii in Malachiam*, PL 25, 1541–1578.
*Epistolae*, PL 30, 13–307.
**Josemaría Escrivá, St**
*The Way*
*Christ Is Passing By*
*The Forge*
*Furrow*
*The Way of the Cross*
**John Chrysostom, St**
*De incomprehensibile Dei natura*, PG 48,
   701–748.
**Justin, St**
*Apologia*
**Leander, St**
*Homilia in laudem Ecclesiae*, PL 72, 894–898.
**Leo the Great, St**
*Sermones*, PL 54, 137–468.
**Melito of Sardis**
*De Pascha*
**Newman, John Henry Cardinal**
*Catholic Sermons*
**Origen**
*Contra Celsum libri VIII*, PG 11, 637–1632.
**Polycarp, St**
*Epistola ad Philippenses*, PL 5, 1005–1024.
**Pseudo-Clement**
*Epitula II ad Corinthos*: in F.X. Funk (ed.),
   *Patres Apostolici*, vol. 1, Tübingen, 1901.
**Teresa of Avila, St**
*Way of Perfection*
**Thérése of the Child Jesus, St**
*Autobiographical Writings*
**Theodoret of Cyrus**
*Interpretatio in xii prophetas minores*, PL 81,
   1256–1546.
**Tertullian**
*Adversus Iudaeos*, PL 2, 595–642.
*Adversus Marcionem libri V*, PL 2, 239–524.
**Thomas Aquinas, St**
*Summa theologiae*

# Headings added to the Biblical Text

## HOSEA

Title 1:1

1. HOSEA'S MARRIAGE 1:2
The prophet's mission and his marriage 1:2
Messianic promises of salvation 1:10
The husband's treatment of his unfaithful wife 2:2
Restoration and a new Covenant 2:14
Husband and wife reconciled 3:1

2. THE SINS OF ISRAEL 4:1
General corruption reproached 4:1
Priests and prophets reproached 4:4
The people's apostasy 4:9
Priests and rulers denounced 5:1
Religious syncretism denounced 5:8
True and false conversion—a call for love, not sacrifice 6:1
Punishment for evildoing 6:8
The people and their leaders denounced for wickedness 7:1

Israel's quest for foreign help 7:8
A severe reproach 7:13
Kings and princes condemned 8:1
Israel ruined by relying on foreign help 8:8
Threat of exile 9:1
The prophet is persecuted 9:7
The crime at Baal-peor 9:10
Evil done in Gilgal 9:15
Israel's idolatry 10:1
Israel reproached for its pride 10:11
When Israel was a child 11:1

3. ISRAEL'S UNFAITHFULNESS 12:1
Israel and Judah steeped in crime 12:1
Biblical history recalled 12:3
Sins of idolatry 13:1
Punishment to come 13:4
The end of the monarchy foretold 13:9
The downfall of Ephraim 13:12
Call to conversion 14:1
A word to the wise 14:9

## JOEL

Title 1:1

1. A TIME OF MISFORTUNE 1:2
The land devastated by a locust plague 1:2
Call to repentance and prayer 1:13

2. THE OUTPOURING OF THE SPIRIT AND THE DAY OF THE LORD 1:19
The Lord's response:the plague ceases 1:19
The day of the Lord is coming "after darkness" 2:1

Invasion by a "powerful people" 2:2
An urgent call to repentance 2:12
The priests entreat the Lord 2:17
Prosperity will return 2:21
The Spirit poured out 2:28
The nations will be judged 3:1
A call to battle 3:9
The day of the Lord 3:14
The future glory of Israel 3:18

## AMOS

Title and introduction 1:1

1. JUDGMENT OF THE NEIGHBOURING COUNTRIES, AND OF JUDAH AND ISRAEL 1:3
Against Damascus 1:3
Against the Philistines 1:6
Against Phoenicia 1:9
Against Edom 1:11
Against Ammon 1:13
Against Moab 2:1
Against Judah 2:4
Against Israel 2:6

2. ISRAEL WARNED AND THREATENED 3:1
Election and punishment of Israel 3:1
The prophet, a messenger of the Lord 3:3
Oracle against Samaria 3:9
Oracle against Bethel and domestic luxury 3:13
Against the women of Samaria 4:1
Israel reproached 4:4
The Lord's warnings have gone unheeded 4:6
Doxology 4:13
Lament for Israel 5:1
"Seek me and live," says the Lord 5:4
Doxology 5:8

Transgressors threatened 5:10
Exhortation 5:14
Lamentation 5:16
The day of the Lord 5:18
Formalism in religion condemned 5:21
The prophet threatens punishment 5:26
A life of luxury gives a false sense of security 6:1
Divine punishment 6:8

3. SERIES OF PROPHETICAL VISIONS 7:1
First vision: the locusts 7:1

Second vision: the fire 7:4
Third vision: the plumb line 7:7
Dispute with Amaziah 7:10
Fourth vision: the basket of fruit 8:1
Exploiters denounced 8:4
A day of judgment 8:9
Fifth vision: the fall of the sanctuary 9:1
Doxology 9:5
Punishment awaits sinners 9:7

4. CONCLUSION: MESSIANIC RESTORATION 9:11

## OBADIAH

Title 1

1. ORACLE AGAINST EDOM 1
Divine judgment pronounced on Edom 1
The ruin of Edom foretold 5

2. CHARGES LAID AGAINST EDOM 8

3. THE DAY OF THE LORD 15
Divine judgment 15
The remnant that shall escape 17
Eschatological restoration of the kingdom of God 19

## JONAH

1. GOD GIVES JONAH A MISSION 1:1
The prophet is charged with a mission and takes flight 1:1
The storm 1:4
Jonah in the belly of the fish 2:1
Jonah's psalm of thanksgiving 2:2

2. JONAH IN NINEVEH 3:1
Jonah preaches repentance in Nineveh 3:1
The people of Nineveh do penance 3:5
Jonah's sense of grievance 4:1
God corrects Jonah and justifies his taking pity on Nineveh 4:9

## MICAH

Title 1:1

1. DIVINE JUDGMENT; SINS CONDEMNED 1:2
Theophany and indictment of Israel and Judah 1:2
Oracle on the downfall of Samaria 1:6
Lament for the cities of Israel and Judah 1:8
The prophet denounces social injustice 2:1
Abuses and evil counsel 2:6
Promise of restoration 2:12
Against rulers who oppress the people 3:1
Against corrupt prophets 3:5
The ruin of Zion foretold 3:8

2. HOPE AND RESTORATION OF ZION 4:1
The nations will come to the mountain of the Lord's temple 4:1
The gathering of the scattered flock on Zion 4:6
Testing and redemption 4:9
The Messiah, the saviour who will be born in Bethlehem 5:2

Assyria repulsed 5:5
The "remnant" of Jacob 5:7
Purification. Destruction of the causes of evil 5:10

3. FURTHER DIVINE JUDGMENT AND PUNISHMENT OF JERUSALEM 6:1
The Lord hands down his sentence 6:6
Formal religion is not enough 6:1
Jerusalem is punished for her sins 6:9
Lament about general corruption 7:1
The prophet's attitude 7:7

4. HOPE AND PRAYER FOR THE FUTURE 7:8
Zion looks forward to the future 7:8
Warning to the nations 7:11
Prayer for Jerusalem 7:14
Hymn to the Lord 7:18

# Headings added to the Biblical Text

## NAHUM

Title 1:1

1. HYMN TO GOD, THE MIGHTY JUDGE 1:2

2. THE FALL OF NINEVEH FORETOLD 1:9

3. NINEVEH ASSAULTED AND OVERTHROWN 2:1
The fall of Nineveh interpreted 2:1
Nineveh sentenced for its crimes 3:1
The destruction of Thebes, an object lesson 3:8
Assyria devoid of power 3:12
Death of the king of Assyria 3:18

## HABUKKUK

Title 1:1

1. DIALOGUE BETWEEN HABUKKUK AND GOD
   1:2
The prophet's first complaint 1:2
God's reply – The Chaldeans are God's scourge
   1:5
The prophet's second complaint 1:12
God's reply 2:2

2. CURSES ON OPPRESSORS 2:5
Greed 2:5

First imprecation 2:6
Second imprecation 2:9
Third imprecation 2:12
Fourth imprecation 2:15
Fifth imprecation 2:19

3. THE PSALM OF HABAKKUK 3:1
Prayer 3:1
Epic psalm: Theophany 3:3
The Lord, a powerful warrior 3:7
The prophet trembles but still he trusts in God
   3:16

## ZEPHANIAH

Title 1:1

1. JUDGMENT ON JUDAH AND ON ALL CREATION
   1:2
Apocalyptic threat 1:2
Judah's idolatry 1:4
The day of the Lord foretold 1:7
The day of wrath 1:14
Call to conversion 2:1

2. ORACLES AGAINST THE NATIONS AND
   AGAINST JUDAH 2:4

Against the peoples to the east 2:4
Against the peoples to the west 2:8
Against the peoples to the south and north 2:12
Against the leaders of Judah 3:1
The nations punished 3:6

3. PROMISES OF SALVATION 3:9
Conversion of the nations 3:9
Salvation of the remnant of Israel 3:11
Psalms of joy in Zion 3:14
Return of the exiles 3:18

## HAGGAI

1. REBUILDING OF THE TEMPLE 1:1

2. THE TEMPLE'S GLORY IN THE FUTURE 2:1

3. WORTHY OFFERINGS 2:10

4. MESSIANIC ORACLE FOR ZERUBBABEL 2:20

## ZECHARIAH

**Part One: Activity of the prophet** 1:1

INTRODUCTION 1:1
Call to conversion 1:1

1. THE BOOK OF THE VISIONS 1:7
First vision: the horsemen 1:7
Second vision: the horns and the smiths 1:18

Third vision: the measurer 2:1
Fourth vision: the high priest and the "Branch" 3:1
Fifth vision: the lampstand and the two olive trees
   4:1
Sixth vision: the flying scroll 5:1
Seventh vision: the woman in the ephah 5:5
Eighth vision: the four chariots 6:1
The crowning of Joshua 6:9

# Headings added to the Biblical Text

## MALACHI